Life between Memory and Hope

The Survivors of the Holocaust in Occupied Germany

Zeev W. Mankowitz tells the remarkable story of the 250,000 survivors of the Holocaust who converged on the American Zone of Occupied Germany from 1945 to 1948. They envisaged themselves as the living bridge between destruction and rebirth, the last remnants of a world destroyed and the active agents of its return to life. Much of what has been written to date looks at the Surviving Remnant through the eyes of others and thus has often failed to disclose the tragic complexity of their lives together with their remarkable political and social achievements. Despite the fact that they had lost everyone and everything, they got on with their lives, they married, had children and worked for a better future. They did not surrender to the deformities of suffering and managed to preserve their humanity intact. Using largely inaccessible archival material, Mankowitz gives a moving and sensitive account of this neglected area in the immediate aftermath of the Holocaust.

ZEEV W. MANKOWITZ is a senior lecturer at the Melton Centre for Jewish Education, the Hebrew University of Jerusalem.

Studies in the Social and Cultural History of Modern Warfare

General Editor
Jay Winter *Yale University*

Advisory Editors
Omer Bartov *Brown University*
Carol Gluck *Columbia University*
David M. Kennedy *Stanford University*
Paul Kennedy *Yale University*
Antoine Prost *Université de Paris-Sorbonne*
Emmanuel Sivan *Hebrew University of Jerusalem*
Robert Wohl *University of California, Los Angeles*

In recent years the field of modern history has been enriched by the exploration of two parallel histories. These are the social and cultural history of armed conflict, and the impact of military events on social and cultural history.

Studies in the Social and Cultural History of Modern Warfare presents the fruits of this growing area of research, reflecting both the colonization of military history by cultural historians and the reciprocal interest of military historians in social and cultural history, to the benefit of both. The series offers the latest scholarship in European and non-European events from the 1850s to the present day.

For a list of titles in the series, please see end of book.

Life between Memory and Hope

The Survivors of the Holocaust in Occupied Germany

Zeev W. Mankowitz

Hebrew University of Jerusalem

CAMBRIDGE
UNIVERSITY PRESS

PUBLISHED BY THE PRESS SYNDICATE OF THE UNIVERSITY OF CAMBRIDGE
The Pitt Building, Trumpington Street, Cambridge, United Kingdom

CAMBRIDGE UNIVERSITY PRESS
The Edinburgh Building, Cambridge CB2 2RU, UK
40 West 20th Street, New York, NY 10011-4211, USA
477 Williamstown Road, Port Melbourne, VIC 3207, Australia
Ruiz de Alarcón 13, 28014 Madrid, Spain
Dock House, The Waterfront, Cape Town 8001, South Africa

http://www.cambridge.org

First published 2002

Printed in the United Kingdom at the University Press, Cambridge

Typeface Plantin 10/12 pt.   *System* LaTeX 2$_\varepsilon$ [TB]

A catalogue record for this book is available from the British Library

Library of Congress Cataloguing in Publication data

Mankowitz, Zeev W.

Life between Memory and Hope: Survivors of the Holocaust in Occupied
Germany/Zeev W. Mankowitz.

        p.   cm. – (Studies in the social and cultural history of modern warfare)
ISBN 0 521 81105 8

1. Jews – Germany – History – 1945–   2. Holocaust survivors – Germany.
3. She®'rit-ha-peleòah in der Amerièaner zone fun Dayòshland – History.
4. Refugees, Jewish – Germany – History – 20th century.   I. Title.   II. Series.
DS135.G332 .M36   2002
943′.004924–dc21   2001043843

ISBN 0 521 81105 8

In loving memory of Gene
and to our children Yonit and Noam,
the light of my life

Contents

Plates

Acknowledgments

This book began as a doctoral dissertation at the Hebrew University in Jerusalem and I wish to thank Yehuda Bauer who introduced me to his pioneering work on *She'erith Hapleitah*. When I decided to follow suit, he helped guide my research with sage advice and challenging counsel. I equally owe a profound debt of gratitude to my teacher Yisrael Gutman who played a critical role in helping this project come to fruition. He has been unflagging in his support and encouragement, and, despite many calls on his time, read the manuscript closely and provided me with invaluable guidance. I, like many others, find his generosity of spirit a source of wonder and inspiration. In my first years as a student of history Professor Yehoshua Arieli took me under his wing and through his teaching and person initiated me into the work and public responsibility of the historian. In those early years I also began to study with George Mosse, a frequent visitor to Jerusalem. Happily, what began as excited admiration matured into a lifelong friendship and each and every time we met over the last decade George urged me to write this book. Given how things turned out, I am especially sorry it was so long in the making. George may sadly be gone but his humanity and unique ability to cut through to the heart of things continues to resonate through my life undiminished.

My association with the International Center for Advanced Studies at Yad Vashem in 1999 allowed me to reenter the world of research while a Koerner Visiting Fellowship at the Oxford Centre for Hebrew and Jewish Studies granted me a year of friendly support and productive peace midst the sylvan beauty of Yarnton Manor. The Melton Center for Jewish Education, my academic home in the Hebrew University, is justifiably known for the intellectual ferment and generous collegiality that I have been fortunate enough to share. I owe a special vote of thanks to my friend and mentor Michael Rosenak, to Carmen Sharon, the Administrative Director, whose friendship and concern went far beyond the call of duty, and Vivienne Burstein who graciously granted me academic assistance every step of the way. I should also like to acknowledge the invaluable assistance of Linda Randall, Elizabeth Howard and their team at Cambridge University Press who have been professionally demanding and wonderfully supportive in preparing the book for publication.

Finally I wish to thank my wife Bella who, when all was dark, gave me the loving care that helped me start anew.

Abbreviations and note on spelling and dates

AACI	Anglo-American Committee of Inquiry on Palestine
AJDC	American Joint Distribution Committee (often shortened to JDC or, simply, the Joint), the charitable arm of American Jews to needy communities overseas
AZA	American Zionist Archive
CDPX	Combined Displaced Persons Executive
CZA	Central Zionist Archives
DP	Displaced person, stateless as a result of the dislocations of the Second World War
FLK	*Fun Letstn Khurbn* (From the Recent Destruction)
FRUS	Foreign Relations of the United States
HHA	*Hashomer Hatzair* Archive
IDF	Israel Defence Forces
IMT	International Military Tribunal, Nuremberg
LLT	*Landsberger Lager Tsaytung* (in the original Polish transliteration '*Caitung*'), the influential weekly of the Landsberg DP camp
NA	National Archives, Washington DC
OHD	Oral History Department of the Institute for Contemporary Jewry, the Hebrew University of Jerusalem
OSE	L'Oeuvre de Secour aux Enfants, a leading French–Jewish philanthropic organization focusing on the health needs of children
PRO	Public Records Office, London
Rec.A-A	Records of the Anglo-American Committee of Inquiry on Palestine
SHAEF	Supreme Headquarters Allied Expeditionary Force
THK	*Tsentraler Historisher Komisiye*, Central Historical Commission
UNRRA	United Nations Relief and Rehabilitation Administration
UZO	United Zionist Organization in Bavaria

YIVO   The well-known Yiddish Institute for Jewish Research that
          was transferred from Vilna, Lithuania, to New York
          in 1939
YSA   Yad Vashem Archive
YT   *Yiddishe Tsaytung* that replaced the *Landsberger Lager
          Tsaytung*
ZK   *Zentral komitet fun di bafreite yidn in datyshland* – the
          Central Committee of the Liberated Jews in Germany (later
          changed to 'in Bavaria')

Note on spelling and dates

She'erith Hapleitah – the Surviving Remnant has been variously translit-
erated and I have retained the variant forms that appear in the diverse
sources I have used.

In the second half of the 1940s the accepted plural acronym for Displaced
Persons was DP's which I have retained when quoting. Elsewhere I prefer
the contemporary usage – DPs.

I have used the European practice of day/month/year throughout.

Introduction

This study sets out to examine the initial responses of Holocaust survivors to the tragedy that overtook them. It focuses on the history of *She'erith Hapleitah* – the Surviving Remnant – in the American Zone of Occupied Germany which, despite its inherent limitations as a group in transit, rose to temporary prominence in the immediate post-war years. While the term *She'erith Hapleitah* refers to all surviving Jews in Europe, it designates most particularly those who converged on Germany between 1945 and 1949.

As the impending defeat of Nazi Germany grew closer and the hope of possible liberation more tangible, the thoughts of the concentration camp inmates in Germany increasingly turned to the fate of those who would be lucky enough to survive. It is in this context that the term *She'erith Hapleitah*, the biblical concept of the saved or surviving remnant, comes to describe those who would survive to see the Allied victory. Apparently the first recorded reference to *She'erith Hapleitah* appears in the Channukah 5705 (November–December 1944) number of *Nitzotz* (The Spark), the underground organ of the *Irgun Brith Zion* in the Kovno Ghetto, which began to appear in Kaufering, a sub-camp of Dachau, to which the last remnants of the Ghetto had been deported five months earlier. In the five extant issues of the paper (two were lost) the term *She'erith Hapleitah* is freely used to describe those who would hopefully survive, suggesting that it was already an integral part of shared language in Kaufering even before *Nitzotz* was reissued. In certain cases the term refers to survivors throughout Europe and in others is restricted to those who would remain alive in Bavaria; sometimes the focus was on physical survival but at other times it was bound up with both personal survival and the rebirth of Jewish life in Palestine, a task for which they, "the generation of the desert," needed to steel themselves.[1] With liberation this multivalent notion of *She'erith Hapleitah* gained immediate acceptance and wide

---

[1] See "D'var hamifkada" (A word from headquarters), *Nitzotz*, no.3(38) (Channukah 5705 – November 1944): 1.

currency. Indeed, when the young American chaplain, Rabbi Abraham Klausner, found himself in Dachau towards the end of May 1945 and began to help the liberated in their desperate search for family, the first in a number of volumes containing the names of thousands of survivors in Bavaria was entitled *Shearit Hapletah*.[2] From 1943 the leadership of Palestinian Jewry also, quite independently, began to refer to those who would hopefully survive as *Sh'erith Hapleitah*.[3]

The earliest mention of the term appears in Genesis 32:9 when Jacob, who was greatly distressed about his imminent reunion with Esau after so many years of estrangement, divided his people and property into two camps saying: "If Esau come to the one camp and smite it, then the camp [*hanish'ar lifleitah*] which is left shall escape." Already this enunciates in a preliminary way the themes of danger, destruction and the survival of a remnant that carries the promise of the future. The redemptive theme becomes central to Isaiah's usage as can be seen in his prophecy to Hizqiyyahu regarding Sanheriv, King of Ashur: "And the remnant that is escaped of the house of Yehuda shall yet again take root downwards, and bear fruit upwards. For out of Jerusalem shall go [*She'erith Upleitah*] a remnant, and they that escape out of mount Ziyyon"(Second Book of Kings 19:30–31). In First Chronicles 4:43 "And they smote the remnant of Amalek who had escaped [*She'erith Hapleitah le-Amalek*]" the term, as it attached to survivors of the Holocaust, appears in a quantitative, almost technical usage. A slightly different version but with the same connotation – *She'erith Yisrael* – the Remnant of Israel appears in Jeremiah 31:7 and from there found its way into the Verses of Supplication in the Daily Prayer Book.

In the aftermath of the Holocaust the term, in its broadest construction, connoted the saved remnant, that is to say, all European Jews who survived the Nazi onslaught including the hundreds of thousands of Polish, Baltic and Russian Jews deported to the interior of the Soviet Union for political reasons or as part of Stalin's "scorched earth" policy. In a more limited sense *She'erith Hapleitah* referred to the collective identity of some 300,000 displaced persons in Occupied Germany, Austria and Italy who turned their backs on their former lives and actively sought to leave Europe for Palestine and many other destinations. Having escaped the unavoidable constraints of rebuilding their former lives and now living temporarily under American protection in a land they despised, it

---

[2] See Alex Grobman, *Rekindling the Flame: American Jewish Chaplains and the Survivors of European Jewry* (Detroit, 1993).

[3] See Dalia Ofer, "The Leadership of the Yishuv and She'erit Hapletah," in Yisrael Gutman and Adina Drechsler, eds., *She'erit Hapletah 1944–1948: Rehabilitation and Political Struggle* (Jerusalem, 1990): 306–310.

was primarily these survivors who publicly identified themselves as the Surviving Remnant. For some of the leaders of this unique community driven by a sense of historical responsibility, *She'erith Hapleitah* was also viewed as the saving remnant who were called upon to play a formative role in shaping the Jewish future. In the words of Samuel Gringauz, one of their prominent leaders:

The Sherit Hapleta sees as its task to symbolize the Jewish national tragedy zzz this task is viewed zzz as one laid upon it by destiny and history regardless of the strength of its bearers zzz The Sherit Hapleta must demonstrate to all Jews everywhere their involvement in a common fate zzz Jewish unity for them is no political program but an actual and living fact of experience. This is why they feel themselves prophets of a national rebirth zzz and of being the backbone of its realization zzz For international Zionism the Sherit Hapleta is an argument, a strength, a reserve zzz Without the situation of the DP's as a basis of appeal, American Jewry could not be mobilized so effectively for the upbuilding of Palestine, nor could the Jews of other lands be nationally awakened and united. Thus the Sherit Hapleta feels today that it is the dynamic force of the Jewish future.[4]

The discussion opens towards the end of 1944 as the Second World War is entering its final stages and in the concentration camps of Germany, the inmates take their first steps towards preparing for liberation. The narrative draws to a close in early 1947 when *She'erith Hapleitah* is well established and the major institutions that will accompany it to its dissolution in 1948–1949 are firmly in place. It has not been our intention, furthermore, to write a comprehensive history of this brief, albeit pregnant moment in history. We wish to focus on the internal history of a unique community that had abandoned its past and was yet to find its future. Much of what has been written to date looks at *She'erith Hapleitah* through the eyes of others and thus has often failed to disclose their richly complex inner life. Our concern is with this dynamic community of survivors itself, its people, movements, ideas, institutions and self-understanding, how it grappled with the unbearable weight of the past, the strains of the present and the shape of a different future. *She'erith Hapleitah* as subjects rather than as objects of history is what we seek to uncover.

Thus, a good few months before the war was over the seeds of survivor organization were germinating in Buchenwald, in the numerous satellite camps of Dachau and elsewhere. On the morrow of liberation of the camps in April–May 1945 we already witness a flurry of activity amongst the survivors that naturally focused on the pressing problems of

---

[4] Samuel Gringauz, "Jewish Destiny as the DP's See It," *Commentary*, vol. 4, no. 6 (December 1947): 501.

food, health, shelter, clothing, the search for family and a safe future but which, over the next few months, rapidly elaborated itself into a network of representative and camp councils, political movements, newspapers, youth groups, children's homes and schools, vocational training and a wide range of cultural pursuits. Amidst this remarkable effort at self-rehabilitation in the most unpromising of circumstances, we also find the first sustained public attempt to grapple with both the implications of the Shoah and some of the major questions of post-Holocaust Jewish life: who would lead the Jewish world with the demise of European Jewry? How would Jewish life and faith change in the aftermath? How should the Jewish people relate to those that turned on them or that stood by in their hour of need? How should they relate to the civilization that for so many Jews held out the promise of a more humane future? In a profound sense She'erith Hapleitah served as a formative bridge between the Holocaust and what was to come after.

Despite its importance and some early attention, the inner history of She'erith Hapleitah has suffered neglect and, until recently, was almost a forgotten history. In 1947 comprehensive reports were published by Leo Srole,[5] the social welfare officer of United Nations Relief and Rehabilitation Administration (UNRRA) in the Landsberg camp, by Koppel Pinson[6] the well-known historian who directed the Education Department of the Joint Distribution Committee in Germany and by Chaim Hoffman (Yachil)[7] who headed the Palestinian Delegation to Occupied Germany. In 1953 Leo Schwarz who served as director of the JDC in Germany from 1946 to 1947 published the first and to date the only full-scale history of She'erith Hapleitah in Germany.[8] It appears that initially only those who worked with the survivors in Germany saw the broader historical implications of their personal engagement.

Over the next twenty years very little was written on the subject and it was in 1970, twenty-five years after the liberation of the camps, that the picture begins to change: Zemach Zemarion who himself served with She'erith Hapleitah in Occupied Germany published his survey of survivor newspapers as an expression of their most pressing concerns[9] while Yehuda Bauer published his study on the Brichah, the illegal or semi-legal

---

[5] Leo Srole, "Why the DP's Can't Wait: Proposing an International Plan of Rescue," *Commentary*, vol. 3, no. 1 (January 1947): 13–24.

[6] Koppel S. Pinson, "Jewish Life in Liberated Germany: A Study of the Jewish DP's," *Jewish Social Studies*, vol. 9 (April 1947): 101–126.

[7] Chaim Yachil (Hoffman), "Peulot ha-mishlachat ha-eretz yisraelit le-she'erith hapleitah, 1945–1949" (Report of the Palestinian Delegation to She'erith Hapleitah, 1945–1949), *Yalkut Moreshet*, no. 30 (November 1980): 7–40, and no. 31 (April 1981): 133–176.

[8] Leo W. Schwarz, *The Redeemers: A Saga of the Years 1945–1952* (New York, 1953).

[9] Zemach Zemarion, *Ha-itonut shel She'erith hapleitah ke-bitui le-ba'ayoteha* (The press of She'erith Hapleitah as an expression of its problems) (Tel Aviv, 1970).

movement of some 250,000 Jews from Eastern Europe primarily to the American Zones of Occupied Germany and Austria.[10] Bauer concluded that from mid-1944 to October 1945, when the first Palestinian emissaries were integrated into this clandestine activity, the *Brichah*, which quietly received financial help from the JDC, was entirely the initiative and work of survivors. This went against the grain of conventional wisdom and, in some quarters, is still looked at skeptically despite additional research that has confirmed Bauer's conclusions.[11] In a parallel study Bauer suggested that in the larger scheme of things this movement was also of critical importance in the creation of the State of Israel, a theme that will be addressed below.[12]

How, then, does one account for this seeming neglect when rich archival material was readily available to historians in both Israel and abroad? First, it was perhaps to be expected that the brief moment of *She'erith Hapleitah* on the stage of history would be overshadowed by the devastation of the Holocaust on the one hand and the revolutionary promise of Jewish statehood on the other. In addition the widespread sense, both secular and religious, that the move from Holocaust to Rebirth was ineluctable, almost preordained, meant that the stormy and uncertain progression of events from May 1945 to May of 1948 was lost from view. If what happened was inevitable, there was scant need to trace the detailed unfolding of events while carefully assessing the concrete contributions of those involved. This lack of attention to detail was reinforced in Israel by the widespread, close to axiomatic assumption that the underground fighting forces had pushed out the British and, in their military victory over the Arabs, achieved statehood.

If it became apparent that statehood was not a direct outcome of the Holocaust and that, in fact, the destruction of the human hinterland of the Zionist movement in Eastern Europe almost precluded the achievement of Jewish sovereignty, this might open the way to new interpretations of the move from Holocaust to Homeland. And, indeed, this is what has happened. A series of new studies tracing the interrelationship of British, American and Zionist diplomacy in the aftermath of the Second World

---

[10] Yehuda Bauer, *Flight and Rescue: Brichah* (New York, 1970).

[11] Shlomo Kless, *Bederech lo slulah: toldot habrichah 1944–1948* (On the unpaved road: a history of the *Brichah* 1944–1948) (Kibbutz Dalia, 1994); in this regard see also David Engel, *Bein shichrur le-brichah: nitzolei ha-shoah be-polin ve-ha-maavak al hanhagatam, 1944–1946* (Between liberation and flight: Holocaust survivors in Poland and the struggle for leadership, 1944–1946), (Tel Aviv, 1996).

[12] Yehuda Bauer, "The Holocaust and the Struggle of the Yishuv as Factors in the Creation of the State of Israel," in *Holocaust and Rebirth: A Symposium* (Jerusalem, 1974), and "From the Holocaust to the State of Israel," in *Rethinking the Holocaust* (New Haven, 2001).

War rendered the compelling story of the phoenix rising from the ashes somewhat suspect and suggested in its stead a story of turbulent ups and downs with no certain outcome.[13] Some historians of Zionism have gone so far as to suggest that Jewish statehood was achieved at the last moment in a political constellation that, in point of fact, did not favor the success of the Zionist endeavor. In his conclusion to *A History of Zionism* Walter Laqueur argues that: "The Jewish state came into being at the very time when Zionism had lost its erstwhile *raison d'etre*: to provide an answer to the plight of east European Jewry. The United Nations decision of November 1947 was in all probability the last opportunity for the Zionist movement to achieve a breakthrough."[14]

Historians of the period, nonetheless, were slow to revise their estimate of the minor role allotted to *She'erith Hapleitah* itself in these developments. Part of the explanation might lie in the focus of these studies which unthinkingly cast the survivors into a subsidiary role of supplicants: their basic necessities were supplied by the US Army, their camps were administered by UNRRA, they were supported by the Joint, inspired by soldiers of the Jewish Brigade, guided politically by the Palestinian Delegation, led over the Alps and transported to Palestine by the *Mossad Le-Aliyah Bet* and their political fate was ultimately determined by the domestic pressure of American Jewry and the creation of the State of Israel. While this description is not without truth it does tend, without ill intent, to cast *She'erith Hapleitah* into a supine role and deprives them of a will of their own.

This image of passivity was rendered more plausible, moreover, by a pervasive stereotype that portrayed survivors as broken and helpless, ground to dust by unspeakable torture, a view that began to circulate

---

[13] See Amitzur Ilan, *America, britania ve-eretz yisrael: reishitah ve-hitpatchutah shel me' uravut artzot ha-brit be-mediniyut ha-britit be'eretz yisrael, 1938–1947* (America, Britain and Palestine: the beginning and development of the involvement of the United States in British policy in Palestine, 1938–1947) (Jerusalem, 1979); Zvi Ganin, *Truman, American Jewry and Israel* (New York, 1979); Shmuel Dothan, *Ha-maavak al eretz yisrael* (The Struggle for Palestine) (Tel Aviv, 1981); Michael J. Cohen, *Palestine and the Great Powers 1945–1948* (Princeton, 1981); Yosef Heller, *Be-maavak la-medinah: ha-mediniyut ha-ziyonit be-shanim 1936–1948* (In the struggle for statehood: Zionist policy in the years 1936–1948) (Jerusalem, 1984); Yoav Gelber, *Toldot ha-hitnadvut III: nosei ha-degel – shlichutam shel ha-mitnadvim la'am ha-yehudi* (A history of voluntary service III: the standard bearers – the mission of the volunteers to the Jewish people) (Jerusalem, 1983); David Sha'ari, *Geirush kafrisin 1946–1949: ha'apalah, ha-machanot ve-chevrat ha-ma'apilim* (Deportation to Cyprus 1946–1949: clandestine immigration, the camps and the social bonding of the illegal immigrants) (Jerusalem, 1981); Ze'ev (Venia) Hadari and Ze'ev Tzachor, *Oniyot o medinah: korot oniyot ma'apilim ha-gedolot "pan york" ve-"pan crescent"* (Ships or state: a history of the large "illegal" immigrant ships the "Pan York" and the "Pan Crescent") (Tel Aviv, no date); Leonard Dinnerstein, *America and the Survivors of the Holocaust* (New York, 1982).

[14] Walter Laqueur, *A History of Zionism* (New York, 1972): 594–595.

in the Yishuv (pre-state Palestinian Jewry) even before the war ended,[15] and that gained wider currency with the first photographs and newsreels of the liberation of the camps: suddenly the "walking skeletons" and "helpless heap of human wreckage"[16] were there for all to see. These images which were repeatedly used by Jewish fundraisers and in the Zionist campaign against British policies in Palestine became fixed in the public mind. The stereotype, in addition, was secretly fed by a dark account of survival which assumed that the virtuous went under while the less worthy survived. After all, even the survivors themselves spoke of a process of "negative selection."[17] These expressions of survivor guilt were often taken at face-value without any sustained attempt to uncover their deeper meaning. Interestingly enough, even when Elie Wiesel, Alexander Solzhenitsyn and Terrence Des Pres[18] succeeded in transforming "the survivor" into a culture hero in an age of mass death, it did not translate into a new understanding of *She'erith Hapleitah*. Their collective enterprise recorded primarily in Yiddish and bearing the profound stamp of East European Jewish life remained a closed book for most. Indeed, even as perceptive an historian as Tom Segev has little appreciation for how the people of *She'erith Hapleitah* organized themselves, fought for recognition and struggled to master their fate. From beginning to end he portrays them as little more than clay in the hands of Zionist envoys quite lacking a face of their own.[19]

Over the last decade or so this picture has begun to change and a slow but steady flow of studies have contributed richly to the brief but remarkably complex history of *She'erith Hapleitah*. In 1985 Yad Vashem devoted its International Historical Conference to the rehabilitation and political struggle of *She'erith Hapleitah*;[20] Juliane Wetzel and Angelika Königseder have written on Jewish life in Munich and Berlin respectively in addition to a general account of Jewish DPs in the aftermath of the war,[21] Jacqueline Giere and Ada Schein have written on education and culture

[15] Yechiam Weitz, "Ha-yishuv ve-she'erith hapleitah: 1944–1945" (The Yishuv and *She'erith Hapleita*: 1944–1945), Master's Dissertation, The Hebrew University of Jerusalem (Jerusalem, 1981): 8, 59.

[16] Leo W. Schwarz, "The DP's: Fiction and Fact," *American Zionist*, vol. 43, no.15 (June 1953): 16–17.

[17] Dr. Shmuel Gringauz, "In tsaykhn fun martirertum hofnung un arbet" (Under the sign of martyrdom hope and work), *LLT*, no. 2 (14) (18 January 1946): 1.

[18] See for example Elie Wiesel, *One Generation After* (New York, 1972); Alexander Solzhenitsyn, *One Day in the Life of Ivan Denisovich* (New york, 1963); Terrence Des Pres, *The Survivor: An Anatomy of Life in the Death Camps* (New York, 1976).

[19] Tom Segev, *The Seventh Million: The Israelis and the Holocaust* (New York, 1993).

[20] Gutman and Drechsler, eds., *She'erit Hapletah 1944–1948*.

[21] Juliane Wetzel, *Jüdisches Leben in München 1945–1951: Durchgangsstation oder Wiederaufbau?* (Munich, 1987); Angelika Königseder, *Flucht nach Berlin: Jüdische Displaced Persons 1945–1948* (Berlin, 1998); Angelika Königseder and Juliane Wetzel, *Lebensmut in Wartesaal: Die jüdischen DPs im Nachkriegsdeutschland* (Frankfurt a.M., 1994).

in the DP camps in Germany,[22] Saul Touster has edited a survivors' Haggadah,[23] Yehudit Tidor Baumel has published her study of *Kibbutz Buchenwald*,[24] Yosef Grodzinski has written a critical left-leaning history of *She'erith Hapleitah*,[25] Joanne Reilly and Chagit Lavski researched the liberation of Belsen and Jewish DPs in the British Zone,[26] Irit Keynan has studied the work of Palestinian emissaries in Germany,[27] Nachum Bogner and Dalia Ofer have examined the Cyprus detainees,[28] Idith Zertal has published a wide-ranging study of Jewish illegal immigration,[29] Hanna Yablonka has traced the absorption and integration of survivors into Israeli society,[30] Yehuda Bauer has continued his research on the JDC with a study of the impact of American Jews on post-Holocaust European Jewry,[31] Haim Genizi has written up the history of the office of the Special Adviser on Jewish Affairs to the American Army,[32] *Yalkut Moreshet* devoted a special volume to *She'erith Hapleitah* and the establishment of the State of Israel,[33] while Aryeh Kochavi, Mark Wyman, Wolfgang Jacobmeyer and Michael Marrus have written about European

---

[22] Jacqueline Giere, *'Wir sind unterwegs, aber nicht in der Wuste': Erziehung und Kultur in den Jüdischen Displaced-Lagern der Amerikanischen Zone im Nachkriegsdeutschland 1945–1949* (Frankfurt a.M., 1993), see also, "We're on Our Way, but We're not in the Wilderness," in Michael Berenbaum and Abraham J. Peck, eds., *The Holocaust and History: The Known, the Unknown, the Disputed and the Reexamined* (Bloomington, 1998): 699–715; Ada Schein, *Homeless Persons as Partners in the Zionist Enterprise: Survivors in German and Austrian Displaced Persons Camps and the Jewish National Fund* (Jerusalem, 1997).

[23] Saul Touster, ed., *A Survivors' Haggadah* (Philadelphia, 1999).

[24] Yehudit Tidor Baumel, *Kibbutz Buchenwald* (Hebrew) (Tel Aviv, 1994).

[25] Yosef Grodzinski, *Chomer enoshi tov: yehudim mul tziyonim, 1945–1951* (Good human material: Jews versus Zionists, 1945–1951) (Tel Aviv, 1998).

[26] Joanne Reilly, *Belsen: The Liberation of a Concentration Camp* (London, 1999); Chagit Lavski, "The Day After: Bergen-Belsen from Concentration Camp to the Center of Jewish Survivors in Germany," *German History*, vol. 11, no. 1 (1993): 36–59.

[27] Irit Keynan, *Lo nirga ha-ra'av: nitzolei ha-shoah ve-shlichei eretz yisrael: germaniyah 1945–1948* (And the hunger was not staunched: Holocaust survivors and the emissaries from Eretz Yisrael: Germany 1945–1948) (Tel Aviv 1996).

[28] Nachum Bogner, *I ha-geirush: machanot ha-ma'apilim be-kafrisin, 1946–1948* (The island of deportation: Jewish illegal immigrant camps in Cyprus, 1946–1948) (Tel Aviv, 1991); Dalia Ofer, "Holocaust Survivors as Immigrants: The Case of Israel and the Cyprus Detainees," *Modern Judaism*, 16 vol. (February 1996): 1–23, and "From Illegal Immigrants to New Immigrants: The Cyprus Detainees 1946–1949," in Berenbaum and Peck, eds., *The Holocaust and History*: 733–749.

[29] Idith Zertal, *From Catastrophe to Power: Holocaust Survivors and the Emergence of Israel* (Berkeley, 1998).

[30] Hanna Yablonka, *Survivors of the Holocaust: Israel after the War* (London, 1999).

[31] Yehuda Bauer, *Out of the Ashes: The Impact of American Jews on Post-Holocaust European Jewry* (Oxford, 1989).

[32] Haim Genizi, *Yoetz u-mekim: ha-yoetz la-tzava ha-amerikani u-le-she'erith hapleitah 1945–1949* (The Adviser to the American Army and *She'erith Hapleitah* 1945–1949 (Tel Aviv, 1987).

[33] "She'erith hapleitah vehakamat hamedinah: leyovel medinat yisrael" (*She'erith Hapleitah* and the establishment of the State of Israel), *Yalkut Moreshet*, no. 65 (April 1998).

refugees in general and displaced persons in particular.[34] While much work remains to be done especially with respect to the internal history of the Jewish DPs in Occupied Germany, a body of research is now available that will help us better to tell and interpret the story of *She'erith Hapleitah*.

One of our guiding goals, therefore, has been to uncover and understand a small but significant chapter of contemporary history. This was also the task that Leo Schwarz set himself some forty-six years ago. He entitled his work *The Redeemers*[35] in order to underscore his reading of *She'erith Hapleitah* as the "saving remnant" that, as part of its own return to life, contributed richly to both Jewish life in general and the creation of the State of Israel in particular. His commitment to *She'erith Hapleitah* together with his dramatic Thucydidean reconstruction of historic occasions, conversations and speeches led Schwarz to a measure of romanticization that historians today find somewhat unsettling. Ironically, the people of *She'erith Hapleitah* themselves were far more open and critical about their own failings and, in truth, their achievements are best understood against the background of the persistent problems they had to overcome. Today, a half a century later with a plethora of rich materials in ready reach it is perhaps easier for the historian to achieve a more balanced perspective. Nonetheless, Schwarz's assessment a decade after publishing his book still rings true: "no matter how objective you attempted to maintain yourself, there was an unconscious identification with the people. You took their side even if you knew they were wrong. And this influenced zzz a great deal."[36]

The question of how to strike the right balance in the portrayal of *She'erith Hapleitah* persists. Like all those who approach this topic sympathetically, I have faced the same temptation and, I am sure, have unthinkingly succumbed to it more often than not. After all, these were ordinary folk who had lived through experiences that beggar description. In most cases they had lost everyone and everything, they were condemned to a protracted stay in grim conditions in the land of their oppressors, they were cast into a debilitating dependence on others and lived in perpetual

[34] Arieh J. Kochavi, *Akurim ve-politika beinleumit: britanya ve-ha-akurim ha-yehudim le-achar milchemet ha-olam ha-shniyah* (Displaced Persons and international politics: Britain and the Jewish *Displaced Persons* after the Second World War) (Tel Aviv, 1992); Mark Wyman, *DPs: Europe's Displaced Persons, 1945–1951* (Ithaca, 1998); Wolfgang Jacobmeyer, *Vom Zwangsarbeiter zum heimatlosen Ausländer: Displaced Persons in Westdeutschland 1945–1951* (Göttingen, 1985); Michael R. Marrus, *The Unwanted: European Refugees in the Twentieth Century* (New York, 1985).

[35] Schwarz, *The Redeemers.*

[36] Leo W. Schwarz, Interview, the Oral History Department of the Institute of Contemporary Jewry, the Hebrew University of Jerusalem, 7(4) 3.

uncertainty about the future. Yet, despite their many failings that were all too human, they, by and large, held fast, they got on with their lives to the degree that circumstances allowed, they married, had children and prepared for the future. Most importantly, they did not surrender, as a rule, to the deformities of suffering and somehow managed to preserve their humanity intact. This is the story we seek to tell.

1 The occupation of Germany and the survivors: an overview

In February 1945 the Allied armies began their full-scale invasion of Germany and on 9 May 1945, after the unconditional German surrender, declared that the war in Europe had come to an end. A month later the Allied Control Commission began administering the country and divided it into four occupation zones in accordance with the principles agreed upon at the Yalta Conference earlier in the year. Germany was in almost total disarray: its large cities had been laid waste, vital services were paralyzed, transport and communications were virtually non-existent and governmental activity had ground to a halt. Returning these vital public services to a minimal level of operation placed an enormous burden on the Allied forces and seriously hindered them in giving their full attention to more than 9 million forced laborers from various countries and 80,000 concentration camp inmates they liberated as they advanced into Germany.

The Allies were fully aware of the large number of forced laborers they would uncover with the conquest of Germany and prepared in advance for the complex problems they expected to encounter. The forty-four states that comprised the United Nations set up UNRRA[1] in November of 1943 and its leaders were party to the discussions of the Supreme Headquarters, Allied Expeditionary Force (SHAEF) as it planned the invasion of Europe.[2] In November 1944 General Dwight Eisenhower, the Supreme Commander of SHAEF, and Herbert Lehman, the Director General of UNRRA, agreed to a division of labor between the two bodies in overseeing the treatment of displaced persons. The military would take responsibility for registration, housing, clothing, medical supplies and security while UNRRA would run the assembly centers where displaced persons would be gathered prior to repatriation and, in addition to health and welfare services, would see to cultural activities and vocational training where appropriate.

[1] For the history of UNRRA see George Woodridge, *UNRRA* (New York, 1950).
[2] For a detailed discussion see Dinnerstein, *America and the Survivors*: 9–38.

The US Army, according to this initial planning, would transfer overall responsibility for the DPs to UNNRA in October 1945 but, as things turned out, this was not to be. In April 1945 the first seven UNRRA teams were advanced into Occupied Germany; by May their number rose to 100 and by mid-July 350. Whereas the original plan called for 6,000 workers, by this date some 2,600 had been called forward and a year later their number had increased to 4,600. The training of these workers had been hasty, the selection process not always effective and, as a result, by the beginning of 1946 about a third were found unsuitable and had to be sent home. The military authorities, in addition, had little patience with a new organization that was dogged by inefficiency and had yet to find its way. In August of 1945 with well over one and a half million DPs still found in Germany, Austria and Italy, UNRRA decided to limit the scope of its activities and, for the time being, left the overall responsibility for the DPs in the hands of the army. One of the important functions relevant to *She'erith Hapleitah* that UNRRA held on to was the supervision and coordination of non-governmental agencies working with the DPs. Workers of the JDC which officially began its operations in Occupied Germany in August 1945 and the emissaries of the Palestinian Delegation who began to arrive in December 1945 both wore military uniforms and operated under the aegis of UNRRA.

With the dismantling of SHAEF in July 1945 the Western powers continued to coordinate their DP policies in the context of the Combined Displaced Persons Executive. By October, however, policy was determined in large measure by the military authorities in each of the four occupation zones and in the American Zone the overall policy of the US Army was straightforward and clear: the massive and speedy return of DPs to their countries of origin. It was a policy driven by a number of goals: to respond to the urgent desire of most DPs to get home as quickly as possible, to lighten the overwhelming administrative burden that tied down the occupation forces, to reduce the heavy costs of caring for millions of DPs and, in pursuit of normalization, to help the resettlement of some 11 million Germans and people of German descent who either fled or were expelled from Czechoslovakia, Western Poland and what was formerly East Prussia. This huge undertaking was expedited by some 8,000 liaison officers from almost every European nation who encouraged their citizens to return home and join in rebuilding their countries. Between May and September 1945 about 6 million DPs left Germany at the rate of 60,000–80,000 a day and by mid-1946 nearly all the West Europeans had been repatriated and, under far less auspicious circumstances, the bulk of those who came from the Soviet Union and its newly acquired satellites.[3] At

---

[3] For a brief survey of this sad and disturbing story see Wyman, *DPs*: 61–85.

this point in time, a little more than half a million DPs remained in the American Zone of Occupation, about 50 percent Poles and Ukrainians, some 90,000 from the Baltic states, approximately 70,000 Jews, 20,0000 Yugoslavs and a smattering of smaller national groups.

The East European DPs who refused to return home were, for the most part, either anti-Communists or Nazi collaborators who followed the retreating German forces westwards for fear of their lives. Ironically and, at times tragically, survivors of the Holocaust sometimes found themselves sharing camp facilities with their erstwhile persecutors. In the second third of 1945, as General Hilldring reported to a Congressional Committee,

procedures were established for eliminating from the camps those persons who were not entitled to receive United Nations displaced persons treatment. Under existing directives, the military authorities are now authorized to screen all displaced persons for pro-Nazi or pro-Fascist tendencies and to discharge people in those categories from displaced persons camps. They are authorized to repatriate without regard to their individual wishes and by force if necessary, those displaced persons desired by their governments who have actively collaborated with the enemy.[4]

However, despite continuing protests on the part of both American Jewish organizations and *She'erith Hapleitah* itself, the screening process remained lax and the military exercised its authority but rarely. Over the last few decades retrospective testimony to this fact can be found in Canadian and American extradition trials of war criminals who succeeded in entering these countries, often with the connivance of their respective secret services, via the DP camps of Occupied Germany.

When we turn to locate *She'erith Hapleitah* midst this welter of forces we should stress, once more, the predominant role of the US Army and the fact that the logic of its policy, designed primarily to deal with the complex challenges of post-war Germany, was often at odds with the special needs of the many survivors who resisted the idea of repatriation. In the first flush of victory and the chaotic conditions that followed, the remaining 50,000–60,000 concentration camp survivors were, by and large, lost from sight. Without taking this general background into account we shall not be able to arrive at a balanced assessment of the army's seemingly insensitive and somewhat summary treatment of *She'erith Hapleitah*. In this context it is instructive to note that studies

---

[4] Statement of Major General John H. Hilldring, Director, Civil Affairs Division, War Department before Subcommittee on War Mobilization and Senate Military Affairs Committee, 6 March 1946, found in the papers of Dr. Chaim Yachil (Hoffman). I thank Professor Leni Yahil for allowing me access to these papers.

of the American occupation of Germany barely mention the presence of survivors.[5] The US Army foresaw the existence of groups with special needs and in the Administrative Memorandum No. 39 of 16 April 1945 laid down that "stateless and non-repatriables ... will be accorded the same assistance granted to United Nations displaced persons. Enemy and ex-enemy nationals persecuted because of their race, religion or activities in favor of the United Nations will receive similar assistance." The directive stated, in addition, "that displaced persons who did not wish to or could not be repatriated, should be collected to special assembly centers. Teams such as the Joint Distribution Committee would be requested for Jewish centers."[6]

Despite their declared intentions, the military authorities were constrained to decide and act under the pressure of unremitting circumstances and, as a result, generally adhered to overall policy directives without allowing for exceptions. At the same time, at least according to one reading of what transpired, the policy of accelerated repatriation accorded with the desires of many survivors in Germany.[7] According to the estimate of Yehuda Bauer, significant numbers of survivors from Western Europe, Czechoslovakia, Romania and Hungary joined the first waves of mass repatriation and returned home.[8] Only a handful of Jews from Poland and the Baltic states followed suit while the majority chose to stay where they were and they, to a great extent, constituted the founding nucleus of *She'erith Hapleitah* in Occupied Germany. Malcolm Proudfoot estimated that in September 1945 there were approximately 32,000 Jewish DPs in Germany and Austria.[9] While Proudfoot based himself on British estimates which did not relate to Jews as a separate group, if we add the 15,000 survivors who crossed over into Italy seeking the protection of the Palestinian Jewish Brigade and in the hope of finding a way to Palestine to his base figure, we arrive at an estimate that is close enough to that of other scholars. The differences that still obtain relate to the first months of liberation and then converge around the figure of 50,000 in late July 1945. At that time, according to Bauer's estimate,

---

[5] Earl F. Ziemke, *The U.S. Army in the Occupation of Germany, 1944–1946* (Washington D.C., 1975) and Edward N. Peterson, *The American Occupation of Germany: Retreat to Victory* (Detroit, 1978).

[6] Memorandum on Stateless and Non-Repatriables, Executive CDPX, 5.8.1945, in Yehuda Bauer, ed., *Machanot ha'akurim be-germaniyah 1945–1948* (DP camps in Germany 1945–1948) (Jerusalem, 1962–1963): 7–8.

[7] Yehuda Bauer, *A History of the Holocaust* (New York, 1982): 237–238.

[8] Bauer appears to base some of his estimates on his research of the death marches in 1944–1945. See Yehuda Bauer, "The Death Marches: January–May 1945," *Modern Judaism*, vol. 3, no. 1 (February 1983): 1–21.

[9] Malcolm Proudfoot, *European Refugees: A Study in Forced Population Movement* (Evanston, 1956): 238–239.

1 The anguish of liberation, Dachau, April 1945

there were 14,000–15,000 Jews in Bavaria, 7,000 in Vienna, 13,000 in Belsen and 8,000 in Berlin.[10]

---

[10] Bauer, *Out of the Ashes*: 48. See also the personal estimate of Chaplain Abraham J. Klausner, "A Detailed Report on the Liberated Jew as He Now Suffers this Period of

The initial steps of those who preferred to remain in Germany were dogged by difficulties: they were forced to resist continuing pressure to return home, they had to fight for recognition as a separate Jewish entity and for the right to live in separate camps. While repatriation policy differed from place to place – in southern Germany the Third Army under the command of General Patton, for example, was notorious for its harsh pressure and lack of consideration – the refusal to recognize the Jews as a separate group was more general. What appeared to hamper the US Army was the absence of a consensual view of the nature of the Jewish group and the fear that dividing them off would be seen as akin to the Nazi policies of separation and exclusion. It was only in August 1945 when the determined struggle of *She'erith Hapleitah* together with the vocal protests of American Jews led to the presidential mission of Earl G. Harrison that real changes came into effect.

Towards the end of 1945, as the stage of mass repatriation drew to a close, the tension between the aspirations of the Surviving Remnant and military policy took on a new guise. With the appearance of the first signs of the Cold War, the strengthening of Germany as a strategic frontier with the Communist bloc became a goal of overriding importance. In practical terms the policy entailed softening the hard line that had been agreed to in Yalta and Potsdam with respect to de-nazification, German reeducation and the neutralization of Germany's industrial power.[11] Against this background, moreover, we can better understand the forbearance shown to East European war criminals who were noted for their strident anti-Communism. The normalization and rehabilitation of Germany came to be seen as an important priority and thus rendered the resolution of the DP problem more pressing. As the months went by the military, most especially those who were new to Germany, increasingly viewed *She'erith Hapleitah* as undisciplined, unforgiving troublemakers who constantly clashed with the local population while enjoying the vocal protection of their brethren in Washington and New York. Most disturbingly of all, from the point of view of the military authorities, their numbers continued to swell until they accounted for about 25 percent of the DP population in Germany. In sum, nonetheless, the enlightened policies of the military high command and the close interest of American Jews served to counter-balance these negative tendencies most especially with

Liberation under the Discipline of the Armed Forces of the United States," in Bauer ed., *Machanot ha-akurim be-germania*: 19–26; Report of the First JDC Team in Germany, Paris, 30.8.1945, AJDC/DP's Germany 1945; Chaim Yachil (Hoffman), "Displaced Persons," *Encyclopaedia Judaica*, vol. VI: 76.

[11] Koppel S. Pinson, *Modern Germany: Its History and Civilization* (New York, 1954): 536–546.

regard to uninterrupted entry of Jewish refugees from East Europe into the American Zone of Occupation in both Germany and Austria.

In September–October 1945 the first groups of Polish Jews organized by the *Brichah* began to infiltrate the American Zone of Occupation. The *Brichah* (the word itself connotes flight and escape) refers to the clandestine organization of the great latter-day exodus from Eastern Europe. It was originally organized by ghetto fighters and partisans in areas liberated by the Red Army in the second half of 1944 and in the next few years succeeded in moving more than 250,000 Jews, primarily from Poland, to Italy and the American Zones of Germany and Austria. In its early phases the founders tried to find a way to Palestine through Romania and, when that proved unsuccessful, they made contact with the Jewish Brigade and opened a route to Italy that was operational – on a small scale – from June to August of 1945.[12]

Once the British Army attempted to block entry to Italy and transferred the Jewish Brigade to Western Europe, the flow of refugees was directed to Germany. At the beginning of 1946 some 40,000 Jews had found their way to Bavaria and by the end of the year their number had grown to 142,000. In the first half of the year a monthly average of 6,550 refugees entered the American Zone via Austria while in July 1946, following the pogrom in the Polish town of Kielce, the monthly average jumped to 17,000 and UNRRA in conjunction with the JDC found themselves unable to cope. At this stage the army intervened and began to move those living in poor and crowded conditions in Austria into transit camps in Germany. Having taken care of 48,000 newcomers in August and September alone, from October to December 1946 some 9,000 refugees were admitted.[13] Of the 127,000 Jews officially registered with UNRRA in November 1946, 71 percent were from Poland, 6 percent Hungarian, 4 percent Czechoslovakian, 2.5 percent German, 2.5 percent Romanian, 2 percent Austrian and 10 percent declared themselves stateless.[14] Clearly, the changing fortunes of the Jews in Poland had a decisive influence on the ebb and flow of refugees guided to Germany by the *Brichah*. Those who left Poland in the latter half of 1945 had been, by and large, directly implicated in the Holocaust: survivors of the concentration camp system, ghetto fighters, partisans and those that had survived in hiding. From the beginning of 1946 the picture

[12] See "Reishitah shel 'ha-brichah' ke-tnuat hamonim be-eduyotav shel abba kovner" (The beginning of the *Brichah* as a mass movement in the testimonies of Abba Kovner), *Yalkut Moreshet*, no. 37 (June 1984): 7–32, and no. 38 (December 1984): 133–146.

[13] Bauer, *Flight and Rescue*: 75–112.

[14] See G.H. Muentz, AJDC Statistical Assistant, to Mr. Leo Schwarz, AJDC Director, American Zone re Jewish Population in US Zone of Germany, YIVO/DPG 70.

begins to change and Polish Jewish repatriates – those who were exiled to the interior of the Soviet Union and fortunately beyond the reach of the Nazi destruction machine – began to return to Poland and to swell the ranks of those moving westwards. In September 1944 the first in a series of Polish–Soviet agreements was reached regarding the repatriation of Polish citizens. Yisrael Gutman estimates that in the framework of this accord some 25,000 Polish Jews returned home during 1945.[15] To this figure we need to add the Jewish soldiers in the ranks of the Polish Army who participated in the liberation of Poland and the 157,420 Jewish repatriates who returned by mid-1946 under the terms of a second accord signed in July 1945. According to this estimate some 195,000 Polish Jews had been repatriated from the end of 1944 to the middle of 1946.

These repatriates put the new Polish government in a delicate situation. They returned from the Soviet Union bereft of all and discovered on their return that their homes, property and places of work had been taken over by the local population. The solution that was found involved transferring 80 percent of this group to the western regions of the country that had been annexed from Germany and emptied of its *volksdeutsche* population. The repatriates, however, did not succeed in striking roots anew. Their numbers were too small to recreate the richness of pre-war Polish Jewish life; they were haunted by memories of the world they had known and an abiding sense of living in a vast cemetery. This and more: they felt threatened by a murderous wave of antisemitism that stemmed, at least in its more immediate causes, from demands for the return of property and popular Polish identification of the new and despised Communist regime as Jewish-inspired. Between November 1944 and December 1945, 351 Jews suffered fatal attacks and by the summer of 1947 the numbers had exceeded 1,500. The high point was reached in the Kielce pogrom in July 1946 when, following charges of the ritual murder of a Polish child, forty-seven Jews were killed and another fifty wounded.[16]

All these factors pushed an increasing number of Jews to leave Poland and to seek refuge in Occupied Germany on their way out of Europe. In its first stages the *Brichah* served a limited number of predominantly Zionist groups but as time went by and conditions in Poland worsened, it became a broad-based, popular movement westwards. In the second half of 1945, 33,275 people departed and by October 1946, a further 78,267. In July 1946, for example, about 19,000 Jews departed and in August a further 30,722 followed suit. From November 1946 to February 1947 the numbers dropped noticeably with altogether 7,180 departing. An

---

[15] This analysis is based on Yisrael Gutman, "Hayehudim be-polin le-achar ha-milchama" (The Jews in Poland after the war), *Yalkut Moreshet*, no. 33 (June 1982): 65–102.
[16] See Bauer, *Flight and Rescue*: 113–151.

additional 20,000–30,000 Jews made their own way to Germany bringing the total to 140,000. One *Brichah* route led through Stettin to Berlin while two others went via Czechoslovakia and Austria.[17]

This being the case, it turns out that by the end of 1946 fully two-thirds of *She'erith Hapleitah* were repatriates who had not been personally and directly caught up in Nazi policies of terror, torture and killing. They had endured harsh and, for some, fatal years of exile; in most cases they lost their families from whom they were separated and, on their return, found their homes occupied by others, their property stolen or confiscated and facing a world that had turned alien and implacably hostile. Their situation, nonetheless, was very different from those who had survived the horrors of the Shoah and their demographic structure, most particularly, was strikingly dissimilar to that of the founding nucleus of *She'erith Hapleitah*. Because their chances of escape and survival had been so slim during the war, no group in post-war Europe had lost so many children and older people. A survey carried out in a number of DP camps at the end of 1945 showed that out of a sample population of 900 there were no children under the age of 5, 3 percent were 6–17 years old and but 0.2 percent were over 65.[18] For the same reasons while two-thirds of the 18–45 year olds – the overwhelming majority – were male, only one third were female.[19] Until February 1946, given that the influx from Eastern Europe was predominantly of direct survivors, the picture remains basically the same. A survey of 30,000 DPs at that time shows that 1.2 percent were children up to the age of 5, 9 percent were of school-going age and the percentage of older people remained at a constant low.

Significant changes began to make themselves felt from mid-1946 in the wake of the large influx of the repatriate population from Poland. By the end of the year 4.5 percent of *She'erith Hapleitah* were infants below the age of 1, 4 percent were 1–5 year olds, 11.8 percent were aged 6–17, the 18–41 year olds accounted for 68.1 percent and 11.6 percent were above the age of 45. The increase in the number of children can also be attributed, in part, to the growing birthrate within the founding survivor group. Whereas couples were common amongst the repatriates, the Nazi policy of sundering men from women only rarely allowed both husband and wife to survive. However, during 1946 many marriages were consummated, indeed from the middle of 1946 the rate of marriage was 27.4 per thousand souls while the parallel rate in the Bavarian population was 2.8.[20] These surprising figures point up the terrible loneliness of the survivors as well as their desire to return to life and to invest, once more, in

[17] Ibid.: 152–189.   [18] See Muentz to Schwarz, YIVO/DPG 70.
[19] Paris Memo 1114 to AJDC New York, 18.12.1945, AJDC/DP's Germany 1945/1946.
[20] See Muentz to Schwarz.

the future. Despite these differences all of the groups making up *She'erith Hapleitah* were united in the feeling that they were, together, survivors of the Holocaust.[21]

For months after liberation many survivors continued to live in primitive, crowded and demoralizing conditions lacking both nourishing food and adequate medical care. Only in August 1945, following the investigation and report of Earl G. Harrison to President Truman, were significant improvements introduced. Others because of their own initiative or the welcome assistance of local officers (oftimes Jewish) managed to improve their lot sooner. The St. Ottilien monastery not far from Munich became a survivor hospital under the direction of Dr. Zalman Grinberg; the army barracks in Landsberg were transformed into a reception camp for those liberated in Dachau and was run effectively by Major Irving Heymont in cooperation with the talented, local leadership group; Feldafing, a Hitlerjugend camp on the shores of Lake Starnberg, was transformed into an absorption center for death march survivors in that region by Lieutenant Irving Smith; Jewish soldiers helped to set up a camp in Zeilsheim in an I.G. Farben housing project near Frankfurt. These camps, together with Föhrenwald which was set up in October 1945, housed 4,000–6,000 inmates each and together served as the driving force behind *She'erith Hapleitah*. In 1945 most of the survivors in the American Zone were to be found in Munich and the large camps nearby while in 1946 we find movement northwards to new camps in Leipheim, Eschwege, Ulm and others in Hessen and Württemberg.[22]

As conditions began to stabilize in the late summer of 1945 the camp inmates had to contend with three major concerns: improving their living conditions which proved to be a long and tedious struggle, establishing separate Jewish camps which began to materialize in September 1945 and official recognition of their right to manage their own internal affairs. In this regard it was Landsberg that led the way and, soon after elections for a Camp Committee in late October 1945, other camps began to follow suit. Of course the authority of the Camp Committees was strictly limited because they had no financial resources to speak of while their

---

[21] On survivors and repatriates see Dr. Joseph J. Schwartz to Moses A. Leavitt, 9.11.1946, AJDC/DP's Germany 1945/1946; Divrei chaim hoffman be-kinus ha-shlichim be-germania (Address of Chaim (Yachil) Hoffman to Conference of Emissaries in Germany), January 1947: 2, CZA/S/4685; Chaim hoffman lehanhalat hasochnut (Chaim (Yachil) Hoffman to the Executive of the Jewish Agency), 19.6.1946, CZA/S/4676; Eli zeirah le-va'adat chutz la-aretz (Eli Zeirah to the Overseas Committee), 25.7.1946, Archive of *Lochamei Hagetaot*, Overseas Committee, Container 10, file 5; Report of Irving Kwasnik, October 1946, YIVO/DPG-215, and Phillip S. Bernstein, Report on Jewish Displaced Persons in the US Zones Germany and Austria to the Five Organizations, New York, 12.5.1947, YIVO/DPG 61.

[22] Pinson, "Jewish Life in Liberated Germany": 107–108.

constituency lacked political clout. On the other hand, they did take responsibility for the quality of life in the camp and many of the able adults were voluntarily employed in caring for cleanliness and sanitation, education and culture, public health, sport, religious needs and, in the larger camps, the publication of a camp newspaper.

In objective terms the achievements of the camp inmates were rather modest but, seen in the context of their singular situation what they managed to do takes on a different aspect. This, on the one hand, is how a Palestinian emissary portrayed the destructive negative side of DP camp life:

On the narrow street you will always find people . . . roaming about in search of something. I think they are seeking content for their lives. In the morning they get up without knowing what for. The day passes and night comes and so on . . . the present is superfluous and its only job is to bridge between the life that once was and what is yet to come. The sense of the provisional is felt at every turn. There is no stability, neither material nor spiritual. Yesterday they were in hell and tomorrow they'll be in an earthly paradise and betwixt and between emptiness and idleness.[23]

After months of intensive work with the inmates of the Landsberg camp this is the way Dr. Leo Srole described what may be seen as the other side of the coin: "The displaced Jews have an almost obsessive will to live normally again, to reclaim their full rights as free men. Their energies and talents have been dramatically exhibited in the vigorous communities they have created in the camps, despite scant material resources and highly abnormal environmental conditions . . . It deserves the world's admiration."[24]

Those who, despite the drawbacks, decided to remain within a camp framework, and they were the clear majority, sought the warmth of a shared life and, equally, the minimization of their direct contact with German society. Those who could no longer bear the unavoidable intimacy of camp life and were willing to forgo UNRRA assistance looked for a modicum of privacy in German homes, usually in the larger cities. In Munich and Frankfurt, for example, there were many thousands living privately while in other cities the numbers were considerably smaller. Thus, of the 47,698 Jewish DPs in the American Zone at the end of January 1946, 30,424 were to be found in camps and 17,274 in open communities.[25] At the end of the year 94,667 were to be found in

[23] Chaim Avni, *Im ha-yehudim be-machanot ha'akurim: rishmei shlichut 1945–1947* (With Jews in the DP camps: impressions of a mission 1945–1947) (Tel Aviv, 1980): 35.
[24] Srole, "Why the DP's Can't Wait": 13.
[25] Jewish Population in the US Zone of Occupation in Germany, 27 January 1946, AJDC US Zone in the papers of Chaim Yachil (Hoffman).

64 camps while 36,426 lived in 143 different communities. At this time, in addition, 4,743 youngsters were living in children's homes, 3,490 youth movement members were stationed in 42 agricultural training farms and a further 2,758 invalids were either hospitalized or recovering in rest homes.[26]

It is nigh impossible for the historian to capture the personal stories of tragedy and pain that hide behind these impersonal figures and it is seldom that we are given access to this hidden world. One such opportunity is afforded us by the diary of Dr. David Wdowinski, an important figure in the Jewish underground movement in Warsaw. Having moved from a camp in southern Bavaria to Feldafing he writes in October 1945:

I'm sad. Everything is getting me down. The general situation of the Jews, the attitude of our American "liberators", the vast tragedy of our people, private tragedies, uprooted people, people without a shadow... how great is the tragedy of each of us. Especially if one is sensitive. How carry this burden, this overwhelming sorrow, this endless pain? There is no past, no present, no future ... Terrible, terrible, without prospects, without hope. Justice and revenge. Justice! Justice? Where is it? [We live in] a world of evil, a world of violence and lies, lies and deceit. How great is the disillusionment! There is no God, no justice, no decency! Just nothing but lies and that alone.[27]

In February 1946 Dr. Leo Srole prepared a report on the mental health of the survivors to the Anglo-American Committee of Inquiry that was investigating the situation of the Jewish DPs and its possible relationship to settlement in Palestine. He focused on two major findings: first, during the Holocaust its victims had suffered terrible psychic damage and, second, their enforced stay in Germany was making it worse and promised few benefits. And yet, he found it surprising that so few had either suffered total demoralization or had fallen victim to mental breakdown: "I was amazed that the imminent threat of violent death, inducing overwhelming anxiety, in combination with reduction by starvation to the demoralized animal level, both suffered thru a period of years, did not induce a high incidence of psychotic ... tendencies, whereas only a few isolated cases with such tendencies in incipient form have been observed."[28]

Srole was profoundly impressed by the resilience of She'erith Hapleitah and their determination to rebuild their lives. This impression is underscored by the lead article opening the first and, as it turned out, the only

---

[26] Jewish Population in US Zone of Germany effective 31 December 1946, AJDC US Zone, in the papers of Chaim Yachil (Hoffman).

[27] Dr. David Wdowinski, *Anachnu lo noshanu* (And we are not saved) (Jerusalem, 1985): 162.

[28] Dr. Leo Srole, Submission to the Anglo-American Commission for Palestine, AJDC/DP's Germany 1946.

number of *Techiyat Hametim* – Resurrection – which appeared in Buchenwald at the beginning of May 1945, just a few weeks after liberation:

> We know: there are various questions which torment us and burn (within) ... we
> are also fully aware that a variety of physical and psychological difficulties have
> become part of us in the course of the hard times (spent) in the camp ... we lost
> contact with normal life and it is our demanding goal to find it again! ... We seek
> to reenter our new lives as healthy and normal people.

In this struggle, wrote the editors, what would serve them well was a
virtue hard earned in the years of terror: "Akshanut – endurance. And
we seek to endure, to hold firm, so that we can start everything afresh
and to bend all our physical and spiritual efforts towards beginning to
rebuild our lives and our world together."[29]

In Srole's view the resilience of *She'erith Hapleitah* did not stand on its
own but was, in many cases, inextricably bound up with their commitment to Zionism. Many of those he questioned about how they managed
to withstand the destructive pressure of Nazi terror almost invariably answered: " What sustained me ... thru those frightful years was ... my
indestructible will to live for the day I could return to Palestine."[30] An
historian might seek to qualify this generalization as it relates to the period
of the Holocaust but there is little doubt that it holds, by and large, in
the immediate aftermath. Hence it is worth noting, with caution, Srole's
dire warning "that if this powerful faith should be shattered, then the
spirit of these people will be broken as Hitler could never break it, and
the psychic damage already done will proliferate."[31] One of our tasks will
be to examine the validity of this sweeping claim, at least in its public
manifestations, and to begin by tracing the first steps taken by *She'erith
Hapleitah* in the months preceding liberation.

---

[29] *Techiyat Hametim: Tsaytung far di bafrayte yidn in lagern, Buchenwald* (Resurrection of the
dead: organ of the liberated Jews in the camps, Buchenwald), no. 1 (4.5.1945): 1.
[30] Srole, Submission.   [31] Ibid.

2 The formation of *She'erith Hapleitah*: November 1944 – July 1945

Towards the end of 1944 the survivors of the Lithuanian ghettos who had been transported to Germany took their first steps toward the organization of *She'erith Hapleitah*. The date, nearly a full six months before liberation, is of some significance because it underscores the crucial role played by the survivors themselves in preparing for liberation long before any help from the outside became available. It also accounts for one of the most surprising features of survivor organization in Germany – the fact that the major institutions of *She'erith Hapleitah* came into being, at least in embryonic form, on the very morrow of liberation. The nuclei of the Central Committee of the Liberated Jews in Bavaria, the United Zionist Organization and the first *kibbutz-hachsharah* in Buchenwald started to coalesce during the final stages of the Allied conquest of Germany and began their actual operations with the liberation.

In the face of the advance of the Red Army in July 1944, the Germans began to transfer the survivors of the Lithuanian ghettos westward. The women were sent to the Stutthof camp while the men were transported, in the main, to the subsidiary camps of Dachau.[1] As the Soviet pressure mounted in January 1945, additional Jews were deported and marched from Auschwitz to Gross-Rosen, Mauthausen, Buchenwald and Dachau.[2] In the chaos which marked the final stages of the war, the survivors were caught in a cruel twilight of conflicting Nazi policies: on the one hand they were used as slave laborers who could also serve as bargaining pawns in Himmler's last-ditch attempt to detach the Western powers from their alliance with the Soviet Union;[3] on the other, they suffered the agonies of the death marches which, in effect, continued

---

[1] Leib Garfunkel, *Kovno ha-yehudit be-churbana* (The destruction of Jewish Kovno) (Jerusalem, 1959): 202.
[2] Bauer, "The Death Marches: January–May 1945."
[3] Yehuda Bauer, "The Mission of Joel Brand," in *The Holocaust in Historical Perspective* (Seattle, 1978): 94–105.

the Final Solution by other means.[4] Two important factors nonetheless distinguish this phase from the preceding period – the cessation of systematic, total annihilation and the approach of the Allied forces. As Jacob Oleiski, a leader of *She'erith Hapleitah* from Kovno, wrote:

> In the last months of the war, even those of us in the camps knew that the German lines were on the verge of collapse. In the last few weeks we actually heard the artillery fire at the front. And the thoughts which had oppressed us in the ghettos became all the more painful: would they not get rid of us in these last moments of the war? This was the question we came back to again and again in the discussions we conducted in our underground barracks late into the night.[5]

For the first time there were real grounds for believing that survival might be possible. There was a palpable need to begin thinking concretely about liberation as the chaotic conditions attending the German collapse opened up new avenues of underground activity. Clandestine groups that had begun to operate in Buchenwald and in the subsidiary camps of Dachau utilized the changing conditions to prepare for the future. In the final analysis, most of the plans put forward at this early stage did not come to fruition – too many unforeseen factors intervened – but a number of leadership groups came into being, groups that were able to take the initiative once conditions made this possible. Here we trace the genesis of these groups and the way in which they laid the organizational and ideological foundations of *She'erith Hapleitah*.

In Buchenwald the Communist underground had taken control of clandestine activities in 1942 and maintained its dominance until the liberation of the camp on 11 April 1945. In the course of time national blocs were formed within the underground movement; however, since Communist doctrine refused to recognize the Jews as a separate nationality, Jewish activists converged on the Polish national bloc. Their presence opened the way to the informal pursuit of Jewish concerns that came to focus on the rescue and education of some 500 Jewish children who had been sent to the camp. Yechezkiel Tidor organized these activities with the active help of Eliyahu Greenbaum who took the lead in the autumn of 1942 when Tidor was transported to Auschwitz. In January 1945 Tidor accompanied by Arthur Poznansky, himself a veteran of "Hechalutz" in Germany, returned to Buchenwald having survived a murderous journey from Auschwitz. The three became the *de facto* leaders of the informal

---

[4] Livia Rotkirchen, "The Final Solution in its Last Stages," in Y. Gutman and L. Rotkirchen, eds., *The Jewish Catastrophe in Europe: Background, History, Implications* (Jerusalem, 1976): 671–683.

[5] Jacob Oleiski, "Fun farknekhtung tsu oysleyzung" (From slavery to redemption), *LLT*, no. 16 (28) (10.5.1946): 4.

Zionist underground and created a commune for mutual help, support and consultation in preparation for the dangers that lay ahead.[6] These activities were supported by numerous non-Jewish groups but never became the official business of the Buchenwald underground.

With liberation an International Committee was set up to oversee the running of the camp but Jews were once again refused separate representation. Consequently, some veterans of the underground, led by Tidor, Greenbaum and Poznansky, took matters into their own hands and established a Jewish Self-Help Committee. A temporary hospital was set up, and the Jewish Committee took the care of the children under its wing and helped the survivors procure food and suitable accommodation.[7] Beyond this, the Committee which was greatly aided by two American chaplains, Robert Marcus and Herschel Schachter, compiled a list of the Buchenwald survivors and at the beginning of May published *Techiyat Hametim* (Resurrection), the first newspaper of Holocaust survivors in liberated Germany.[8] When the first team of the American Jewish JDC and OSE arrived in Buchenwald from France in mid-June in order to transport some of the surviving children to Switzerland, the French director was able to report that the Jewish Committee was effectively taking care of Jewish affairs with the blessing of the military authorities. Indeed, a week or so after liberation Rabbi Schachter organized Sabbath prayers in the "Sports Hall" which had earlier served as an oversized punishment area. More than a thousand survivors participated and, as Yehudit Tidor Baumel writes, it turned into "a massive demonstration of Jewish identification in Buchenwald."[9]

From the outset the question of "where to now?" gave the survivors no rest:

The Jews suddenly faced themselves. Where now? Where to? They saw that they were different from all other inmates in the camp. For them things were not so simple. To go back to Poland? To Hungary? To streets empty of Jews, towns empty of Jews, a world without Jews. To wander in those lands, lonely, homeless, with the tragedy before one's eyes ... and to meet, again, a former Gentile neighbor who would open his eyes wide and smile, remarking with double meaning, "What! Yankel! You're still alive!"[10]

[6] Ruzka Korczak, "Yeladim be-machaneh rikuz buchenwald" (Children in the Buchenwald concentration camp), *Yalkut Moreshet*, no. 8 (1968): 42–74.

[7] In this regard see the following testimonies Chaim Tzamit, YSA/03/3116; Yaakov Verber, *Moreshet* Archive/A/421; Chaim Tzamit, Meir Ahuviah, Eliyahu Greenbaum, Avraham Lindenbaum, *Moreshet* Archive/A/428.

[8] *Techiyat Hametim*, no. 1 (4.5.1945); see also Zemarion, *Ha-itonut shel she'erith hapleitah*: 64–68.

[9] Yves Lyon, Rapport sur le voyage de Buchenwald de l'Equipe Joint-OSE (13–23 June 1945): 2, AJDC/DP's Germany; and Baumel, *Kibbutz Buchenwald*: 24.

[10] "Homecoming in Israel: Journal of Kibbutz Buchenwald," in Leo W. Schwarz, ed., *The Root and the Bough: The Epic of an Enduring People* (New York, 1949): 310.

2 Liberation: the first Sabbath prayers in Buchenwald led by Chaplain Zvi Schachter.

Generally speaking, the Jews of Hungary and Romania decided to return home, at least as a first step prior to determining what their final destination would be.[11] The Polish Jews, who constituted some 90 percent of the survivors, were deeply divided on this issue, and many of the discussions of the Jewish Committee, as given expression in the pages of *Techiyat Hametim*, focused on this question. The Bundist faction demanded the return of the Jews to Poland where, as Baruch Goldberg put it at a 1st of May celebration for the children of the camp, "we wish further to develop the traditions of Yiddish culture and education as part of the national freedom struggle for a just, independent and democratic Poland, a struggle wherein the Jewish workers ... have already inscribed a heroic and bloody chapter."[12] In no way was this illusionary, argued Goldberg (apparently in response to his Zionist critics), for a new order was rising in Europe on the ruins of fascism and the Jews were called upon to take an active role in this development.

[11] Yves Lyon, Rapport sur le voyage de Buchenwald: 5–7.
[12] Baruch Goldberg, "Mir viln boyen" (We want to build), *Techiyat Hametim*, no. 1 (4.5.1945): 2.

There were those, however, who viewed the projected return of Jews to Poland rather differently. Perhaps French or Hungarian Jews could put down roots once again, but when it came to Polish Jews, wrote one of Goldberg's detractors, "matters were somewhat different! . . . How can I go back there, to that land where every stone tells me and reminds me of the blood of my brother and sister . . . The spirits of my dear departed ones will appear before my eyes and ask: Why, why did you return in order to erect your wedding canopy on our graves?"[13] And, even if the returning Jew did manage to overcome his repulsion, his Polish neighbors would not leave him alone, for he would be seen as an accuser, risen from the grave, who had come to remind them of their sins of yesterday – handing the innocent over to the Nazis and then claiming their property.

The Zionists had no doubts as to their final destination and, within a week of liberation, published a call to the Jewish world to provide them with immigration certificates to Palestine. There was nowhere else they could go, there was nowhere else they wanted to go.[14] The more vigorous survivors sought to join the Jewish Brigade so as to participate in the final defeat of Nazi Germany but practical difficulties prevented this and, in truth, it was more of a symbolic gesture than a realistic option.[15] The activists of the Jewish Self-Help Committee who began to fear the demoralizing impact of inactivity and uncertainty in the unhealthy surroundings of the camp requested the help of Rabbi Schachter in locating a farm where they could set up a *kibbutz-hachsharah* – a cooperative agricultural training farm – where young people could prepare themselves for life in Palestine. Rabbi Schachter won over the local G-5 officer responsible for DPs to the idea and he, in turn, procured a farm in nearby Eggendorf which allowed this remarkable experiment to get underway in late May 1945.

Kibbutz Buchenwald, as the young survivors called it, formally set out to embody the lessons of the Holocaust and, at the same time, served as a substitute family for those whom the war had left orphaned. The founders decided that their *kibbutz* would not limit itself politically or religiously and would open its doors to all who wished to join. During the war, so they reasoned, the Jews had, without distinction, suffered one

---

[13] Motele S., "Un vos vayter?" (And what next?), *Techiyat Hametim*, no. 1(4.5.1945): 4.
[14] An die Zionistische Oeffentlichkeit, Juedischer Hilfsausschuss, Buchenwald (22 April 1945), CZA/S25/5235.
[15] Ibid. In addition see Joseph W. Eaton, The Jews Surviving in the Buchenwald Concentration Camp (21.4.1945), CZA/S25/5235; on the early attempts at Zionist organization in the camp see the letter from the Committee of Pioneer Youth in Buchenwald (in Hebrew, undated), Archive of *Lochamei Hagetaot*, Overseas Committee, Carton 11, file 2; for a detailed and sympathetic history of Kibbutz Buchenwald see Baumel, *Kibbutz Buchenwald*.

fate. This raised questions about the validity of old divisions in Jewish life in general and in the Zionist movement in particular, leading to the suggestion that the unity which had been imposed as a common fate should now be embraced as a central value of their shared future. This reading of the Jewish Catastrophe became the ideological cornerstone of *Kibbutz Buchenwald*.[16] A second lesson underscored the central pioneering value of self-labor – the one and only answer to the devastation wrought by the Germans was Jewish independence and this, in turn, rested on the willingness of the pioneers to shoulder the heavy burdens of independence. In a letter written to the representatives of the Jewish Agency in Paris in mid-1945, the leaders of the *kibbutz* explained their basic philosophy:

So far, we are a preparatory *kibbutz*, but do you believe that we need physical and spiritual training before we can live in Palestine? No. We have had a six-year course of preparation that has made us hard like steel . . .

Some of our people have become demoralized through their years of suffering . . . Still, there were . . . many who did not lose their pride and convictions. These people have built *Kibbutz Buchenwald*. Most of us are Zionists of old; the rest, through prison and suffering, have come to the realization that the only place for us is our own national home.

Through our physical labor in this *kibbutz*, we have meant to demonstrate that we are not yet destroyed, but that we have the will to live and build. We have meant to demonstrate our dislike of philanthropy and dependence on others.[17]

In early June 1945 the *kibbutz* got formally underway and before long there were some forty–seven members in training and a start was made in the study of Hebrew.[18] When the surrounding area was slated for Russian occupation, the group moved to Geringshof, a former Zionist training farm situated near Fulda in the American Zone of Occupation. In its new setting *Kibbutz Buchenwald* elicited much favorable comment and soon became a focus of inspiration for the young survivors. When the first group left for Palestine in late August, its place was immediately taken by a new and even larger group of youngsters, thereby ensuring continuity to a unique venture which started in Buchenwald but came to serve as a model for education and rehabilitation in *She'erith Hapleitah* as a whole.[19]

Another focal group in the early organization of *She'erith Hapleitah* were the survivors of the Kovno Ghetto who had been deported to the Dachau area in late 1944. One of the figures in encouraging clandestine activity in Kaufering, a subsidiary camp of Dachau, was Michael

---

[16] "Homecoming in Israel": 316.   [17] Ibid.: 319.

[18] Akiva Skidell, "Im ha-tzava ha-amerikai be-germaniya ha-kvushah" (With the American Army in Occupied Germany), *Yalkut Moreshet*, no. 30 (November 1980): 164.

[19] Ibid.: 167.

Burstein, the Yiddish writer from Kovno. With the downfall of Germany now in sight, Burstein, who did not survive the war, suggested setting up an organization that would both maintain morale and begin to plan for what was going to happen after liberation. The group, which included Leib Garfunkel and Dr. Zalman Grinberg, launched some clandestine cultural activities and began to explore the possibilities of cooperation with a Communist group moving in the same direction. As the end of the war grew closer there were also discussions with Dr. Rudolf Valsonok and Beinisch Katsch, both of whom had served as officers in the Polish Army, about capturing the armory during the evacuation of the camp. These plans did not ultimately materialize but the discussions which took place boosted morale and helped create a group of leaders who stepped into the breach when the time was ripe.[20]

On the eve of liberation this group found itself near the village of Schwabhausen after the rapid advance of the American forces had frustrated the Nazi design to move them to the Tyrolean Alps. There, in a small wood beside their train which had been immobilized by American strafing, a number of the leaders hastily conferred with one another. Israel Kaplan, the historian from Riga who was also present, sees this hurried meeting of Grinberg, Oleiski, Dr. Samuel Gringauz, Dr. Nachum Katz, Rudolf Volsonok, Shlomo Frankel and others as the founding act of *She'erith Hapleitah*.[21] Grinberg, who had studied medicine in Switzerland, was sent to the village head in order to obtain help for the wounded. He took full advantage of the proximity of the American forces and managed to extract some aid from the local population. Grinberg also contacted a military hospital in the nearby monastery of St. Ottilien and here too the threat of American reprisals served to secure ambulances and hospitalization for the badly wounded. With the arrival of the American forces on the following day, Grinberg was charged with directing the hospital which immediately opened its doors to all needy Jews in the area.[22] In short order, some 400 Jews from Hungary, Greece, Slovakia, Lithuania and Poland found refuge in St. Ottilien which almost immediately became one of the first centers of survivor organization.

The new and surprising role of the erstwhile monastery-cum-SS hospital came to the attention of the public with the Liberation Concert that was held on 27 May 1945. Some 800 survivors from St. Ottilien

---

[20] Dr. Zalman Grinberg, *Our Liberation from Dachau*, a private translation by Israel Eiss from *Kamah*, Yearbook of the Jewish National Fund (Jerusalem, 1948): 28–36, and, in addition a personal interview with Dr. Shlomo Shafir (Frenkel), 17.5.1999.

[21] Israel Kaplan, "Marsh fun kaufering lagern" (The march from the Kaufering camps), *Fun Letstn Khurbn*, no. 5 (May 1947): 22.

[22] Dr. Z. Grinberg, Bericht an den Juedischen Weltkongress (31 May 1945), YIVO/DPG 21.

and the camps in the area participated and a number of representatives from the Military Government and UNRRA were also present.[23] In his speech to the gathering Grinberg gave voice to the pain of personal loss and national destruction while addressing the terrible doubts of the few who had survived. Those who remained alive were the pitiful remnants of the great centers of European Jewry:

> Millions of members of these same communities have been annihilated. What is the logic of fate, then, to let us live? We belong in ... the common graves of those shot in Kharkow, Lublin and Kovno; we belong to the millions burnt and gassed in Auschwitz and Birkenau; we belong to the tens of thousands who died under the strain of the hardest labor; we belong to those tormented by millions of lice, the mud, the starvation ... We are not alive – we are still dead.[24]

The sole purpose of the living was to serve as a voice for the dead, to tell the world what had befallen an innocent people and "what brutal hellishness is concealed within a human being and what a triumphant record of crime and murder has been achieved by the nation of Hegel and Kant, Schiller and Goethe, Beethoven and Schopenhauer."[25] Grinberg's words were followed by *Kaddish* – the Prayer for the Dead – and the program ended on an affirmative note with a concert given by the remnants of the Kovno Ghetto orchestra.

No operative discussions took place at the Liberation Concert and no formal decisions were taken. The importance of the event is to be found in the gathering itself, in the sense of sharing the burden of the past and beginning to shoulder responsibility for what lay ahead. What emerged from the meeting was a feeling of community, the sense that this was a group of people with a shared identity and purpose rather than a random collection of survivors. At a deeper level this purposefulness seems to be a reaction to the profound helplessness experienced during the Holocaust. On a more immediate level, however, it was a response to the perceived absence of representatives of the Jewish world and stemmed from a painful sense of abandonment. This was an issue that Grinberg addressed when he wrote to the World Jewish Congress a few days later; "Four weeks have now passed since our liberation and no representative of the Jewish world ... has come, in the wake of the greatest tragedy of all time, to be with us and to lighten our burden ... and so we have been forced to take care of ourselves with our own meager resources."[26] This was something that the

---

[23] An account of the occasion is to be found in the New York *Forverts* (14.6.1945): 10.

[24] Speech given by Z. Grinberg, MD, Head Doctor for Political Ex-prisoners in Germany at the Hospital Liberation Concert in St. Ottilien on 27 May 1945, PRO, FO 371 55705/YIN 08304: 1.

[25] Ibid.

[26] Dr. Z. Grinberg, Apell an den juedischen Weltkongress, St. Ottilien (31.5.1945), YIVO/DPG 21.

survivors could neither understand nor forgive, it was a sore point that surfaced repeatedly in the months to come and was seen as an important factor in forcing *She'erith Hapleitah* to take matters into its own hands.

A Zionist group, somewhat younger in composition, was also operative in Dachau. Its members were formerly active in the *Irgun Brith Zion*, a middle-of-the-road Zionist youth movement in the Kovno Ghetto.[27] From September 1944 members of the movement who had been deported to Germany strove toward renewed association in an attempt to combat the debilitating inhumanity of camp life. The first tangible step they took was the renewed publication of their underground newspaper *Nitzotz* (The Spark) which they had first put out during the Soviet invasion and which continued to appear under Nazi rule. Seven issues of the paper appeared in Dachau-Kaufering prior to liberation in what seems to be an unprecedented venture in concentration camp life.[28] The twelve to nineteen pages of each issue were written in fine, flowing Hebrew by Shlomo Frenkel (today Shafir) and then, using writing materials smuggled out of the camp office where his father worked, five copies were copied by Ya'akov Lipschitz and circulated in the Kaufering and other neighboring camps. Frenkel managed to preserve five copies under his belt, in his socks or hidden in their primitive dug-out in Kaufering I while the two issues produced in Kaufering II were lost. Each issue contained political articles that engendered lively debate, memoirs of ghetto life in general and of the *Irgun Brith Zion* in particular and, remarkably, literary contributions. On the eve of liberation as his group was herded into the main camp of Dachau, Frenkel met Monsignor Jules Jost of the Red Cross, whom he knew from earlier visits to Kaufering. Fearing that they were to be gassed, Frenkel asked him to look after the five issues of *Nitzotz* that he was carrying with him. Jost, in turn, passed on the material to an old-time Spanish Republican inmate for safekeeping. A few days after liberation just before the first repatriation train left for Spain, Frenkel managed to track him down and to retrieve his precious parcel.[29] The very act of putting out a Hebrew newspaper and circulating it in a concentration camp is noteworthy. But our concern with *Nitzotz* goes beyond the courage that informed this daring initiative and focuses primarily on a remarkable first attempt to sum up the meaning of what the paper called

---

[27] For a narrative *cum* documentary history see Dov Levin, *Bein nitzotz ve-shalhevet: "irgun brith zion" be-milchemet ha-olam ha-shniyah* (Spark and the flame: "Irgun Brith Zion" during the Second World War) (Ramat Gan, 1987).

[28] Zemarion, *Ha-itonut shel she'erith hapleitah*: 129–133.

[29] Interviews of the author with Mr. Shlomo Shafir (Frenkel) on 18.5.1979 and 17.5.1999; see also Shlomo Shafir, "Ha-'nitzotz' she-lo kaba" (The spark that was not extinguished), *Kesher*, no. 9 (May 1991): 52–57.

"the Catastrophe," in the light of which efforts were made to plan for the future. A few months later members of this group, including Abraham Melamed, a future member of the Knesseth, came to occupy a number of key positions in *She'erith Hapleitah* and played an active role in determining its initial policies.[30] There are, as we shall see, some important lines of continuity between the ideas first aired in *Nitzotz* and policies pursued after liberation.

The surviving members of *Irgun Brith Zion* were persuaded that a determined fight against the physical and moral debilitation of concentration camp life was the necessary precondition for any serious collective activity. The cruel battle for survival in the camps generated a selfish nihilism that threatened to weaken the bonds of solidarity necessary for any social organization. The first step in the struggle for humanity – and here these younger leaders fell back on their movement ethos and their ghetto experience – was for them to set an example of caring for others and to safeguard their individual integrity. The second step entailed the setting up of underground cells that would concern themselves with both education and mutual help. The Zionist education envisaged by the *Nitzotz* group was to provide both spiritual sustenance and tangible guidelines for the future and it was the latter that gave rise to painful heart-searching. What, they asked, did the future hold for the Zionist movement? What was the future of Zionism now that European Jewry had been annihilated?

For Frenkel the dilemma was stark: on the one hand the subjective attraction of Zionism was greater than ever before,[31] while on the other, the objective chances of achieving its goals had dimmed considerably:

Before our eyes Zionism has begun to lose the claim to the political title of being the movement that will save the remnants of our people. There is no point in dreaming anymore about the liquidation of European Jewry for it has been wiped out already by the fire and swords of German soldiers ... The Jewish question has already been solved by Adolph Hitler; he has, without doubt, succeeded in achieving his goal. Even if he has not destroyed all of world Jewry he has nonetheless reduced our national strength to a minimum and has brought us to a critical pass from which there is no certainty that we will recover.[32]

---

[30] Samuel Gringauz and Zalman Grinberg were prominent leaders of *She'erith Hapleitah*, Leib Garfunkel headed the Organization of Survivors in Italy while many of those associated with *Nitzotz* were instrumental in the creation of the United Zionist Organization and *Nocham*; Shlomo Frenkel, in addition, continued to edit *Nitzotz* and later *Dos Vort* as well.

[31] Cohen (Chaim Cohen), "Lishelat ha-zman" (On the question of (this) time), *Nitzotz*, no. 5 (40) (Purim 5705 – March 1945): 49. (Page numbers follow the more accessible copy of the paper found in the CZA. The original is deposited in the Yad Vashem Archives.)

[32] Ivri (Shlomo Frenkel), "Al parashat drachim" (At the crossroads), *Nitzotz*, no. 3 (38) (Channukah 5705 – December 1944): 14–15.

Beyond this fatal blow to the biological and cultural heart of the Jewish people two additional factors reinforced this gloomy prognosis: the constant attrition of Jewish life in the Soviet Union taken together with the fact that American Jewry lived at ease and could not be expected to raise, en masse, the flag of Zionist realization. Political Zionism had therefore lost its *raison d'etre* and what remained was the possibility of a spiritual, minimalist Zionism that would seek a national center in Palestine for the creation of a revitalized and free Jewish culture.[33] This shift of the emphasis from the problem of the Jews to the problem of Judaism was also politically wise. In all its international appearances the Zionist movement supported its claims by focusing on the plight of European Jewry. This line of argument, however, had become tragically anachronistic since the problem of European Jewry "had already been solved by Adolph Hitler." The international situation in Frenkel's estimate, was not propitious for a Zionist breakthrough. Britain and the Soviet Union, each for their own reasons, did not favor the creation of a Jewish state, while the United States, despite its sympathy for the Zionist cause, lacked direct influence in the Middle East. It was imperative to formulate a new and realistic approach to Zionism so that the survivors would not have to experience the dangerous disappointment of yet another failure.

It should be noted that in April of 1945, those who secretly listened in to the BBC in Kaufering II reported that the Allies had invited representatives of both the World Jewish Conference and the World Zionist Organization to the forthcoming peace conference in San Francisco. This generated much excitement and comment for it was seen as tantamount to international recognition of the Jewish people as a nation and of the Yishuv as its political embodiment. For Frenkel it opened the way to a guarded return to the central Zionist goal of Jewish statehood: "The Zionist movement finds itself, fifty years after the appearance of 'The Jewish State', standing before the realization of its critical aim – the founding of a Hebrew state. In the upcoming international conference it could gain all or lose all. The decisive moment has arrived." Nonetheless, a profound sense of loss continued to inform the thinking in *She'erith Hapleitah* long before its significance was either understood or internalized by many others.[34]

Frenkel's analysis gave rise to keen debate and his views were hotly contested by Leib Garfunkel, a veteran Zionist who had served on the *Judenrat* of Kovno and was soon to become one of the preeminent leaders

---

[33] Ibid.: 15.

[34] Ivri (Shlomo Frenkel), "Le-or ha-metziut ha-chadashah" (In the light of the new reality), *Nitzotz*, no. 6 (41) (Pesach 5705 – April 1945): 22–23.

of *She'erith Hapleitah* in Italy. Garfunkel saw the policy of striving for a spiritual center without a Jewish majority in Palestine as mistaken. Even the 600,000 Jews of the Yishuv would not suffice for this minimalistic aim. At least one to one and a half million Jews were needed for this limited purpose, which meant that mass immigration remained the foremost Zionist priority. Frenkel, in Garfunkel's view, needed to qualify his predictions with respect to the post-war situation in Europe: the European Jews had not been totally annihilated and there were substantial communities that would need to be rescued. Many Jews in Hungary, Romania and the Balkans had been deprived of their homes and livelihood, and it was hard to see them putting down roots again in places where "the earth had not yet . . . managed to soak up the Jewish blood that had been shed."[35] Where the victimization had been substantial, on the other hand, those who survived did not have the numbers or the will to rebuild the communal structures that had been the pride of European Jewry before the war.

Garfunkel also advised against the premature dismissal of Soviet Jewry. The Jews of Russia had become aware that a great divide continued to separate them from the population as a whole despite twenty years of Soviet rule. This hard-learned lesson could ignite a Jewish national awakening that could possibly benefit from the new flexibility which the Soviet regime had demonstrated in its wartime relations with the West. One had to take into account the negative attitude of Jews in the Yevsektsiya – the Jewish section of the Communist party – to changes of this kind but their direct influence on the formulation of high policy was strictly limited. Either way, the question of Soviet Jewry should enjoy high priority on the national agenda. Neither was Garfunkel willing to forgo the constituency of idealistic Jews in America who would be able to make a critical contribution to the creation of a Jewish state. This, then, is how he saw things as the end of the war drew near:

In the light of our terrible situation there should be neither talk about the question of the Jews nor of Judaism. The tragic and unprecedented question on our agenda relates to the very existence of the Hebrew nation. For if we do not see the creation of an independent and viable Jewish center in the Land of Israel in the near future it will spell the beginning of the final decline and fall of our people.[36]

The Zionist movement should not lower its aims, therefore, and had to appear before the world with a comprehensive plan of action that would include a call for mass immigration. In point of fact, it was this approach

[35] Aryeh (Leib Garfunkel), "Le-birur emdateinu" (Towards a clarification of our position), *Nitzotz*, no. 5 (40) (Purim 5705 – March 1945): 63.
[36] Ibid.: 67.

that was adopted by the leaders of *She'erith Hapleitah* in the months to come.

While general assessments of what the future had in store differed, the Zionists in Dachau-Kaufering were of one mind when it came to formulating the practical steps that needed to be taken in preparation for liberation. Their most important task was to move toward the unification of their ranks. In the Kovno Ghetto the *Irgun Brith Zion* had made Zionist unity its main goal, and now that the end of the war was in sight it had become all the more pressing. All agreed that the extreme factionalism of Jewish life had added to their disarray in the fact of the Nazi onslaught. This could not be allowed to continue once the war was over. The Nazis did not distinguish between rich and poor, religious and secular, nor did they concern themselves with different ideological positions – all Jews, no matter where they stood, were subject to one and the same fate. This lesson stood at the center of their reading of the great Catastrophe and served as the guiding principle in all their public activity. In order to open its ranks to others, the group sought to reconstitute itself as the Association of National Youth and to coordinate its activities with other factions in preparation for liberation.[37]

Fearing that they would be caught between an American drive to expedite repatriation and Soviet disregard for their Jewish needs, they aimed to forge a united leadership that could legitimately claim to represent the Jewish survivors and thereby protect their vital interests:

we ... stress ... the need to create an organizational power and leadership group here in the concentration camp prior to our liberation ... We have to be ready – both externally and internally for what the future has in store for us. The Zionist group should take the lead and this it will be able to do only if the foundations are already laid now.[38]

Taking the lead included working for the realization of the strategic aims of the united Zionist camp: free immigration into Palestine and the immediate establishment of a Jewish state. This was more than a political demand, it was a moral claim on the civilized world, a demand that it see the creation of a state as somehow compensatory for the millions of Jews who had been senselessly slaughtered.[39] The willingness of the world to acknowledge its responsibility would be a token of its moral stature and a precondition for the return to basic trust and a sense that life has meaning. Garfunkel wrote in April 1945:

[37] See *Nitzotz*, no. 4 (39) (Tu B'Shvat 5705 – February 1945): 19.
[38] *Nitzotz*, no. 5 (40) (Purim 5705 – March 1945): 19.
[39] *Nitzotz*, no. 6 (41) (Pesach 5705 – April 1945): 71.

While in this Nazi hell one burning question racks our brains and gives us no respite: what was it all for, why the murder of millions and a sea of blood? A vain sacrifice from which nothing good will come? Or will this revolutionize our lives and lead to a fundamental change in the way the world relates to us? Perhaps both they and we will come to the realization that the Jewish people can no longer live without a national center of its own.[40]

In time, we should add in parentheses, many in *She'erith Hapleitah* came to see that no redeeming purpose could be found in the destruction. The terrible question "What was it all for?" could not be answered. Their task, as they perceived it, was to redeem the future and the return to Zion was regarded as the critical first step in this endeavor.

The move to Jewish sovereignty represented a self-conscious attempt to shake off the abject status of being the millennial objects of history, and take on, instead, the responsibility and risks of being its subjects. This essentially ideological stand mirrors an important feature in the psychological makeup of this group of survivors. Most descriptions of human behavior in extreme situations focus on the debilitating effect of totalitarian terror.[41] We have come to recognize a reverse phenomenon worthy of attention. Robert Lifton approximates a description of this special quality when he writes that "the survivor can retain an opposite image of having met death and conquered it, a sense of reinforced invulnerability."[42] Those who had lived through the unprecedented trials of the Holocaust emerged with self-assuredness, determination and extraordinary daring. David Wolpe, a young poet from Kovno, while still in Kaufering described the survivors as:

> ... the saved remnants of Israel
> A small band
> Bold, brave and strong
> As reinforced concrete
> Tempered by a thousand trials.[43]

It should be noted that this feeling of being beyond fear could easily have come to serve destructive ends and this, indeed, happened on occasion. In this Zionist group, however, the very opposite took place: their protracted immersion in a world of suffering and pain strengthened their devotion

---

[40] Aryeh (Leib Garfunkel), "Petach tikvah" (The gate of hope), ibid.: 72–73.

[41] For example Bruno Bettelheim, *The Informed Heart* (London, 1960): 106–107.

[42] Robert J. Lifton, *Death in Life: Survivors of Hiroshima* (New York, 1969): 481.

[43] David Wolpe, "Tikvat hagolah" (The hope of exile), *Nitzotz*, no. 6 (41) (Pesach 5705 – April 1945): 93. In this regard see David Wolpe, "Meine tsvay ivrit-shirim in katset" (My two Hebrew poems in the concentration camp), *Forverts* (14.5.1999): 16.

and deepened their sense of historical responsibility. It was this willingness to work for the commonweal that helped them gain the respect of their fellows and endowed them with the moral authority to take the lead when liberation came.[44]

On 27 April 1945 a train carrying Jewish prisoners being moved out of Kaufering I to Dachau was strafed from the air. As many as 200 deportees were killed or wounded; some who escaped and went into hiding eventually reached St. Ottilien; yet another group arrived in Dachau and was liberated there on 29 April in the afternoon. Among these were Frenkel and Hayim Kagan, a more senior leader of the *Irgun Brith Zion*, who immediately set up a Zionist group which brought the Jewish survivors together, organized mutual help and even began preparing lists of prospective immigrants to Palestine.[45] On a more symbolic level they clashed head-on with the International Committee, representing the 30,000 liberated inmates of Dachau, which refused to recognize the Jews as a separate national group. The Zionist group would not back down and persisted in its protests until the blue-and-white flag was hoisted at the entrance of the camp alongside those of all the other nationalities.[46] A few days after liberation Samuel Goldsmidt, an Anglo-Jewish journalist reached Dachau and met with Frenkel and Kagan.[47] On his return to London in mid-May, Goldsmidt gave a full report of his trip to David Ben-Gurion, the chairman of the Jewish Agency, and handed him a letter from Kagan. Ben-Gurion was visibly moved by what he heard and immediately arranged for fifteen immigration certificates to be placed at the disposal of the Dachau group, which enabled some of its members to set out for Palestine in September 1945. Through his meeting with Goldsmidt, furthermore, Ben-Gurion learnt of the presence of an active Zionist group in Bavaria, a group with views similar to his own and the ability to play a significant role in the Zionist strategy he had decided upon toward the end of the war.[48]

In the initial period of liberation Frenkel and his companions found themselves pitted against Communists and Soviet liaison officers who

---

[44] Chaim (Chaim Aleksandrovitz), "Al miftan meuraot machri'im" (On the threshold of momentous events), *Nitzotz*, no. 7 (42) (25.4.1945): 107.

[45] S. Goldsmidt, "Shichrur dachau" (The liberation of Dachau), *Haboker*, (13.5.1945): 1. See also the cable of I. Schwartzbart to E. Dobkin (10.5.1945), CZA/S25/5231.

[46] Goldsmidt, "Shichrur dachau".

[47] Details about this meeting and the meeting with David Ben-Gurion were contained in a personal letter to the author from Samuel Goldsmidt sent on 22.6.1980; see also S. Goldsmidt, *Jews in Transition* (New York, 1969): 64–78.

[48] See minutes of the *Mapai* Executive (15.3.1945), Ha'avodah – Labor Archive, 23/45: "Our ties with the remnants of European Jewry are liable to be one of the decisive factors in settling the question of Palestine."

attempted to persuade the survivors to return to the countries of Eastern Europe.[49] They argued that the repatriates would forfeit their freedom in vain while the Zionist movement would lose desperately needed reinforcements at a critical moment in its history. Following their refusal to be associated with the Soviet contingent, they were joined to a group of right-wing Lithuanian nationalists who were imprisoned in Dachau following clashes with the German Occupation forces in the latter part of the war. Fearing Soviet retribution, they also declared themselves to be stateless. Not surprisingly, many of the survivors sought to leave Dachau: the infirm found refuge in St. Ottilien and Gauting, a German tuberculosis sanitorium, while several others made their way to the fledgling camp in Landsberg and the Freimann-Flakkaserne, an international assembly center on the outskirts of Munich.

In this endeavor they were greatly assisted by a young and determined chaplain, Rabbi Abraham Klausner, who chanced to arrive in Dachau in May 1945. What struck him forcibly in the course of his initial conversations with survivors was the remarkable vitality they demonstrated, their urge to locate their families and their drive to rebuild their lives. Klausner soon began to identify with the survivor's reading of their situation and agreed that there was no public body of any stature able to extend help to them forthwith. He thus decided to take matters into his own hands and for the next eighteen months devoted himself to working for *She'erith Hapleitah*. Klausner's courage and unconventional resourcefulness earned him the esteem of the survivors and the enmity of the larger organizations that served the displaced persons within the limiting restraints of standard procedure. He focused his considerable energy on the immediate needs of the survivors and became the moving force in the establishment of the Jewish Information Office in Dachau which set out to locate, register and publish the names of all the Jews who had survived in Bavaria.[50] By 26 June 1945 he had already managed to publish the first volume of *She'erit Hapleta*, a list, organized by a camp of survivors in Bavaria, which was followed, in the months to come, by four updated editions. Klausner also played an important role in the initial organization of *She'erith Hapleitah* and served as the honorary president of the Central Committee of the Liberated Jews in Bavaria until his departure from Germany in December 1946.

[49] Interview with Shlomo Shafir (17.5.1999).
[50] See testimony of Abraham J. Klausner, OHC, 4 (4). See, in addition, letter of M. Dortheimer and Yaakov Zilberstein (Chairman and Secretary of the Jewish Information Office) to Nathan Schwalb in Geneva, CZA/S6/4560, and the report of Hyman Yantian who served in the British Jewish Relief Unit (9 June 1945), CZA/S25/5238, and also Abraham J. Klausner, A Detailed Report on the Liberated Jew.

During the visits he paid to other camps in the area, Klausner discovered that the situation of the liberated Jews continued to be indescribably bad. In Mittenwald to the south, for example, the ex-prisoners almost rebelled against their American guards in protest against their poor nourishment and degrading living conditions. The Jews in the camp organized a Zionist Committee under the leadership of Dr. David Wdowinski who had been chairman of Betar (the right-wing Revisionist youth movement) and played an active role in underground activities in the Warsaw Ghetto.[51] Soon after liberation they had been visited by Dr. Saly Mayer, the representative of the Joint in Switzerland, but no help had been forthcoming. They needed food, clothing and medicine and asked in addition for Jewish newspapers, religious items and books for the study of Hebrew and English. Wdowinski reported, furthermore, that a Polish Committee had taken upon itself to represent the Jewish survivors but this was something they would not tolerate.

We have had enough of being the objects of foreign politics. It should be known that almost no Polish Jews wish to return to Poland. For us Poland is a large cemetery without graves and bereft of tombstones. Of the three and a half million Polish Jews perhaps 15,000–20,000 are still alive ... Most want to settle in Palestine and the remainder in North and South America.[52]

The only way to an effective Jewish politics, argued Wdowinski, was by concentrating all the Jews spread over Germany in one area.

A similar situation obtained in Buchberg where a few hundred Jews separated themselves from a large number of Russians awaiting repatriation. A makeshift committee was organized and recommended that the Jewish survivors move en bloc to a Lithuanian camp in Bad Toelz. Levi Shalitan, a young journalist who had been an underground activist in the Siauliai ghetto and later in Dachau, supported the move for it could lead to meeting other Jews and joining them in the pursuit of common goals. In Bad Toelz, as it turned out, Shalitan met up with Yitzchak Ratner, a veteran Zionist leader from Kovno, and Yosef Leibowitz who had been a member of the Judenrat in the Siauliai Ghetto and served as the underground liaison with *Irgun Brith Zion* in Kovno.[53] The three were in basic agreement as to the tasks which awaited them: the pitifully few survivors had to be brought together under a united leadership that would stand

---

[51] Saly Mayer, Über Besuch der Lager in Vorarlberg, Bericht Österreich, 24. Mai, Württemberg, Bayern und bis 29. Mai, 1945. See also Ergänzende Mitteilungen zu unserem Bericht über Besuch der Lager in Deutschland vom 29. Mai 1945. These documents were made available to me from the private collection of Prof. Yehuda Bauer.

[52] Report of Dr. D. Wdowinski, CZA/S6/4560.

[53] See testimony of Yosef Lavi (Leibowitz), OHC, 37(4).

above party strife and work together for immigration to Palestine and the creation of a Jewish state.

Toward the end of May 1945, Ratner and Leibowitz arrived at the Freimann-Flakkaserne in pursuit of this aim. They immediately set about creating a local Zionist Committee, initiated the creation of support groups, assisted in organizing the search for relatives and began registration for immigration to Palestine. Here, too, a major effort had to be invested in the fight against repatriation, but their work was made easier by the return of some survivors who had made the trip east in order to search for family and salvage some of their personal property. They brought back dreadful stories of threat and attack that quickly spread through Bavaria and deterred many from venturing back to their previous homes. As a JDC worker reported in July 1945:

I have come across a number of people who have already been home to their native countries and now returned without any status of any kind to Germany because of the terrible pogroms that are in constant progress, I am now in contact, for instance, with a group of eight men – Jews – from Poland. They fled back to Germany because the Poles and the Ukrainians are killing the Jews left and right when they return, it seems they are terrified of having the Jews reveal to the Russians those who have been working with the SS, Gestapo, etc., as well as their natural love of Jew killing.[54]

On 9 June, Ratner sent a short memorandum to the Zionist Executive in Jerusalem detailing some of the initial activities of the "Zionist Secretariat in the DP Camp near Munich." He was able to report that Zionist groups were operating in all the camps in their vicinity and that a Central Committee had been set up in Munich.[55] Their work, however, was suffering for lack of regular contact with some official Zionist body that would both provide guidance and help them overcome their sense of isolation. "Our people are under the impression that nobody cares for us. We have no one to turn to ... and desperately await news from you."[56] Their major concern, wrote Ratner, was the combined American and Russian pressure for repatriation, and this was a question of vital urgency for the Zionist movement. There was no way of knowing what would become of these people if they did return to Eastern Europe, and according to their reading of the situation, "the tragedy of European Jewry and the future of our work in Eretz [Israel] require us to save every Jew possible

---

[54] Helen Waren to Eli Rock (2 July 1945), YIVO/DPG 226.
[55] Yitzchak Ratner to the Zionist Executive in Jerusalem (9.6.1945), CZA/S5/829; a toned down version of the letter was also published in *Davar* (18.7.1945).
[56] Ratner to the Zionist Executive (9.6.1945), CZA/S5/829.

for our cause ... We fear that the day may dawn when there will just not be enough immigrants for the country."[57]

Already in June 1945, therefore, the local Zionist groupings that sprung up after liberation began to move toward a more comprehensive, regional organization. Equally noteworthy is the political thinking which underpinned this organization. These survivors understood that the Zionist movement had lost its human hinterland in the Holocaust and that their primary task was to keep the Saved Remnant together in the hope that the majority would avoid the uncertainties of dispersion and, when the time came, would be able to make their way to Palestine. What we have here, in embryonic form, is the idea of concentrating *She'erith Hapleitah* in one area, a concept that was further reinforced with the arrival in Germany of representatives of the Jewish Brigade.

At the end of the war the Palestinian Jewish Brigade that had fought in Italy was stationed in Tarvisio on the Austro-Yugoslavian border. At that time the leadership of the Yishuv was divided as to the future of the Brigade and debated whether it should remain in Europe or be returned home as soon as possible. The position of the political leadership within the Brigade itself was emphatic. Chaim Ben-Asher, editor of the Brigade newspaper *Ba-ma'avak,* wrote in a letter to his wife:

A rumor has reached us about a decision to return home at once. This would be a grave error both politically and Jewishly ... We did not burn with the ghettos when they rebelled, surely we should do something to save the remnants??? And this would be a step backwards in terms of Jewish dignity ... While there are still Jews here the Brigade must do everything to be close to them. What our people are able to do will not be done by anyone else – and things are far more serious than anyone ... imagines. Without these Jews how will we hold out at home?[58]

As it turned out, the decision taken in Palestine concurred with this analysis and the Brigade was given two major assignments: to make its presence as the military representative of the Jewish people felt in Germany and, perhaps more importantly, to do everything possible to help the survivors. Thus, from the end of May the soldiers of the Brigade, in addition to Palestinian soldiers in other units, began to fan out over Europe in search of relatives and survivors. Very soon contact was established with a group of survivors in Klagenfurt just over the Austrian border, while at the end of May, Hyman Yantian reached Dachau and met with the Jewish Committee there.[59] In his wake the Brigade sent Martin Hauser, an RAF intelligence officer, to seek out Jews in Austria

---

[57] Ibid.   [58] Chaim Ben-Asher to his wife Chana (10 June 1945), CZA/A-292/22.
[59] See report of Hyman Yantian (8.6.1945).

and southern Germany, and he was able to make contact with the Zionist groups that had sprung up in the Munich area.[60] Through the networks that were established information began to flow to the Brigade and toward the end of June, Ben-Asher reported on pockets of antisemitism in UNRRA and among the American forces, and told of attempts to break the spirit of the survivors in order to ensure compliance with the policy of repatriation. The best answer to this pressure, in his view, was the "lively [Zionist] movement in Bavaria which had demonstrated political acumen and the ability to hold its own in the face of bewildering change."[61]

The first official delegation of the Brigade to *She'erith Hapleitah*, under the command of Captain Aharon Hoter-Yishai, visited the Freimann-Flakkaserne on 20 June 1945. Its arrival was a source of comfort and inspiration to all, and in a meeting with Hoter-Yishai the representatives of the Zionist Center decided to hold a festive conference in order officially to welcome the Palestinian soldiers. As it moved from camp to camp the delegation passed on the word, and on 24 June representatives from Zionist groups in Feldafing, Buchberg, St. Ottilien, Landsberg, Schleißheim and Munich met in the Freimann-Flakkaserne. Ya'akov Lipschitz, rabbi of the Brigade, was moved to provide the following description of the occasion:

slogans of redemption, land, settlement and immigration cried out from the walls. Dark, wasted eyes are cast upward and hungrily take in what is written. There is a podium bedecked with pictures of Herzl, the Zionist fathers and the movement flag. On the chairs sat shrunken skeletons with dry, thin hands, wearing tattered caps. Many are still in their prisoner garb. On the faces of all the immobility of death ... an expression of apathy. They represented the millions of Zionists who had been asphyxiated, hung and burnt in Europe. The delegates bore a strong resemblance to their dead constituents.[62]

This description captures the eerie, outward unreality of the early stages of liberation but completely overlooks the vitality and determination that made the Zionist movement in Bavaria a force to be contended with. Lipschitz identified in every way with these people and their plight, but, at the same time, his perceptions are in line with the widespread stereotype of the survivors as broken spirits listlessly awaiting a redeeming hand. However, the representatives in the hall drew their moral authority, their right to speak for others, as was the case throughout liberated Europe,

---

[60] See Gelber, *Toldot ha-hitnadvut III*: 409.
[61] Chaim Ben-Asher to his wife Chana (20 June 1945).
[62] Yaakov Lipschitz (Gil), in *Sefer ha-brigada ha-yehudit* (The book of the Jewish Brigade) (Tel Aviv, 1950): 382.

from their underground activities during the war and their public role after liberation.

After a full day of presentations and discussion, the participants formulated a public statement that gives us a sense of Zionist thinking in *She'erith Hapleitah* at this formative stage. The "First Conference of Zionists in Bavaria" called upon the survivors to embrace the one clear lesson from what had befallen them: "to liquidate the European *Galut* [exile] and to go on aliyah [immigrate] to Eretz-Israel."[63] This negation of exilic life in Europe was not only a preface to aliyah but an act of significance in and of itself. This was an expression of self-respect and a refusal to submit any longer to the indignities of minority life. From their point of view, it was also the most meaningful form of revenge against those who had attempted to destroy them. "For two thousand years we unstintingly gave of our substance to this accursed Europe" and after they had toiled, built and even shed their blood, wholesale murder was their reward. All Jewish energies should be directed, henceforth, to the rebuilding of their own people and this would be their proud response to all those who had sought their downfall.[64]

In view of the fact that the Nazis had destroyed the human hinterland of the Zionist movement, the liquidation of the European *Galut* also implied the rescue of the National Home by those who had been fortunate enough to survive. This, in turn, could be achieved only on condition that the residual resources that remained to European Jewry could be galvanized into unified action. The demands of the conference, however, went beyond this and they aspired to see *She'erith Hapleitah* leaving its mark on the Yishuv, as was the case with earlier waves of immigration to Palestine, and on the Jewish people as a whole: their task was to bring the message of unity to the Yishuv in an attempt to marshal its depleted forces in the fateful struggle for sovereign statehood. As for the rest of the Jewish world, it was their solemn duty to inform them that the defeat of Hitler did not in any way signify the demise of antisemitism. Severe trials still awaited the Jewish people and only a state of their own would be able to ensure the creative continuity of Jewish life. This too was the moral foundation of their claim upon the world – Zionism held out a solution to the problem of both Judaism and the Jews, and represented the only sure way to prevent the danger of recurrence.[65]

---

[63] "Derklarung fun kinus tsiyonei bavaria in minkhen dem 25.6.1945" (Declaration of the Zionist Conference in munich, bavaria, 25.6.1945), in Ze'ev Hering, *Tsvishn khurbn un geulah: in gerangl far der she'erith hapleitah* (Between destruction and redemption: midst the struggle for *She'erith Hapleitah*) (Munich, no date): 79–80.
[64] Ibid.   [65] Ibid.

Toward the end of the war the term *She'erith Hapleitah* referred to those who remained alive, to the survivors.[66] With liberation additional shades of meaning were attached, and it came to denote, especially in Germany, a group with a special status, ideology and identity. The key element in the shaping of this shared identity was the commitment to national rebirth and the desire to be an active and unifying force in its fulfillment. In the months following liberation this entailed a stubborn struggle against repatriation and thus inevitably led to a series of clashes with the American forces in Occupied Germany. However, the early protests of survivors, chaplains and Palestinian officers were to little avail, and it was only in August 1945, following the report of Earl Harrison, that some change became evident. *She'erith Hapleitah* suffered further disabilities because it was officially defined as a religious rather than a national group. Jews were registered in the DP camps according to their country of origin, and for many East European Jews this form of classification was both cruel and degrading. Thus it often happened that the former victims of the Nazis found themselves bunking down with fascists who had happily collaborated with the German Occupation forces a few weeks earlier. The irony became almost unbearable when Jews born in Axis countries had to struggle to avoid being defined as enemy nationals. Three months after liberation, therefore, most of the survivors in Bavaria found themselves living on enemy terrain, without freedom of movement or national recognition. They were hungry, poorly dressed and desperately uncertain as to their future. "When the blood flowed in the torture camps of Auschwitz, Treblinka, Dachau, Buchenwald," wrote Chaim Cohn, one of the activists from Kovno, "we were a people, a separate entity. But now, as the day of reckoning draws closer, the relationship to us is rather different."[67] The survivors were, as they so often claimed, "liberated but not free," and expressions of anger, frustration and, at times, despair became far more noticeable.

The gap between the nigh utopian dreams of liberation and the flawed reality encountered by the survivors engendered the disappointment and their desire to take charge of their lives again in despite the debilitating dependence of DP life fired their sense of frustration. When Ratner, by way of illustration, once dreamt of liberation, he imagined the loving embrace of the peoples of the earth and their ready assistance in the realization of Jewish national aspirations. In the real world they encountered, however, little resembled the object of their dreams. Russia was experiencing a

---

[66] Chaim (Chaim Aleksandrovitz), "Al miftan meuraot machri'im": 107.
[67] Chaim Cohn, "An Appeal from a Concentration Camp", *PM* (Thursday 27.9.1945): 9, CZA/S25/5214.

wave of post-war nationalism that was implicitly antisemitic; in Poland Jews lived in fear; in Romania and Hungary they were denied their former jobs and the return of their property; Czechoslovakia refused recognition to any minority group; and in Western Europe, too, anti-Jewish feeling ran high. Thus, concluded Ratner, "We have lost our faith in the justice and conscience of humanity ... Our hope has come to naught ... Alone we blunder through a world of blight."[68]

Over and above the troubles of the hour, each survivor also carried a private burden from the past. Many were indeed ready to inform outsiders about what had happened to them, but these stories told of externalities and generally did not reveal experiences that were far more intimate.[69] After many and lengthy conversations with Dr. Wdowinski in Mittenwald, Ben-Asher described him as "a man who emerged from those years unsullied and sound in mind and spirit."[70] Wdowinski's personal diary gives us a very different sense of what weighed on his heart at the time:

There is no belief, no hope. I spoke today with a rabbi, a man of faith. "I study in order to forget, and not because I was commanded to." Without faith, helpless, without a future, without a link to life. Black despair. What is the point of our lives? Why and to what end? For what? Uprooted, without a shadow, a ridiculous figure, a tragic man. Inner emptiness. And if others say that they have something substantial [to hold on to] – that is also a lie: they are mouthing empty phrases from ten years ago. They speak with their mouths and not with their hearts. It is cerebral, everybody is lying, everybody. There are but two ways out: to commit suicide or to surrender to the forces of darkness; to drink, get drunk, to eat and copulate. And that is what most are doing. They commit suicide by killing their humanity, unknowingly. A lost people ... What and who do I have in the world? Friends? An empty phrase, just words. A people? A people? This is a people?[71]

It is difficult for an outsider to plumb the depths of the darkness that envelops Wdowinski's words and all that we are able to infer is that the maintenance of a facade of affirmative normalcy was not an automatic reflex but rather the outcome of a determined struggle.

Raw pain of this kind did not suffer easy comfort and the leaders of She'erith Hapleitah were especially wary of allowing these feelings to

---

[68] Y.R. (Yitzchak Ratner), "Ha-achzavah ha-gedolah u-maskanateinu" (The great disappointment and our conclusion), *Nitzotz*, no. 9 (44) (20.7.1945): 5.

[69] "To work with them," complains David Shaltiel, a Jewish Agency emissary who got to France after the liberation, "one has to steel oneself because we keep hearing the same things about what they went through in the ghettos, how the deportations began, that their wives and children were sent to the gas chambers while their father was shot to death." Report to the *Mapai* Executive, *Ha'avodah* – Labor Archive, 24/25.

[70] Chaim Ben-Asher to his wife Chana (4.7.1945): 8.

[71] Wdowinski, *Anachnu lo noshanu*: 159–170.

fester for, where anguish overcame all else, moral breakdown or corrosive self-pity could not be far behind. Only affirmative deeds would be able to counter these dangers, and thus the survivors were called upon to share in the attempt to concentrate the remaining Jews of Eastern Europe in Germany, to maintain camp activity at a high pitch, to go south into Italy *en route* to Palestine, and to keep up the fight for international recognition of their basic rights.[72] It was nonetheless clear that this attempt to harness anger and frustration to constructive ends could be sustained only if *She'erith Hapleitah* coalesced around leaders who they saw as their own and who could be recognized as the elected representatives of a separate national group.

One of the subjects that came up for discussion at the Zionist gathering in the Freimann-Flakkaserne was the need for an overall representation that would be able to protect vital Jewish interests. Thus Klausner's proposal to convene a meeting of camp representatives from all over Bavaria met with general approval and the consent of the Military Government. Forty-one representatives gathered in Feldafing on 1 July 1945 and set about creating an elected body that would serve as the official representative of *She'erith Hapleitah*.[73] Feldafing was at that stage the only Jewish camp in Bavaria and owed its existence to the persistent efforts of its Jewish commander, Lieutenant Irving Smith. The medical attention, nutritious food and reasonable accommodation it offered soon attracted thousands of liberated Jews, and thus Feldafing as the largest camp in the area was the natural site for the conference.[74]

The participants agreed that their primary task was the establishment of an effective representative body; they were somewhat divided, however, as to its political affiliation. Dr. Rosenthal, who apparently represented a Bundist group, argued that his constituents intended to return to their countries of origin and thus could not see their way clear to working with a body that was Zionist by definition. He suggested the creation of a non-political organization that would concern itself with the immediate needs of the survivors. The Zionist majority at the gathering agreed that the body should be universal in its membership and concerns, but at the same time they insisted on the crucial significance of Eretz-Israel for the rescue of the survivors in particular and for the future of the Jewish people in general. Accordingly, the constitution of the Association of Surviving

---

[72] See address of Yitzchak Ratner at the special session of the Center for the Diaspora of the Jewish Brigade on the arrival of the first organized group that departed Bavaria for Italy in July 1945, *Ha'avodah* – Labor Archive, 33/14.

[73] See Protocol, Feldafing, YIVO/DPG 21.

[74] See the report of Major Caspi to the Center for the Diaspora of the Jewish Brigade, early July 1945, *Ha'avodah* – Labor Archive, 33/14 and the testimony of Abraham J. Klausner in A Detailed Report on the Liberated Jew.

Jews in the American Occupied Zone of Bavaria that was drawn up in Feldafing defined its major task as the representation and protection of *She'erith Hapleitah*. At the same time, a clause was inserted that promised close cooperation with the Zionist movement in Bavaria and, in point of fact, there was a large overlap in the leadership of the two groups both then and later.[75] On a more practical level it was decided that the camp representatives (proportional to the number of their constituents) would serve as the plenum of the Association and elect a Council of twenty-one members to determine overall policy and an Executive Committee of eight to carry this out.[76] The Council included eight Lithuanian Jews, five from Poland, four from Hungary, three from Romania and one from Greece. Rabbi Klausner was appointed, by way of recognition, as the honorary president of the Council, while Dr. Grinberg was elected as chairman of the Executive. The proceedings concluded with the formulation of a resolution addressed to the Allies on the eve of their conference in Potsdam, expressing profound appreciation for the Allied victory, stressing the Jewish contribution to the war effort, and demanding that the 1939 White Paper be annulled and the gates of Palestine be thrown open to unrestricted Jewish immigration.[77]

A few days later the Executive Committee met in the Freimann-Flakkaserne and shortly thereafter moved to more permanent offices in the Deutsches Museum in Munich. Seven makeshift departments were set up to deal with the most urgent needs of the survivors, including repatriation, medical care, nutrition, clothing and housing.[78] On the broad political front two interconnected concerns engaged the attention of the Committee: the need to build up an effective organization and to receive recognition as the legal representative of a separate national group from the US Army. After Klausner failed in his efforts to secure some form of recognition, the Committee sought the help of Joseph Dunner, a Jewish officer who supervised newspaper publication in Munich. Dunner participated in the first working sessions of the Committee and hoped to be able to bring their requests to the personal attention of General Eisenhower.[79]

Chaim Ben-Asher and Aryeh Simon, the emissaries of the Jewish Brigade who had been touring the camps of Germany from the beginning

---

[75] See the testimony of Yosef Lavi (Leibowitz), OHC, 37 (4).

[76] See Zitsung des farbandes der iberlebendn yidn in der amerikanishn bezatsungszone (Session of the Association of Surviving Jews in the American Occupation Zone), YIVO/DPG 21.

[77] See Oyfruf (Appeal), YIVO/DPG 21.

[78] See the minutes of the session of the Praesidium (5.7.1945) and (12.7.1945) as well as the sessions of the Executive Committee on 5, 9 and 13 July 1945, YIVO/DPG 94.

[79] See minutes of the session of the Praesidium (5.7.1945), YIVO/DPG 102.

of July, urged the Committee to step up its activity. In point of fact, several initiatives had already been set in motion at this early stage: some representatives had left for Bergen-Belsen to make contact with the survivors there; others had traveled to Poland to assist in the search for relatives; while a third group had gone south into Italy in search of a way to Palestine. The Brigade emissaries nonetheless felt that the time was ripe for a dramatic initiative that would capture public attention – Britain was on the eve of elections, Earl Harrison, who had met with Simon, was touring the DP centers, the Zionist Executive was about to convene in London for the first time since the war and a meeting of the governing body of UNRRA was also in the offing. This was a propitious moment for a concerted campaign that would bring the plight of *She'erith Hapleitah* to the attention of the world and thereby pressure the British Government to revise its White-Paper policy of May 1939 severely limiting Jewish immigration to Palestine and purchase of land.[80] This would help the Committee gain publicity and credibility in the survivor communities spread through Germany. They recommended convening a broad-based conference to include communities in the British Zone and others not yet represented on the Committee. In the end, two of these developments were especially significant for *She'erith Hapleitah*: the tour and subsequent report of Harrison and, internally, the convening of an expanded representative conference.

The Conference of Representatives of the Surviving Jews in Germany convened in St. Ottilien on 25 July 1945, bringing together ninety-four delegates representing some 40,000 Jews from forty-six centers spread over Germany and Austria.[81] The organizers, who were well aware of the importance of public relations, invited a number of reporters and ranking American officers to participate in the opening ceremony. Eliyahu Dobkin, head of the Jewish Agency's Immigration Department, also took part in the conference and, indeed, was the first Jewish figure of public standing to reach *She'erith Hapleitah*. Grinberg captured the tragic aspect of the gathering in his opening remarks when he recalled the impressive conferences of the pre-war years attended by representatives from the proud communities of Vilna, Warsaw, Prague and Berlin, who had assembled in pursuit of shared aims. "Now the delegates are from Dachau and Bergen-Belsen, Schleißheim and Landsberg ... representing the handful that survived the extermination camps."[82] What brought them together was the tragic fact that despite their suffering and the very real

---

[80] See minutes of the sessions of the Executive Committee on (13.7.1945) and (14.7.1945), YIVO/DPG 94.

[81] For some records and minutes of the Conference in St. Ottilien see CZA/S6/4560 and S25/5232; a detailed description of the Conference can be found in YIVO/DPG 61.

[82] For Grinberg's opening address see CZA/S25/5231.

contribution of the Jewish people to the war effort, they were moldering, orphaned, on German soil, without the possibility of realizing the one thing that still gave meaning to their lives – the return to their historic homeland. In this fateful endeavor, stressed Grinberg, the survivors were not only representing themselves – they also spoke for those who had made their last wishes known before they perished:

> We, the innocent victims, were put to death on the altar of a historic injustice ... for over the generations we never had the opportunity to root ourselves in our own ... land. The flame that rises from our burning bodies will bring a new light to the world that will enable the leaders of the nations to perceive the sufferings of a people bereft of a home and open the way for the return to our historic homeland. This will and testament embodies the sole ... meaning of the most ghastly catastrophe in the history of man.[83]

The reports of the delegates and resolutions carried at the conference focused on two major demands: free and immediate immigration to Palestine and, in view of the small likelihood of this happening, preparations for a more extended stay in Germany. In this regard the conference recommended concentrating the Jews in separate camps with internal autonomy and possibilities for both education and vocational training on the model of *Kibbutz Buchenwald*. A further resolution called for collecting testimonies and evidence which would help bring Nazi criminals to trial; this material would later be shipped to Palestine and could serve as the foundation stone for a memorial to the destroyed communities of Europe. Germany, moreover, was called upon to compensate the victims for both physical disabilities and the loss of property. The intensive deliberations were brought to a conclusion with a symbolic ceremony held in the Bürgerbräukeller in Munich. There, amidst desecrated Torah scrolls, twenty of the delegates assembled and read an official declaration calling for an independent state and equality of rights for the Jewish people worldwide.[84]

There can be little doubt that given these inauspicious circumstances the St. Ottilien Conference was a remarkable success. The verve, the courage and vitality deeply impressed the foreign observers.[85] The historian, nonetheless, should inquire whether the event is best likened to the demonstration that took place in the Bürgerbräukeller, i.e., a symbolic gesture, or whether it had a real impact on the history of *She'erith*

---

[83] Ibid.   [84] See YIVO/DPG 61.

[85] See N. Stern, "Im veidat ha-sridim al admat germaniyah" (At the Conference of Survivors on German Soil), *Be-ma'avak: iton hachativah hayehudit halochemet* (In battle: organ of the Jewish Brigade), nos. 4–5 (1945): 20–24; A. Galoz, *Ish ha-chativah ha-yehudit ha-lochemeth* (A member of the Jewish Brigade) (Tel Aviv, 1972): 148–160.

Hapleitah. At St. Ottilien the survivors were yet frail, vulnerable and inexperienced. Soon thereafter, moreover, the survivors in Bergen-Belsen and Austria broke away from the Committee in Munich, leaving it as the representative of some 18,000 survivors in Bavaria. It is thus not a little surprising that a year and a half later, when some 175,000 Jews from Eastern Europe had converged upon the American Zone of Occupation, they were absorbed by a large and impressive network of organizations that had risen from the tenuous foundations laid at St. Ottilien.[86] As Shlomo Frenkel wrote in April 1946 of the leadership of *She'erith Hapleitah*:

Without help from outside they set about creating an organization and frameworks wherein those rescued from the flames could regroup. The movements and committees ... that were established gathered up the surviving remnants, addressed their problems and attempted to deal not only with their physical disabilities but also with the spiritual disfigurement they had sustained.[87]

The Central Committee, which remained largely faithful to the basic policies determined at St. Ottilien, was further strengthened in mid-1946 following its recognition by the American Army as the official representative of the Jews in Occupied Germany. These developments, taken together, made it possible for *She'erith Hapleitah* to have an impact on events in Germany and far beyond. It was during the visit of Earl Harrison to the DP camps in July of 1945 that the survivors took their first faltering but significant steps into the arena of world affairs.

---

[86] Dobkin's remarks appear in Konferenz der Vorsteher der Ueberlebenden Jueden in Deutschland (25.7.1945), CZA/S25/5232.

[87] Ivri (Shlomo Frenkel), "Bimlot shanah lashichrur" (The first anniversary of liberation), *Nitzotz*, no. 14 (59) (29.4.1946): 3.

3 *She'erith Hapleitah* enters the international arena: July–October 1945

As the Allied armies uncovered the hastily abandoned concentration camps, the shocking truth about the murder of the Jews of Europe was, for the first time, widely publicized. Newspaper reports and photographs, newsreels, soldiers writing home and chaplains informing Jewish organizations of what they had found quickly supplanted the vague images and protective disbelief which had lent wartime reports an air of unreality.[1] The horror and anger these reports engendered were compounded by descriptions of the hostility and ill-treatment that survivors continued to encounter after their liberation. As Chaplain Samson M. Goldstein reported to the American Jewish Welfare Board already in April 1945: "Some Jews are being found but they are completely destitute. So are the other freed prisoners. But in the case of the Jews the mental attitude is worse. The war has not done away with the antisemitic feeling among antisemites. The faster these Jews can be evacuated from here the better they will be."[2] Soldiers wrote of the harsh conditions that those who barely remained alive had to contend with, especially if they originally come from Axis countries:

Instead of preserving the few Jewish survivors and taking care of their needs better ... because they represent the remnants of the millions who have been murdered ... these poor people are put in the category of the German civilians who have been their worst enemies. The victims of Nazism are made to suffer all the "inconveniences" – to put it mildly – meant for the reeducation of the Germans.[3]

All these reports which emphasized the urgency of immediate intervention and the need for massive aid awakened powerful emotions and drove

---

[1] See Eliyahu Eilat, *Ha-maavak al ha-medinah: 1945–1948* (The struggle for statehood: 1945–1948) (Tel Aviv, 1979): 72–74, and Dinnerstein, *America and the Survivors*: 34.

[2] Chaplain Samson M. Goldstein's Report (April 1945), AJDC/DP's Germany 1945/1946.

[3] Rudolf Callman, American Federation of the Jews from Central Europe, to Max M. Warburg (11.6.1945), AJDC/DP's Germany 1945/1946; D.J. Eizenberg to Mrs. Louis Friedman (21.6.1945), AJDC/DP's Germany General, January–July 1945.

the larger Jewish organizations in America to seek ways and means of alleviating the plight of the survivors.[4]

As part of this effort in early June 1945, Meyer Weisgal, head of the Jewish Agency office in New York, suggested to Henry Morgenthau, Secretary of the Treasury, that the administration should send a representative to Europe in order to check on these disturbing reports. Morgenthau adopted the idea and succeeded in persuading the State Department of its urgency and importance for the American Jewish community.[5] James MacDonald whom Morgenthau and Weisgal had suggested for the job was turned down by the State Department because of his outspoken pro-Jewish views and in his stead they appointed Earl G. Harrison who had served as the American Commissioner of Immigration and Naturalization and continued to represent his country in the Intergovernmental Committee on Refugees. According to the terms of reference laid down by the State Department on 21 June 1945 his task was "to ascertain the needs of the stateless and non-repatriables, particularly Jews, among the displaced persons in Germany and to what extent those needs are being provided at present by military authorities, international, national or private organizations. Mr. Harrison has also been directed to determine in general the views of the refugees with respect to their future destinations."[6] Prior to his departure Joseph Grew, the Acting Secretary of State, obtained a letter of interest and support from President Truman emphasizing this last point: "It is important to the early restoration of peace and order in Europe that plans be developed to meet the needs of those who for justifiable reasons cannot return to their countries of pre-war residence."[7]

This letter, in effect, made Harrison into the personal envoy of the President thus extending both the reach of his authority with the

---

[4] See Eilat, *Ha-mavak al ha-medinah*; Louis Lipsky, Chairman of the American Jewish Conference Executive, to Thomas M. Cooley, Joseph Hyman, Executive Vice Chairman of the AJDC, and to Congressman Benjamin J. Rabin (14.6.1945), AJDC/DP's Germany 1945; Abraham J. Klausner, A Detailed Report on the Liberated Jew. Yehuda Bauer correctly asks how sufficient reports were received early enough to precipitate the reaction they did. We do not have a full answer except to suggest looking at the readiness of American Jewish leaders to respond precipitately. If it is true that American Jewry, on the whole, came to respond to the Holocaust in its aftermath we might assume strong feelings of missed opportunities and deeds undone. This may have been a goad to quick action even without a significant accumulation of eye-witness reports. See Bauer, *Out of the Ashes*: 47 n. 6.

[5] For a variety of documents in this regard see CZA/ S25/5124.

[6] See Memorandum for the President from Joseph Grew, Acting Secretary of State (21.6.1945), NA/800.4016 DP/16-2145: "Private groups in this country interested in these refugees are pressing urgently for information concerning their present situation and plans for their care. Agencies of the Federal Government require this information in order to deal effectively with the problem through military channels and the international organizations in which this government participates as a member."

[7] Ibid.

US Army[8] and, later, the resonance of his findings. The fact that he had been personally sought out by the State Department, furthermore, lent his mission a credibility it might otherwise have lacked. From the outset the Jewish leaders who had set the process in motion felt comfortable with the appointment but recommended, nonetheless, that he be accompanied by an advisor familiar with European Jewry who would be able faithfully to convey what the survivors thought and wanted.[9] It was agreed that Dr. Joseph Schwartz, the well-known Director of the JDC in Europe, would accompany Harrison and fill this role. As part of his preparations Harrison met with Weisgal and Henry Montor, a key figure in the United Jewish Appeal, and prior to leaving for Europe received both a minute of the meeting and a memo discussing the goals of his mission.

Weisgal's aim was twofold: to widen the scope of the mission in order to prevent it from exclusively limiting itself to immediate questions of rehabilitation and so as to indicate the relevance of Zionism to the broader, long-term perspective. "The problem ought to be seen for the long-range one it is," he wrote,

and not merely as a temporary, transitional crisis. The world is planning for the security of all men. It ought to give thought to the insecurity of the Jews who have had the least of it. Provision for current economic and social needs is only a part, a small part of the problem. It is the political basis of security which is the indispensable element in the solution of the problem.[10]

He asked Harrison to be sure that he made direct contact with the survivors in order to ascertain what their true feelings were. From his point of view, argued Weisgal, there were but three major options facing the Jews of Europe: one was the completion of their demise, perhaps by other means, the second was full equality and the third emigration. Of the two options open to discussion Weisgal felt that true equality was unattainable because both sides, each for their own reasons, were not prepared to make the effort. The only real option was emigration and the cardinal question was: to where? Weisgal was persuaded that the majority would opt for Palestine and would be willing to pay a heavy price in order to find inner peace and quiet in their historic home. The war, in addition, had created a tragic reality that had to be taken into consideration: following the murder of the Jewish people the dimensions of the Jewish question had been drastically reduced for now, but 1,250,000 Jewish refugees were to be found throughout Europe. "The world now has an opportunity,"

---

[8] Harrison made a point of stressing this in his conversation with Abraham J. Klausner in Dachau. See Rabbi Abraham J. Klausner, Interview, OHD/4: 91.

[9] M. Weisgal to H. Morgenthau (14.6.1945), CZA/S25/5124.

[10] See CZA/ Z5/991.

concluded Weisgal, "of adopting a permanent solution for the problem of Jewish homelessness. The framework of the problem has been reduced so that it can be much more adequate than before."[11] Harrison who responded affirmatively to these ideas took Weisgal's correspondence with him to Europe. It is difficult to assess the extent to which Weisgal's efforts bore fruit but there is no doubt that some of the themes he articulated are to be found in Harrison's final report and most especially his reference to the reduced state of the Jewish people in Europe in the wake of the Holocaust. "Now that such large numbers are no longer involved and if there is any genuine sympathy for what these survivors have endured, some reasonable extension or modification of the British White Paper of 1939 ought to be possible without too serious repercussions."[12] Harrison, however, carefully argued the case for Palestine, over and above the express desires of the survivors, on humanitarian rather than Zionist grounds.

Harrison and Schwartz together with Patrick Malin of the Intergovernmental Committee on Refugees and Herbert Katzki, a JDC man who was then working for the War Refugee Board, accompanied by a team of assistants arrived in Frankfurt in early July 1945. In order to cover more ground they divided into two teams with Joseph Schwartz writing independent reports which Harrison integrated into his final document. Their liaison officer from UNRRA was its Deputy Director in Germany, E. E. Rhatigan while their itinerary had been set up by the G5 Displaced Persons Department in SHAEF. One of the officers who played an active role in facilitating Harrison's visit, Colonel Richmond, quietly informed Rabbi Klausner of the group's travel plans emphasizing that the formal program, as it stood, focused on high level policy discussions and kept the mission away from what was happening on the ground. Klausner asked for Harrison to seek him out when he visited Dachau.[13]

In Frankfurt Harrison invited Ben Klotz, the resourceful head of the local Jewish Committee, to come and see him.[14] Their conversation revolved around the situation of the Jewish DPs in the area and the attempts to transform the housing estate in nearby Zeilsheim into a reception center for survivors. Harrison, who was warm and sympathetic, promised to do all he could to help.[15] At the same time Lieutenant Aryeh Simon, who was on a tour of duty in Germany on behalf of the Jewish Brigade, also arrived in Frankfurt and heard by chance from a survivor that a presidential envoy had come to study their situation. Laboring under the

---

[11] Weisgal to Morgenthau.   [12] Report of Earl G. Harrison, CZA/S25/5214.
[13] See Klausner, Interview: 91.
[14] See Ben Klotz's unpublished *Memoirs: 1939–1946*, deposited in Yad Vashem: 50.
[15] Ibid: 53–54.

impress of what he had already seen, Simon succeeded in arranging a meeting with Harrison in order to share his experiences and his sense of what should be done.[16] In his meeting with the Executive of the Central Committee in Munich on 13 and 14 July 1945 Simon reported on the two topics he raised for discussion: the temporary concentration of the Jews in separate camps and the cardinal question of free and immediate immigration to Palestine. With respect to both he had found Harrison to be both forthcoming and extremely supportive.[17]

Simon's summary report of his trip gives us a sense of the tone and substance of his meeting with Harrison. He found the sight of survivors behind barbed wire, under armed guard, degradingly dressed, suffering from malnutrition and living in constant fear of forced repatriation to be profoundly disturbing. The US Army refused to recognize that they were Jews, a group apart, who in the wake of the Holocaust had special needs and therefore turned a deaf ear to all requests for separate camps that would make more adequate treatment possible. Indeed, he reported "a feeling, whether justifiable or exaggerated, in almost all camps: 'The occupation authorities are against us.'"[18] But their most urgent need, given their untenable situation, was to open the way for emigration in general and to Palestine in particular. Simon estimated that 90 percent of the Jews from Poland and the Baltic states, the majority of the survivors, rejected the idea of going back home and had set their hearts on Palestine. Among the more assimilated Jews of Hungary he estimated that about 60 percent sought repatriation while the other 40 percent wished to return in order to search for family and would then seek their future elsewhere including Palestine. The longing for the Land of Israel, in Simon's view, was not primarily motivated by ideology: "There is an urge, almost instinctive, to go home to their own people where they will be among folk that understand them and want to help them and who are only too ready to give them that kindness and love which they so much need."[19] Aryeh Simon sensed the vitality that pulsed beneath the surface in *She'erith Hapleitah*, a drive to life that found expression in what they had already achieved and their powerful desire to start anew. At the same time these signs of hope could not be simply be taken for granted, they needed to be nursed and encouraged in order to keep the terrible traumas of the past at bay. Jewish Palestine, in Simon's view, was the one place in the world where

---

[16] Conversation of the author with Aryeh Simon (30.10.1980).

[17] Protokol der Zitsung di Eksekutiv Komitet (Protocol of the Executive Committee) (14–15 July 1945), YIVO/DPG 94.

[18] Aryeh Simon, "Report on the Position of Jewish Refugees in Southern Germany: From a Tour of the Camps, 6–14 July, 1945," IDF Archives, Spektor Collection. My thanks to Prof. Yoav Gelber who directed me to this source and many others.

[19] Ibid.

this huge project of rehabilitation could be undertaken with some hope of success.

This analysis that appears to have left its mark[20] gives us a sense of what Harrison heard informally and how it might have helped to both shape and organize his perceptions. An additional source of information and influence was Joseph Dunner who served as the head of the Press Office in the Military Government in Munich and developed close ties with the Central Committee of the Liberated Jews.[21] Dunner had been called upon to assist Jewish DPs in the Buchberg camp who were going to be forcibly moved into a Polish camp by the Third Army and then sent on their way to Poland. On the basis of vague undertaking by the Military Governor, Dunner drafted an official letter delaying the transfer by three days. The letter was duly produced when the army trucks arrived and when Dunner personally intervened he was threatened with a court martial. Deeply disturbed by what he had seen, Dunner traveled to Frankfurt and handed in a written report on the situation of the Jews in Bavaria to Colonel Gurfein who headed the Intelligence Section of the Information Control Division.[22] In his report Dunner highlighted the shameful injustice of the Third Army's refusal to recognize the Jews as a separate group especially in view of the fact that the Jews of Eastern Europe had always seen themselves as a distinct people and fully willing to pay the price of the opprobrium this attracted. The army, in addition, continued to treat survivors of the Holocaust shabbily and, despite their protestations and the palpable dangers that faced them, insisted on their forcible repatriation.

According to Dunner, Colonel Gurfein passed on his report to Harrison who "immediately came down to the Munich area, checked on my report and reported it personally to President Truman. The President in turn made the well known statement about the treatment of the Jews which contained an exact quotation from my report."[23] Dunner is apparently referring to the passage in the Harrison report which indeed made the headlines and which President Truman quoted in full in his follow-up letter to General Eisenhower in late August 1945: "As matters now stand, we appear to be treating the Jews as the Nazis treated them except that we do not exterminate them."[24]

---

[20] Aryeh Simon in his conversation with the author (30.10.1980) told of hearing a report to this effect not long after his meeting with Harrison.

[21] See Joseph Dunner to Edward Grusd (25.10.1945), YIVO/DPG 61.

[22] We did not succeed in tracking down the report itself but its contents are mentioned in the letter to Edward Grusd (ibid.) and in the following: Joseph Dunner, *The Republic of Israel: Its History and Its Promise* (New York, 1950): 61–63, and *Zu Protokoll Gegeben: Mein Leben als Deutscher und Jude* (Munich, 1971): 122–141.

[23] See Dunner to Grusd.

[24] Harry S. Truman to General Eisenhower (31.9.1945), CZA/S25/5214.

Harrison and his party traveled throughout Germany and met many of the army and UNRRA personnel who were working with DPs. As planned, Harrison met with Rabbi Klausner in Dachau, conferred with him and met representatives of *She'erith Hapleitah* in Landsberg, Feldafing, St. Ottilien, Munich and elsewhere.[25] To round out the picture Joseph Schwartz paid a brief visit to Poland, Hungary, Romania and Czechoslovakia at the end of July. Harrison, in the meantime, cabled his principal findings to Henry Morgenthau: "In general found complete confirmation of disturbing reports concerning Jews in SHAEF Zone of Germany," and ended his brief account by expressing the wish that "These are only few highlights sent now in hope actions can be taken to indicate to relatively small number of survivors that they have in fact been liberated as well as saved."[26]

Harrison and Schwartz proceeded to write independent reports and in the latter half of August, Harrison combined them into one document which was then dispatched to President Truman.[27] A comparison between the two reveals that with respect to the overall content they essentially saw eye to eye with Harrison relying heavily on Schwartz when it came to assessing the mood of the survivors and their hopes and plans for the future. The differences that emerge are more a question of style: whereas Schwartz maintained quiet restraint throughout, Harrison wrote with a prophetic passion that presented the plight of the survivors with clarity and force. Thus, while thanking the US Army for its remarkable achievements in expediting the return of millions of displaced persons to their former homes, he also made it clear that he held the army directly responsible for the harsh and degrading conditions of forced isolation in which survivors of the Holocaust continued to live three months after liberation.

Because they had been "the first and the worst victims of Nazism," the few who survived the ordeal emerged from the war with special needs that demanded unconventional care. It was the refusal of the army to recognize this elementary fact that led to the sad neglect of urgent questions of health, nutrition, clothing and assistance in the search for family; it explained why the Jews were not granted a differential status midst the other DPs and why the army avoided expropriating German property in order to alleviate their situation. The disparity between the seemingly normal lives of many Germans, especially in rural areas, as compared to the continuing misery of the victims of Nazism angered Harrison greatly.

---

[25] See Klausner, Interview: 91.
[26] Cable for Secretary Treasury from Earl G. Harrison (28.7.1945), NA/800.4016 DP/8–145.
[27] Joseph Schwartz, Paris (9.8.1945), AJDC/DP's Germany.

Here was a golden opportunity to put into practice the Potsdam policy of holding all Germans responsible for the crimes perpetrated by the Nazis and instead, wrote Harrison in fury, "we appear to be treating the Jews as the Nazis treated them except that we do not exterminate them. They are in concentration camps in large numbers, under our military guard instead of S.S. troops. One is led to wonder whether the German population seeing this, are not supposing that we are following or at least condoning Nazi policy."[28]

The first step in order to put things straight was officially to recognize the Jews as a separate group with its own special needs. This would immediately open the way to a coordinated program of assistance on the part of the army, UNRRA and private Jewish organizations. Harrison recommended, secondly, that those Jews so desiring be allowed to create their own camps and that the army should not hesitate to requisition living quarters from the local population for those who wished to live outside out of a camp framework. The primary and most urgent need of these people, however, was to leave Germany as soon as possible. Their preferences with regard to destinations were often a function of background: "Very few Polish or Baltic Jews wish to return to their countries; higher percentages of the Hungarian and Rumanian groups want to return, although some hasten to add that it may be only temporarily, in order to look for relatives. Some of the German Jews, especially those who have intermarried, prefer to stay in Germany." With regard to possible places of resettlement for those who did not wish to return to their former homes, Palestine was, for a variety of reasons, the preeminent first choice:

Many now have relatives there, while others, having experienced intolerance and persecutions in their homelands for years, feel that only in Palestine will they be welcomed and find peace and quiet and be given an opportunity to live and work. In the case of the Polish and Baltic Jews the desire to go to Palestine is based in the great majority of cases on a love for the country and a devotion to the Zionist ideal.[29]

Knowing what they did of prevailing immigration restrictions in the postwar world, not many believed that they would succeed in reuniting with their families outside of Europe.[30]

Now that the great wave of mass repatriation was drawing to a close, Harrison recommended that both care for the Jews and the facilitation of their speedy emigration become an American priority. For purely

---

[28] Report of Harrison.   [29] Ibid.

[30] Harrison who had an excellent grasp of immigration possibilities hardly related to this topic in his report.

humanitarian reasons, therefore, it was necessary to deal with the question of Palestine despite the fact that the 75,000 immigration certificates allocated under the terms of the 1939 White Paper had just run out. In accordance with the widespread sympathy for the victims of Nazi persecution, the international consensus favoring the unification of families, the small number of people actually involved, traditional Labour sympathy for the Zionist cause and the absorptive capacity of the Yishuv, Harrison believed this to be well within the realm of possibility. In concrete terms he suggested embracing the demand of the Jewish Agency for 100,000 immigration certificates[31] as a significant contribution to solving the problem of the Jewish DPs in Germany, Austria and the neighboring countries.

Despite his generous praise of the US Army and his understanding of objective difficulties it had to contend with, there is no escaping the fact that Harrison's report was a stinging and painful criticism of its failure to grant the survivors either the consideration or the treatment they deserved. The high military command responded with anger and it took months for the hurt to subside.[32] Even Chaplain Judah Nadich, who was soon to be appointed as Special Adviser to General Eisenhower on Jewish affairs in the wake of the report, felt constrained to write that

Mr. Harrison, his broad humanitarianism enraged by the deplorable and miserable conditions characteristic of so many of the displaced persons camps, had let his feelings run away with him. After, all, no matter how one judged the situation, it was patently unjust, unfair and untruthful to state that Americans were treating the Jews as the Nazis did with the one exception of not exterminating them.[33]

It is instructive to compare this assessment with the views of Jacob Oleiski, one of the leaders of the Landsberg camp: "Mr. Earl Harrison, not himself Jewish, indeed one of the righteous of the nations, who came to us with warm sense of humanity and fraternity, presented our situation objectively."[34] It can plausibly be argued that one can only understand the report if we see that Harrison made the language and the views of *She'erith Hapleitah* his own. For reasons hard to reconstruct today, he chose to see reality through the eyes of the survivors and to describe it in their terms.

---

[31] M. Shertok to the British High Commisioner for Palestine (18.6.1945), CZA/S25/7679.

[32] At the end of October 1945 General Bedell Smith was still smarting with anger at what he saw as false charges. See Ben-Gurion's report to the Central Committee of *Mapai* (22.11.1945), *Ha'avodah* – Labor Archive.

[33] Judah Nadich, *Eisenhower and the Jews* (New York, 1953): 116. It could be argued that Harrison in focusing on German perceptions was referring to appearances, to a possible construal of reality rather than reality itself and thus his formulation "we *appear* to be treating the Jews"(my emphasis). However justified, this misses the point: Harrison was understood as making a direct and explicit accusation.

[34] Jacob Oleiski, "Undzer tayne tsu der velt" (Our claim against the world), *LLT*, no. 7 (19) (22.2.1946): 4.

Thus, what was understandably "unjust, unfair and untruthful" for Judah Nadich was, at the same time, simply the objective truth for Jacob Oleiski. If our assumption is correct, in a very unique way the voice of a small group of survivors reached the ears of the President of the United States of America at a fateful hour and was responded to with humanity.

The report of Earl G. Harrison set in motion a series of important developments and played an important role in improving the plight of *She'erith Hapleitah*. Already at the end of July 1945 Harrison's summary cable of his first findings to Henry Morgenthau began to set the wheels of change in motion. General Marshall who was Chief of Staff US Army passed on some of Harrison's findings to General Eisenhower and asked for clarification.[35] On 10 August 1945 Henry Stimson, the Secretary of State, also wrote to Eisenhower expressing his department's concern and asking for swift action.[36] At this time Eisenhower received a further cable from Rabbi Stephen Wise who had met with a number of Jewish chaplains serving in Germany at the beginning of August. On their advice Wise asked Eisenhower to appoint a liaison officer to coordinate all military activity regarding the Jewish DPs.[37]

Most important of all was the sharp response from President Truman who read the report and also conferred at length with Harrison. In his letter to Eisenhower on 31 August 1945, Truman stressed the failure of the army to ensure that action on the ground would faithfully reflect the thrust of national policy while emphasizing two further points: the humanitarian obligation to stand by those who had suffered grievously at the hands of the Nazis and the need to demonstrate to the German population that they bore their share of responsibility for the crimes of the past.

> I know that you will agree that we have a particular responsibility toward those victims of persecution and tyranny who are in our zone. We must make clear to the German people that we thoroughly abhor the Nazi policies of hatred and persecution. We have no better opportunity to demonstrate this than by the manner in which we ourselves treat the survivors remaining in Germany.[38]

On the international front Truman renewed his efforts to lift the British restrictions on Jewish immigration to Palestine by raising again, contrary

---

[35] Nadich, *Eisenhower and the Jews*: 34.   [36] Ibid.: 35.

[37] Ibid.: 35–36. In May 1945 a similar request had been directed to the State Department by the five leading Jewish organizations in the US. See Dinnerstein, *America and the Survivors*: 45–46.

[38] Harry S. Truman to General Eisenhower (31.8.1945), CZA/S25/5217.

to the advice of the State Department, a request he made of Churchill at Potsdam in this regard.[39] On 31 August 1945 Truman turned to Clement Attlee, Britain's newly elected Prime Minister, with a request to allow 100,000 survivors to enter Palestine forthwith. Adopting the content and tone of Harrison's reasoning "that no matter is so important for those who have known the horrors of the concentration camps as is the future of immigration policies into Palestine" the President emphasized that "The American people as a whole firmly believe that immigration into Palestine should not be closed."[40] This diplomatic initiative in the wake of the Harrison report proved to be of great significance for it set in motion, without anyone knowing what the end result would be, a series of developments which finally led to the creation of the State of Israel in May of 1948.[41]

President Truman was convinced that the entry of 100,000 survivors into Palestine would not essentially change the demographic balance of the country, would not incite widespread opposition and hence would not lead to a British request for the deployment of American troops in the Middle East. The President knew full well that the chances for large-scale immigration to the United States or elsewhere, for that matter, were slim; he also knew that despite serious divisions amongst American Jews with regard to the advisability of establishing a Jewish state, there was a broad consensus in support of free immigration to Palestine.[42] In his response Attlee dissented from the view that the Jewish DPs constituted a special problem, he spelt out the dangers of lifting immigration restrictions and informed Truman that no far-reaching changes would be forthcoming until his new government had formulated its Middle Eastern policies.[43] Not wanting, for both political and economic reasons, to enter into a confrontation with the American side, he suggested, instead, the creation of an Anglo-American Committee of Inquiry that would look into the question of immigration in the larger context of the future disposition of Palestine.

The moment Britain acceded to Truman's request that the problem of the Jewish displaced persons in Europe be central to the work of the

---

[39] Harry S. Truman to Winston S. Churchill (24.7.1945), *FRUS*: 716–717.
[40] Harry S. Truman to C. Atlee (31.8.1945), *FRUS*: 737–739.
[41] Ilan, *Amerika, britania ve-eretz yisrael*: 189.
[42] See Menachem Kaufman, "Atida shel she'erith hapleitah ve-she-elat eretz yisrael be-einei ha-irgunim ha-lo-tzionim be-artzot habrit bishnat 1945" (The future of She'erith Hapleitah and the question of Palestine in the eyes of non-Zionist organizations in the United States in 1945), *Yalkut Moreshet*, no. 21 (June 1976); also Eilat, *Ha-maavak al ha-medinah*: 172–178, and for background and context, Ganin, Truman, *American Jewry and Israel*.
[43] C. Atlee to Harry S. Truman (16.9.1945), *FRUS*: 740.

Committee, the President accepted the proposal and in a public statement on 13 November 1945 emphasized that

among the important duties of this committee will be the task of examining conditions in Palestine as they bear upon the problem of Jewish immigration ... this committee will make possible a prompt review of the unfortunate plight of Jews in those countries in Europe where they have been subjected to persecution, and a prompt examination of questions related to the rate of current immigration into Palestine and the absorptive capacity of the country. The situation faced by the displaced Jews in Europe during the coming winter allows no delay in this matter.[44]

While it would not be realistic to suggest that Truman's concern for the Jewish DPs was not informed by political considerations, it could be plausibly argued that at this early point in his presidency genuine humanitarian concern came first. A year later when the President had been initiated into the critical complexities of American global policy, his humanitarian ardor began to cool somewhat and from then on it was primarily the concerted pressure of the American Jewish community that held him to his word.[45]

The Harrison report was also an important catalyst in helping to ameliorate the living conditions of *She'erith Hapleitah* in Germany and Austria. The senior command of the army who were especially sensitive to public criticism immediately set about improving matters and, of course, as the following comment of Jacob Oleiski bears out, the survivors themselves were the first to register the change: "Following the visit of Mr. Harrison conditions in the camps were made much easier."[46] On 10 August Eisenhower sent his response to the report to the State Department[47] and detailed the action he was initiating. Jews who could not or would not return to their countries of origin (excluding citizens of the Soviet Union)[48] would be gathered into separate camps on the model of Feldafing. The responsibility for running the camps would be handed over to UNRRA reinforced by JDC workers who would be in direct contact with the DPs. Eisenhower, moreover, ordered his officers to take full advantage of their authority to requisition property in order to make sure that the standard of living in the camps was not inferior to what was accepted on the outside. He informed the State Department, in addition, of the creation of a central office that would coordinate the

---

[44] Statement by the President (13.11.1945), NA/Anglo-American Committee of Inquiry, RG-43, Box 1.
[45] See Michael J. Cohen, "Truman, the Holocaust and the Establishment of the State of Israel," *Jerusalem Quarterly*, no. 23 (Spring 1982): 79–94.
[46] Oleiski, "Undzer tayne."   [47] Nadich, *Eisenhower and the Jews*: 39–40.
[48] This was for public consumption and not adhered to in practice. See ibid.: 118–119.

search for missing persons. On 22 August 1945 this policy, spelt out in unambiguous language, was published as an order of the Supreme Command.[49]

Over and beyond these steps Eisenhower set aside his opposition to the appointment of an adviser on Jewish affairs as recommended by Rabbi Stephen Wise.[50] He informed the State Department of his decision to appoint a Jewish chaplain on a temporary basis and requested that a public figure of stature be found to fill the post. Chaplain Judah Nadich was appointed Special Adviser on Jewish Affairs with the responsibility for maintaining on-going contact with the Jewish concentrations in Germany and attending to their current concerns; he was to report regularly to General Bedell Smith, Eisenhower's Chief of Staff and to advise both the Supreme Command and UNRRA on questions of policy; the Adviser had also to oversee the operations of Jewish organizations that wished to enter the zone in order to work with *She'erith Hapleitah*.[51]

Nadich, accompanied by Joseph Schwartz, immediately set out on a tour of the major Jewish centers in Germany: Frankfurt, Zeilsheim, Feldafing, Munich, Landsberg and St. Ottilien, at each site met with the DPs and their representatives and inquired extensively into what they felt, thought and wanted. All his conversations with the army and UNRRA focused on what he had heard and seen with the express purpose of bringing General Eisenhower's policies to fruition. When Eisenhower received President Truman's comments on the Harrison report in mid-September Nadich was recalled to Frankfurt to report on his findings. The Special Adviser reported on the flaws he had found and made a number of policy proposals regarding living conditions, food and clothing. He related to the questionable behavior, sometimes explicitly antisemitic, of the Third Army under General Patton's command. Nadich recommended expanding the work of the JDC and creating more agricultural training farms by bringing in additional Palestine teams under the aegis of the Jewish Agency.[52]

On the Day of Atonement in mid-September 1945 General Eisenhower paid a personal visit to the Jewish centers in Stuttgart and Feldafing and was enthusiastically received in both.[53] Following his visit Eisenhower published a further set of commands that attempted to address many of the issues Nadich had raised.[54] Beyond ordering his senior staff to make regular site visits to the various Jewish centers, Eisenhower had the armed camp guards removed and replaced them with internal security

---

[49] Ibid.: 43–44.   [50] Ibid.: 37–38.   [51] Ibid.: 48.   [52] Ibid.: 123–127.
[53] See *Undzer Veg* (Our Way), no. 1 (12.10.1945): 2.   [54] NA/800.4016 DP/16–2345.

arrangements. These initiatives did not always achieve what they set out to do for an unforeseen change was beginning to insinuate itself into the American occupation: a growing number of officers who had arrived in Europe in the recent past tended to identify with the German population and increasingly saw the Jewish DPs through their jaundiced eyes. Eisenhower's new policies, on balance, left their mark and introduced important changes.

Interestingly enough, Truman's public expression of concern for the survivors together with the news of improved conditions in the camps served to draw more refugee groups from Eastern Europe to the American Occupied Zone.[55] While the general trend in mid-1945 was to seek refuge in Italy, with the removal of the Jewish Brigade to Western Europe the flow began to move towards Germany and by the end of the year some 200–600 refugees were entering the American Zone daily via Berlin so bringing the Jewish DP population to about 45,000.[56] The attempt to transform Germany into a temporary refuge and way station had been initiated by Zionist groupings on the morrow of liberation as part of their campaign against repatriation. The soldiers of the Jewish Brigade, on their part, had begun to pursue a similar policy and these initiatives were given a great boost by David Ben-Gurion's visit to Germany at the end of October 1945.

The British Army, not wanting the Jewish Brigade so close to both the shores of the Mediterranean and the heart of Germany, ordered its transfer to Holland and Belgium at the end of July 1945. At the beginning of August, therefore, the Jewish Brigade sought to renew its contacts with the Jewish concentrations in Hungary, Italy and Germany. Zvi Shiloah (Langzam), one of those sent to Munich, participated in the Zionist conference held in Landsberg and two things happened there to shape his thinking about the flow of refugees from Eastern Europe.[57] On the one hand he met Abraham Klausner and understood that together with the Joint the newcomers could be accommodated. He also met a group of members of the *Dror* youth movement from Poland who had been sent to

---

[55] See Din ve-cheshbon shel ch. weizman le-chavrei misrado (Report of Ch. Weizmann to the members of his bureau) (22.10.1945), CZA/Z/4.

[56] In September 1945 the members of the Central Committee of the Liberated Jews in Bavaria were unable to estimate the overall number of Jews in the American Zone because of the continual influx of refugees from the East. See Nadich, *Eisenhower and the Jews*: 78; in October 1945 Nadich was told of an influx of 200 refugees a day while Dinnerstein in *America and the Survivors*: 46, talks of a daily influx of 500–600 at the end of the year.

[57] Zvi Shiloah, Interview, OHD/4 (64):13, and in his book *Eretz gedolah le-am gadol* (A great land for a great people) (Tel Aviv, 1970): 44. Shiloah believes the meeting to have taken place in Feldafing but other evidence makes Landsberg the more likely venue.

spy out the land. Their dilemma was the following: should they remain in Poland until they had a sure passage to Palestine or should they move westwards, get closer to the Mediterranean and wait for an opportune moment to set sail? Shiloah, innocent of any knowledge of the operation of the *Brichah*, had begun to understand the possibilities of using Germany as a temporary refuge and thus urged a few of them to return to Poland in order to persuade the movement coordinators to send out additional groups to the American Zone.[58]

On their return to base the teams sent out by the Brigade came together in the *Mercaz La-Golah* – the Center for Diaspora Communities – in order to think through the question of the growing exodus from Poland. The cardinal issue was whether to direct the flow to Italy or to move towards an intermediate stage by helping to create a sizeable concentration of refugees in the American Occupation Zone.[59] Those favoring the Italian option wanted the survivors to be close to ports of embarkation for Palestine and far from the tainted soil of Germany. Aaron Hoter-Yishai, on the other hand, supported the German option because of its symbolic, political advantages. A large concentration of Jews in Germany, he assumed, would be useful in mobilizing world opinion to oppose British policies in Palestine.[60] Shiloah who also favored this approach developed some of the ideas he had begun to think about on his recent visit to Germany:

Herzl justified his proposal of Uganda in terms of the urgent need to provide the Jews of Eastern Europe with a temporary haven. It is doubtful whether Uganda could have served as a temporary haven to the Jews of Eastern Europe at that time, but the idea itself still has validity. The few that remained after the Shoah are in urgent need of a temporary haven on their way to Eretz Yisrael and Bavaria could serve this purpose: the American army is stationed there, there is no civilian government and there are warm-hearted Jewish officers; the Joint can extend assistance and there is a nucleus of Zionists that will get things organized locally.[61]

In the wake of this meeting of the *Mercaz La-Golah* Meir Argov, Secretary of the Jewish Brigade, sent a cable to the Jewish Agency in Jerusalem recommending that Germany be transformed into a temporary place of concentration "for Jews who will come from the East"[62] and suggested negotiating with the military authorities in the American Occupation Zone in order to receive their official blessing. Ruth Klinger, the representative of the Jewish Agency in Paris, was also contacted in this regard and

---

[58] Shiloah, Interview: 15–16, and *Eretz gedolah*: 45.
[59] Aaron Hoter-Yishai, Interview, OHD/4 (22): 13–14.   [60] Ibid.: 14–15.
[61] Shiloah, *Eretz gedolah*: 47.   [62] Shiloah, Interview: 18.

requested to raise the matter with David Ben-Gurion. These developments helped pave the way for Ben-Gurion's visit to Germany at the end
of October 1945.[63]

Ben-Gurion was invited as the personal guest of General Eisenhower
and in his conversations with both his host and his second-in-command,
Walter Bedell Smith, presented a series of proposals aimed at expediting the rehabilitation of the Jewish DPs. He requested that the Jews be
granted a measure of self-rule, local and central, and additional possibilities of physical, agricultural and vocational training that would better
prepare them for their future lives in Palestine. He even suggested concentrating the Jewish DPs in one area so as to both minimize contacts with
the German population and enable the internal leadership of *She'erith
Hapleitah* to run their own affairs. Ben-Gurion also recommended sending Palestinian teachers and instructors to assist in the various training
programs.[64]

Eisenhower and Bedell Smith refused to create an enclave that would
be exclusively Jewish but warmly embraced many of Ben-Gurion's other
suggestions.[65] At their final meeting Ben-Gurion told Bedell Smith a
little haltingly about the daily influx of Jews from the East. Smith answered that he had been apprised of what was happening, he was aware
of the antisemitism rife in Eastern Europe and insisted that the American
army was duty-bound "to save these Jews."[66] Ben-Gurion immediately
grasped the far-reaching implications of what he was being told, namely,
that Jewish refugees could enter the American Occupation Zone freely
and that the army would see to their security and maintenance. Here
was a green light to realize what the leadership of *She'erith Hapleitah*
had been struggling to achieve in its campaign against enforced repatriation and a way to create a politically significant presence in Occupied
Germany.

Eisenhower was also willing to send a special plane to Palestine to
bring over the first group of emissaries to *She'erith Hapleitah* thereby
transforming Bavaria into an ideal training ground for the Zionist
movement.[67] Moreover, Ben-Gurion foresaw that a large concentration
of East-European Jews on German soil would be of great political value
"for the Americans know that that they will not be able to remain in
Munich forever. The one place [these Jews] will be able to go to is

---

[63] Shiloah, *Eretz gedolah*: 47.
[64] See Report by David Ben-Gurion on his Visit to the Camps (6.11.1945), CZA/ S25/ 5231.
[65] See W. B. Smith to D. Ben-Gurion (November 1945), CZA/ S25/5232.
[66] Report of Ben-Gurion to the Central Committee of *Mapai* (22.11.1945): 14.
[67] Report by David Ben-Gurion (6.11.1945).

Palestine and that will generate American pressure, they'll push and they [*She'erith Hapleitah*] will be allowed to go."[68] Ben-Gurion, in his later report to the Central Committee of his party, *Mapai*, clearly hinted that Bedell Smith understood what he was driving at and, without anything being made explicit, indicated his willingness to play his part in helping this happen.

[68] Ibid.

4   Hopes of Zion: September 1945 – January 1946

From the outset the dream of a Jewish home in Palestine permeated the public life of *She'erith Hapleitah*. The bitter fate of the Jewish people during the war was accounted for in terms of the vulnerabilities of minority life; Jewish resistance to the Nazis was celebrated as a primarily Zionist enterprise while the creation of a Jewish state in the Land of Israel was taken to be the last will and testament bequeathed by the dead to the living. The frameworks set up by the survivors in and around the DP camps – local and regional committees, the Central Committee of the Liberated Jews in Bavaria, political parties, youth movements, schools and training farms – were infused with the same spirit. For many, their almost intuitive Zionism stood for the warmth, unquestioning acceptance and security of home; for the more politically minded it signified the only real hope for the rescue and rehabilitation of the little that remained of European Jewry and, in the longer term, the promise of the Jewish future.

Edward Shils has suggested that

[the] need for an ideology is the intensification of the need for a cognitive and moral map of the universe... An ideology arises because there is a strongly felt need for an explanation of important experiences which the prevailing outlook does not explain, because there is a need for the firm guidance of conduct which, similarly, is not provided by the prevailing outlook, and because there is a need, likewise strongly felt, for a fundamental vindication and legitimation of the value and dignity of the persons in question.[1]

Thus, what we appear to be witnessing in *She'erith Hapleitah* is a shared effort to bring order into their disrupted lives, to make sense of what had befallen them and to find a way of moving forward. In the debilitating context of DP life the survivors desperately needed to restore their sense of human worth which had been so mercilessly trampled by the Nazis. Their Zionism was an attempt to reconstruct their chaotic lives, a bid for meaning and dignity.

[1] Edward Shils, "Ideology," in *The Intellectuals and the Powers and Other Essays* (Chicago, 1972): 29.

The acute need for an ideology is therefore clear. What needs to be clarified is why it was Zionism rather than communism or Bundist socialism or religious Orthodoxy that was called upon to fill the breach. The historian Koppel Pinson who directed the educational services of the JDC in Germany between October 1945 and September 1946 related to this issue as follows:

The events of 1939–1945 seemed to discredit completely those philosophies of Jewish life prevailing before the war which were not centered around Palestine. The Zionists were the only ones that had a program that seemed to make sense after this catastrophe. The Zionists were organized, active and militant. Prospects for immigration to Palestine in the earlier period seemed more imminent... Without Palestine there seemed to be no future for them. Anti-Zionism or even a neutral attitude towards Zionism came to mean for them a threat to the most fundamental stakes in their future.[2]

The leading role played by Zionist underground groups in active resistance to the Nazis also counted for a lot: these were unsung heroes who in the eyes of many survivors had saved the honor of the Jewish people. After liberation, moreover, these young Zionist activists together with movement leaders repatriated from the Soviet Union came to play a significant and often prominent role in the life of the Surviving Remnant. Secondly, there was no real competition of groups ideologically opposed to Zionism in the formative period of *She'erith Hapleitah*. Understandably, a fair number of Communists and Jewish socialists returned to Eastern Europe upon liberation and, indeed, called upon their fellow Jews to follow suit. Those who remained behind or arrived in Germany at a later date, such as the Bundist group in Feldafing, maintained a low profile and, at times, found temporary refuge among left-wing Zionists. To add to this, anti- and non-Zionist Orthodox groups were hardly in evidence at this stage, lacked leadership of stature and, in certain cases, were even sympathetic to Zionist aspirations. In this spirit Rabbi Eliezer Burstein claimed that "The only aspiration of Agudat Yisrael is to struggle with other Jews for the establishment of our own Jewish home in Eretz Yisroel in the spirit of the Torah."[3] In October 1945, Meir Gavronsky, the editor of *Dos Fraye Vort* – The Free Word – which served as shared platform for Zionists, Bundists and Agudat Yisrael in Feldafing, confidently wrote that: "Eretz Yisrael is no longer a question that concerns only Zionists. Today all Jews, be they religious, socialist or even Communist, are concerned with this problem."[4]

[2] Pinson, "Jewish Life in Liberated Germany": 117.
[3] Rabbi Eliezer Burstein, "Undzer lebens oyfgabe" (Our task in life), *Dos Fraye Vort*, no. 11 (20.12.1945): 2.
[4] M. Gavronsky, "Di zogen in lib haben kost nit kayn gelt" (Said in love doesn't cost anything), *Dos Fraye Vort*, no. 3 (19.10.1945): 2.

Zionism, of course, did not gain its preeminence simply by default. What made it especially compelling over and beyond immediate and existential concerns was the interpretive key of Jewish history it offered. A review of opinion in *She'erith Hapleitah* at this time points to a widely held belief that the destruction of European Jewry was continuous with the major trends of Jewish history and in no way *sui generis*. It was but the latest link in the long chain of suffering that had dogged the Jews in the lands of their dispersion. The Nazi annihilation of European Jewry was, undoubtedly, the greatest tragedy to have overtaken the Jewish people. In essence, however, it did not differ from the tragedies that had come before. The common source of this continuous persecution had to be sought in a structural flaw of Jewish life that repeatedly exposed the Jews to attacks from without. This flaw, following the classic Zionist analysis, was to be located in the ubiquitous minority status of a people without a land of its own. As a homeless minority they were vulnerable, helpless in the face of force and always dependent on the uncertain favors of others in order to secure their very existence.

For some it was the cultural tension between the Jews and their surroundings that underpinned antisemitism: as a minority their insistence on being a people apart generated suspicion and antagonism which, in times of crisis, escalated into open persecution. According to this interpretation the history of antisemitism could be read as a long series of clashes between those who sought to make an end of Jewish uniqueness and those who chose doggedly to preserve it, no matter the consequences.[5] This was the hard core of emnity to which economic rivalry, opposition to Jewish intrusiveness and self-serving expectations of saintly behavior attached themselves.[6] Shlomo Frenkel who continued to serve as the editor of *Nitzotz*, elaborated on this theme during Chanukah, 1946:

The period of the Maccabees shows us that Hitler was not the first to set about destroying our nation... There was no fundamental difference between Antiochus Epiphanes and Adolf Hitler. On numerous occasions in the history of our people persecutors have declared their purpose of doing away with us... The antisemitism which reached its high point during Nazi rule has its roots in the fateful historical clash of the Maccabean period except that physical extirpation was added to the opposition to religious and national apartness and climaxed in organized murder that was scientifically executed down to the last detail.[7]

---

[5] See Ivri (Shlomo Frenkel), "Chanukah," *Nitzotz*, no. 5 (50) (30.11.1945): 1. Those writing for *Nitzotz* underground disguised their identity for fear of disclosure. We place their clandestine noms de plume first and their full names in parentheses.

[6] Meir Gavronsky, "Far vos men hat unz faynt?" (Why are we hated?), *Dos Fraye Vort*, no. 9 (30.10.1945): 3.

[7] Ivri, "Chanukah."

The destruction of European Jewry, in this view, was part of the long tradition of antisemitism whereas its unprecedented dimensions were closely bound up with the new dangers the twentieth century introduced to the well being of minorities. The socio-economic turbulence that emerged in the wake of the First World War together with the Russian Revolution and the economic crises of the 1920s unleashed forces radically inimical to Jewish life. With the closing off of immigration possibilities, in addition, the safety valve of demographic mobility was no longer available and so by 1925, the Jews of Europe were to all intents and purposes trapped. Finally, when an antisemitic party driven by a racial ideology gained access to the awesome power of a centralized and technologically advanced state, a deadly pass was reached wherein the Jews were brought to the brink of total physical destruction.[8] There were two connected lessons to be learnt: on the one hand, "Jews can no longer live in *Galut* [Exile]"[9] and on the other, "A people with a land cannot be destroyed."[10] The refusal to face up to this elementary truth because of the endemic myopia of life in Exile had exacted an horrific price. The time had come, as Meir Gavronsky put it succinctly, for radical treatment: "The Jewish people is sick... The best specialists have presented us with a diagnosis: statelessness. The cure is our own soil, our own home, our own state."[11]

This analysis suggested a rhetorical question much asked in *She'erith Hapleitah*: if murderous antisemitism did not begin with Hitler, "Who can assure us that what transpired in Germany will not ever happen again in other lands?"[12] Events unfolding in Europe seem to bear out Zalman Grinberg's observation that the Allies defeated Hitler but antisemitism remained unvanquished.[13] The Jews of Eastern Europe who had begun to trickle into Occupied Germany brought frightening tales of hatred run rampant while from its modest beginnings the survivor press carried numerous reports of anti-Jewish acts in Poland, Romania, Czechoslovakia,

---

[8] Dr Shmuel Gringauz, "In tsaykhn fun martirertum hofnung un arbet" (Under the sign of martyrdom hope and work), *LLT*, no. 2 (14) (18 January 1946).

[9] Moshe Zilberberg, "Haynt oder keynmol" (Now [today] or never), *Dos Fraye Vort*, no. 14 (4.1.1946): 3.

[10] Aronovitch, "Mir vilen nit keyn nedavos" (We don't want any charity), *Dos Fraye Vort*, no. 8 (23.11.1945): 2; see also the report that appeared in *Dos Fraye Vort*, no. 4 (26.10.1945): 2, of Ben-Gurion's address to the camp residents on 21 October 1945 in which he emphasized that while all peoples under Nazi conquest had suffered, the Jews suffered most because they did not have a land of their own. "Up to the present," concluded Ben-Gurion, "no enemy has succeeded in destroying a people that has its own state, [that is] firmly rooted in its own soil."

[11] Meir Gavronsky, "Men heilt di krankayt – nit di simptom" (One treats the disease – not the symptom), *Dos Fraye Vort*, no. 14 (4.1.1946): 2.

[12] Ibid.

[13] See the report on Zalman Grinberg's speech in *Undzer Veg*, no. 6 (16.11.1945): 2.

France, Britain and the Argentine. The pogrom that swept over the Jews of Tripoli in November 1945 excited widespread and sympathetic interest in the DP camps and was commented on widely.[14]

The general feeling was that the situation of the Jews relative to the First World War was tenuous in the extreme. Then Britain had used the Balfour Declaration to win over Jewish support whereas now, given the palpable weakness of the Jewish people in the aftermath of the war, the White Paper policy could be continued and historic undertakings ignored; then the League of Nations took it upon itself to protect minority rights and now the lesson of Nazi subversion was the wholesale expulsion of ethnic minorities midst a wave of intolerant nationalist fervor whipped up by the war. To this sad accounting two further considerations had to be added: the residue of Nazi propaganda during the long years of occupation and, most notably, the Communist presence beyond the borders of the Soviet Union.[15] The outlook, overall, was gloomy: the Jewish role in the war effort and the grievous losses it sustained seemed to make little difference for the doors of Palestine remained closed, the hopes for 100,000 immigration certificates were fading and there appeared to be scant international support for Jewish statehood.[16] The feeling among many survivors was that they had been placed before an impossible dilemma: either to voluntarily dismantle their historic identity or to be ravaged by another wave of persecution. The operative conclusion to be drawn was equally stark: "If the Jewish people fails to prosecute the historic process of liquidating the *Galut* and creating a Jewish state then what awaits it is either assimilation or its final demise. In this mighty struggle of 'to be or not to be' we need to understand that for *She'erith Hapleitah* there is no third way."[17]

From this point of view all the historic strategies which sought to bolster Jewish life in the Diaspora had exhausted themselves and, given the absence of opposition from the religious groupings, the arrows of Zionist criticism were primarily directed at the anti-Zionist left in general and what remained of the Bund in particular. "We had come to think that the Bund as a movement that had given up the spirit, that the course of history and reality had left it without a way . . . It turns out, however, that the lesson has not been learnt . . . and once more people are embracing

---

[14] For example see the following reports: B. Takatsch, "Fun reize kein Polin" (From a journey to Poland), *Undzer Veg*, no. 6 (16.11.1945): 5, and Yisrael Blumenfeld, "Signaln" (Signals), *Undzer Veg*, no. 15 (11.1.1946): 5.

[15] See Levi Shalitan, "Fun farshlosene tirn tsu ge-efente toyern" (From closed doors to open gates), *Undzer Veg*, no. 1 (12.10.1945): 1.

[16] Ivri (Shlomo Frenkel), "Le-or ritzinut ha-matzav" (In view of the seriousness of the situation), *Nitzotz*, no. 4 (49) (16.11.1945): 6.

[17] Zilberberg, "Haynt oder Keynmol."

the theory of the everlasting *Galut* and wish to revitalize it."[18] Bundists in America who spoke thus could be forgiven for they had not experienced the catastrophic war years at first hand. "But Bundists who were strung up on the same pine that grew in the soil they wished to hold on to forever, Bundists who saw their theory of exilic existence refuted in the most horrible way...pop up again and publicly declare 'Follow us.'"[19]

The Zionist critique was equally directed at both the left-wingers who remained behind in Poland and the group that sought temporary refuge in Occupied Germany. The Jewish repatriate settlements set up in the western territories newly annexed to Poland were run by Communist appointees totally out of touch with their constituents who had strong Zionist sympathies. The insistence of this imposed leadership that "Jews view Poland as their homeland" or that "Jews are not thinking of leaving" flew in the face of a threatening and despairing reality.[20] Their ideological presuppositions that could not cope with the complexities of the Jewish situation had been tragically misleading during the war and now, again, in aftermath. The Bund had not prepared the Jewish masses for their abandonment in the time of killing or for the widespread collaboration with Nazi designs on the part of those who were believed to be brothers and allies.[21] The ideology that based itself on class solidarity could not deal with the absurd reality that even Jews willing to sacrifice themselves for the commonweal found their sacrifice unwanted.[22] After the war nothing changed and these distorted expectations persisted, compounded now by an additional misreading of the internal Jewish situation. The war had swept aside the class structure of Jewish life and created a situation where instead of exploiters and exploited Jews found themselves "belonging to one class: the persecuted and the homeless."[23]

The Zionists in *She'erith Hapleitah*, accordingly, found the soul-searching of M. Tsanin, a veteran Bundist journalist who had settled in Palestine, very close to their own point of view.[24] At the beginning of 1946 after a visit to Europe Tsanin unburdened himself in the Palestinian press:

---

[18] Sh. D., "Niftar ha-mefarfer" (The moribund has died), *Nitzotz*, no. 6 (51) (17.12.1945): 3.

[19] Ibid.

[20] Baruch Hermanovitch, "Firer un farfirer" (Leaders and misleaders), *LLT*, no. 7 (19) (22.2.1946): 3.

[21] See Dr. Y. Nover, "Di eintsige leizung fun der yidishe frage – a yidishe melukho in erets yisroel" (The only solution to the Jewish question – a Jewish State in Eretz Yisrael), *Dos Fraye Vort*, no. 14 (4.4.1946): 3.

[22] Zilberberg, "Haynt oder Keynmol."   [23] Nover, "Di eintsige leizung."

[24] M. Tsanin, "Mul pnei ha-metziut" (In the face of reality), *Davar* (17.1.1946): 2.

The world view... of the Bund was based on the belief that humanity was progressively moving towards equality and freedom and that we could therefore build our national life midst these liberated peoples. Today this beautiful belief is buried in the mass graves of our people in the fields of Poland, the Ukraine, White Russia and Lithuania. These countries on which we pinned our hopes have become the graveyards of both millions of Jews and of our hopes, the hopes of our party.[25]

The persecution continued apace with the local population often expressing their gratitude for what the Germans had managed to do and sorrow for what they had left undone. Thus, in opposition to the hopeful "wait and see" approach of the Bund in Poland, Tsanin insisted that there was but one item on the agenda of the Jewish people: emigration. It distressed him that while the doors of the world remained firmly shut his fellow Bundists persisted in turning their backs on Palestine. "You, my friends, have stopped the clock... even now, you continue to embrace the views that perished with the first victims of the first gas-chamber erected by the Germans in Poland. Instead of facing up to reality you hide behind these moribund views."[26]

It was precisely this issue of emigration that drew the ire of Zionist publicists in *She'erith Hapleitah* and became the active focus of the debate with the Bundist group. In the light of their decision not to return to Poland for reasons not far removed from those of Tsanin, these Bundists moderated their ideological formulations and adapted, somewhat, to prevailing opinion. They were encouraged to do so furthermore, by developments in Poland: as the Communists strengthened their hold over the country, it became increasingly difficult for the Bund to maintain an independent presence. In a passionate speech against British Middle Eastern policies, for example, N. Gerovitch, one of the Bundist leaders in Feldafing declared that "With regard to the question of Palestine all Jews stand united,"[27] and in the elections for the local Camp Committee the Bund recognized the Yishuv as a progressive Jewish force and spoke in favor of aliyah.[28] When it came to emigration, however, the Bund stuck to its guns and called for free emigration worldwide as opposed to the Zionist commitment to focusing the public campaign on opening the doors of Palestine. The Zionists were in no way opposed, so they claimed, to each individual seeking out their own future wherever they pleased. At the same time, it was wrong to blur the principled division between personal desires and national policy. The very decision of the Bundists not to return to Poland and to seek their future in America or elsewhere demonstrated their uncertainty about the future. If they could

[25] Ibid.   [26] Ibid.   [27] N. Gerovitch, *Dos Fraye Vort*, no. 10 (11.12.1945): 2.
[28] See Sh. D., "Niftar ha-mefarter."

not hold out the promise of security and well being, their public commitment to life in dispersion had to be seen as selfish and even irresponsible. Palestine, far from being just another immigration possibility, was, instead, a daring bid to provide a comprehensive solution to the problem of Jewish homelessness. The program of the Bund, on the other hand, failed to offer a persuasive answer to the existential concerns of the nearly 2 million Jews who remained in Europe and it lent support to the British claim that Palestine could not offer a comprehensive solution to the Jewish problem.[29]

These reservations about the Bund did not necessarily translate into a critical stance vis-à-vis the Soviet Union. As opposed to many other groups of DPs whose countries were now under communist dominance, many in She'erith Hapleitah were profoundly grateful for the role played by Russia in the defeat of Nazism and stood in awe of the human price exacted by victory. While this attitude might affirm that the Russian Revolution changed the course of human history and identify with its quest for social justice it argued that the new regime had failed, nonetheless, to find a satisfactory answer to the problems of the Jews living in its midst. The political challenge was to recognize the new status of the Soviet Union as a world power and to win over its active sympathy for the Zionist cause. This complex relationship was reflected in an almost comic headline in the Landsberger Lager Tsaytung describing a local ceremony to commemorate the October Revolution: "The workers of Landsberg marked the day of the great Soviet Revolution with an impressive demonstration in favor of Palestine and Jewish unity."[30] The speakers enthusiastically saluted the liberation of Russia and stressed that Zionism sought to do the same for its people. This affirmative tone which was fairly common in the latter half of 1945[31] changed by the end of 1946 when the majority of She'erith Hapleitah consisted of people who had not been liberated by the Red Army and who had spent most of the war in exile in the interior of the Soviet Union.

The survivors' relationship to Great Britain, by comparison, became openly hostile as 1945 wore on and it became clear that the White Paper policy was not going to change. Two weeks after the surrender of Nazi Germany, Chaim Weizmann requested of Churchill to set the White Paper aside and to reopen the doors of Palestine to Jewish immigration. Churchill refused claiming that the matter was best dealt with in

---

[29] Ibid.
[30] See LLT, no. 5 (12.11.1945): 1.
[31] Ibid. For an interesting testimony on the affirmative relationship to the Soviet Union see A. Ethel Ostry, After the Holocaust: My Work with UNRRA, ed. Elizabeth Fisher (1978): 127–128. deposited in Yad Vashem Archives.

the context of the upcoming peace talks. In the general elections held in Britain on 5 July 1945, the Conservatives were defeated and Labour that had traditionally opposed the White Paper came to power. Clement Attlee, the new premier, and Ernest Bevin, the Foreign Minister left things as they were, however, and the early hopes of August were transformed into despairing rage by November. On 13 November 1945 Bevin told Parliament that the White Paper policy was to continue until the newly formed Anglo-American Committee looked into the situation of the Jewish DPs and the role that Palestine might play in solving their problems. At a press conference that evening he advised the Jews that it would be unwise to attempt to push to the head of the queue and proposed, instead, that they utilize their unquestioned talents in helping to rebuild a new Europe.[32] His unfortunate choice of words ignited a wave of angry protest in Palestine and throughout the Jewish world. On 16 November *Undzer Veg* – Our Way – in Munich reported that:

> When Bevin's declaration was received it generated a tremendous stir in *She'erith Hapleitah*. There was a great sense of disappointment. Spontaneous protest meetings were held in Landsberg, Foehrenwald and Feldafing while the Central Committee of the Liberated Jews in Bavaria went into extraordinary session together with the Zionist Executive; the Association of Rabbis in Bavaria took counsel with all the camp and local rabbis.[33]

Given its urgent significance for the survivors, Bevin's declaration led to a radicalization of Zionist sentiment and an escalation of the public campaign against what was termed "The Black White Paper".[34] *Undzer Veg* commented that in the protest in Munich on 15 November "a new tone was heard that had little in common with the conventional rhetoric of protest speeches up to that point. It was set in the resolute addresses of Jewish fighters and partisans, heroes of the underground movements in the ghettos and became the dominant voice within *She'erith Hapleitah*."[35] The policy of the Labour government was a betrayal of British undertakings given in the Balfour Declaration and in the conditions of the Mandate as laid down by the League of Nations. Bevin had gone back on the ringing promises of his party in support of Zionism and had supplanted the socialist tradition of Labour with cold imperialist calculation.[36] How

---

[32] For these developments see Christopher Sykes, *Crossroads to Israel: Palestine from Balfour to Bevin* (London, 1965): 315–317; Nicholas Bethell, *The Palestine Triangle: The Struggle between the British, the Jews and the Arabs, 1935–1948* (London, 1979): 194–239.
[33] See *Undzer Veg*, no. 6 (16.11.1945): 1.   [34] See *Dos Fraye Vort*, no. 10 (11.12.1945): 1.
[35] *Undzer Veg*, no. 6 (16.11.1945): 1.
[36] See the report on the protest in Feldafing against Bevin's Palestinian policies "Ale yidn einig in erets yisroel frage (All Jews stand united on the question of Palestine), *Dos Fraye Vort*, no. 10 (11.12.1945): 1–2.

else could one account for the injustice of ignoring the contribution of the Jewish people to the war effort and its rightful share of the fruits of victory? "A million Jewish soldiers fought in the ranks of the Allied armies," argued Samuel Gringauz, "30,000 Jewish volunteers proudly donned the insignia of the Jewish Brigade . . . Tens of thousands of Jewish partisans did battle in the forests of Poland, Lithuania and Russia, throughout France and in the deadly confines of the ghettos."[37] The Arabs in Iraq, Egypt and the Mufti in Jerusalem, on the other hand, demonstrated sympathy for the German cause. How ironic that those who did next to nothing for the Allied victory were now to partake of its fruits. And Britain, which stood by when the Jews of Europe were being slaughtered and had further added to the dimensions of the killing because of its Middle Eastern policies, calmly washed its hands of any responsibility and condemned the handful of survivors to a sad end.[38]

The Zionists in Occupied Germany were persuaded that Bevin's call for a European solution to Jewish homelessness was a recipe for disaster: those who would not fall away through internal collapse would be ultimately wiped out by murderous antisemitism. Were this to happen the Yishuv, now deprived of the remnant of its human hinterland, would be condemned to perpetual minority status and would finally go under in a sea of emnity. This would spell the end of the two centers that could possibly have ensured the future of the Zionist enterprise and with it the resurgence of Jewish life in general. Against this backdrop we can better understand the harsh judgment of Bevin "as the deputy standing in for our destroyers, an heir of Hitlerite violence"[39] and the despairing call for the English to reactivate the crematoria and to continue where the Nazis left off.[40] The request of the Jews to help in rehabilitating Europe simply added insult to injury. "Bevin seeks to send us back to our destruction and demise," wrote the editor of *Undzer Veg*, "back to Polish antisemitism, to the graves of [what has become] a cemetery. Hitler paved the roads of his new Europe with our bodies and now Bevin seeks to build his new Europe with what is left of our lives."[41]

---

[37] Dr. Samuel Gringauz, "Finfakhike bgido" (Five-fold betrayal), *LLT*, no. 7 (22.11.1945): 3.

[38] Moshe Zilberberg, "Tsinitsism un farrat" (Cynicism and betrayal), *Dos Fraye Vort*, no. 8 (23.11.1945): 2.

[39] Shimon Rafike, "Vesof metifim yetufun" (In the end, they that drowned thee shall be drowned), *Undzer Veg*, no. 9 (16.11.1945): 5.

[40] See Zilberberg, "Tsinisism un farrat": 2.

[41] Levi Shalitan, "Oyfgedekt di korten" (Showing one's cards), *Undzer Veg*, no. 6 (16.11.1945): 1.

What has been discussed thus far, both in terms of broad interpretive schemes and the reading of current events, is fully consonant with the mainstream of Zionism and reflects important lines of personal and ideological continuity that bound *She'erith Hapleitah* to pre-war Europe and the Yishuv. In a brief inventory of these themes of continuity we would list the centrality of peoplehood in the Jewish experience, the view that Jewish interdependence of fate was both an inescapable fact and a value, the assumption that antisemitism was a permanent feature of Diaspora life which led to the negation of exile and a yearning to return home to a life of dignity and freedom in the Land of Israel. There were, however, certain emphases peculiar to the Zionist commitment of the survivors, a tangle of understandings, feelings and beliefs that bore the mark of their tragic circumstances.

In the first instance, the victims of the Holocaust were a pervasive presence for *She'erith Hapleitah* and a potent force in their Zionism. "Everything we do is done under the shadow cast by our holy dead," proclaimed Samuel Gringauz at the beginning of 1946, "Neither the inhabitants of Landsberg nor those of Feldafing give us our marching orders. We are commanded by the millions of our fallen martyrs."[42] The agony of the innocent dead served as the collective conscience of the survivors, their last will and testament constituted a categorical imperative that demanded implicit loyalty.[43] The primary duty of those who remained alive was to continue their lives as Jews so as to endow those who died with symbolic perpetuity and to serve, thereby, as their "living monument."[44] Somehow their senseless deaths had to be redeemed, if only fragmentarily, by saving the Jewish people from a similar fate. This was to be achieved through the realization of the lessons embraced by the victims in the face of death that for many in *She'erith Hapleitah* came to one thing: a national home in Eretz Yisrael that would ensure the survival of the Jewish people and restore the possibility of living with dignity and hope. In short, the Zionist vision was perceived as embodying the deepest aspirations of those who had perished during the Holocaust.

In this fashion, a halting attempt was made to transform the paralyzing terror of the past into a source of spiritual strength in the present. "The strength of a people does not always lie exclusively in its physical power. The strength of millions of slaughtered Jews is much greater today, in moral terms, than the force which Jews were able to muster in 1917."[45]

[42] Gringauz, "In tsaykhn fun matirertum."
[43] See Zalman Grinberg, *Undzer Veg*, no. 4 (2.11.1945): 1.   [44] Ibid.
[45] Levi Shalitan, *Undzer Veg*, no. 4 (2.11.1945): 1.

David Wolpe, the yiddish poet, echoed these sentiments of Levi Shalitan in one of his rare Hebrew poems:

> A command, brother a command
> Forward forward!
> The bridge is burnt –
> Blood sweat and tears
>
> Fragment on fragment
> The destruction is great
> Behind – the grave
> Before us the Land.
>
> A home for the people
> Will arise forever
> The command is the blood
> Building – our vengeance[46]

This attempt to turn tragedy to constructive ends did not come easily to those who saw "A sea of tears behind, a great question mark up ahead while today is once again crowded with sad troubles, darkness and gray."[47] With the temptation of destructive nihilism so close at hand, many asked themselves how the Jews of *She'erith Hapleitah* found the strength to go on living.[48] Marek Gutman, the head of the Jewish Committee in Stuttgart saw this affirmation of life as flowing out of the Jewish tradition:

Our Jewish world-view is basically optimistic. It is bound up with faith in mankind and hope for a better tomorrow. This spiritual attitude served as the force behind our lives, it reinforced our courage and will-to-live so helping us to withstand the unheard of torture and persecution that descended on us during the six years of war.[49]

Others, as Israel Kaplan declared, saw survival as an active attempt to foil Nazi designs: "The world must know that we are alive, that we saw it through!... indeed but a small fraction, altogether ruined... but with a determined will to keep on living – and to survive."[50] The renewal of Jewish life in Palestine, moreover, raised endurance to a new level worthy of those who had perished for, no matter how tempting, the biblical

---

[46] Davis Wolpe, "Tzav" (Command), *Nitzotz*, no. 5 (50) (30.11.1945): 6.

[47] Shammai Waks, "Oyf der frei" (In freedom), *Oyf der Fray*, no. 1 (December 1945): 3.

[48] For an example of nihilistic behavior see Simon Shochet, *Feldafing*, (Vancouver 1983): 24–25. See also Jacob Oleiski, "Undzer tayne tsu der welt" (Our claim against the world), *LLT*, no. 7 (19) (22.2.1946).

[49] Marek Gutman, "A yor nokh der bafreiung: a pruv fun a sakh-hakol" (A year since liberation: an attempt at a summation), *Oyf der Fray*, no. 3 (February–June 1946): 2.

[50] Israel Kaplan, "A tsaytung, a tsaytung" (A newspaper, a newspaper), *Undzer Veg*, no. 1 (12.10.1945): 3.

injunction of "an eye for an eye" went beyond their moral restraints and desperate imaginings.[51] In a *Yizkor* memorial address in the Landsberg camp synagogue Samuel Gringauz gave voice to this approach:

But you, the youth, cannot and should not live in a situation of memory and sorrow. You must live and build, work and liberate yourselves . . . for you, our young people are the agents of our revenge which ought to be a proud assertion to continue life. You must readily show the world and all our enemies that despite everything we are here to stay. Your revenge must be in working and toiling for your own land. You must create and build, dance and sing, open yourselves to life, to living and labor.[52]

In a world in which survivors carried scars that often rendered them insecure, manipulative and self-centered, leaders like Gringauz were engaged in a constant and not always successful struggle to rebuild both trust and the capacity to look ahead with hope. The way to the future meant leaving Europe but also entailed a withering critique of its culture and civilization that, especially during these first months after liberation, was held directly responsible for Auschwitz. The notion of *Galut* as far as *She'erith Hapleitah* was concerned, encompassed all countries of the Diaspora for no community was exempt from the dangers of recurrence. Existentially, however, *Galut* meant Europe and some observers went so far as to suggest that the Zionism of the survivors had more to do with their rejection of Europe than with their love of Eretz Yisrael.[53] Indeed already in May 1945 this issue was being publicly aired and became, in a variety of permutations, a persistent theme in the outlook of the Surviving Remnant.

We should recall in this regard that in the nineteenth century the Jews of Eastern Europe were introduced to Western ideas through German mediation and since then Germany had been viewed as the acme of European culture and its descent into barbarity signaled the collapse of Western civilization as a whole. How could it be that after 2,000 years of Christian culture and the advances of modernity "professors and writers, priests and philosophers, artists and judges . . . almost the entire elite of Germany rapturously cheered on the blood-drunk murderers."[54] Against this background we can better understand the harsh edge in the one-sided critique of the Bund and the call for the survivors even to desist from

---

[51] See in this regard Ivri (Shlomo Frenkel), "Hatzatzah min ha-tzad" (A glimpse from the sidelines), *Nitzotz*, no. 6 (51) (17.12.1945): 7, and B.H., "Hasneh" (The burning bush), *LLT*, no. 18 (2.12.1945): 7.

[52] Samuel Gringauz, "Yizkor" (Remember–prayer for the dead), *LLT*, no. 1 (8.10.1945): 3.

[53] Yisrael Efros, "Nesiyah le-machanot ha-akurim be-germaniyah" (A trip to the DP camps in Germany), *Hadoar*, no. 38 (10.4.1946): 965.

[54] Gringauz, "Jewish Destiny as the DP's See It": 506.

using European languages in public forums.[55] Those who were abandoning Europe unfortunately persisted in carrying the language of their
persecutors with them. "In our speech we bear with us the shame of *Galut,*
the shame of enslavement – for all to see. Elementary self respect should
bring us to remove this blight . . . especially in the light of the enormities
we experienced."[56]

In the same vein numerous voices decried the call of the well-known
writer, Sholem Asch, for a Jewish Christian rapprochement in his tract
One Destiny: An Epistle to the Christians.[57] To talk of Jewish–Christian
understanding in the light of the Nazis' deeds and the willing help they
received from so many Christians was to make a mockery of the martyrdom of European Jewry. Asch, without attempting to conceal the darker
side of the Church's relationship to the Jews in the past, had argued that
Christianity could not be held responsible for a movement that was essentially pagan and that many Christians had suffered grievously during the
war as well. He hoped that this shared fate would presage a new Jewish–
Christian partnership for they ultimately shared one destiny. Joseph Gar,
a historian resident in Landsberg, also took a less hostile position but one
that ultimately flowed from considerations of expedience: on the eve of
the fateful struggle for Jewish statehood closer relations with Christianity
could prove to be useful.[58] The more characteristic response was one
of outrage and rejection. Wrote Moshe Zilberberg, a Zionist leader in
Feldafing:

Asch the Polish Jew got it in his head, in a world in which millions of Jews were
murdered, to write such drivel. Has he not heard of what the Germans did to
his brothers in the crematoria, the concentration camps and the ghettos? What
the Poles, Lithuanians, Estonians, Ukrainians, Romanians, Hungarians got up
to? . . . Was Asch living on Mars when he rolled his eyes at the Christian God and
went on about brotherhood between Jews and Christians.[59]

It would be fair to say that when it came to issues of this kind, at least
in the public realm, the more militant voices easily overcame appeals for
moderation and balance.

Within this reassessment of the survivors' relationship to the world
around them Zionism had one further advantage. When it came to immigration there was no avoiding the appearance, cap in hand, before state
officials and the feeling that one was pleading for a charitable handout.

[55] See M. Neuberger, "An efene briv" (An open letter), *Undzer Veg*, no. 4 (2.11.1945): 4.
[56] Ch.D., "Klapei pnim" (Turning Inwards), *Nitzotz*, no. 7 (52) (31.12.1945): 3.
[57] See Sholem Asch, *One Destiny: An Epistle to the Christians*, (New York 1945).
[58] Yosef Gar, "Wegn unzere kheshbonos mit der kristlekher velt" (Concerning our accounting with the Christian world), *LLT*, no. 8 (2.12.1945): 6.
[59] Moshe Zilberberg, "Shalom asch: quo vadis?," *Dos Fraye Vort*, no. 16 (18.1.1946): 3.

Aliyah to Eretz Yisrael, on the other hand, was a matter of right based on the historic and judicial standing enjoyed by the Jewish people. The leaders of *She'erith Hapleitah*, therefore, had little patience with humanitarian gestures and demanded free entry to Palestine as a basic entitlement. The almost formulaic "The Land of Israel belongs to us ... it was promised to us by God, recognized by the Balfour Declaration and accepted, in turn, by the nations of the world"[60] was axiomatic for the survivors in Occupied Germany. After years of helplessness and total dependence on others they shared a strong distaste for charity and had one recurring demand: "For once and for all to shape our own history in our own land."[61] The underground forces in Palestine and the soldiers of the Jewish Brigade were a living example of this commitment to independence but pride of place was given to the ghetto fighters and partisans as the true exemplars of the struggle for dignity. Thus, in sum, both the call of those who fell victim to the Nazis and "the inspiration of Warsaw and Czestochowa combined with the heroism of the Jewish men and women who fought in the forests of Poland and Lithuania must show us the way."[62]

What further distinguishes the Zionism of *She'erith Hapleitah* is the remarkable overlap between ideological postulate and personal situation. Antisemitism, the disabilities of life in exile, degrading dependence and the sharp pain of homelessness were not only abstract coordinates on a cognitive map of Jewish life but had become an intimate and pressing reality for every survivor. We can best illustrate this by considering the various usages of the term *heimlozikayt* – homelessness – in their lives. On an abstract level, homelessness served as an overall explanatory scheme for the tragedy that had befallen European Jewry. Their exposure and vulnerability stemmed from the fact that they had nowhere to go and no country that made caring for Jews a national priority.[63] Existentially, homelessness was the most urgent problem of each survivor: their homes had been irretrievably lost, their present status as displaced persons required no further commentary while the question of where and when they would finally be able to strike root again remained agonizingly uncertain. Thus they prayed for *a heim, a heim*, a warm corner and a life lived amongst one's brothers and sisters, a family home that promised permanence, a place of freedom and repose.[64]

[60] Levi Shalitan, "Recht oder z'est" (Right or gesture), *Undzer Veg*, no. 14 (4.1.1946): 2.
[61] Ibid. See also Aronovitch, "Mir vilennit keyn nedavos."
[62] Levi Shalitan, *Undzer Veg*, no. 1 (12.10.1945): 1.
[63] Gringauz, "Finfakhike begido."
[64] See Marek Gutman, "Mir veln nit vartn" (We don't want to wait), *Oyf der Fray*, no. 1 (December 1945): 11; M. Gavronsky, "A blik oyf der virklekhkayt" (A look at reality), *Dos Fraye Vort*, no. 2 (14.10.1945): 5, and Baruch Hermanovitch, "Tsu a nayem leben" (To a new life), *LLT*, no. 11 (21.12.1945): 3.

Psychologically, too, the yearning for home made what was often merely a figure of speech painfully real. The most powerful need of those bereft of family, observed Leo Srole,

is to find refuge in the Jewish "nation," which must be understood as the Jewish family extended, writ large. Hence, they think of Palestine in family terms as "home," and their settlement there as a "return home." In effect their feelings are:

1. "We Jews must be an integrated family again, for our scatter has been our weakness and our undoing."
2. "We cannot be a family again except in a home of our own."
3. "We can really be at home only where our fathers struck their first and deepest psychological and cultural roots."

As one survivor expressed it: "Our illusion that we could live as a stranger in the house of others was totally exploded by the Nazis' own atomic bomb which they devised to destroy us all. And we see now that such atomic bombs are no monopoly and no secret."[65]

On another level *She'erith Hapleitah* sensed that they were situated at a fateful crossroads, an orienting event in Jewish history that would determine the future of their people. They were persuaded that the Exodus from Egypt and *Yetziat Europa* – the Exodus from Europe – were fully analogous. It could be said that in their minds historical symbols tended to actualize themselves, or, put more cautiously, that these symbols took on an immediacy that colored their thoughts and deeds. So, for example, in Chanukah 1946 many declared that the days of the Maccabees had not passed and told stories of Jewish mothers who had refused to hand over their children to Christian families in the face of death as Hannah had done with her seven sons in days of yore. Or as Meir Gavronsky wrote in honor of the Chanukah candles:

> To you little lights
> You tell of days past
> Deeds without number
> Deeds that were once
> . . . .
>
> You tell of bloodiness
> Of heroes so brave
> Deeds that were once.
> No. Not only past
> But also today.[66]

---

[65] Dr. Leo Srole, Submission to the Anglo-American Commission for Palestine, JDC/DP's Germany 1946: 4.
[66] Meir Gavronsky, *Dos Fraye Vort*, no. 9 (30.11.1945): 2, and, in addition, "Khana un

Perhaps this sense of the confluence of tradition with the contemporary is best seen in the special significance attached to the celebration of Passover in 1946, the first *Pesach* celebrated in freedom after six years of war that brought tragedy, destruction and annihilation. In the numerous *Haggadot* written for a communal celebration of the second *seder*, the traditional text sprang to life. When survivors adorned their contemporary text with traditional passages like: "for not only one has risen up against us to destroy us," or "Pour out Your wrath upon the nations that do not recognize You . . . For they have devoured Jacob and destroyed his habitation . . . Pursue them with anger and destroy them from beneath God's heaven," they did so because of their overwhelming relevance. As Shalom Herschkopf from Feldafing told it:

Fate determined that the celebration of both the Exodus from Egypt and the heroic Warsaw Ghetto Revolt would take place on the same day when the Jewish father sits down for the *seder* and tells his children of the miracles that happened once and, when he has told of those who went out of Egypt, he then goes on to describe and tell of the heroic Jewish battle in the streets of the Warsaw Ghetto which was the start of the Exodus from Europe.[67]

On the other hand, in the Haggadah written by the young members of Kibbutz "Nili," an agricultural training farm that had been symbolically set up on the estate of Julius Streicher, the central narrative theme became the Holocaust, a chronological retelling of ghettoization, forced labor, disease, abandonment, resistance and relentless destruction. The root cause of this terrible travail was to be found in the prolonged enslavement of the Jews following the loss of political independence and the self-delusion that: "All that befell our brothers yesterday, all that happened to them . . . will not befall us." The lessons these young people derived from their experience still gives one pause:

All that was done to us by Amalek has been engraved in our memory, the memory of an ancient people as have [the deeds] of their collaborators, all those who stood by, heard our screams and did nothing to help. Through all this time, however, we have never faltered in our dream and yearning for national and human awakening. Our people has ever been the victim of reactionary sadism and bestial barbarism. Nonetheless, we have persisted in believing that instead of the beast will come forth man, that after the darkness of night a new day will dawn . . . that we shall yet be a great and free people in our own liberated land.[68]

ire 7 kinder" (Chanah and her seven sons), *Feldafinger Magazin*, no. 1 (Chanukah – 7.12.1945): 11.

[67] Shalom Herschkopf, "Betrachtungen vegn varshaver oyfshtand" (Reflections on the Warsaw revolt), *Dos Fraye Vort*, no. 28 (26.4.1946): 3.

[68] Passover Haggadah, Kibbutz "Nili," Pleikershof, 1946, HHA.

Perhaps the most explicit and self-conscious attempt to read the orienting past as present is to be found in the United Zionist Organization and *Nocham* Supplement to the Haggadah that was arranged and illustrated by Y. D. Sheinson with woodcuts by Miklós Adler (signed Ben Benjamin).[69] The printing of the Haggadah was organized by Chaplain Klausner who conducted the public *seder* in Munich on 15 and 16 April 1946. In Sheinson's text traditional passages are accompanied by contemporary transpositions – Egypt becomes Germany, Pharaoh is transformed into Hitler and the concentration camps supplant the pyramids as the locale of slavery – and all this is interwoven with dreams of humanly achieved redemption in Zion. The main narrative line tells in mock biblical prose of the horrors visited on the Jewish people, of the callous indifference of both the Allies and the bystanders, liberation, the trauma of returning home, flight and the hope of aliyah. The story as told by Sheinson was close to canonical among the survivors and thus worth quoting at length:

"And they afflicted us and laid upon us hard bondage." When the righteous among the nations saw that Hitler had decided to exterminate Israel, their great assembly came together and out of their great sorrow decided to keep silent . . . All the while Hitler sets his hungry dogs at the babes of Israel and they tear them to pieces. That evil man went on to build gas chambers and crematoria in which to annihilate the people of Israel . . . And the people of Israel, in the attempt to save their children, hand them over to Christians to hide them. Some hide them for money; some, demanding money, hide them and later bring them out to be killed. Others hide them not for money, but out of conviction. And still others convert [the children] and turn them into idol worshippers. The fathers of these children are dragged by the murderers into camps, where they are made to perish by hard labor, by hunger, and by all kinds of torture and disease . . . Finally, the enemies of that man of evil grew indignant, girded themselves and unleashed . . . great wrath, rage, fury, disaster and a band of avenging angels . . . And a multitude of chariots . . . sweep across the land of that evil man, and destroy him, and *She'erith Hapleitah* in the camps are liberated and redeemed.

. . .

The surviving remnants came out of caves, out of forests, and out of death camps, and returned to the lands of their exile. The people of those lands greeted them and said: We thought you were no longer alive, and here you are, so many of you . . . And the people of Israel ran for their lives, smuggled themselves across borders . . . and they went to Bavaria in order to go up to our Holy Land.[70]

Thereafter the didactic structure of the Haggadah is used to teach the Zionist interpretation of what had befallen the Jewish people – the bitter herbs of exile and the dubious sons speaking the part of the detractors of

---

[69] See Touster, ed., *A Survivors' Haggadah.*   [70] Ibid.: 27, 29, 31.

Zionism – and the story draws to a close with a ringing affirmation of the universal value of human freedom:

From parents to children, from generation to generation, the story of the Exodus from Egypt is passed on as a personal memory; it never pales or loses its luster. "In each and every generation one should regard oneself as though he had come out of Egypt."

... Can anything be greater than the wisdom of the ancient commandment? Is there any literary creation that better teaches us to hate and despise slavery and to love freedom, than the story of the bondage and exodus from Egypt? Does there exist any ancient memory that could better serve as a symbol for the present and the future.[71]

Sheinson as a strong advocate of Jewish and Zionist unity also used his supplement to settle accounts with those who, from his point of view, were sowing senseless dissension among the youth of *She'erith Hapleitah*. This drive to create a unitary framework in the search for a new politics brings us to our final port of call in our attempt to delineate the unique contours of survivor Zionism.

[71] Ibid.: 49, 51.

5   In search of a new politics: unity
versus division

With liberation there were repeated efforts, formal and informal, to establish a united Zionist movement in Bavaria. The quest for a new order
that would set aside old divisions had already been part of the ethos of the
Irgun Brith Zion in the Kovno Ghetto; it reappeared in both Buchenwald
and Kaufering as preparations for liberation got underway and moved
on to center stage as an ideal evoking deep resonance in the early organization of *She'erith Hapleitah*. In the latter half of 1945 it looked like
these efforts, with all their ups and downs, might be crowned with success
but, by the beginning of 1946, the hopes of those favoring unity began
to recede. From October to November 1945 various groupings seeking
to preserve their independence began to break away from the general
framework and once this happened others were tempted to follow suit.
In the first half of 1946, therefore, the unity camp while still believing in
value and necessity of a broader framework slowly became, by default,
one movement among others.

The quest for unity that animated survivors throughout Europe in the
immediate aftermath of the war appeared in different guises in Poland,
Hungary, Czechoslovakia and, in its most sustained form, in Germany.
The loneliness and pervasive sense of loss, the experience of being abandoned by all, the remembrance of Jewish disarray in the face of Nazi
aggression and the fear of continued vulnerability created a community
of fate that sought to bind itself in a protective cover of unity. Unity in its
most primary sense meant the familial warmth of belonging, of being simply welcomed and accepted with no questions asked. It sprung, secondly,
from a more reflective feeling that what had happened had irrevocably
changed the course of Jewish history, was a watershed event that rendered many antediluvian conceptions and divisions irrelevant and waste-
ful. Sadly, the moral compulsion often generated by academic stature,
professional ethics, refined cultural taste, enlightened politics and even a
Christian upbringing had failed to stand in the way of cruel inhumanity.
Indeed, the faith of so many Jews in brotherhood and progressive human
solidarity had served to disarm them in their hour of need. The writing on

the wall was simple and clear: away with the old debilitating divisions for you have no one to depend on but yourself! *She'erith Hapleitah*, ravaged, scattered and weak, was therefore called upon to stand together in the face of dangers that were yet to pass and the challenges that still lay ahead.

The drive to unity was articulated in a variety of ways in accordance with the background and war experiences of its protagonists. Those who had already shed factionalism as part of their armed resistance to the Nazis in the ghettos and forests of Eastern Europe followed the lead of Abba Kovner in setting up the Division of East European Survivors which sought to create an inclusive framework for the mass exodus of those seeking to make their way to Palestine.[1] Those who had experienced the extremities of Nazi terror in the concentration camps and death marches sought overarching frameworks that could accommodate all: religious and secular, left and right, militant and moderate. Equally strong in their advocacy of unity were a number of socialist Zionist repatriates from the interior of the Soviet Union and survivors from the eastern regions of Poland who had both experienced at first hand what they saw as the deceit, rot and endemic antisemitism of the Soviet Union. Disabused of their erstwhile belief in the communist world of tomorrow, they sought to supplant it with an ethos of solidarity derived from Jewish sources. On the other hand, those who had received vital aid from the Communist underground in Warsaw and the western regions of Poland during the war took a more moderate position and remained committed to a framework of socialist cooperation in the Zionist movement. Finally the bitter experience of the Soviet occupation of Lithuania followed closely by the annihilatory policies of Nazi Germany confirmed the veterans of the Kovno Ghetto in their belief that the politics of Emancipation which, following the European model, divided Jews between left and right had become anachronistic and meaningless. While those advocating a new politics were not always clear about what they meant, they were quite certain that they no longer wished to model themselves on movements that had failed the test of humanity.

In its initial phases, therefore, the attempt to create a united Zionist movement in Occupied Germany evoked excitement and wide support and by September 1945 the United Zionist Organization and its youth movement *Nocham* – the United Pioneering Youth – were established and running. The official Declaration of the Founding Conference gave brief expression to the new movement's guiding philosophy:

We who were transformed by years of terrible suffering into a community of fate, we who were brought together by our clandestine activity and fought with the

[1] See Kless, *Bederech lo slulah*: 15–74.

partisans in the forests and swamps of Eastern Europe . . . and midst the ruins of the ghetto . . . turn to Jews everywhere and to the Yishuv in Palestine in particular and demand that the lesson to be learned from great catastrophe visited on our people is the unification of all our creative forces for the upbuilding of our land.[2]

They were impelled by a sense of urgency and disappointed to learn that elsewhere in the Jewish world "the fact that in 1939 our people entered a new and decisive period"[3] was yet to sink in.

The most active allies of the UZO were the emissaries of the Jewish Brigade, especially those who were members of *Mapai* and followers of Berl Katznelson and David Ben-Gurion. Foremost among these was Zvi Langzam (Shiloah) who coordinated the Brigade's activities in *She'erith Hapleitah*.[4] Shiloah had enlisted into the British Army in 1941 and, in consultation with Berl Katznelson, helped set up an ideological, non-party forum for Palestinian soldiers serving in the British forces. When the Jewish Brigade was sent to North Africa in 1944, the distance from home together with the shared experiences of a fighting unit created an atmosphere far more conducive to talk of political rapprochement. This tendency was reinforced by the emotional meeting of the Brigade with Jewish communities in North Africa and Italy and especially in the first encounters with survivors of the Holocaust in Germany and Austria, climaxing in the rescue operation launched to care for thousands of Jewish refugees who had been encouraged to move towards Tarvisio in northern Italy where they were stationed. These tendencies were cast into a dramatic new light in July 1945 with the arrival of the Division of East European Survivors led by Abba Kovner. Here was a group of heroic figures who sought a new form of unity that expressed itself in the radical rejection of exilic life, the organization of a latter-day exodus from Eastern Europe and an unqualified commitment to the goal of Jewish statehood.[5]

---

[2] 'Hatzharah' shel ha-veidah ha-tzionit ha-rishonah shel she'erith hapleitah begermaniyah (Declaration of the first Zionist Convention of She'erith Hapleitah in Germany), CZA /S25/1988. Material on the Founding Convention is found in CZA /S5/829 while a copy of the Constitution of the United Zionist Organization of *She'erith Hapleitah* in Germany is located in S5/1988. See also Kol koreh vehachlatot shel ha-kinus ha-tzioni hasheni shel she'erith hapleitah (Proclamation and resolutions of the second Conference of She'erith Hapleitah), CZA /S5/829 and S25/1988, which includes a list of the participants. See, in addition, Zvi Shiloah, Interview, OHD/4 (64): 13–16.

[3] Ivri (Shlomo Frenkel), "Le-or ritzinut ha-mtzav" (In view of the seriousness of the situation), *Nitzotz*, no. 4 (49) (16.11.1945): 6.

[4] My thanks to Mr. Zvi Shiloah for placing his private papers at my disposal. See there Hanachot yesod (Basic assumptions) and also Shiloah, *Eretz gedolah*: 34–36. For a broader description see Yoav Gelber, "Hamifgash im she'erith hapleitah" (The meeting with She'erith Hapleitah), in *Toldot ha-hitnadvut III*.

[5] On the Brigade of East European Survivors see Bauer, *Flight and Rescue*: 35–40; and Kless, *Bederech lo slulah*: 15–74. For details on the meetings between the two groups

When Abba Kovner argued in his now famous address to the soldiers of the Jewish Brigade that the horrors of the past and the dangers of the future should create a new community of souls, the advocates of unity felt that he was talking their language. The feeling that a new phase of Zionism was in the making was further reinforced when Zvi Shiloah came to discover that important voices in *She'erith Hapleitah* were "saying the same thing. While none of them have forgotten their political roots they seek to organize themselves in one framework of a general nature that will include all regardless of their past."[6] The sense of affinity between these emissaries of the Jewish Brigade and the leadership of the UZO had one further dimension: they shared an almost messianic belief that, despite all indications to the contrary, the catastrophe would bring redemption in its wake, that the vast suffering would not be in vain, that a new day would dawn.[7] The emissaries of the Brigade carried this message to Italy, France, Holland and Belgium but it was only in Germany that it found a ready ear and was warmly received.

The leaders of the major kibbutz movements in Palestine not associated with *Mapai* strongly objected to involvement of their youth groups in the new unitary frameworks. In view of the destruction of their European hinterland, this was very clearly an attempt to protect and nurture the little that was left of the human reserves so vital for the maintenance and growth of their *kibbutzim*. They feared, and not without cause, that the call for unity would surreptitiously help *Mapai* recruit new supporters and thereby help perpetuate its hegemony in the Palestinian labor movement. Their opposition flowed, in addition, from a different reading of the catastrophe of European Jewry and its aftermath. The Palestinian leadership of *Hashomer Hatzair*, to take but one example of many, refused to grant normative status to the world of death over and above the responsibilities and continuing demands of the world of the living. This approach is clearly delineated in a letter they sent to Mordechai Rosman,

---

see Yehuda Toubin to Yaari, Chazan and Kobah (15.7.1945, 16.7.1945), Meir Yaari Collection, *HHA*. See also Abba Kovner, "The Mission of the Survivors," in Y. Gutman and L. Rotkirchen eds., *The Jewish Catastrophe in Europe: Background, History, Implications* (Jerusalem, 1976): 671–683. For an eyewitness record of this historic meeting see also the *Moreshet* Archive/A.388

[6] Shiloah, Interview: 14.

[7] See Amitzur Ilan, "Messianism and Diplomacy: The Struggle for a Jewish State 1945–1948," *Wiener Library Bulletin*, vol. 30 no. 41/42 (1977): 36–46; see also Prateikol shel yeshivat va'adat ha-brigada bi-sh'elat derech shlichuteinu beshe'erith u-ba-noar be-eropa (Protocol of the Brigade Committee on the question of our mission to the remnant and youth in Europe) (15.8.1945) and the contribution of Y. Duvdevani to Moetzet ha-kibbutz ha-meuchad (Council of the United Kibbutz movement), Haifa (3.2.1946), in the Zvi Shiloah papers; Matza shel histadrut ha-tzionit ha-achida shel she'erith hapleitah be-germaniyah (Platform of the United Zionist Organization of She'erith Hapleitah in Germany), *Ha'avodah* – Labor Archive, Division 126v11, folder 13a.

a veteran member of the movement who had been exiled to the interior of the Soviet Union, moved westwards with the Division of East European Survivors and agreed to help coordinate *Hashomer Hatzair* in Occupied Germany:

> The necessities of life take hold of us . . . each person and people seeks and should seek to live even when those who hate us close in on us from all sides. We are obliged to make an accounting of the life of our people, an accounting of our future . . . those who led the fighters . . . can unite to form a powerful force . . . if they understand that they now need to devote themselves to the living, to build-ing . . . their blessing, and we stand in need of it, will be all the greater only if it merges with historical movements that have a well founded and on-going world view.[8]

The Palestinian leadership was profoundly suspicious of views born in "the life of the bunker and the ways of the partisan"[9] which, working on First World War analogies, conjured up images of fascism and le-gionnaires. This was the background to their categorical negation of the integrally Jewish ethos embraced by both the Division of East European Survivors and *Nocham*. Jewish unity which cancelled out considerations of class, the dismantling of Jewish life in Eastern Europe without due regard for the progressive role of the Soviet Union and working for Jew-ish statehood despite the bi-national goals of their mother-movement could not be countenanced. As Meir Yaari put it sardonically: "Satan has hatched us a Revisionist[10] version of *Hashomer Hatzair*."[11] Ever sensitive to his reading of the past Yaari feared that the resistance fighters would scorn the "heroism of the quotidian" and seek to translate the powerful experiences of the underground into a civilian idiom.

Furthermore, the members of *Hashomer Hatzair* were among the ini-tiators and organizers of the *Brichah*.[12] Their Palestinian leaders who em-braced the goals of rescue and expanding the Jewish presence in Palestine were clearly supportive of this activity but they had reservations about the undue haste and sense of impending doom that appeared to inform the mounting exodus from Eastern Europe. For one thing they feared that not enough of their key people would remain behind to absorb returning repatriates from the Soviet Union into the ranks of the movement. They were equally anxious lest a large-scale population flow westwards, prior

---

[8] See Chief Directorate of *Hashomer Hatzair* to Bela, Gershon and Mordechai (1.9.1945), *Moreshet* Archive/D.1.4879, and Shiloah, Interview: 15–16.

[9] Adam Rand to Mordechai Rosman (26.7.1945), *HHA*/*Hanhagah Elyonah*, Correspon-dence with *shlichim* (emissaries) 1945/1946 (2)3.32.

[10] Referring to the right-wing Zionist Revisionist movement founded by Zeev Jabotinsky.

[11] Meir Yaari to Yehuda Toubin (24.7.1945), Meir Yaari Collection, *HHA*.

[12] See the testimony of Moshe Meiri (Ben), *Moreshet* Archive /A.471.

to the opening of the gates of Palestine to free immigration, would entail a long debilitating stay in DP camps for those already scarred by long years of untold suffering.[13] When masses of Jews voted with their feet in favor of flight, in addition, it reflected poorly on the new socialist regimes that had come to power in Eastern Europe under Soviet tutelage. Shutting the door on progressive Europe, in the eyes of the Palestinian leadership, was both politically unwise and a further inducement for Jews to turn in on themselves and be caught up in a "false messianism" that had pervaded the Zionist movement in the aftermath of the war. Headlong flight from Europe was tantamount to giving up on the possibility of human redemption and thereby abandoning one of the foundation stones of socialist Zionism. "There is a Zionism of false messianism in flight from the frying pan to the fire and fixated on the forces of yesterday. And there is the other Zionism – that of militant, creative pioneering and socialist fraternity. It is for the other Zionism that our movement is working."[14] This call to regulate the *Brichah* did not and, indeed, could not have had a significant impact on those poised to depart: the weight of the past, the grim reality of post-war Poland and the fear of the iron curtain being rung down again pushed many to leave just as soon as they could.

Given that the official policies of *Hashomer Hatzair* were diametrically opposed to the basic course of events in Europe, keeping the movement strictly apart from others was critical to the maintenance and promotion of the "other Zionism". Despite the initial reluctance of the European leaders of the movement, Yaari and Ya'akov Chazan carried the day and by the latter half of 1945 *Hashomer Hatzair* was running its own educational seminars and in the process of setting up independent, collective training farms in order both to escape the unhealthy atmosphere of camp life and to encourage the crystallization of a stronger movement identity.[15]

Hashomer Hatzair's breakaway from *Nocham* encouraged the leaders of *Dror* (Freedom), the youth movement of the United Kibbutz to follow suit. After the great destruction everything had to be started anew for only a separate movement would serve as a reserve for the kibbutz while unity meant, in effect, "lining up politically with those in power [who are] using devious means to siphon off new immigrants into their own framework."[16] Similarly, *Hanoar Hazioni* (the Zionist Youth) affiliated

---

[13] Meir Yaari to the Conference of the Oranizations of *Hashomer Hatzair* in Europe (31.12.1945), *HHA*/(2)3.32.

[14] Ibid.

[15] See Yehuda Toubin to Yaari and Chazan (30.10.1945, 11.12.1945), Meir Yaari Collection, *HHA*. See also Zelig Shoshan to Adam Rand (27.12.1945), *HHA*/(2)3.32.

[16] Secretariat of *Dror* to Yisrael Karolinsky (no date), Archive of *Bet Lochamei Hagetaot*, Overseas Committee, Container 11, folder 2, in response to Yisrael Karolinsky to Yosef Korniyansky (25.9.1945), Archive of *Bet Lochamei Hagetaot*, Overseas Committee,

with the liberal wing of the centrist General Zionist party who initially joined *Nocham* soon became disenchanted with the unified framework that appeared to hold out great promise but, in point of fact, undercut loyalty to *Hanoar Hazioni* and its struggling settlements.[17] When the first group of newcomers from Germany arrived in Palestine and failed to join the movement *kibbutzim* Moshe Kolodny, the Palestinian General Secretary of *Hanoar Hazioni*, underwent a change of heart and advocated immediate secession from *Nocham*. Kolodny attributed the disappointing results of the first group of newcomers to the "chaos," "illusions and confusion" that the attempts at unification had generated. The problem, at bottom, stemmed from the preference for impressive numbers joined together in synthetic union as opposed to investing in the more modest and dedicated membership of a tighter and more organic movement. All the idealism invested in striving for unity had been in vain. The notion that they would serve as an example to the vying parties in Palestine was "a dangerous illusion because it would end up in disillusionment and despair. This union could come into being in Palestine on the basis of a shared ideological platform. If it does not happen here it will not come from abroad."[18]

How, then, did the leaders of the UZO and *Nocham* respond to these incessant pressures that threatened to tear apart the delicate fabric of unity? In the first instance they distinguished between threats from within that related to developments in Europe itself as opposed to external threats which referred to the attempts by Palestinian parties to politicize *She'erith Hapleitah*.[19] In the last third of 1945 the leadership of the UZO fought a losing battle in their attempt to make political activity off limits for the Palestinian emissaries and to mobilize public support for their position in the Yishuv. "If *shlichim* are going to come to us so as to organize their parties," warned Yizchak Ratner, the Chairman of the UZO, "we shall not accept them. Since we have to make every effort to establish a Jewish state, and now as the struggle unfolds and we make our final effort to achieve our goal, we very definitely have to be united and not divided."[20]

Container 11, folder 2. And also, Chaim Avni to the *Dror* Secretariat (28.12.1945), Archive of *Bet Lochamei Hagetaot*, Overseas Committee, Container 10, folder 5, and Chaim Avni to the *Dror* Secretariat (25.1.1946), Archive of *Bet Lochamei Hagetaot*, Overseas Committee, Container 10, folder 2.

[17] See Yitzchak Ratner to Moshe Kolodny (10.8.1945), *Masuah* Archive, *nun tzadi*-26–1; for a review of *Ichud Hanoar Hazioni* in Germany see "Tza'adeinu ha-rishonim" (Our first steps), *Biyulatin Informativi* (Kislev 1947): 3–8, published by *Hotza-at histadrut chalutzit olamit – ichud hanoar hazioni ve-akiva be-germaniya*.

[18] See Moshe Kolodny, *Iggeret le-chaverim ha-pe'ilim ba-golah* (A letter to movement activists in the *golah*) (6.1.1945), *Masuah* Archive/*Aleph*:62/1.

[19] See Yitzchak Ratner to the Zionist Executive (3.9.1945), CZA/S25/1988.

[20] Ibid.

As the danger of division began to grow it was further recommended that emissaries only be allowed to work within the organizational and ideological constraints of the United Zionist Organization, an idea that was actively embraced by the Jewish Agency which was effectively controlled by *Mapai*.[21]

In the internal battle for unity the moral imperative of joining forces and creating an atmosphere of openness and sharing was given prominence. The fight for survival in impossible circumstances had left its scars: many were unable to settle down to a regular regimen, could not face the prospect of work and had became prey to either the deformations of prolonged idleness or blackmarket activity. Without adequate and sympathetic attention, warned the leaders of the UZO, these future immigrants could easily become a burden that the Yishuv could ill afford. Even more acute were the potential problems of the young who hung on the every word, personal and political, of the young leaders that had guided them through the *Brichah* escape routes to a temporary haven in occupied Germany. "The child survivors of our people," wrote the leadership of UZO to the Jewish Agency in Jerusalem,

are not unclaimed property and certainly not the personal possession of a movement in which a seventeen-year-old leader can do with them as he pleases. The children whose health, for the most part, is frail in the extreme, whose education is non-existent and whose upbringing has been terrible, require us to concentrate our scarce, remaining teaching staff on developing educational activities. This requires having general and combined resources: joint schools and youth movements and concerted action on the part of the executive of the UZO.[22]

In the same vein, Ben-Gurion who participated in the First Congress of *She'erith Hapleitah* in January 1946 was struck by the passionate claim of one of the participants that educating the young to movement affiliation was to make a mockery of their real needs which were "first of all to make them [decent] people who need to know what cleanliness is, that they shouldn't steal from each other . . . (they need) a humane education that would restore to them the image of man."[23]

In the UZO–*Nocham* Survivors' Haggadah Y. D. Sheinson reflected on both the distorted education of the young and the divisive role of the Palestinian *shlichim*:

---

[21] See both the circular of the Aliyah Department of the Jewish Agency (8.11.1945) and Eliyahu Dobkin to the Executive of the United Zionist Organization (9.11.1945), CZA/S5/829.
[22] The Executive of the United Zionist Organization to the Executive of the Jewish Agency (25.12.1945), CZA/S25/5232.
[23] D. Ben-Gurion in the *Mapai* Secretatiat (20.2.1946), *Ha'avodah* – Labor Archive.

Now that the Saved Remnant is redeemed, the orphaned children of Israel are taken in. Each group of the Remnant makes a claim on the children and is envious of the other groups on their account, because each group wants to increase its number. And while the children of Israel are being collected like abandoned eggs, the contention increases as each group tries to pull them its way... And so it happens that the non-Orthodox snatch the children of the Orthodox, and the Orthodox snatch the children of the non-Orthodox. And each group has its own school where children learn "Torah." And after they study for a time, they grow clever; and a child behaves like a man of seventy who has opinions about how the world should be run, or how or when to settle the [Promised] Land and manage affairs of state. The children argue, and all are eager to advance their own positions and views, so that brothers are set apart, unable to agree on the question of [politics], unable to sit peacefully together. The emissaries come to meet the remnants, and when they meet Israel, they ask: Which group do you belong to? But the survivors do not understand them and... reply: What is the meaning of this? Are we not, all of us, Israel? The emissaries say: You must have been sleeping for seventy years, because the unity of Israel is a fable. It is no longer possible; each person must join a group. The remnants answer: But was not all of Israel slaughtered together? Is not all of Israel to build the Land together? The emissaries say: The unity of Israel is fable. The land of Israel is being built by different factions.[24]

In the last months of 1945 *Nocham* and the United Zionist Organization struggled mightily to protect their vision of a new politics but to no avail. Neither persuasion nor political pressure sweetened with the promise of material benefits were sufficient to protect and maintain what had been achieved under the banner of unity. Movement after movement, each at its own season and for its own reasons, broke away from the shared framework, dissolved the UZO and reduced *Nocham* to but one movement among others. How then can one explain the demise of an idea that was initially so powerful?

Any accounting must begin with the determined effort of Palestinian settlement movements to restore their youth divisions in Europe to functioning independence which, unavoidably, generated opposition to the vision of unity. For some of the proponents of unity in *She'erith Hapleitah* the distance of the Yishuv from both the war and the destruction of European Jewry explained their inability to grasp the root experiences of the survivors. As Yitzchak Ratner wrote in September 1945: "We understand that in the Yishuv the rot [of division] can and will continue because the Yishuv, thank God, did not suffer in this world war and, on the contrary, prospered and, therefore, goes on kicking out at all we hold dear and holy."[25]

[24] See Y. D. Sheinson's comments in Touster, ed., *A Survivors' Haggadah*: 33, 35.
[25] Yitzchak Ratner to the Zionist Executive (3.9.1945), CZA/S25/1988.

One should not overstate the case, however, by claiming that the leaders of the Yishuv did not face up to the destruction of European Jewry and its implications. Their personal background, family ties, sense of movement responsibility and the critical consequences of what had happened for the whole Zionist enterprise simply did not leave room for this kind of disregard. It would be more correct to assume that what we have here is a different interpretation of the catastrophe, a reading colored by local realities and the fundamental assumption that the very future of the Jewish people would be determined by developments in Palestine and that, accordingly, the leaders of the Yishuv should be the ones to decide what that would be. It should be noted, moreover, that the suspicion aroused by the enthusiastic support of *Mapai* for Zionist unity was not without foundation. On the one hand, the policies pursued by *Mapai* cannot simply be reduced to a question of political expedience. The quest for unity certainly flowed from a sense that in the wake of war the Zionist movement was confronting its most fateful hour. Basing himself on the analogy of the changes wrought by the First World War, Ben-Gurion was fully convinced that if a Jewish state did not arise as part of the new world order, the Zionist enterprise would be condemned to a slow but sure death.[26] On the other hand it would be disingenuous to pretend that a united Zionist movement in *She'erith Hapleitah* would not have been most advantageous as far as *Mapai* was concerned.

Briefly put: while the opposition to Zionist unity could be variously interpreted, it was generally agreed, both at the time and later, that the Yishuv was the primary factor in undermining the efforts of *She'erith Hapleitah* in this regard.[27] This perception needs to be qualified because in the absence of any real powers of coercion, the willingness to accede to pressure from Palestine came from the survivors themselves and they did so in order to satisfy deep and abiding needs of their own. Chaim Hoffman (Yachil) sought to account for the different approaches to unity in terms of different experiences undergone in the war years.[28] The survivors of the death camps had undergone the most extreme of experiences that undercut many of their preconceptions including the religious and political convictions that had once divided the Jewish people into rival camps. They had to be distinguished from "the Jews in the forests, the partisans, those in hiding...that operated in small units and groups. They were

---

[26] See Shiloah, Interview: 30.
[27] See David Ben-Gurion, meeting of the *Mapai* Secretariat (20.2.1946): 2, *Ha'avodah* – Labor Archive.
[28] See Yachil (Hoffman), "Peulot ha-mishlachat ha-eretz yisraelit," *Yalkut Moreshet*, no. 30: 18.

saved thanks to the cohesiveness of these groups and thus valued the special qualities of their movement groups above the unity of a shared Jewish fate. The idea of unity struck them as a blurring of their unique values."[29] Yachil's explanatory scheme could be further supported by the example of repatriates who had fought to preserve their movement frameworks while in exile and were loathe to surrender their separate identity for the sake of unity.

One difficulty that this approach runs into is that its categories are too broad and fail to pick out the significant differences within the reference groups identified. Abba Kovner, for example, was a ghetto fighter and partisan but, nonetheless, was the key figure in the Division of East European Survivors that was without compare in its radical commitment to Zionist unity. "Antek" Zukerman, by comparison, played a leading role in the Warsaw Ghetto Revolt and, in line with Yachil's analysis, was the driving force behind the reemergence of *Dror* as an independent movement in post-war Europe. When talking about partisans and resistance fighters in this context, therefore, we need to clarify the structure of the resistance organization as it operated during the war, the nature of the group's experience with left-wing and Soviet forces and, finally, the personal characteristics of those taking the lead.

Beyond these factors and beyond the loyalties of movement veterans to both their own past and their comrades who had perished, the decisive factor driving movement affiliation – and here we return to a theme enunciated earlier – was the sense of home, family and belonging that these frameworks offered. The social cohesion and mutual help, the shared experiences of crossing Europe together, the feeling of belonging to something defined with a tangible foothold in Palestine and, furthermore, a record of heroic conduct during the war, these were the factors that endowed particular movements with their powerful valence. The UZO and *Nocham* emerged out of a profound sense of loneliness and Jewish interdependence but, precisely because they were late products of the war, they lacked the intimacy of particularity, of a shared story and tradition in both Europe and Palestine. What is being suggested is that in most cases movement belonging was more a matter of psychology than of ideology – the *kibbutz* communes in Europe were able to compensate in part for what had been lost forever. The following testimony gives us a better sense of what belonging to a movement really meant. The writer, Yamima Rudnik, aged sixteen and a member of *Hashomer Hatzair*, traveled from Palestine to Lithuania to visit her father and was trapped in Europe at the outbreak of war:

[29] Ibid.

To the soldier Yehoshua *chazak*![30]
A girl who is a complete stranger is answering your letter. Strange, that is to say because the letter and parcel did not reach me but came to a woman Yehudit lying beside me here in hospital – I really liked your letter and especially the photos because I am also a member of a *kibbutz* of *Hashomer Hatzair* and the name of the *kibbutz* is *lochamei hagetaot* [The Ghetto Fighters]. For the letter and pictures you sent... I would have paid anything just to get hold of them – and what happened was that I gave her something she needed and she gave me your letter and those dear pictures. I was really overjoyed and felt myself so happy... because the pictures are so close to us and we feel your friendship from the letter, it is so good that we know that we are welcome in the Land of Israel and the *Kibbutz Artzi* [of *Hashomer Hatzair*].[31]

The local *kibbutz* clearly served as a family with the group leader, no matter how young, cast as a father figure and, to the chagrin of many outsiders, with the readily accepted authority to guide his wards in matters big and small.[32] In this constellation the task of the emissary was to serve as a living bridge between the local commune and the larger movement home in Palestine. As Chaim Hoffman described it:

People now want to be in a *kibbutz*, camp, collective, because they feel themselves to be safer in a large concentration... at the same time they have a strong need for a private corner or perhaps, more correctly, for a concretization of their future place. It is not enough for them to know that they're coming to Palestine... They want to know something a little clearer, more defined. For this reason they are so keen to belong to a particular *kibbutz* in the Yishuv... I am saying this because I want to explain why the work of division is so successful... this is how they see the Land of Israel... you can enter... a *kibbutz* and find that the only map is of the settlements of *Hakibbutz Hameuchad* and that is the map of Palestine.[33]

If we take different outlooks, personal loyalties, various war experiences and the deep need for familial warmth and then add the drive of movements to ensure their future, their mutual mistrust and fear of losing out, we shall come close to explaining why by the middle of 1946, the forces of division in *She'erith Hapleitah* emerged triumphant. Eventually both *Nocham* and the UZO had to come to terms with reality and, having moved closer to *Mapai*, adapted themselves to the new situation:

---

[30] A movement greeting derived from Joshua 1:9–1 "Chazak ve-ematz" (Be strong and of good courage).
[31] Yamima Rudnik to the soldier Yehoshua (6.12.1945), *Moreshet* Archive/ D.1.2481.2.
[32] See the following: Zelig Shoshan to Adam Rand (8.4.1946), *HHA*/(2)3.32; Y.D. Sheinson, "Ha-alahah be-chinuch: le-ba'ayat ha-manhig ve-ha-madrich bi-tnuat ha-noar" ("Deification" in education: the problem of the leader and the guide in the youth movement), *Nitzotz*, 6 (51) (17.12.1945): 5; Ben-Gurion, meeting of the *Mapai* Secretariat (20.2.1946).
[33] Chaim Yachil (Hoffman), meeting of the *Mapai* Secretariat (4.7.1946): 12, *Ha'avodah –* Labor Archive.

the youth movements cooperated with one another in the federative framework of the Coordination of Pioneering Youth while the United Zionist Organization closed down and was supplanted by seven Zionist parties that jealously guarded their independence and became the basic unit of organization in the life of *She'erith Hapleitah*.[34] As Chaim Hoffman summed up the post-unity phase in the life of *She'erith Hapleitah*: "All authority was given to the parties and every institution was organized in accordance with a party key and was in effect a federal institution made up of different parties."[35]

What emerged in retrospect was that in terms of both cooperative settlement and party affiliation the yield from the aliyah of *She'erith Hapleitah* was often rather meagre.[36] It appears that the strains of life in transit did not allow for the intensive and planful education that could produce a significant cohort of rooted movement members. The only way to have reached this goal would have been to focus on the intensive education of a chosen few. None of the movements, given both the pressure from Palestine and their sense of responsibility to those who were in need, chose to adopt this elitist strategy.[37] Ironically, it turned out that those who bent their best energies to creating independent movements ultimately landed up serving the general cause of Zionism. One might hypothesize that in the wake of the Holocaust the Zionism of *She'erith Hapleitah* – the quest for the "Jewish family writ large" – stood the test of time while its more particular movement embodiments rested on urgent but more transient needs that either dissipated or were otherwise satisfied upon arrival in Palestine.[38]

---

[34] See Yachil (Hoffman), "Peulot ha-mishlachat ha-eretz yisraelit," *Yalkut Moreshet*, no. 31: 141.

[35] Ibid.

[36] See Aaron Berdichevsky, "Yoman meshek yagur" (The Yagur Kibbutz diary), Archive of *Bet Lochamei Hagetaot*, Overseas Committee, Container 10, folder 2.

[37] See the interview with Eli Zamir, *Sefer Ha-shlichut* (The book of movement missions), Archive of *Bet Lochamei Hagetaot*, Container 2, file 7: 26a–29.

[38] In this respect we should draw attention to the opinion of Rabbi Abraham Klausner who was skeptical about both the depth and steadiness of the political commitments of the survivors. The key point in his analysis is that we are dealing with a unique group of people whose potent but unpredictable responses were largely conditioned by their ghastly experiences. See Abraham J. Klausner Interview, OHD, (4) 4.

6 The Central Committee of the Liberated Jews in Bavaria

In the second half of 1945, building on the momentum generated at the St. Ottilien Conference, the *Tsentral Komitet fun di Bafreite Yidn in Daytshland* – the Central Committee of the Liberated Jews in Germany (*Zentral Komitet* in the transliteration of the time and thus *ZK*) – continued to expand the scope of its activities and to shape its organizational structure. This development was outwardly symbolized by the transfer of the offices of the Central Committee from Feldafing to the headquarters of UNRRA in the Deutsches Museum in Munich and from there to 3 Sieberstraße which also became home to the JDC and a central drawing point to *She'erith Hapleitah* as a whole.[1] Perhaps a more substantive and telling measure of this process of expansion and growth would be to compare the first hesitant steps taken at St. Ottilien with the public notice, local and international, that attended the impressive Congress of *She'erith Hapleitah* at the end of January 1946.

On 8 August the Council of the Liberated Jews in Bavaria met for the first time and elected the new Central Committee which consisted of five representatives from Munich, three each from Landsberg and Feldafing with Dr. Zalman Grinberg who continued to direct the St. Ottilien hospital reelected as chairman.[2] Dr. Samuel Gringauz, the President of the Council, and his colleagues understood that the great distances between the various parts of the occupation zones together with difficulties of travel and regular communication meant that the Central Committee would have to restrict its sphere of competence to Bavaria. Deciding this

---

[1] Irving Heymont, *Among the Survivors of the Holocaust – 1945: The Landsberg Camp Letters of Major Irving Heymont, United States Army* (Cincinnati, 1982): 20–21, and also Rabbi Abraham J. Klausner, Interview, OHD/4: 15.

[2] Protokoll nr. 6 der sitzung des rates der befreiten juden in bayern (Protocol no. 6 of the Meeting of the Council of the Liberated Jews in Bavaria) (8.8.1945), YIVO/DPG 94. The members of the *Tsentral Komitet* chosen by the Council were: Dr. Zalman Grinberg – St. Ottilien; Dr. Samuel Gringauz – Landsberg; Moshe Segalson – Landsberg; David Treger – Landsberg; Azriel Berkman – Munich; Dr. Yisrael Jochelson – Munich; Eng. Yosef Leibowitz – Munich; Adv. Marian Pucyz – Munich; Yitzchak Ratner - Munich; Moshe Grinbaum – Feldafing; Mendel Forstenfeld – Feldafing; Alex Katz – Feldafing.

meant that relations with Bergen Belsen, which had already developed its own representative structure, would be based on a looser arrangement of intermittent visits and the periodic coordination of policy.[3] The *ZK*, moreover, extended its authority to all of Bavaria while, in point of fact, its membership was to be primarily found in Munich and its environs. Only in January 1946 with the growth and spread of *She'erith Hapleitah* was the electoral base broadened to include representatives from the new areas of settlement.

The Central Committee viewed itself as the democratically elected representative of the Surviving Remnant, responsible for their welfare and rehabilitation while in Germany and committed to expediting their early departure for either Palestine or any other destination. To put it a bit more precisely: the *ZK* by virtue of its composition and articulated goals saw itself as a Zionist body that was bound to take care of one and all. What this meant, in the first place, was for it to serve as the voice of *She'erith Hapleitah* vis-à-vis the American Army and UNRRA and to fight for the official recognition of the Jews as a people, for separate camps with internal autonomy and an improvement of supplies and services. They were in constant touch with international bodies, Jewish and general, in order to promote and explore possibilities of speedy immigration. Regular contacts were maintained with the International Red Cross and local German authorities and they worked hand in glove with the Jewish agencies granted entry by the occupation authorities. Over and above these numerous assignments, the Central Committee played host to influential guests from the Jewish world including David Ben-Gurion, Nachum Goldman and Ignaz Schwartzbart of the World Jewish Congress, Lady Reading and numerous delegations from the major Jewish organizations in North America.

The functions filled by the Central Committee within *She'erith Hapleitah* were many and diverse and included the work of the *Zukhdienst* – the tracing service – that built up an impressive body of information to help in the search for missing relatives thus complementing Rabbi Klausner's five volumes of "Shearit Hapleta" that listed survivors and their personal details; medical services were provided at St. Ottilien and the Jewish wing of the hospital in Gauting while tuberculosis patients were treated in the Babenhausen sanatorium headed by Dr. Pesachovitch who was also in charge of the Health Department of the *ZK*;[4] schools were opened in all of the major camps and numerous vocational training courses were set in motion; a great deal of energy was expended

---

[3] Protokoll nr. 9 des *ZK* (Protocol no. 9 of the Central Committee) (2.9.1945), YIVO/DPG 94.

[4] See Klausner, Interview: 16–21.

on the procurement of more nutritious food, decent clothing and less crowded living quarters; in the cultural sphere a makeshift orchestra was expanded and placed on a sounder footing while in November 1945 the first steps were taken towards establishing an "Historical Commission" charged with collecting personal testimonies, documents, photographs, books and memorabilia that would both serve future historians and be of help in bringing war criminals to justice.[5] In order to cope with its growing responsibilities the *ZK* opened a number of additional departments to deal with Economics, Education and Culture, Emigration, Health, Religious Affairs and, at a slightly later stage, a Legal Bureau and a Comptroller's Office.[6] In this early period workers were paid with food and goods contributed by the larger DP camps in the Munich area. A noteworthy achievement of the Central Committee was the weekly publication of *Undzer Veg* (Our Way) under the editorship of its founder, Levi Shalitan, a young journalist from Shavli (Siuliai) in Lithuania. When the first number was issued on the 12 October 1945, 20,000 copies were distributed and in short order *Undzer Veg* became an important force in galvanizing *She'erith Hapleitah* from within and representing it to the Jewish world without.[7]

In the last third of 1945 two important matters dominated the agenda of the Central Committee: the proposal to transfer the children of *She'erith Hapleitah* out of Germany to England, France and Switzerland and, at the same time, the question of how to cope with the swelling flow of refugees being guided by the *Brichah* to the American Zone of Occupation. The proposal of the Jewish Refugee Committee in Britain to move 10,000 children to England before the onset of winter was first discussed at the beginning of August and two weeks later there is a report of initial registration in Landsberg and Feldafing.[8] At this meeting of the *ZK* no objections were noted and it appears that towards the end of September the children were gathered together in St. Ottilien. At the last moment the trip was cancelled due to difficulties in the travel arrangements and the upset children were temporarily returned to whence they had come.[9] In mid-October Zvi Langzam, who appeared before the Council

---

[5] See M.Y. Feigenbaum, "Tsu vos historisher komisyes" (To what end historical commissions), *Fun Letstn Khurbn*, no. 1 (August 1946).

[6] Protokoll nr. 7 des *ZK* (12.8.1945), nr. 8 (19.8.1945).

[7] On the planning of the paper and setting up the Editorial Board see Protokoll nr. 8 des *ZK* (19.8.1945), nr. 11 (20.9.1945), nr. 12 (7.10.1945). For the dramatic background story see Schwarz, *The Redeemers*: 57–62, and the letter of Levi Shalit to Leo Schwarz in 1951, YIVO/DPG 167. See also Levi Shalit, *Beyond Dachau: Memories and Reflections* (Johannesburg, 1980).

[8] Protokoll nr. 6 des rates (8.8.1945), Protokoll nr. 8 des *ZK* (19.8.1945).

[9] See Klausner, Interview: 13–14, and the report of Marian Pucyz to the Council in Protokoll nr. 13 des rates (14.10.1945).

of the *ZK* to report on the outbreak of widespread resistance to the British in Palestine, related this to the question of the children. At a time when the Palestinian Jewry was taking to arms in order to fight for its future and thus, by extension, the future of *She'erith Hapleitah*, the transfer of the children to England would be a moral victory for the British and a blow to the Yishuv.[10] Up to that point the concern of the participants had focused on the immediate welfare and comfort of the children but having the issue placed in the larger context of the struggle against the White Paper led to a sudden *volte face*. Feelings ran high and the Council now took a strong and widely publicized stand against the transfer of the children to anywhere except Palestine:

In view of what is taking place in Palestine where the English armed forces have decided to use arms and detention against Jews saved from the jaws of death, the sad remnant of the terrible destruction of European Jewry who seek to rescue themselves in the one corner in the world which is theirs in the Land of Israel so as to return to a normal and peaceful life we declare as the representatives of the Jews in Bavaria that we do not place the slightest trust in the helpfulness and hospitality that English society seeks to display to our children and we impose our stringent veto on sending them there.

The Council authorizes the *ZK* to take care and be on guard lest one single Jewish child be transferred to anywhere else except directly to its only possible home – Palestine.[11]

Although the decision of the *ZK* was taken in the context of the struggle against the British it was formulated as a matter of general principle applicable elsewhere. Thus, when Zerach Warhaftig, the representative of the *Mizrachi* national religious party in Europe, suggested on behalf of the Union of Orthodox Rabbis in the United States and Canada that 500 children accompanied by 50 educators be transferred to France, it was rejected outright.[12] Towards the end of November Shlomo Adler-Rudel came to Munich on behalf of the British Jewish Refugee Committee in the hope of being able to persuade the *ZK* to revoke its decision.[13] When his request was turned down Adel-Rudel accepted the decision in principle but asked to exempt those children who had already been prepared for the journey. In the vote that was taken one was in favor, one abstained and twelve voted against.[14] The subject came up again in January 1946 when a request was received from the Swiss Jüdische Jugend-Hilfe to take in a number of orphans so as to contribute to their

[10] Protokoll nr. 13 des rates (14.10.1945).   [11] Ibid.
[12] See Resolution of the Central Committee of the Liberated Jews in Bavaria (7 November 1945), YIVO/DPG 2204, and David Ben-Gurion's report to *Mercaz Mapai* (The *Mapai* Central Committee) (22.11.1945), Ha'avodah – Labor Archive: 16–17.
[13] See Protokoll nr. 19 des *ZK* (25.11.1945).
[14] See Protokoll nr. 20 des *ZK* (2.12.1945).

rehabilitation and preparation for immigration to Palestine. In the discussion which took place there were members of the *ZK* who sought to limit the earlier decision to Britain alone while those who were still opposed stressed the total dedication to the children's well being together with the symbolic importance of their presence for *She'erith Hapleitah*. The proposal was not turned down but, as things turned out, the plan did not materialize.[15] These were not easy decisions, neither psychologically nor in terms of its public reception given the strong opposition even on the part of some of the children to this policy. Despite this pressure the *ZK* stood firm and it was only in April 1946 that 476 orphans received governmental grants for early immigration to Palestine.[16]

The second issue that engaged the Central Committee with increasing frequency was the growing number of East European Jews seeking refuge in the American Occupation Zone. Already in September 1945 the *ZK* word had been received of thousands of Jews held up in Czechoslovakia on their way to Bavaria and a representative was sent out to extend assistance.[17] At the same time additional representatives were sent to Poland in order to verify the disturbing reports received from those newly arrived and to look into ways and means of expediting their departure.[18] The basic strategy of the *ZK* was to alert public opinion in the West to the situation in Poland and to make sure, at the same time, that the entry to the American zone remain untrammeled.[19] In October the Council held a wide-ranging discussion regarding the *Brichah* and Zalman Grinberg presented his views on what was happening:

The flow of all Jews from all lands is already underway. The remnants of Polish Jewry are seeking to cross borders illegally in order to get here. And that is because each Jew possesses political intuition. Here what is left of Jewry is gathering, this is

---

[15] See Protokoll nr. 30 des *ZK* (20.1.1946), YIVO/DPG 95.

[16] On the opposition to the decisions of the *ZK* see Simon H. Rifkind to Colonel Guyler (14.11.1945), UNRRA German Mission/RG17/66,641 and Harold G. to Director UNRRA, US Zone (21.1.1945), UNRRA German Mission/RG17/66,641. For an historical reading strongly critical of the Zionist "exploitation" of the children for political ends see Grodzinsky, *Chomer enoshi tov*: 71–86. Grodzinsky's argument rests on one unproven assumption – that keeping the children back was clearly hazardous to their health and happiness and that both the Central Committee and the Jewish Agency made their decisions in full knowledge of this fact. This appears to be implied in his comparison between Ben-Gurion's position and the front-line role allotted to children by the Palestinian Arab leadership during the *Intifada*, ibid.: 85; for a different appreciation of Ben-Gurion see his conversation with the Jewish leaders of the British Zone in Bergen Belsen where his advice to them turns precisely on this point – the welfare of the children, ibid.: 79.

[17] See Protokoll nr. 9 des *ZK* (2.9.1945).

[18] At least three people were dispatched on this mission – see Protokoll nr. 13 des rates (14.10.1945).

[19] Protokoll nr. 10 des *ZK* (14.9.1945) and nr. 11 (20.9.1945).

to be the waiting station. It certainly is a poor waiting station but we hope the day will come when we can get our people in this temporary abode better organized.[20]

This assignment was all the more urgent in view of Grinberg's assessment that the influx to Germany would grow while the possibilities of departure would remain limited. What emerged from this analysis was the immediate need to open up new avenues of gainful employment and vocational training, to expand opportunities of study and to ensure that the cultural life of She'erith Hapleitah be rich and rewarding. All this was necessary in order to stave off demoralization of what they hoped would be a vital, albeit transient, community. Grinberg hoped that the Brichah would add the decisive weight of numbers to the qualitative edge of She'erith Hapleitah as a politically aware and cohesive community of fate.[21]

The ZK was called upon to develop a number of strategies in order to absorb those who had already arrived and to persuade others to follow suit. In the first instance this entailed taking a strong stand against the initial refusal of the US Army and UNRRA to recognize the basic entitlements of what they termed "infiltrees." In response to this official differentiation between "displaced persons" possessed of rights and "refugees" or "infiltrees" denied them, the leaders of She'erith Hapleitah argued that the geographic location of a survivor at the end of the war was totally arbitrary and without moral weight: the Jews of Europe were equally victims of annihilation and thus were equally entitled to assistance from their allies, the United Nations.[22] The ZK was critical of the continuing resistance of the army to the expropriation of German property which certainly would have helped in alleviating the plight of both those who were seeking refuge in Germany and those who were constrained to share their already overcrowded quarters with them. It was a topic that was repeatedly brought to the attention of Joseph Schwartz and Judge Simon Rifkind who had been appointed as the army's Special Adviser on Jewish Affairs to the Commander of the European Theater.

The response of the army to these diverse pressures was initially cumbersome and although a new transit camp was set up in one of the suburbs of Munich and the large camp in Foehrenwald was opened, these actions were not adequate to the constant growth of the Jewish DP population. In the last third of October, for example, the ZK was informed that 1,400 newcomers had arrived: 1,080 were directed to Foehrenwald while the rest chose to make their own arrangements. At the time both

[20] Protokoll nr. 13 des rates (14.10.1945).

[21] "In the political struggle it is very important that numbers here increase: then our demands will carry more weight," Z. Grinberg, in ibid.

[22] Ibid.

3 Polish repatriates from the Soviet Union began streaming into the DP camps from mid-1946. Despite the harsh conditions in Asiatic Russia some of the families managed to remain intact.

Landsberg and Feldafing were housing 1,000 people above their normal capacity so generating many administrative difficulties, group tensions and individual hardship. The policy of the *ZK* was to let matters take their course until a crisis would awaken public opinion in the United States, embarrass the army and shame it into more decisive action.[23]

This policy helped to a degree but it also highlights the immanent limitations of the Central Committee, the nagging gap between the ambitions of these leaders and their real power. The *ZK* had to work within the constraints of a military occupation zone, bereft of official recognition[24] and independent funding and always beholden to others. Thus, whereas the question of the children was largely an internal affair subject to their authority, when it came to the *Brichah* there was no possibility of independent action without the help of others. In the complex and fluid

[23] See Zalman Grinberg's comments in Protokoll nr. 24 des *ZK* (23.12.1945). On the opening of Foehrenwald see Eli Rock, Interview, OHD/28 (119): 13–16.

[24] The only document that served the *ZK* as an informal sign of recognition was the letter of thanks sent by General Eisenhower after he received the first number of *Undzer Veg*. See *Undzer Veg* (7.12.1945): 1.

reality of Occupied Germany, any attempt to cope with a population increase of more than 20,000 refugees[25] over a few short months required unremitting pressure on both UNRRA and the US Army. The basic approach of the high command to this influx, as Bedell Smith had promised Ben-Gurion, remained sympathetic and, in addition, General Truscott who had supplanted Patton in the Third Army proved to be open and generous in his dealings with *She'erith Hapleitah*. The army, however, was weighed down by a myriad of concerns, many of its officers in the field lacked the human sensitivity of their superiors and, in the absence of clear directives from Washington, its relations with the fractious Jewish DPs was not high on its list of priorities. In view of the ever increasing influx of Jewish refugees General Smith proposed that the War Department authorize the closing of the borders but in view of his continuing reluctance to take concrete action in this regard his recommendations may have been an attempt to elicit a clearer articulation of policy.[26] Despite a basically positive approach, therefore, policies fluctuated and there was a need for constant prodding, persuasion and pressure.

UNRRA, too, was unable to take decisive action in the absence of an agreed policy with regard to the Jewish infiltrees. Generally speaking, the *Brichah* was viewed as flowing from anxiety in the face of an uncertain future as opposed to a direct and palpable threat to life and limb.[27] It was also generally known that the refugees were crossing Europe in organized groups, according to carefully chosen routes and under the guidance of well-informed operatives with the insistent impression "that the whole movement is not spontaneous but that it is part of a deliberate plan to bring the question of the future of the Jews and of Zionism to a head."[28] General Morgan who was in charge of UNRRA operations in Europe went even further and at a press conference in January claimed that this was a Zionist conspiracy aimed at embarrassing the British government for, according to his sources of information, the so-called refugees were arriving in an organized fashion, well-dressed and carrying considerable sums of money.[29] The leaders of *She'erith Hapleitah* and Jewish public

---

[25] Chaim Yachil (Hoffman) estimated that by January 1946 the *Brichah* had brought in a minimum of 20,000 infiltrees into Bavaria – see Chaim Yachil, Interview, OHD/4: 28.

[26] See Dr. Ignacy Schwartzbart, Report on the Visit to the American Zone in Germany (January 1946), CZA/S25/5232: 21–23, and Genizi, *Yoetz u-mekim*: 48–49.

[27] See Jay B. Krane, Observations on the Problem of Jewish Infiltrees (18.1.1946), UNRRA German Mission/RG17/66,021: 3–4.

[28] Ibid.: 7.

[29] See "Er glaybt nit" (He doesn't believe), *Undzer Veg*, no. 14 (4.1.1946): 1, and "Pratim vegn Morgans derklarung" (Details about Morgan's declaration), *Undzer Veg*, no. 15 (11.1.1946): 6.

opinion worldwide were outraged by what they saw as blatant anti-semitism and demanded Morgan's immediate resignation.[30] At the same time most UNRRA field workers followed the formulation of their colleague Jay B. Krane who looked into the question of "infiltration" and concluded that "whether the movement is organized or not is not the main point of issue. The more compelling fact is that there is a large number of people with legitimate reasons for wishing to emigrate from their countries who require temporary care and assistance."[31]

Many in *She'erith Hapleitah* had scant respect for UNRRA given its total dependence on the army, chronic inefficiency and inability to articulate a refugee policy of its own.[32] The exceptional field workers, and they were not few, were able to notch up important achievements to the extent that they took the initiative and were willing to deviate from the limitations of routine action. Perhaps the most prominent of these was Dr. Leo Srole, a senior member of the UNRRA team stationed in Landsberg. Srole resigned his commission in early January as an act of protest against what he considered to be the dangerous and inexcusable overcrowding in the camp.[33] In order to ensure the maximum impact to his demonstrative act, Srole forewarned Rabbi Klausner who passed on the information, in turn, to the *ZK*.[34] Klausner saw to widespread press coverage of the resignation while the *ZK* sent a strongly worded protest to Judge Rifkind.

Undoubtedly the most important channel of the communication between the Central Committee and the higher echelons of the army ran through the office of the Special Adviser to the Theater Commander on Jewish Affairs.[35] Judge Simon H. Rifkind, the civilian successor of Rabbi Judah Nadich who began his term of office in October 1945,

---

[30] See, for example, Levi Shalitan, "Chachamim hizharu be-divreichem" (Wise men watch your words), *Undzer Veg*, no. 15 (11.1.1946): 2, and Ben-Gurion's opening speech at the Congress of *She'erith Hapleitah* on 27.1.1946 when he engaged in a sharp polemic with Morgan in CZA/S25/5232. For a more general discussion see Bauer, *Flight and Rescue*: 194–198.

[31] Krane, Observations on the Problem of Jewish Infiltrees: 7.

[32] See the Report by Judge Simon H. Rifkind, Special Adviser to the European Theater Commander on Jewish Affairs (8.4.1946), CZA/S25/5232: 6.

[33] See "Dr. Leo Srole, direktor fun 'UNRRA' in landsberg demisonirt" (Dr. Leo Srole, director of "UNRRA" in Landsberg resigns), *Undzer Veg*, no. 11 (14.12.1945): 2.

[34] See Klausner, Interview: 51–52.

[35] This applies equally to the JDC, the Palestine Mission and various bodies that visited Germany on behalf of the American Jewish community. See, for example, the Report of Eli Rock to Judge Simon H. Rifkind (8.11.1945), AJDC /DP's Germany 1945/1946, and the Interim Report of American Jewish Conference Representatives in American Occupation Zone of Germany with Reference to Jewish Displaced Persons Centers sent to Judge Simon H. Rifkind (13.12.1945), AZA/American Jewish Conference Overseas Liaison, 1943–1945. For an overall assessment of Judge Rifkind's contribution see Genizi, *Yoetz u-mekim*: 35–57.

played a critical role in caring for and promoting the interests of *She'erith Hapleitah*.[36] Over and beyond his personal qualities and Zionist passion, Rifkind was greatly helped by his stature as a federal judge. The *ZK* turned to him with regard to sensitive questions of principle and his interventions with the military authorities were generally successful most markedly in dealing with the complex issues raised by the *Brichah*.[37] Rifkind concurred with the refusal of the *ZK* to accept the official differentiation between DPs and refugees and he was able to get the Supreme Command to grant all of the survivors in Germany the same rights irrespective of their date of entry or their personal fate during the war. This claim overrode earlier attempts of the army to deny full rights to those Jews who had not been imprisoned in concentration camps and the importance of this achievement became even more apparent during 1946 when the flow of repatriates from the Soviet Union began.[38]

Following the resignation of Srole – which he was eventually persuaded to retract – Rifkind accompanied General Bedell Smith on an inspection tour of the Landsberg camp and arranged a private interview for David Treger, chairman of the UZO, who himself lived in the camp.[39] The General refused to accept the validity of Srole's dire warnings but he did issue new orders with regard to the absorption of newcomers that were encouraging and effective.[40] As a first step the existing camps were expanded so as to take in thousands of newcomers, new centers were prepared in Munich-Neu Freiman, Bamberg, Ainring, Schwandorf, Tirschenreuth, Pöking and Ansbach while a number of farms were expropriated to make way for new training farms.[41] However, the move into the new facilities was slow and uncertain: some feared the notion of resettlement, others took umbrage at orders imposed from above while in the case of Feldafing, the Camp Committee itself opposed the new arrangements.[42] During his term of office which ran from October 1945 to April 1946, Judge Rifkind was active in many different endeavors which included greater personal freedom for the Jewish DPs, enlarging

---

[36] See Chaim (Yachil) Hoffman's urgent request to Ben-Gurion to help in finding a replacement for Rifkind: "We feel his absence very much" – Chaim Hoffman to the Jewish Agency (5.5.1946), CZA/S25/5232.

[37] See Klausner, Interview: 67.

[38] See the Report of Marian Pucyz, the General Secretary of the *ZK* to the First Congress of *She'erith Hapleitah* in the private collection of Professor Yehuda Bauer and also the Interview with Judge Simon H. Rifkind and his adjutant Mr. Eno in OHD/11(4).

[39] See Levy Becker, Interview, OHD/94 (119): 38–39.

[40] See Levy Becker to Jacob L. Trobe (26.12.1945), YIVO/DPG 64.

[41] See Chaim (Yachil) Hoffman to Eliyahu Dobkin (25.12.1945), CZA/S25/10164, and Dr. Chaim Hoffman to Miss Gertrude Richman, UNRRA Welfare Division, US Zone (February 1946) in the private papers of Chaim Yachil (Hoffman).

[42] Becker to Trobe.

the scope of their self-rule and speeding up retraining programs in the camps. He saw the latter as part of a critical shift from short-term rescue to a longer process of rehabilitation that implied new standards and priorities in army policy. The Special Adviser also worked hard at educating the officer corps as to the special characteristics of the people they were dealing with: these people, he stressed, were not a random collection of individuals but the last vestiges of a rich civilization possessed of a highly developed political awareness and a sense of historical mission.

They know what they want: they want to quit Europe, they want to live together, not dispersed among a population that regards them as aliens; They desire to live in the pattern of their own historic culture; they visualize the realization of their desires in Palestine. It is a strange phenomenon that the Jewish displaced persons in Germany and Austria, because they have a policy and program have emerged as the vanguard of East European Jewry.[43]

Viewing the Jewish survivors in this light, suggested Rifkind, would help better to understand how they differed from the other DPs in Germany: their feverish political activity, lively press, their burning desire to get out of Germany and on with their lives. In this context it was important to emphasize the subjective distaste of She'erith Hapleitah for economic ties with the surrounding population and the relatively light but justified burden they imposed on the Germans personally and on their economy in general. The Germans had first killed and subsequently inherited the property of their victims and now that a tiny fraction of those murdered were temporarily living on German soil "the question whether the presence of the Jews constitutes too heavy a burden on the German becomes irrelevant. Their claim is second only to the occupation forces."[44] Judge Rifkind, therefore, generally sympathized with the views of the Central Committee, accepted the legitimacy of what they, the elected representatives of the survivors in Occupied Germany, sought to achieve and spared no effort in helping military policy-makers understand their way of looking at things.

A second group that worked closely with the leadership of the ZK and came to play an important role in the life of She'erith Hapleitah was the Palestinian Mission headed by Dr. Chaim Hoffman (Yachil).[45] As the war drew to a close, the Jewish Agency attempted to get an initial support mission to Europe by teaming up with UNRRA. In 1944 a Council for Welfare Divisions in the Dispersion had been set up in Jerusalem and after protracted negotiations it was agreed that it could send its first team

[43] Rifkind, Report: 3.   [44] Ibid.: 3–4.
[45] See the republication of Chaim Yachil's summary report originally written in the summer of 1949 "Peulot ha-mishlachat ha-eretz yisraelit." See also Yachil Interview.

to Greece on a general mission. Using this as the thin edge of the wedge it was then suggested that a Palestinian Mission be sent to Germany and eventually a thirty-six strong welfare team was agreed to. In September 1945 the US Army, after a series of delays, gave its consent and an advance party finally arrived in mid-December. After an initial period of orientation the twenty members of the Palestinian Mission were requested by the army to help out in the absorption of the refugees arriving in ever greater numbers from Eastern Europe. During its initial period of orientation the influence of the Mission which was to grow by leaps and bounds after January 1946 was still rather peripheral.

The structural weakness of the *ZK* in the official realm was also evident, if less noticeably, on the local level for despite their palpable desire to respond to numerous requests for help, there was little they could actually do. In this regard the indefatigable Rabbi Klausner made a critical contribution to the work of the *ZK* for the simple reason that he was "able to control aspects of the programme which these people could not control... No member of the Committee was able to meet with any of the military representatives. At best they could meet with a DP officer... and they were constantly mistreated by them. In other words, they were patronized."[46] There were those who warned against excessive dependence on Klausner but, given his role in the genesis of the *ZK* and his unfailing devotion to *She'erith Hapleitah*, most gladly accepted his indispensable centrality and agreed with Levi Shalitan that "he has become one of us."[47]

The feelings of sharing and trust that attached to Klausner did not always characterize the complex relations of the *ZK* with the American Joint Distribution Committee Mission which played a decisive role in funding and supporting the work of the Central Committee. The contribution of the JDC was viewed with gratitude and respect but when the two bodies clashed over questions of competence and authority that, in the nature of things, happened quite often, it generated feelings of suspicion and ambivalence. When the war ended the European office of the JDC was moved from Lisbon back to Paris and Dr. Joseph Schwartz and his team worked hard to gain early access to Occupied Germany. In the first phase the plan was to send in twenty-one workers to extend immediate assistance to camp survivors and in mid-June after long negotiations with UNRRA a JDC team got to Buchenwald.[48] Their major

---

[46] See Klausner, Interview: 12.

[47] Levi Shalitan, "Ayner fun aykh" (One of us), *Undzer Veg*, no. 1 (12.10.1945): 3.

[48] The formal requests presented to the US Army Supreme Command were initially turned down by the commands of both the Third and Seventh Armies that controlled the entry of welfare teams into the occupied zone. In this regard see YIVO/DPG 145 and Joseph

aim was to arrange the transfer of hundreds of children to Switzerland but they were also able to expedite the repatriation of survivors from Romania and Hungary or, when it came to Polish Jews, the transfer of 600 of their number to Landsberg in the American Zone of Occupation. Irene Lowy who headed the team stayed on in Germany and reached an agreement with both the Third Army in Munich and the Seventh Army in Heidelberg to move forward an additional eight teams. The first permanent team arrived in Feldafing in early August and its leader, Eli Rock, later moved to Munich and took charge of the entire JDC operation. By the end of August an additional team was stationed in Landsberg and individual representatives were sent to Stuttgart, Frankfurt and Kassel so that by October there were thirteen JDC workers, operating under the aegis of UNRRA, in the American Zone and by December 1945, their number had doubled.[49] In these first stages their work focused on the primary needs of the survivors: medical treatment, food, living quarters and clothing. In the absence of funding and independent supply lines, however, they were totally dependent on the army and UNRRA for everything they had to offer. Given the army's very different priorities and the singular lack of enthusiasm in UNRRA their initial impact was rather modest. The dedicated JDC workers did their best to help in the search for relatives, guidance with respect to immigration procedures, personal welfare and legal counsel.[50]

While the JDC workers were warmly received and their assistance much appreciated, the survivors were initially ambivalent towards Jews from a very different background, far removed from their experiences and wearing military uniforms. Phillip Struchan who headed the team in Landsberg attributed these feelings to more objective factors:

In view of . . . the very apparent hostility to the Joint for failing to be on the scene earlier, the task of the . . . Joint representatives at Landsberg has been . . . most difficult all the way. No Joint supplies were received here until four weeks after the first personnel came in so there was very little to offer as answer to the harsh charges levelled against the Joint . . . a good deal is yet to be done before the Joint can reclaim some of its former prestige and reputation.[51]

Hyman to Benjamin Rabin (14.6.1945), AJDC/DP's Germany 1945; see, in addition, Report of the First JDC Team in Germany (30.8.1945), AJDC/DP's Germany 1945, and Rapport sur le Voyage de Buchenwald de L'Equipe Joint-OSE and Arthur D. Greenleigh to Joe Schwartz (23.6.1945), AJDC/DP's Germany General, 1945/1946.

[49] On the first phases of the work of the JDC in Germany see the Rock, Interview.

[50] See the general report and more detailed accounts of Landsberg and Foehrenwald in the AJDC Staff Conference (21.10.1945), AJDC/Germany DP Camps 1938–1945.

[51] Phillip Struchan, Landsberg Report, AJDC Staff Conference. The absence of supplies was a source of embarrassment and frustration for the senior JDC staff in Europe. See, for example, Joseph Schwartz's cable to the head office in New York (3.12.1945), AJDC/DP's Germany 1945/1946.

The same combination of cooperation and tension appeared to inform the working relations between the JDC and the Central Committee. When Eli Rock set up his headquarters in Munich he did so, in part, because of the importance he attributed to the *ZK*.

This organization has steadily grown both in influence and services rendered until it has come to represent one of the most significant factors in the entire life of the Bavarian Jewish community... the Committee has had great significance as a manifestation of self-aid and to that extent has represented a great step forward in the spiritual rehabilitation of the Jewish DPs.[52]

In view of this both Rock and his successors based their work on close cooperation with the *ZK* and from very early on the Joint provided the lion's share of the Committee's budget, coordinated its policies with them and set up its headquarters in the same building. On the other hand, because the *ZK* had its finger on the pulse of *She'erith Hapleitah*, this arrangement gave it unique access to what was happening in the field and a strategic base for effective intervention.

The first formal meeting between the two took place in August, just after the first team arrived, and already on this occasion we have a first hint of the ambivalence referred to above.[53] Over and above the limited means at the JDC's disposal what seems to have caused the friction was the disparity between the impatience of those who had survived by evading or bending the rules and what they perceived as legalistic bureaucrats in awe of military authority. Besides this, some of the militant Zionists in the *ZK* were concerned about the hidden agenda of a philanthropic organization run by, in their view, assimilated Jews.[54] These attitudes made it difficult for the leaders of the *ZK* to lend credence to the counter claims of the JDC side which highlighted the advantages of being part of the military and the fact that they were volunteers and thus not subject to political directives from New York.[55] There seemed to be something else at work here as well. When the Joint representatives were asked: "Where were you?" the question went beyond its immediate reference to the period immediately after liberation and seemed to say something critical about those who watched Europe from the safety of a distant shore, understood

---

[52] "The Jewish Community of Bavaria", AJDC Staff Conference.

[53] See the Protkoll nr. 6 des rates (8.8.1945).

[54] This emerges from Levy Becker's report to the Congress of *She'erith Hapleitah* at the end of January 1946: "It is true, that many assimilated people participate in the Joint in America and are involved in straightforward philanthropic work. Also, they are not great Zionists. They obviously have no direct say about what we should be doing. This allows us to do, therefore, what we hold to be necessary." See Bericht van Levy Becker, Direktor van AJDC in der Amerikanischen Zone in Prof. Bauer's private collection.

[55] See the comments of Holzer, Heitan and Rock at the Council meeting as recorded in Protokoll nr. 6 des rates.

so little of what had happened and now wanted to make policy for those who had seen it all. As Yitzchak Ratner put it at this first encounter with the JDC workers:

The representatives of the AJDC claim that it is too soon to give a report. However, what did the AJDC do during the six years that we were burnt in the crematoria? And why did the AJDC not come before today, even if it had to be illegally? Things have happened from the side of our brothers which cannot be forgotten, that is, the fact that during the war they never got directly involved [in our fate]. [Also] much could have been spared us if the AJDC had come earlier. They must know that we do not want rations, the only thing we want is to be able return to a normal life. The only place we want to go to is Palestine.[56]

Levy Becker who replaced Eli Rock as director of the JDC operations in Germany readily agreed that anyone who had not been "there" could not grasp what the victims of the Nazis had been through. At the same time he was persuaded that the barrier was not totally impenetrable, that an empathetic outsider could achieve a glimmer of understanding and, with good will on both sides, this could serve as a bridge to fruitful cooperation.[57] Many years later Becker, who had earned the respect of the *ZK* through his unstinting dedication to their cause and a willingness to be party to the illegalities of the *Brichah*, recalled not without a touch of bitterness that no matter what you did or tried to do, disillusionment and disappointment had become the prevailing norms of *She'erith Hapleitah*. "They just felt that they had been done out of a portion of their lives and that therefore the whole world should have been at their knees begging the understanding of the DPs who suffered."[58] These tensions that knew ups and downs came to focus on one cardinal question: which body, the *ZK* or the JDC, would enjoy primacy in the distribution of funds, goods, and services to *She'erith Hapleitah*? Already at the first meeting with the team that began to operate out of Feldafing Rabbi Klausner, speaking on behalf of the *ZK*, suggested a way of joining forces, a proposal he returned to in early September at a meeting of the Committee with Rabbi Judah Nadich and Joseph Schwartz.[59] The Joint, according to this proposal, would finance the Central Committee and utilize its organizational structure to promote its own policies which would lead to three desirable outcomes: the JDC would be able to cut its costs, the *ZK* would forestall the creation of a threatening competitor while this arrangement would avoid the undignified relationship of givers and takers while leaving the real control in *She'erith Hapleitah* in the hands of its leaders.[60]

---

[56] Ibid.
[57] Levy Becker's report to the Congress of *She'erith Hapleitah* at the end of January 1946.
[58] Becker, Interview: 41.   [59] See Protokoll nr. 9 des *ZK* (2.9.1945).   [60] Ibid.

In point of fact, both Eli Rock by virtue of his inexperience and Levy Becker on the basis of a conscious choice allowed the *ZK* to take the lead and avoided close administrative supervision of its operations.[61] Blurring the boundaries between the two and their respective areas of competence did not please the European office of the JDC in Paris[62] and equally disturbed UNRRA workers who were at a loss to decide "who was controlling who, the *ZK* the Joint or the Joint the *ZK*?"[63] The growth of the JDC staff and budget in the first part of 1946 led to repeated demands for budgetary restraint and a closer scrutiny of expenditures which also meant a closer watch over the work of the *ZK*. In April 1946 when Leo Schwarz took over from Levy Becker, the latent tensions between the two organizations burst out into the open.

After years of total helplessness the members of the *ZK* desperately sought to return to the elementary dignity of taking responsibility for themselves and running their own affairs. In their estimate the achievement of a greater measure of autonomy depended on their recognition as the legitimate representatives of the Jewish DPs by the US Army. Towards this end it was necessary to demonstrate beyond dispute that the *ZK* was indeed the sole, democratically elected representative of *She'erith Hapleitah* in its entirety. As the end of 1945 approached, therefore, the Committee began to push for local elections in order to ensure that the Camp and Community Committees would be truly representative and reflect the rapidly changing composition of *She'erith Hapleitah*.[64] These elections were to be held by mid-December and each 500 voters would send one representative to the Congress at the end of January when a new Central Committee would be elected.[65] In another move aimed at bolstering its public standing, the *ZK* decided to extend its area of competence beyond Bavaria and to include survivors throughout the American Zone of Occupation in the forthcoming elections.

The *ZK*, we should add, were not the only ones pressing for new elections. One group of Polish Jews led by Advocate Friedheim, a resident of Feldafing, objected strenuously to the "dictatorship" of the Lithuanian Jews in the *ZK* arguing that but two members of the Committee represented more than 90 percent of *She'erith Hapleitah*.[66] A second group

---

[61] Becker, Interview: 27.   [62] Ibid.   [63] Protokoll nr. 27 des *ZK* (8.1.1946).

[64] See Protokoll nr. 15 des *ZK* (4.11.1945).

[65] See Protokoll nr. 18 des *ZK* (21.11.1945) and nr. 22 (16.12.1945). The counter-suggestion of one representative for every 1,000 voters was turned down because it would exclude the smaller centers.

[66] According to Ignacy Schwartzbart who saw himself as the spokesman of Polish Jewry, the imbalance flowed from objective factors and did not reflect any discriminatory intentions. See Schwartzbart, Report Part 1: 27, 29, 33 and Part 2: 6.

with a very different agenda was committed to the educational value of elections as an antidote to the moral havoc wrought by a corrupt leadership that had been foisted on the Jews by the Nazis who then exploited them to serve their own destructive purposes. "The continual contact with the 'kapos' and 'forarbeter,' 'lager-polizei' and other camp prominents . . . so weakened and dragged down the moral fibre of our people that stealing, lying, and dishonesty have lost their forbidding aspect and have become the current coinage of daily encounters."[67] The democratic process could serve as a salutary starting point on the journey back to responsibility and integrity.[68] A third group advocating speedy elections was centered mainly in Landsberg and found the ZK lacking in the essential attributes of leadership: vision, courage and initiative and thus sadly unequal to the unprecedented challenges of the hour. Rudolf Valsonok, the editor of the *Landsberger Lager Tsaytung*, for example, protested against the pallid efforts of the ZK that focused on everyday concerns and looking after its own as against galvanizing *She'erith Hapleitah* for concerted political action. But this meant understanding that "the time for welfare committees is past and that *She'erith Hapleitah* finally deserves to have active, political representation."[69] For Valsonok, therefore, the feverish activity in Sieberstraße 3 – the meetings, discussions, decisions, circulars and paperwork – were nothing more than a facade that concealed the fact that the critical issues of the day were not being addressed. The Congress would hopefully bring forth a leadership that would be able to show the way.

No matter how far apart in terms of style and substance, all these competing factions joined forces on the question of Palestine and the struggle for Jewish statehood.[70] On the eve of the Congress Samuel Gringauz sketched out his reading of "The fateful turning point"[71] that had been reached in the history of the Jewish people as a result of the destruction of European Jewry and gave voice to the deep concern and sense of urgency prevalent in *She'erith Hapleitah*. In all the years of its exile which were often accompanied by insecurity, persecution and even expulsion, wrote Gringauz, one external factor had always helped the Jewish people

---

[67] Dr. Shmuel Gringauz, "In tzaykhn fun martirertum hofnung un arbet" (under the sign of martyrdom hope and work), *LLT*, no. 2 (14) (18 January 1946): 1.
[68] See Levi Shalitan, "Demokratizatsye" (Democratization), *Undzer Veg*, no. 15 (11.1.1946): 2, and Jacob Oleiski, "Problemen fun she'erith hapleitah" (Problems of *She'erith Hapleitah*), *LLT*, no. 2 (14) (18.1.1946): 2.
[69] Velvele Tamarkin (Rudolf Valsonok), "Sieberstraße 3 . . . ," *LLT*, no. 8 (2.12.1945): 4.
[70] Levi Shalitan, "Di she'erith hapleitah hat dos wort" (The She'erith Hapleitah has the floor), *Undzer Veg*, no. 16 (25.1.1946): 2.
[71] Dr. Samuel Gringauz, "Di goraldike vendung" (The fateful turning point), *LLT*, no. 2 (14) (18.1.1946): 7.

survive: the geographic mobility that allowed endangered communities to seek a safe haven elsewhere. Following the First World War the doors of the world were shut fast against mass emigration and precisely at this moment the Jews of Europe "fell into the bloody maelstrom of a satanic program of destruction – and was all but totally annihilated."[72] Thus Polish Jewry, the biological reservoir of the Jewish people, had been wiped out, the communities of Central and Western Europe had largely disappeared while the large concentration of Jews in western Russia had been decimated and its remnants dispersed throughout the country which further reduced their chances of holding out against the assimilatory pressures of the Soviet regime. The chances of the Jews in America being able to maintain themselves had also sustained a serious blow given the critical importance of continued European immigration to Jewish survival in the land of the melting pot. Broadly speaking then: "One Jewish center remains which – even though it is quantitatively the smallest – concentrates in itself at present the historical potential of the Jewish people for moving into the future ... Today the national fate of of our people rests on the solution of the question of Palestine."[73]

The *churban* had brought down the curtain on the history of the Jewish people in Europe and opened a new era that would be dominated by Palestinian and American Jewry and thus the relations that would bind the two was of decisive importance for the Jewish future. The young and vulnerable Yishuv would stand in need of the political and financial aid of American Jewry while the latter would be able to moderate the impact of assimilation to the extent that it organized itself to serve the Zionist cause. Gringauz hoped that the sense of an interdependence of fate that united the Congress delegates around the question of Palestine would come to prevail in the Jewish world as a whole.

The opening of the Congress of *She'erith Hapleitah* on 27 January 1946 in the historic Rathaus of Munich with 112 representatives from the entire American Zone of Occupation, many honored guests and wide press coverage was an impressive demonstration of Jewish resilience and solidarity.[74] In his opening address Zalman Grinberg made reference to

---

[72] Ibid.   [73] Ibid.
[74] For descriptions and analyses of the Congress see "Drite konferents fun she'erith hapleitah in amerikaner zone" (Third Conference of *She'erith Hapleitah* in the American Zone), *LLT*, no. 4 (6) (1.2.1946): 5–6; Baruch Hermanowich, "Mentshen un verter: notitsen un ayndrukn fun der she'erith hapleitah konferents" (People and words: notes and impressions from the Conference of *She'erith Hapleitah*), ibid.: 3; Lozer Diler, "Ayndrukn fun der minkhener konferents" (Impressions from the Munich Conference), ibid.: 7; Yosef Gar, "Notitsen fun der minkhener konferents" (Notes on the Munich conference), ibid.: 2; Jacob Oleiski, "Kultur un produktivizatsye – hoyft-fragen oyf der konferents" (Culture and productivization – key issues in the conference), ibid.: 8; "Fayerlekhe

the symbolism of holding the Congress "in the impure city of Munich, capital of the Hitlerite movement":

Here have assembled the remnant, those Jews who miraculously survived in order to make their accounting of the past and to consult with one another about the future. We are, all of us, broken and shattered by the tragedy of the last 6 years... We have come together to take counsel on how we can, for once and for all, put an end to our abnormal life so that what happened to us will never happen again.[75]

During the war, continued Grinberg, now directing his comments to the representatives of the military and UNRRA, the Jews in Occupied Europe neither lived nor died like others. Indeed, millions of soldiers had tragically fallen in battle but it was a tragedy open to rational explanation. Not so the Jewish catastrophe where an entire people was tortured, broken and murdered for no visible rhyme or reason. Moreover, all this took place on the soil of enlightened Europe in full view of the Allies who knew what was going on but refused, apparently because they felt it was not their concern, to extend any help whatsoever. The Jewish accounting with the nations of Europe and the Allies was long and hard and led to one inescapable conclusion: "Not to remain any longer in Europe [for] our home is in the Land of Israel."[76]

In this spirit the political resolutions of the Congress were primarily directed against the British Government and the continued adherence to the White Paper policy that "has shut the doors of Palestine before the wounded Jewish people and is creating a Jewish ghetto in Palestine on the pattern of the Nuremberg race laws."[77] This stood in sharp contradiction to the great fight for freedom that the English people had waged with the Allies against Nazism and fascism. The Congress went on to condemn the antisemitism rampant in Eastern Europe, sent its warm greetings to the American people, its president and army, saluted the soldiers of the Jewish Brigade and the Yishuv and called on the Jewish people "to unite all of its forces in the battle for its historic goal."[78]

The second and third day of the proceedings were devoted to the internal affairs of *She'erith Hapleitah* and, as Jacob Oleiski reported, "There was a veritable storm of criticism and complaints from nearly all the

derefnung fun kongres" (Festive opening of Congress), *Undzer Veg*, no.18 (1.2.1946): 2; "Kongres zitsungen" (Congress sessions), ibid.: 3; "Lebedike vilen lebn" (A lively will to live), ibid.: 6.

[75] "Rede fun dr. grinberg" (Speech of Dr. Grinberg), *LLT*, no. 4 (16) (1.2.1946): 4.

[76] Ibid.

[77] "Polityshe rezolutsies fun der konferents" (Political resolutions of the conference), ibid.: 3.

[78] Ibid.

delegates with respect to the ineffective activity and neglect of the important areas of culture, productivization and organization of the outgoing Central Committee."[79] Dr. Grinberg did not deny the validity of these claims but laid the blame at the door of the objective weakness of the Committee which the Congress was attempting to set right. Interestingly enough the election of the new Central Committee on the last day of the Congress did not bring about any radical changes in the leadership of She'erith Hapleitah. Zalman Grinberg was reelected as Chairman and Samuel Gringauz returned to serve as President of the Council. The Landsberg faction succeeded in increasing their representation while the achievements of the Polish group were more modest and the leadership remained primarily Lithuanian. Among those chosen to serve in the new departmental committees there were a sprinkling of representatives from newly created and more distant communities like Neu Freiman, Leipheim, Zeilsheim. As the influx of Jews from the east continued through 1946 there were repeated requests, well exploited by the opposition to the ZK, for new elections. But, whereas the newcomers were integrated, almost immediately, into local politics the next elections of the central institutions of She'erith Hapleitah were held a year later, as planned.

As its first order of business the new Central Committee set about tightening up its organizational structure and developing a wide variety of new initiatives. In terms of relations with the army the ZK took advantage of the participation of a delegation from Bergen Belsen in order to set up a joint political representation close to the US Army headquarters in Frankfurt.[80] A meeting was held with the local Munich community so as to map out areas of competence with respect to the thousands of Jews living in the city.[81] There were consultations with Camp Committees with regard to efficiency and democratic procedures,[82] and in order to improve education, vocational training and cultural activity the Committee succeeded in procuring daily support for 300 teachers from UNRRA and the use of fifteen classrooms from a Bavarian charity.[83] In terms of its political responsibilities the most important item on the agenda of the new Committee was hosting the representatives of the Anglo-American Committee of Inquiry who arrived in Germany on 5 February 1946. In many ways this was the end result of what had been achieved as a result of Earl Harrison's visit in July 1945. In the wake of the Harrison report President Truman had requested of Attlee to allow 100,000 survivors to settle in Palestine: "As I said to you in Potsdam, the American people as

[79] Oleiski, "Kultur un produktivizatsye."   [80] See Protokoll nr. 31 des ZK (29.1.1946).
[81] Ibid.   [82] See Protokoll nr. 34 des ZK (5.2.1946) and nr. 35 (7.2.1946).
[83] See Protokoll nr. des ZK 35 (7.2.1946).

a whole firmly believe that immigration to Palestine should not be closed and that a reasonable number of Europe's persecuted Jews should, in accordance with their wishes, be permitted to resettle there."[84] Because Truman was initially driven by mainly humanitarian concerns, his first tendency had been to turn down Attlee's counter-proposal to set up a joint body to make a thorough investigation of the matter including the situation of the Jews in Europe, an estimation of the number of Jews unable to return to their previous homes and the suggestion of ways and means to alleviate their situation. This proposal that pointedly steered attention away from Palestine was the subject of intensive negotiation until the British side put forward a formulation acceptable to President Truman.[85]

In the new version the first and third clauses in the Terms of Reference of the AACI focused on the question of Palestine and the possible impact of increased Jewish immigration on its inhabitants. The second clause instructed the Committee to examine the situation of Holocaust survivors in Europe and to estimate the number that would seek to emigrate to both Palestine and other countries. The fourth clause sought recommendations on both improving the situation of the Jews in Europe and expanding the possibilities of emigration.[86] These contradictory instructions reflect the competing policies of the two governments: Bevin, in presenting the agreement to Parliament on 13 September 1945, expressed his doubts about the capacity of Palestine to provide a solution to the problems of the Jewish DPs and appealed to the Jews of Europe to join in the effort to rebuild their countries of origin. President Truman, on the other hand, made no secret of his preference for the Palestinian solution and urged the twelve members of the Committee to finish their work as soon as possible. The British contingent, at the outset, tended to separate off the problems of the Jewish DPs from the question of Palestine and were, according to the description of Richard Crossman, "not emotionally pro-Jew but only rationally anti-antisemitic – which is a very different thing."[87] The American contingent who did not carry the burden of Great Britain's imperial commitments maintained an attitude of neutral sympathy towards the Zionist cause and tended to view the problems of the survivors and the question of Palestine as one.

The Anglo-American Committee of Inquiry began its work in Washington and in terms of *She'erith Hapleitah* the three important voices

[84] Harry S. Truman to Clement Atlee, 31 August 1945, Rec. A-A, NA, /RG43/Box 1.
[85] Michael J. Cohen, "The Genesis of the Anglo-American Committee of Inquiry on Palestine," *Historical Journal*, vol. 22, no. 1(1979): 185–207.
[86] Statement by the President (13.11.1945), Rec.A-A/Box 91.
[87] See Richard Crossman, *Palestine Mission: A Personal Record* (London, 1946): 27.

heard in the initial hearings were those of Earl J. Harrison, Joseph Schwartz, who provided a comprehensive, up-to-date survey of Jewish life in post-war Europe, and Judge Proskauer, the Chairman of the non-Zionist American Jewish Committee who saw the Yishuv as an immediate answer to a burning human problem:

> Go to work and get these people out of the misery they are mired in . . . we have no time to delay the discussion . . . until you find out if these poor people will be able to emigrate to Australia, or Canada or the United States or Great Britain for it is a fact, a first premise that the only place they can go to immediately is Palestine.[88]

The testimonies gathered in England, by comparison, focused on the future of Palestine and the British–Arab–Jewish triangle. The question of *She'erith Hapleitah* came up frequently but did not command special attention. Sir Herbert Emerson, the British delegate to the Intergovernmental Committee on Refugees described the plight of East European Jewry and the *Brichah* while others provided demographic data on the Jewish DPs. However, the distance between the members of the Committee and the realities of Europe came into sharp relief during the testimony of Rabbi Leo Baeck when his personal stature and unique role in the face of destruction passed largely unnoticed and thus there was no effort to elicit his perspective and views on the questions at hand. In fact the only issue that received special attention were allegations regarding the role of Palestinian emissaries in whipping up Zionist sentiment in *She'erith Hapleitah*.[89]

Initially the Zionist movement had viewed the AACI with open suspicion. There was no real reason for a further study of the Palestinian issue and thus the creation of the Committee was seen as another delaying tactic on the part of the British while attempting to neutralize the Americans. Nonetheless, in December 1945 the Zionist Executive decided that it would be wiser to appear before the Committee in the hope that Truman's sympathy, the spiraling costs of the protracted stay of a growing number of Jewish DPs in Germany and Austria and the English desire for Anglo-American cooperation would produce a positive outcome.[90] Ben-Gurion and Moshe Shertok, furthermore, fearing both the closing of the exits from Eastern Europe and the dwindling of Zionist

---

[88] Azriel Carlebach, ed., *Va'adat ha-chakirah ha-anglo-amerikanit le-inyanei eretz yisrael* (The Anglo-American Committee of Inquiry on Palestine) (Tel Aviv, 1947): 98.

[89] Ibid.: 254–256.

[90] See the study by Yosef Heller, "Ha-mediniyut ha-tzionit ba-zirah ha-beinleumit le-achar milchemet ha-olam ha-shniyah – parashat va'adat ha-chakirah ha-anglo-amerikanit 1945–1946" (Zionist policy in the international arena in the wake of the Second World War – the case of the Anglo-American Committee of Inquiry 1945–1946," *Shalem: Studies in the History of Palestine and its Settlement*, vol. 3 (Jerusalem, 1981): 213–293.

enthusiasm in *She'erith Hapleitah* agreed that Gideon Rufer (Raphael) of the Political Division of the Jewish Agency would work in liaison with the Committee. Accordingly Raphael visited Prague, Bratislava, Budapest, Vienna and Frankfurt in an attempt to persuade the local community representatives to support the Zionist cause.[91]

At the same time, preparations for the possible visit of the Committee to the American Zone of Occupation got underway in late December. On 31 December 1945 the Presidium of the *ZK* decided to extend an invitation to the Committee members to come to Germany in order to learn about their situation at first hand.[92] The organized preparations continued two weeks later when the Central Committee and United Zionist Organization met with Nachum Goldman, President of the World Jewish Congress, in order to discuss the forthcoming visit.[93] When Sir Frederick Legett and Bartley Crum came to visit Germany as representatives of the larger Committee, they primarily came as guests of the *ZK* and it is interesting to note that even Chaim Hoffman was not able to gain direct access to the sessions they held.[94] The most important links to the sub-committee were Judge Simon Rifkind and his assistant Rabbi George Vida. Rifkind accompanied Legett and Crum in their travels and meetings while Vida served as their interpreter and became an important source of inside information.[95]

The sub-committees which fanned out over the continent after their sessions in London, also visited France, Austria, Slovakia, Poland and Italy. At each of their stops they questioned survivors and their representatives and spoke to army officers, UNRRA workers, politicians and clergy. Thereafter the sub-committees met in Vienna in order to compare notes and to reach their first conclusions with regard to the future of *She'erith Hapleitah*. The impact of the European visit was not uniform but, as Richard Crossman put it: "each of my colleagues had undergone a violent personal experience . . . they had smelt the unique and unforgettable smell of huddled, homeless humanity. They had seen and heard for themselves what it means to be isolated survivors of a family deported to a German concentration camp or slave labour."[96]

---

[91] See Protokoll nr. 26 des presidium beim *ZK* (13.12.1945), YIVO/DPG 94; for a more critical approach see L. S., "Dervartendik di komisye" (Awaiting the commission), *Undzer Veg*, no. 12 (21.12.1945): 1.

[92] Protokoll nr. 26 des presidium beim *ZK* (13.12.1945).

[93] Protokoll nr. 28 der Gemeinzamen Zitzung des *ZK* un des Zion. Mercaz (The joint meeting of the *ZK* and the Zionist Central Committee) (9.1.1946), YIVO/DPG 94.

[94] Chaim (Yachil) Hoffman to the Jewish Agency (28.2.1946), CZA/S25/6449.

[95] George Vida, *From Doom to Dawn: A Jewish Chaplain's Story of Displaced Persons* (New York, 1967): 133.

[96] Crossman, *Palestine Mission*: 86.

This is a fairly apt description of what happened to Legett and Crum on their brief visit to the American Zone. In Frankfurt, their first stop, they received the results of the census conducted by UNRRA as to the "desired place of ultimate residence" of the Jewish DPs. The referendum embraced 19,311 respondents above the age of fourteen and of the responses that were counted, 13 desired to stay in Germany, 95 wished to move to another West European country, 393 wanted to immigrate to the United States and 18,702 indicated Palestine as their one and only destination.[97] In their many and diverse meetings the two Committee members sought to work out what these results really meant: what were the motives guiding the way the overwhelming majority voted? Were they subject to political pressure? Was everyone aware of the dangers that awaited them in the Middle East? Indeed, any attempt to unravel why the people of She'erith Hapleitah voted as they did is a complex undertaking given the various and often contradictory forces at work. Numerous Bundists and Communists, for example, gave their votes to Palestine so as not to harm the hopes of others. Others identified with the Zionist cause even if they were not planning to settle in Palestine themselves. There were also cases of political pressure but it was local, sporadic and, by virtue of the confidentiality of the questionnaires, limited in its impact. There was also a report of Palestinian emissaries forging questionnaires[98] but this was an individual case that did not reflect the policy of the Jewish Agency Mission. Chaim Yachil, as he made clear in his confidential reports, believed that the results faithfully reflected the commitments of She'erith Hapleitah:

She'erith Hapleitah is, generally, Zionist. I would even say, completely Zionist . . . as came to light in the Anglo-American Committee. It was not as a result of propaganda that 96 percent voted for Eretz Yisrael. And many answered that their second place of choosing was the "crematorium." We asked people whom we knew were leaning towards America why they had voted for Palestine and they answered us that it was their own concern that they were going to America but the Jews needed the Land of Israel.[99]

Further evidence of the lack of a concerted plan to influence the results can be found in the complaint of Samuel Gringauz, on the eve of the

[97] For details of the organization of the census see J.H. Whiting to UNRRA Team Directors (29.1.1946), Rec.A-A./Box 12, and for the questionnaire and results see Analysis of Census taken in the Jewish Camps on or about 31st January 1946, UNRRA Headquarters, US Zone.
[98] See Ze'ev Tzachor, "She'erith hapleitah ke-gorem politi" (She'erith Hapleitah as a political factor), in Machanot ha-geirush be-kafrisin: yom iyun mukdash le-zichro shel menachem oren (The detention camps in Cyprus: a study day dedicated to the memory of Menachem Oren), no. 62 (Efal, 1986): 24.
[99] The Mapai Secretariat (24.7.1946), Ha'avodah – Labor Archive/24/46: 13.

arrival of the Committee representatives, that the leadership had done nothing to alert their people to the decisive importance of the impression they would leave.[100]

Ultimately, Legett and Crum received the most telling answer to their questions from the stories of the survivors. They noted that those conversing with them were often the last surviving member of a family and community that thirsted for the warmth and security of a home of their own. They spoke to people who had experienced at first hand the collaboration of the nations of Europe in the destruction of their Jewish neighbors and interviewed recent arrivals who told of the circumstances that brought them to flee Poland. The survivors were well aware that millions of Jews lived securely in England and America but, as one of them put it to Bartley Crum: "We have suffered too much to take another chance. The end of our road is Palestine – a Jewish land with Jewish people who are simply Jews and nothing else. We are too tired to go to any country where, someday, someone may say 'Jews get out. Go to Palestine.'"[101] They took strong exception to any attempt to define them as a religious community, a view that informed the thinking of some members of the Committee, and equally rejected talk of the contribution they could make to the rebuilding of Europe. Or, as Jacob Oleiski asked rhetorically when the sub-committee visited Landsberg: if after 2,000 years of coexistence European culture was unable to prevent the annihilation of its Jewish population "then who can give us an undertaking that . . . what took place will not happen again sometime in the future? We are leaving Europe light of heart for it has been a source of deep and bitter disappointment."[102]

The testimony of Dr. Zalman Grinberg left a lasting impression on Legett and Crum. He told them his own personal story which accounted for his desire and that of his fellow survivors simply to go "home." This dream of home gave them the strength to see through the last terrible months of the war and now "months after liberation, we have come

[100] Dr. Samuel Gringauz, "Dos vos der kongres hat nit geton" (That which the conference did not do), *LLT*, no. 4 (16) (8.2.1946): 2.

[101] Bartley Crum, *Behind the Silken Curtain: A Personal Account of Anglo-American Diplomacy in Palestine and the Middle East* (New York, 1947): 91; on the visit of the Committee to Germany see "Anglo-amerikanishe erets-yisroel komisye in landsberg" (The Anglo-American Committee on Palestine in Landsberg), *LLT*, no. 5 (17) (15.2.1946): 9; "Di english-amerikaner erets yisroel komisye in stuttgart" (The Anglo-American Committee on Palestine in Stuttgart), *Oyf der Fray*, no. 3 (February – June 1946): 17; "Der erets-yisroel komisye in greifenberg" (The Palestinian Committee in Greifenberg), *LLT*, no. 7 (19) (22.2.1946): 9; "Di english-amerikaner komisye forsht unz oyfn ort" (The Anglo-American Commission investigates us on the spot), *A Haym*, no. 1 (19.2.1946): 2.

[102] "English-amerikaner e"y komisye in landsberg" (The Anglo-American Committee on Palestine in Landsberg), *Undzer Veg*, no. 20 (15.2.1946): 2.

to realize, with such agony of spirit and soul as I cannot describe to you, that the world has built an even higher barbed-wire fence around Palestine."[103] Grinberg stressed the therapeutic value of being part of a national endeavor for those who had gone through so much and his words were underscored by a visit to the "Nili" training farm. The enthusiasm, seriousness and lively commitment of the young pioneers surprised and inspired the visitors. In Landsberg, too, this very point stood at the center of David Treger's presentation:

> Having gone through such an agonizing life experience, people could so easily fall into a life of killing and stealing and become the dregs of humanity. Only the inspiring idea of building the Land of Israel as a homeland give both young and old the courage and belief to prepare themselves for a new life based on social justice.[104]

The members of the Committee were also struck by Dr. Leo Srole's report that highlighted the mental damage inflicted by protracted exposure to extreme conditions of deprivation and danger.[105] Srole went to great pains to explain that the damage was not irreversible but rather a natural reaction to threatening circumstances that would recede in a warm and supportive environment. This clinical diagnosis led him to his emphatic demand to get the survivors out of Germany forthwith and his enthusiastic support for making Palestine their destination. Whoever had the welfare of the survivors in mind, warned Srole, would have to move quickly: "it is my considered opinion that if steps are not taken before next winter to restore these people to a normal milieu the United Nations, by default alone, will probably bring to a final completion the designs envisioned by Hitler, albeit in a somewhat different form."[106] Crum, who had been deeply moved by what he had seen and heard, adopted Srole's position and decided to use the meeting of the sub-committees in Vienna to push for an interim report that would recommend the immediate removal of the Jewish DPs from both the camps and Germany. He demanded, in addition, that "The displaced persons must be permitted to go where they wanted to go and if that was Palestine, so be it. If they did not get out . . . they would be utterly demoralized."[107] Crum who anticipated strong opposition from his British colleagues planned to hold a press conference in order to bring pressure to bear on the Committee.

---

[103] Crum, *Behind the Silken Curtain*: 99.

[104] "English-amerikaner e"y komisye in landsberg": 2.

[105] Leo Srole to the Anglo-American Commission for Palestine, February 1946, AJDC DP's Germany 1946.

[106] Ibid.: 3.

[107] Crum, *Behind the Silken Curtain*: 121; see also "Intervu mit der erets-yisroel komisye" (Interview with the Anglo-American Commission), *Undzer Veg*, no. 20 (15.2.1946): 2.

His initiative supported by Legett and Crossman set off a rather bitter debate with Sir John Singleton and Major Manningham-Buller who were strenuously opposed claiming that a declaration of this kind would undercut their credibility in the Arab world. They threatened to publish an intermediate report of their own if Crum persisted but he agreed to stand down.

On their arrival in Jerusalem in March 1946, Lesley Rood, the secretary to the AACI, wrote a summary of the visit to Europe.[108] According to their estimate there were about 1,200,000 Jews remaining in Europe outside of the Soviet Union: 140,000 were in the USSR awaiting repatriation, 80,000 in Poland, 570,000 in Romania and Hungary, 380,000 in Western Europe and Scandinavia and some 100,000 in Germany and Austria. If the overall situation in Europe was bad, wrote Rood, the situation of the Jews was terrible. What they had suffered during the war beggared description and in the aftermath they found strong resistance to their reintegration into the countries they had lived in. They feared for their lives and according to a number of forecasts one could expect to see 400,000–500,000 Jews departing Europe in the next few years. The reasons for this were patently clear to the members of the Committee: the Jews felt themselves to be living in a cemetery, surrounded by enemies who had profited from their destruction and abandoned by governments who could not or would not return their property or guarantee their safety.

One cardinal fact emerged from the work of the Committee: nearly all the Jews sought to leave Europe and according to varying estimates between 60 percent and 98 percent wished to emigrate to Palestine. The depth of the Zionist commitment of the survivors was not in question and, at times, its very unquestioning intensity did not sit well with some members of the Committee.[109] Rood was circumspect but practical in his attempt to plumb the sources and nature of survivor Zionism: "Among most of the people Zionism has always been popular; events of the last few years have destroyed their faith in much of the rest of the world. Their incipient thoughts have been skillfully guided in the last year. The desire to reach Palestine, however it may have been induced, has now become a passion."[110] Richard Crossman was not quite as diplomatic in his formulation. The Jews, after all, knew that the Western democracies did not want them and that Bevin's suggestion of participating in the reconstruction of Europe struck them as cruelly hypocritical:

---

[108] Leslie L. Rood to Mr. Vincent and Mr. Loud, Jerusalem (19.3.1946), Rec.A-A./Box 12.
[109] Ibid.: 26.   [110] Ibid.: 39.

They were not Poles any more; but, as Hitler had taught them, members of the Jewish nation despised and rejected by "civilized Europe." They knew that far away in Palestine there was a national home willing and eager to receive them and to give them a chance of rebuilding their lives not as aliens but as Hebrews in their own country. How absurd to attribute their longing for Palestine to organized propaganda! Judged by sober realities, their only hope of an early release was Palestine.[111]

The members of the Committee of Inquiry had traveled first to Cairo and then to Jerusalem. They were very soon inveigled in Middle Eastern politics but they were constantly reminded of what they had seen and experienced in Europe. On one hand, the plight of European Jewry figured prominently in the evidence given by the heads of the Jewish Agency;[112] on the other, in their meetings with representatives of the Jewish communities in Syria and Lebanon members of the Committee heard stories of fear and insecurity deeply reminiscent of what they had heard in Europe.[113] At the end of March the Committee members retired to Lausanne in order to write their final report. Despite the political and personal differences that divided them, they were able to reach a consensus on two important matters: the intolerable situation of European Jewry and their moral responsibility to suggest an immediate answer to their special problems and, secondly, a deep appreciation for all that the Yishuv had achieved and a commitment to ensuring its future.[114] The path to detailed agreement, however, was long and arduous because the conflicting political interests of their countries needed to be taken into account in addition to the rights and political ambitions of the Palestinian Arabs in the context of a volatile Middle East. The Anglo-American Committee of Inquiry completed its work in late April and its recommendations were published at the beginning of May 1946.

The newspapers in She'erith Hapleitah carried banner headlines as they welcomed the report and the recommendations that were music to their ears: "100,000 Certificates: The Jewish Camps Must Be Liquidated by 1 January 1947."[115] Working on the assumption, furthermore, that the lion's share of these immigration certificates were destined for the DPs in Germany and Austria the papers reported on feverish activity throughout She'erith Hapleitah and in the Palestinian Mission in particular.[116] At

---

[111] Crossman, Palestine Mission: 88.

[112] See for example the testimony of Chaim Weizmann in Carlebach, ed., Va'adat ha-chakirah: 298–301.

[113] Crum, Behind the Silken Curtain: 238–246.

[114] Crossman, Palestine Mission: 184.

[115] "100 toyzent sertifikatn: di yidishe lagern muzn likvidirt wern bizn 1 yanuar 1947" (100 thousand certificates: the Jewish camps must be liquidated by 1 January 1947), LLT, no. 15(27) (3.5.1946): 1.

[116] "Der tsugraytung fun der groyser aliyah fun daytshland" (The preparations for a large aliyah from Germany), Undzer Veg, no. 31 (3.5.1946): 1.

this point in time the hopes and expectations of the Jewish DPs were in line with the general prognosis of the Committee members themselves. Colonel Mickelsen who was in charge of DP affairs in the Supreme Command of the US Army had been personally invited to Lausanne to testify on the logistics of transporting 100,000 people to Palestine and Richard Crossman confirmed that "we believed it was only a matter of weeks before the displaced persons would be on the boats."[117] The second topic that drew the attention of public opinion in She'erith Hapleitah were the recommendations to rule Palestine in accordance with guiding principles of the Mandate and to lift the stringent restrictions on the land purchases of Jews which, taken together, spelt the undoing of the 1939 White Paper.[118]

After a more sober reading of both the report and the first official responses to it, however, more balanced and often critical appraisals began to be heard. By 10 May 1946 many began to grasp that making the grant of certificates conditional on the willingness of the Palestinian underground movements to lay down their arms was an attempt by the British to frustrate the implementation of the central recommendation of the report.[119] As the evidence supporting this pessimistic reading mounted, more and more voices expressed their displeasure and reservations about different aspects of what had been recommended. Mordechai Karnowsky, for example, opposed the reduction of the Jewish tragedy to the problems of the DPs in Central Europe and feared that even the "prize" of 100,000 certificates would be rationed out without lifting the restrictions of the White Paper and so blocking the way to Jewish independence when it was so desperately needed.[120] By the middle of 1946, the great wave of initial excitement had dissipated and given way to a debilitating despair that eroded the hopes pinned on a Zionist solution and sent many people in search of personal solutions to their problems.

In view of these developments, the second half of 1946 was marked by renewed efforts of the Central Committee to bolster its public standing in order to deal more effectively with the multiple and often intractable problems that continued to beset She'erith Hapleitah. The huge wave of infiltrees that fled Poland in the wake of the pogrom in Kielce had to be absorbed and cared for; education, vocational training and productive employment had become urgent priorities now that the hopes for

---

[117] Crossman, *Palestine Mission*: 193.

[118] "Baricht fun komisye: forgeshlogn 100,000 sertifikatn – erets-yisroel ibergebn uno . . . frayer bodn-aynkoyf" (Report of committee recommends 100,000 certificates, Palestine to be handed over to un . . . free land purchase), *Dos Fraye Vort*, no. 29–30 (3.5.1946): 1.

[119] Chaim Goldzamd, "Tsu di resultatn fun der oysforshungs-komisye" (Regarding the results of the Committee of Inquiry), *Undzer Vort*, no. 8, (10.5.1946): 2.

[120] Mordechai Karnowsky, *Hamedinah* (The state), no. 2 (10) (14.6.1946): 2.

early immigration had been dashed; the growing hostility of the German population had to be addressed and, following the lead of Palestinian resistance, a more organized and sustained campaign to break the British blockade on Palestine had to be mounted.

An overall assessment would suggest that in the face of these numerous challenges, *She'erith Hapleitah* and its leadership stood the test. The repatriates, in the first place, appropriated the reigning ethos of the direct survivors, rapidly integrated into the existing structures of *She'erith Hapleitah* and filled them with new energy and determination. The survivor press continued to play an important role in informing the public and providing a sober analysis of changing realities. New patterns of commemoration suggested that the inner identity of *She'erith Hapleitah* had reached a new level of maturation and the rapid expansion of educational opportunities opened diverse possibilities of recovery and growth for those who had been deprived of the innocence of childhood and the stirrings of youth. This ability to stand firm and not to collapse into incoherent demoralization owed not a little to a homegrown leadership that had proved its mettle.

Among the remnants of European Jewry both the young and the old were conspicuous by their absence. They – the vulnerable, the weak and the unprofitable – were the first victims of the cold, hunger, disease, forced labor and systematic murder. This helps account for the profound concern of *She'erith Hapleitah* for the handful of surviving children like the four-year-old Yosef (affectionately called "Yosele") Schleifstein who, according to the number tattooed on his arm, was Prisoner No. 116543.[1] By December 1945 there were still few children under the age of five and those between six and seventeen years old made up some 3 percent of the survivor population in Bavaria.[2] From February 1946 the picture began to change, with the very young accounting for 2 percent of the population and the children of school-going age 9 percent. The big change came that summer when many families with infants and young children began arriving in Bavaria,[3] a flow that only slowed down towards the end of the year. At this point and through 1947 the surprisingly large, natural increase of the original core of *She'erith Hapleitah* also began to be felt.[4] At the beginning of 1946 there were an estimated 39,902 Jews in the American Zone of Occupation and by the end of the year the count has risen to 142,084.[5] In December 1945 there were 1,800 children, 16,000 in August 1946 and, in December of that year, 26,506 according to the following distribution of age and place:

---

[1] "Yosef schleifstein, 'heftling no. 116543'" (Yosef Schleifstein, prisoner no. 116543), *Undzer Veg*, no. 11 (14.12.1945): 4.

[2] See G.H. Muentz to Leo Schwarz, "Jewish Population in the US Zone of Germany in 1946" (January 1947), YIVO/DPG 70.

[3] Ibid.

[4] Ibid., including "The Natural Increase of Jewish Population during the Last 6 Months of 1946."

[5] G.H. Muentz, AJDC Statistical Office to Mr. Schwarz, "Summary Analysis of the AJDC Program in the US Zone of Germany" (January 1947), YIVO/DPG 70.

	Infants	1–5	6–13	14–17	Total
Camps	4,716	4,886	6,055	5,899	21,556
Communities	356	225	291	464	1,336
Children's homes	24	136	1,613	1,376	3,149
Hospitals	127	60	124	154	465
Total	5,223	5,307	8,083	7,893	26,506[6]

4 Sarah Robinson feeding her daughter Alice, Zeilsheim, DP camp near Frankfurt a.M., Germany.

Thus the story of education in *She'eith Hapleitah* has two foci: the ongoing need rapidly to integrate large numbers of newcomers into the system and the complex task of dealing with the deep scars of the past left on body and soul within the inauspicious context of Occupied Germany. The first attempts to set up kindergartens, schools and vocational courses were carried out in the large DP camps in the Munich area. In September 1945 Landsberg had 18 children in early education and 381 at school.[7] A further 244 had begun to study in a variety of vocational courses organized by Jacob Oleiski, the former director of the "Ort" in Lithuania who also helped Föhrenwald and Feldafing to follow suit. In Foehrenwald which had been assigned the task of absorbing children, 350 children

---

[6] Ibid.   [7] Phillip Struchan, Landsberg Report, AJDC Staff Conference: 5–6.

5 Mothers and children in Zeilsheim. The marriage and birthrate in the DP camps was, remarkably, one of the highest per capita in the world.

studied at the general school while a further 180 were registered at the Agudat Yisrael school under the guidance of Yechiel Halberstam, the Klausenberg Rebbe.[8] At the beginning of 1946 the 110 children in Deggendorf were well cared for but the education system in Feldafing and Stuttgart still left much to be desired.[9] The children in smaller

---

[8] Ibid., and see Report on Camp Foehrenwald AJDC Staff Conference (21.10.1945): 254, and M.J. Joslow, "Report of Education Survey American Third Army Area, Germany" (26 December–5 January 1946), YIVO/DPG 438.

[9] See Edith Lambert, "Camp Feldafing Report" (8.9.1945), YIVO/DPG 236; on the improvement at the beginning of 1946 see Gershon Gelbart, "Notes on Feldafing" (11.1.1946), YIVO/DPG-236.

6 Miss Waldman in Waldstadt is teaching a Hebrew class. The acquisition of Hebrew and English was a major component in the education of young and old.

communities and newly established camps were caught in a difficult situation because they lacked frameworks of their own while their parents would not allow them to attend German schools in the area.[10] Generally speaking the very young were well cared for, the level of the primary schools varied and almost everywhere there were difficulties in accommodating both high school students and the 18–25-year-olds. The latter group, where not enrolled in institutions of higher learning, was primarily interested in studying Hebrew and English.[11]

These bare facts fail to give a real sense of all that was achieved during this early period despite the numerous problems that had to be overcome. There was a severe lack of classrooms, exercise books, pencils and textbooks. The teachers were generally unqualified, barely rewarded for their efforts and bereft of teaching aids. Often there was no shared language in the classroom and those who had been deprived of their education for the duration of the war had, in many cases, forgotten how to read and write and lacked the discipline and patience to buckle down to

---

[10] See Joslow, "Report of Education Survey."   [11] Ibid.

serious learning. Thus, as Leo Schwarz summed it up, despite "The annihilation of intellectuals and teachers by the Nazis ... the loss of schooling during six years of war and slavery and ... the almost total lack of
educational facilities and materials ... [a]n extraordinary vitality and in-
genuity has been displayed by the people."[12]

In the first half of 1946 the educational arrangements in *She'erith
Hapleitah* went through an impressive period of growth and development. The pioneers of the early period were now joined by teachers who
had arrived from Eastern Europe, in May the *Kulturamt* of the Central
Committee began to operate, "Ort" was critical in making vocational
training possible, the Joint provided counsel and funding while many of
the Palestinian emissaries were roped into educational work.[13] In Furth,
for example, a school with fifty pupils, half of them Polish speakers, and
the other half Hungarian, was set up in April 1946. At the outset the small
staff focused on teaching English and Hebrew but by July eight teachers had been recruited and a full study program was set in motion.[14] By
March a first primer for the study of Hebrew was printed and by then,
in addition, over 200 students had registered for a variety of courses in
German universities.

In the second half of 1946 the *Kulturamt* prepared a curriculum for
the first five grades of the primary school and appointed an inspectorate
to guide teachers in their work and the implementation of the study
program.[15] At the end of November 1946 a regional conference was held
in Stuttgart for forty-four teachers followed by a training seminar for
nursery school teachers.[16] The increasing demands on teachers with the
growing institutionalization of the system also led to a teachers' strike in
protest against both inadequate pay and benefits, the latter being the most

[12] Leo W. Schwarz to Dr. Joseph Schwartz, "Summary Analysis of AJDC Program in
the US Zone of Occupation, Germany" (13.1.1946), YIVO/DPG 9; in this regard see
also Nachum Levin, "Al ba'ayot chinuch ve-tarbut shel she'erith hapleitah" (On the
problems of education and culture in *She'erith Hapleitah*), *Yoman mishlachat ha-sochnut
ha-yehudit le-eretz yisrael be-germaniyah ha-kevushah* (Journal of the Jewish Agency for
Palestine Mission in Occupied Germany) (8.4.1947), CZA/S86/32; Y. Kaplan, "In shul
arayn" (Back to school), *Undzer Veg*, no. 15 (11.1.1946): 3, and *Undzer Veg*, no. 16
(18.1.1946): 3.

[13] See M.J. Joslow, "Report of Activities" (26.3.1946), YIVO/DPG 439. For developments
in the area of vocational training see M.J. Joslow, "Vocational Training in the US Zone
of Occupation, Germany" (4.4.1946), and "Quarterly Report" (31.8.1946), ibid.

[14] See Helen Witkin to Leo Schwarz (1.5.1946), YIVO/DPG 224.

[15] See A. Blumovicz, "Baricht fun der tetikayt fun tsentral komitet farn kadents yor 1946",
YIVO/DPG 20.

[16] Filip Friedman to Leo Schwarz, "Report of the Educational and Cultural Department"
(31.10.1946), YIVO/DPG 1; Dr. P. Friedman to Leo W. Schwarz, "Monthly Report"
(November 1946), YIVO/DPG 439 and "Monthly Report" (31 December 1946),
ibid.

common form of remuneration. The preparation of textbooks on Hebrew, mathematics, literature, Jewish festivals and the historical geography of Palestine also proceeded apace and thousands of copies were distributed throughout the Zone.[17] At the end of 1946 the Department of Education and Culture of the JDC estimated that of the approximately 15,000 children of 6–17 years old, about 10,000 were registered in schools while the remainder had not managed to find either a high school or a Jewish framework in their particular area. The following was the distribution of schools, students and teachers by region at the end of 1946:

Region	Schools	Students	Teachers
Stuttgart	8	1,355	78
Frankfurt	10	2,169	133
Bamberg	7	791	51
Regensburg	9	927	59
Munich	20	4,657	266
Total	54	9,899	587[18]

By this time 581 students were studying at German universities, mainly in Munich and with a fair number in Frankfurt.[19]

In terms of their guiding philosophy most of the educational institutions adhered to the dominant Zionist norm of *She'erith Hapleitah* and in this regard it is instructive to follow Koppel Pinson's endeavor to plan out an alternative educational approach on behalf of the JDC in Germany.[20] The Joint by virtue of its inclusive approach saw any group operating within the Jewish sphere as deserving of its support. In the context of Germany this meant extending a helping hand to the non-Zionist minority given the abundant evidence "of undue pressure being exercised by either majorities upon minorities or organized minorities upon unorganized majorities. Totalitarianism has left its impress even upon Jews."[21]

The JDC was duty bound to intervene so as to ensure a fair chance to all while seeking to address the major educational concerns that Pinson had identified: helping students make up for lost time, broadening horizons so as to lessen the obsessive focus on self, providing language and vocational

---

[17] Friedman, "Monthly Report" (31 December 1946).
[18] Blumovicz, "Baricht fun der tetikayt."
[19] Friedman, "Monthly Report" (November 1946).
[20] Friedman, "Monthly Report" (31 December 1946).
[21] Koppel Pinson, "General Directives for Educational Program of AJDC in Germany and Austria" (25 April 1946), YIVO/DPG 10.

courses to prepare *She'erith Hapleitah* for emigration, trying to undo the debilitating effects of prolonged idleness and providing "a complement to the deep Jewish consciousness which up till now is based almost entirely upon martyrdom and suffering and thus most of the time hysterical in character, with deeper knowledge of Jewish culture thus giving a healthier foundation to their Jewish consciousness."[22] Pinson was generally affirmative about the achievements of the school system in *She'erith Hapleitah* but sought to broaden and balance a curriculum devoted almost exclusively to Hebrew and Jewish history. He recommended adding units on geography, general history, world literature, art and music.

> A determined but indirect and subtle effort must be made by our JDC workers to modify the now dominant spirit in these children's schools which keeps harping on the gruesome experiences of the past years, on ideas of revenge, on fanatical contempt for the rest of the world and an unrealistic feeling of complete self sufficiency against the rest of the world. There is still time for some of the youngsters to be children.[23]

The policies that flowed from these principles generated a degree of tension with the Jewish Agency Mission and often led to acrimonious relations with the *Kulturamt* of the *ZK*. In early 1947 Eliyahu Dobkin and Joseph Schwartz agreed to create a joint Jewish Agency-JDC European Center for Education and Culture.[24] The plan never materialized but it did open the way to an agreement between these two bodies and the *ZK* regarding the management of education in the American Zone.[25] An autonomous Education Council was to be set up with each of the three organizations delegating two representatives while the chairman was to be chosen in accordance with the recommendation of the Jewish Agency. The first tasks of the newly formed Council were to open new facilities, prepare additional curricula and focus on teacher training.[26] With respect to overall policy the curriculum was to be Jewish, national, general and non-partisan with special emphasis on the study of Hebrew and English.[27] The Council undertook, in addition, to provide full religious education for children from traditional families. The JDC took primary responsibility for the budget and the Jewish Agency committed itself to recruiting 100 additional Palestinian teachers for work amongst *She'erith Hapleitah*. Many JDC workers saw the agreement as relieving them of an onerous responsibility for a sensitive and demanding area of work

---

[22] Ibid.: 1.   [23] Ibid.: 2.   [24] Ibid.: 3.
[25] See Kultur amt beym tsentral komitet (Culture Office at the Central Committee), *Proyekt* (Project) (24.12.1946), YIVO/DPG 19.
[26] See M. Beckelman to AJDC Munich (9.1.1947), CZA/S86/54, and M.N. Beckelman to E. Dobkin (15.1947), ibid.
[27] C. (Yachil) Hoffman to E. Dobkin (8.2.1947), CZA/S86/54.

while the Jewish Agency Mission viewed it as a victory for the Zionist camp.[28]

Against this backdrop we can now turn to a more detailed discussion of the educational institutions established in Germany. Children's homes designated to care for orphans and children who had been separated from their parents enjoyed a special standing in *She'erith Hapleitah*. The first frameworks were set up in early 1946 in order to accommodate nearly a thousand children who had come mainly from Hungary.[29] A further 2,458 "unaccompanied children," as UNRRA designated them, arrived from Poland with the large wave of infiltrees that entered the American Zone in the wake of the pogrom in Kielce in July 1946 and by the end of the year their number had grown to 5,703. Many of these children had been located after long and arduous searching in monasteries, orphanages and private homes and, in some cases, had left their new homes with great reluctance.[30] They were joined by children who had been sent westwards by their parents in the hope that they would be bettering their chances for an early immigration to Palestine. In most cases the *kibbutzim* that provided the protective framework in which the children traversed Europe numbered fifty to seventy youngsters from two to eighteen years old, came together under the banner of one or another movement, made the difficult journey together and planned to maintain their close ties after reaching the Land of Israel. Children who arrived with their parents were sent with their families to DP camps, those who arrived unaccompanied were placed in children's homes. The first institution of this kind was opened in Strüth bei Ansbach in January of 1946 and by October there were five more with an additional four in the last stages of planning. From the moment of their arrival the children were granted preferential status and all those concerned with their welfare did everything in their power to attend to their every need.[31] "This is something precious given to our safekeeping," editorialized *Nitzotz* in January 1946, "We shall protect them from all evil and give them everything of the good and the light that survived in us until the day of their aliyah arrives."[32] In September 1946 UNRRA headquarters appointed Susan Petiss to serve as its coordinator to the children's care programs. At the same time the UNRRA workers were well aware that "The Jewish people considered themselves the ones

[28] Beckelman to AJDC Munich (9.1.1947).

[29] (Yachil) Hoffman to E. Dobkin (8.2.1947).

[30] Ibid. See also Minutes of Monthly Meeting of Regional Directors and Zonal Consultants, 15–16 February 1947, YIVO/DPG 19.

[31] Susan Petiss, UNRRA Child Welfare and Care Division, "Infiltration of Jewish Children" (25.6.1947): 1–3, UNRRA German Mission/RG 17/66,048.

[32] C.D., "Le-hatzalat yaldei yisrael" (Saving Jewish children), *Nitzotz*, no. 8 (53) (21.1.1946): 32.

to decide the destiny and destination of their children"[33] and therefore made do with a consultative role and left the strategic decisions to the *ZK* working in conjunction with the Jewish Agency and the Joint.[34] In actual fact it was the Jewish Agency that took the lead and in October 1946 it had established a local Youth Aliyah department that would dedicate itself "to care for children and adolescents wherever they may be; to prepare them for their life in Palestine and educate them accordingly, to register them for immigration and to allocate to them certificates for immigration."[35] So as to expedite matters, a Jewish Child Care Committee was established on 16 January 1947 so seating all the major agencies, including UNRRA, around one table. The Committee met once a week and oversaw the current administrative, medical and educational concerns relating to the children's homes.[36]

When the flow of "infiltrees" grew exponentially in the second half of 1946 a children's absorption center was set up in Rosenheim so as to provide a warm environment where the children could rest on arrival, receive medical attention and have all their paperwork done. Within a few weeks the children were divided out to the various children's homes according to their formal movement affiliation.[37] Initially the *ZK* and the Palestinian Mission had sought to keep politics out of the children's homes and this policy became one of the key issues in the great debate on Zionist unity. When the supporters of separation in *She'erith Hapleitah* carried the day it was just a matter of time before the unity camp would have to give up on the children's homes as well. The UNRRA people found it difficult to swallow the division of infants and young children according to a party key but any attempt they made to guide placement by age or special needs met with ferocious resistance. In the end they, too, bent with the wind and found extenuating circumstances to justify the acceptance of what their common sense resisted:

1. The group pattern was adopted before the children came into Germany, and will probably continue in Palestine. By breaking it up during the stay there is the danger of tearing down some emotional security that the children have been able to acquire.
2. Eliminates the possibilities of subjecting the children to conflicts set up by the competition of the groups...
3. Facilitates programming planning usage of facilities and personnel...

---

[33] Petiss, "Infiltration of Jewish Children": 4.
[34] Moshe Kliger interviews Eli Zamir, *Sefer ha-shlichut* (The book of missions abroad), Archive of *Bet Lochamei Hagetaot*, Container 2, file 7: 9.
[35] Petiss, "Infiltration of Jewish Children": 9.
[36] Minutes of Meeting of Jewish Child Care Committee Held at UNRRA US Zone Headquarters, Heidelberg (16.1.1947), YIVO/DPG 159.
[37] Susan Petiss, Report on Jewish Infiltree Children (5.12.1946): 4–5, UNRRA German Mission/RG 17/66,646.

4. Anticipates emigration when children will probably move forward in these assimilated groups.[38]

A rather sensitive problem came to light when it turned out that in some of the groups nearly 50 percent of the children had parents who had independently made their way to Germany. Because the *Brichah* gave priority to unaccompanied children, parents handed their children over to *kibbutzim* in order to expedite their departure from Poland. They also hoped that their children would receive preferential treatment and be granted, in addition, priority in terms of their aliyah. When the parents learned, on arriving in Germany, that their children's aliyah had been indefinitely postponed they either demanded their return or found accommodation near the children's home. Their presence complicated the workings of the homes that were not designed to deal with adults and created a conflict of interest when it came to dealing with their children. Everyone welcomed the reunification of families but it could not be left at that. Both in terms of on-going care and chances of early emigration there were advantages for the child to stay in the organized framework; on the other hand, it was not always clear that those who claimed to be the parents were *bona fide* – at times children were persuaded to pretend in order to promote the interests of adults who were exploiting them.[39] It was finally decided that in all such cases children should be returned to their parents but only after a thorough investigation of the facts.

In each children's home great efforts were expended on creating a coherent system of education and the obstacles that had to be overcome were no different to those plaguing all of *She'erith Hapleitah:* an absence of qualified teachers, textbooks, teaching aids, a basic curriculum and a stable environment. But far more intractable than any of these was the challenge of dealing with the debilitating scars left by the catastrophic war years on the young. A complicating factor was that in many cases those in a position to influence the children were 17–18-year-old *madrichim* – youth movement leaders who in Eastern Europe had gathered the children into what were in fact surrogate families. They were totally devoted to their wards, saw them through the difficulties and dangers of the *Brichah* and brought them safely to Germany. Nobody doubted their devotion but they themselves needed help and in a more stable environment where both a steady routine and formal knowledge moved to the fore, their power remained great but their ability to contribute to the advancement of those in their care was significantly reduced.[40]

---

[38] Ibid.: 4.
[39] Ibid.: 9, and see also Leo Schwarz to Joseph Schwartz (13.1.1947): 17–18.
[40] See Moshe Kliger interviews Eli Zamir, *Sefer ha-shlichut*: 9.

Generally speaking, the Palestinian emissaries found a shared language with the *madrichim* and were able to be of help without undercutting their authority. Their relations with the UNRRA workers in the children's homes, on the other hand, were complex and tense. There was a great disparity, first, between a quasi-military organization that worked according to standard operating procedures with its professional focus on formal education and individual needs as opposed to the collectivist ethos of the youth movement with its emphasis on value education in an informal context. The encounter between the two almost unavoidably generated strong disagreement as emerges from this report of Toby Schefter in Strüth:

Campfires, hikes, nature study and camping out form part of the scouting program. These activities stem from the program of the Zionist Youth Movement. In essence, Strüth is almost an exact duplicate of any Hashomer Hatzair or Poalei Zion Moshava [summer camp] ... that could be found in the United States, Palestine or in any other country ... imagine if you can the effect of superimposing an UNRRA team on a Hashomer Hatzair [summer camp] at home. Some of these devastating effects have been achieved at Strüth.[41]

A constant bone of contention between the *madrichim* and the UNRRA staff revolved around the attempt to render the group orientation of the young leaders more flexible and to sensitize them to the individual needs of each child. The Department for Child Care set up a course of study in mental health and sought to give the *madrichim* a rudimentary grounding in the world of developmental psychology and learning disabilities. They wanted their help with the children when it came to dealing with personal hygiene, problems of concentration and sustained application, chronic exhaustion and, where necessary, gaining access to the inner world of the child. The professional staff, for example, wanted better to understand why in art classes so many children would draw diminutive figures in a bottom corner of the page leaving the rest blank.[42] In October 1946 these programs were expanded and the Jewish Council attached to UNRRA took the entire initiative under its wing.[43] At the end of November a five-week training course was to be held at Rosenheim and the following were the topics to be covered: DPs, their camps and the role of UNRRA; welfare and health; education, psychology and counseling; leisure time activities; education in Palestine; the social structure of the Yishuv; the history of Zionism and settlement of the land; the Jews in the lands of

[41] Toby Schefter to Leo Schwarz, Report on the Children's Center Strüth bei Ansbach (9.5.1946), YIVO/DPG 225.
[42] Miss Lotte Lotheim, Principal Welfare Officer in Muehldorf to UNRRA District 5 Headquarters (19.2.1947), UNRRA German Mission/RG17/66,646.
[43] See Jewish Council Meeting Held in Munich (22.10.1946), YIVO/DPG 451.

Exile; teaching the Bible, Jewish history, Hebrew literature; the geography of Palestine and mathematics.[44] The substance of the seminar provides a graphic illustration of how the two worlds, while pulling in very different directions, were constrained to accommodate one another.

The on-going tension also expressed itself in the conflict between professional detachment and ideological commitment. Thus, by way of illustration, Miss Lotheim the Principal Welfare Officer was asked to run a seminar at Porten 1 on social work in the USA. Some forty *madrichim* participated in what was a largely factual presentation but they refused to be party to the question and answer session that followed and transformed the discussion into an ideological debate. As one of the young leaders put it: "We do not need social work, we need Nationalism."[45] This response led to great consternation and on the following day the UNRRA workers pointed out the dangers of a narrow nationalistic education and criticized the obsessive exploitation of the horrors of the past to help bind the *kibbutzim* together in the present. As Miss Lotheim described it,

Those who are called upon to "lead" held on to their provoking experiences of the past – with such great emotional need – that it is difficult for them to be "objective." Intellectually they admit to this and find the following excuse: "We must hold on to it – in order to keep alive among our people that our goal is Palestine."[46]

The same dynamic came to the fore when strong social pressure was brought to bear on the children who did not want to go to Palestine. As Susan Petiss reported at the end of 1946:

It has become a major problem in many instances, sometimes necessitating removing a child from the group to avoid serious emotional consequences. It is UNRRA's policy that a child's wishes should be recognized in this matter and pressures be eliminated. At any time that such a situation becomes evident the child is removed to an international children's center into a neutral environment.[47]

Koppel Pinson saw this "totalitarian" pressure as indicative of rather dubious tendencies that had become ingrained in *She'erith Hapleitah*. In many of the DP camps he discerned a disproportionate emphasis on

---

[44] See Training of Madrichim and Personnel in Jewish Children's Centers (25.11.1946), YIVO/DPG 451.

[45] Miss Lotte Lotheim (19.2.1947).

[46] A new account of youth movements in the DP camps points to a very different reality in 1947. We shall need further research to establish if, indeed, obsession can turn into avoidance. See Yehoyakim Cochavi, *Shoresh la-akurim: tnuot ha-noar be-machanot ha-akurim be-germaniyah 1945–1949* (Roots for the uprooted: youth movements in Jewish refugee camps in Germany 1945–1949) (Kibbutz Dalia, 1999): 105–107.

[47] Petiss, Report on Jewish Infiltree Children: 10.

discipline, a monolithic conception of group life, educational techniques carried on in a military drill-like fashion, concern with marching, demonstrations, banners and uniforms, the widespread resort to agitation, propaganda and indoctrination and the persistence on the whole of a certain kind of regulated intolerance . . . in most camps all betray, perhaps unconsciously the effects of living for many years under Totalitarian rule.[48]

As Pinson read it, the survivors felt that their war was not yet over – their problems had still to be solved, their future yet to be assured. It was premature to let down one's guard, too early to relax the readiness to do battle on behalf of Zionism and the Jewish future. This combined with the impress of the years spent under totalitarian rule had brought forth highly undesirable patterns of behavior that came to "dangerously resemble that of their former masters."[49]

It is certainly true that in the closed camp society powerful conformist pressures were generated and further hardened by the widespread sense of emergency. It is equally true that these tendencies were even more prominent in the tightly organized youth groups informed by a collectivist ideology. The notion, however, that these were traces, even unconscious, of a residual Nazi influence invites closer examination. This could have stemmed from a misinterpretation of the drill elements – uniforms, parades and ceremonies – that some Zionist youth movements traditionally employed, especially for their younger members. The error in judgment here appears to flow from a confusion between the substance of Nazism as opposed to the unfortunate residue of life *in extremis*. There is a fundamental distinction between the scars of terror and identification with the oppressor. Pinson's thesis, furthermore, does not relate in any way to the countervailing survivor "neo-humanism" as articulated by Samuel Gringauz.[50] The survivors turned their backs on a Europe that had let them down but they had not rejected the universal values which had become part of a shared Jewish–Western heritage. Thus on all levels the institutions of *She'erith Hapleitah* were democratically elected, their traditional abhorrence of bloodshed survived all they had been through and the ideal of cooperative settlement in the Land of Israel served as a widely shared symbol of a worthy life. The "totalitarian" thesis, therefore, appears to miss the critical issue: how was the burden of the past, the suspicion and lack of trust dealt with and neutralized in the children's homes and elsewhere in *She'erith Hapleitah*? How did it become possible to turn the energies of the young to more constructive ends? We shall be able to deal more effectively with these questions after we consider

---

[48] Pinson, "Jewish Life in Liberated Germany": 113–114.   [49] Ibid.
[50] See Gringauz, "Jewish Destiny as the DP's See It": 506.

the role of the *kibbutzim* in general and, by way of illustration, those of *Hashomer Hatzair* in particular.

The role of the *kibbutzim* in the aftermath of the war was *sui generis*. What had once been an elitist formation of the pioneering youth movements broadened out to include many and diverse groups in a framework of group living, study, vocational training and work in preparation for aliyah. The youth movement *kibbutzim* that were set up in Eastern Europe moved westwards as a group and on arrival in Germany, were sent, in accordance with their composition, to children's homes, DP camps or agricultural training farms. The age range in the *kibbutzim* was extremely broad and, at times, even included families. There were, first of all, *kibbutzim* made up of young folk, the backbone of the Zionist youth movements; there was a second, older variety sometimes including families that were also politically defined and a third, unusual group of ex-partisans and ex-servicemen whose political affiliation gave rise to protracted controversy. Generally speaking the degree of cooperation and social cohesion within the *kibbutz* was a function of the age of the members: the younger ones tended to create tight frameworks, the older people preferred a looser arrangement that allowed for piecemeal cooperation.[51]

In the DP camps the *kibbutzim* received separate quarters and tried hard to protect their independence. At the same time they were active in the public affairs of the camp, a high percentage of their members took advantage of the study courses being offered and when it came to cultural and political activities they were equally prominent. Because they were such a constructive presence, the *kibbutzim* were held in high regard throughout the survivor community as the following report from Feldafing bears out: "The members of the whole camp and the elected board of the camp recognize the *kibbutzim* as one of the main factors in the social and cultural work in and for the camp and as organized groups which strive for the common aim of the whole of Jewry in Palestine."[52] From September 1945, with the appearance of the first *kibbutzim* in Landsberg and Feldafing, their number steadily increased and by the beginning of 1947 numbered 276 with 16,328 members.[53]

The *kibbutzim* proved to be a compelling option in *She'erith Hapleitah* both because they answered deeply felt needs and provided a protective framework for those who did not wish to face what they felt to be a hostile world alone. While *Kibbutz Buchenwald* had shown the way in Bavaria and was in many ways unique, the deep needs it responded to were felt

---

[51] "Kibbutzim", AJDC Statistical Office (20.5.1947), YIVO/DPG 204.
[52] Max Munk, "Feldafing" (30.3.1946), YIVO/DPG 234.   [53] "Kibbutzim": 2.

by many. Throughout Europe these mobilized family groups sprung up in answer to the losses of the past and the challenges of the future. By the end of 1945 this new role of the *kibbutz* and *kibbutz hachsharah* in the post-war world was being given its reformulation. Aliyah to the Land of Israel was the major, hard-learned lesson of the destruction of European Jewry and as many claimed, the shared dream of the survivors. Palestine, furthermore, was not only conceived as a place of refuge but also the beginning of a revolution that demanded extended preparation. What was novel was that this classic formulation of pioneering Zionism had now taken on a new meaning: the aim of the Nazis had been "to oppress, to confuse and to kill us spiritually and socially before casting us into the crematoria ... the cruel, murderous conditions in the exterminatory regime that reigned in the ghettos and concentration camps set out to destroy every fine human sentiment; that is what these criminals were aiming to do."[54] Many and especially so the young whose education had been prematurely interrupted were infected by "camp ways" that were further exacerbated by living conditions in liberated Germany. In the DP camps educators had to contend with corrupting dependence, soul-destroying inactivity and a situation where "work and coercion had become synonymous."[55] Only productive work and educational training projects could help to restore labor to its erstwhile standing as a central value and precondition for the upbuilding of the Yishuv. In the collective regime of the *kibbutz* it would be possible to recreate "a life of work, simplicity, making do with a little, mutual help, responsibility and respect for one's fellow human being."[56] The shared framework could also be used to cultivate a forward-looking culture so allowing the young constructively to distance themselves from those that had so grievously harmed them in their hour of need. In terms of these goals the *kibbutzim* in the camps provided the vital scaffolding for rehabilitation while agricultural training farms offered even greater opportunities for a return to physical and moral health.

In February 1946 when Dr. Grinberg was touring the US as a guest of the American Jewish Conference, he met with General Hilldring who was in charge of DP affairs in the War Department and raised the question of agricultural training farms. He underscored the importance of gainful employment for both the morale and the future of the younger survivors in particular and reported on their lack of success in persuading the Military Government to expropriate German farms to this end. As it was reported to the Interim Committee of the American Jewish Conference,

---

[54] C.D., "Klapei pnim" (Looking inwards), *Nitzotz*, no. 7 (52) (13.12.1945): 3.
[55] Ibid.   [56] Ibid.

7 The *Kibbutz Buchenwald* Agricultural Training Farm in Geringshof. The sign in the library reads: "People of the Book take care of your books."

"General Hilldring expressed great surprise pointing out that this request was absolutely within the framework of policy. On February 27th we learned that General Hilldring had dispatched two cables to the theatre command, strongly advising setting up farm installations ... at the earliest possible date."[57] The Palestinian team, it goes without saying, were strongly in favor of setting up *kibbutzei hachsharah*. At the same time they understood that the program had no chance of success without UNRRA and the US Army being persuaded that it would be both beneficial and its political and economic price not too high. The various arguments put forward were well received and at the very first meeting of the "Jewish Council" it was decided to give priority to training projects with a special emphasis on agricultural training farms.[58] As Jack Whiting, the Director of UNRRA in the US Zone, argued the case in presenting it to the army in March 1946, it would relieve pressure in the overcrowded camps, help the youngsters regain their health and keep them away from

---

[57] Minutes of the Interim Committee (20.3.1946): 3–4, American Jewish Conference Archives.
[58] J. Whiting, "Memorandum on Jewish DP's – Persecuted – Infiltrating – Agricultural Training Projects" (5.3.1946), UNRRA Headquarters US Zone, UNRRA German Mission/RG17/66,483.

the temptations of the black market. These training farms were primarily aimed at

Jewish youths who are in organized groups called Kibbutzim, whose aims are to train themselves for their future life work, especially in agriculture. They are well-disciplined, have high moral standards and have dedicated themselves to undertake the hardest and often the nastiest assignments. They are willing to cooperate in the life of the general community but they have asked for and have been led to expect that their great need for agricultural training would be met.[59]

Whiting estimated, having tactically inflated the figures somewhat, that there were about 10,000 members of *kibbutzim* half of whom sought to move without delay to an agricultural training commune. The army was favorably impressed by the desire of the young people to be productively engaged but feared the political price of expropriation and the economic costs of handing over viable enterprises to rank amateurs who would any-way resist selling their produce on the open market.[60] In the negotiations it became clear that rational economic calculations would sink the whole project and when the issue was subsequently referred to the adjudication of the War Department a positive answer was received.[61] While many obstacles slowed down the process of implementation, by the summer of 1946, twenty-four *kibbutzei hachsharah* accommodating over 2,000 young pioneers had been made operational.[62] Optimally, farms which had pre-viously been owned by either Nazis or, more happily, Jews were handed over *tout court*, but in 20 percent of the cases the German owner stayed on creating a complex web of arrangements. In addition, where Palestinian instructors could not be found, German managers were appointed in their stead. By and large, the training farms received the warm backing of UNRRA and invaluable aid from the JDC.[63]

As 1946 drew to a close, forty communal farms with over 3,000 trainees were operating but by the end of April 1947, a distinct falling off could be noticed.[64] The Military Government had begun to return property to their original owners and, given their chronic lack of economic viability, refused to open any new sites. On the other hand, pressure from the movements also began to subside: some of their members had already left

[59] J.H. Whiting to the Commanding General, Third US Army Headquarters (17.3.1946): 1–2, UNRRA German Mission/RG17/66,483.
[60] See David J. Eizenberg to Celia Weinberg (19.11.1946), YIVO/DPG 208.
[61] Yachil (Hoffman), "Peulot ha-mishlachat ha-eretz yisraelit," *Yalkut Moreshet*, no. 20: 29.
[62] See Shmuel Zimri, "Hachsharot", Minutes of the Conference of Emissaries in the US Zone of Germany, Munich (20–21.5.1946), CZA/74/10095.
[63] See *Hashomer Hatzair*, Germany, Memorandum for the Director of the "Joint" in the American Zone (24.9.1946), YIVO/DPG 159; also Report on the Bamberg Region as of July 31, 1946, YIVO/DPG 229.
[64] "Kibbutzim": 9.

for Palestine, those who despaired of an early aliyah began to leave and the numbers of new groups arriving from Eastern Europe had also begun to dwindle. The attempts by the Central Committee and Jewish Agency to create inter-movement training farms running at higher profitability were not able to turn the situation around and thus the slow decline continued unabated.[65]

While the *kibbutzei hachsharah* were hardly ever profitable, their achievements in dealing with the deformations of the past were often impressive. Together with the *kibbutzim* in the camps they had to contend with problems in the physical development of their wards, the loss of many years of schooling and, most acutely, the undermining of their sense of trust in themselves and the world around them. At least in terms of immediate attention, the physical problems were the most amenable to treatment. These were disabilities that stemmed from long periods of confinement in places of hiding, starvation and disease from the period of the ghetto and the terror and deprivation of the concentration camp regime. The more difficult cases were treated in the general medical facilities of *She'erith Hapleitah* but, generally speaking, those in need could be offered neither special nourishment nor physiotherapy.[66] At the same time the *kibbutzim* devoted a lot of time and effort to physical education, active games, hiking, the martial arts and, of course, physical labor.[67] The following report from *"Kibbutz Lochamei Hagetaot* in memory of Tusia Altman" in Eschwege gives us a vivid sense of the human composition of the group and the kinds of educational problems this presented:

The *Kibbutz* numbers today 57 members here in Exile and 57 in Palestine or on their way there. Of the present number 17 new members have arrived in the last few months. In the *Kibbutz* here there are 24 boys and 33 girls... 50 percent have reached the level of primary school while the other 50 percent have done 3–4 classes. During the occupation 40 percent were in concentration camps, 20 percent – in bunkers or the forest. 30 percent in Russia or Romania, 10 percent had Aryan papers or fought with the partisans.[68]

---

[65] See Protkol fun der zitsung fun a spetsial komisye fun *ZK* un sokhnut wegn landvirtshaftlekhe hakhsharot (Protocol of the meeting of the Special Commission of the Central Committee and Jewish Agency on agricultural training farms), YIVO/DPG 703, and Yachil (Hoffman), "Peulot ha-mishlachat ha-eretz yisraelit," *Yalkut Moreshet*, no. 20: 29.

[66] Petiss, "Infiltration of Jewish Children": 8.

[67] S. Weinberg, "Hatza'ah le-tochnit avodah le-kibbutzei ha-noar be-mizrach u-mercaz europa" (Proposal for a work plan for the *kibbutzim* of youth from Eastern and Central Europe), *Hashomer Hatzair, Hanhagah Elyonah*, Circular no. 10 (Merchavia, 1.12.1946): 1–3, HHA/(4).32.3.

[68] "Skirah Klalit" (General survey), *Kibbutz Lochamei Hagetaot* in memory of Tusia Altman, Eschwege (no date), HHA/(2).8.13.1.

In terms of formal education, therefore, the educators had to deal with illiteracy, a general lack of learning, bad study habits, difficulties in abstract thinking, and, at times, the absence of a dominant mother tongue.[69] To this one needs to add two additional factors: these youth who were so deficient in their formal education had come to early maturation through the shocking events they experienced and witnessed. As Akiba Lewinsky put it: "A fifteen-year-old boy often possesses the verbal proficiency of a first-grader in Palestine, the general education of a ten-year-old, and the life experiences of an adult."[70] This disturbing imbalance made it very hard for them to settle into an arduous routine of long hours of study while the endemic instability of life in the aftermath rendered serious, systematic learning all but impossible. The *kibbutzim* set up in Eastern Europe brought together young people from varied backgrounds who after an initial period of organization moved westwards, chopped and changed their abode in Occupied Germany and impatiently awaited their departure for Palestine.

The story of the "*Kibbutz* in memory of the United Fighting Organization" (in the Vilna Ghetto) provides a further example of this unique form of social organization. Six members of *Hashomer Hatzair* in Western Poland founded the *kibbutz* in February 1946 and by May had succeeded in attracting a further seventy members.[71] Of this number, 88 percent were repatriates from the Soviet Union, a third of whom had served in the Red Army and the remainder were death camp survivors. In this first period all members of the *kibbutz* worked in order to maintain themselves but from the outset there were also daily Hebrew lessons followed by lectures on Zionism, the labor movement and questions of defense with all learning to use firearms.[72] The *kibbutz* participated in all the activities of *Hashomer Hatzair* in Poland and in May 1946 adopted a group of twenty-five children aged 6–18 who arrived from the Soviet Union. On the 8 June 1946 they set out for Munich via Bratislava, Vienna and Ainring. On arrival in Munich they were dispatched to the training farm in Holzhausen and very quickly buckled down to a regime of work and study. Over a period of six months, therefore, they had traveled from the Asiatic steppes to Poland, via the *Brichah* to Germany where they readied

[69] See Benjamin Grinbaum, "Noar palit u-ba'ayat chinucho be-aretz" (Refugee youth and the problem of their education in Palestine) *Alon La-moreh* (The Teachers Journal), An Organ for *Hashomer Hatzair* Teachers and their Supporters, Munich (March 1947): 8–9, *Moreshet* Archives/D5./54.25.

[70] Akiba Lewinsky, Bericht Ueber seine Arbeit in Europa, gehalten vor den JDC, quoted in Giere, "We're on Our Way but We're Not in the Wilderness": 702.

[71] Report of the "*Kibbutz* in memory of the 'United Fighting Organization in the Vilna Ghetto'" (30.7.1946), *HHA*/(2).8.13.2.

[72] For a similar story see *Kibbutz Lochamei Hagetaot* in memory of Tusia Altman.

themselves for what they hoped would be the final leg of their long journey. Against this background their success in maintaining regular regime of study was a remarkable achievement.

All of the movements prepared educational materials for their respective *kibbutzim*. The educational program of *Hashomer Hatzair* was devised in Palestine by Shaike Weinberg who had worked with *She'erith Hapleitah* while serving in the Jewish Brigade.[73] The general studies included geography, world history, mathematics, physics, zoology, anatomy and biology. Jewish studies consisted of Jewish history including Zionism, Palestine studies, Hebrew and movement ideology. What this "cultural work" looked like in actual fact can be learned from the following report of "*Kibbutz Lochamei Hagetaoth* in memory of Yosef Kaplan" in Yordenberg:

> The Hebrew classes consist of three beginner classes, two classes for the more advanced and one for those who can more or less use Hebrew freely. This class focuses on Hebrew literature. All members, without fail, participate. In addition there are classes for mathematics four of which are studying arithmetic and a fifth algebra. *Attendance in both mathematics and Hebrew is mandatory*.
> Every Monday there are classes on geography, materialism, either history or the history of our people in two separate classes. The classes are run by *kibbutz* members five days a week. They begin at 2pm and finish at 6.30pm.[74]

In all of the *kibbutzim* Hebrew enjoyed top priority – it was critical to creating a shared language, it served as a symbolic form of disassociation from a harmful and hostile world and it embodied the promise of the future. As a young leader writing of her work in Bad Salzschlirf put it: "I should have liked to have written more but my Yiddish is poor and I don't wish to use Polish. P.S. I am personally studying a bit of Hebrew and working on the history of settlement in the land (that is to say Zionism)."[75] Indeed, the history of Jewish settlement in the Land of Israel and the history and geography of the country were also in great demand. Each movement, in addition, devoted a lot of time to their own history, ideological commitments and political stand on questions of the hour. In *Hashomer Hatzair* these concerns were especially pressing for, as S. Weinberg argued, what these young people had gone through during the war

---

[73] See Weinberg, "Hatza'ah le-tochnit avodah."

[74] *Kibbutz Lochamei Hagetaot* in memory of Yosef Kaplan, Yordenberg, to the Movement Leadership of *Hashomer Hatzair* in Bavaria (16.3.1946), *HHA*/(2).8.13.2.

[75] A Report on Work with the *Bnei Midbar* (Children of the Desert) Unit in Bad Salzschlirf, *HHA*/(1).9.13.2, and, in addition, *Kibbutz Hashomer Hatzair "Ma'apilim"* in memory of Zvi Brandes, Feldafing, to the Movement Leadership in Munich and *Kibbutz "Bechazit"* in Waldstadt, to the Movement Leadership (August 1946), *HHA*/(2).8.13.2.

had led to approaches and a way of thinking that often contradicted the ideological path of the movement. The close encounter with the Soviet reality under abnormal circumstances and most especially the brushes with antisemitism in the peasant, the partisan and Russian soldier had given rise to a profound sense of hostility towards the Soviet Union and deep skepticism about the idea of socialism altogether. Experiences of the war had supposedly demonstrated the inevitability of a cruel war of survival between nations and between each man and his fellow. This was a war in which the weak was condemned to extirpation while the strong came out on top. The fact that that the peoples of Europe assisted in the destruction of the Jews reinforced this hatred of non-Jews.[76]

Many in the Palestinian leadership of the movement feared that the impact of the war would call forth an intolerant, integral nationalism diametrically opposed to everything they held dear. It was more than apparent that a sustained effort would be required in order to be able to educate towards pioneering activism guided by what George L. Mosse was wont to call nationalism with a human face. These young people according to Weinberg's reading "did not need any proof that Zionism was the only solution to the Jewish problem. Zionism was taught to them by their own bitter life experience. On the other hand, it was necessary to explain to them the justice of our particular way within the Zionist movement."[77] Amongst many of the movement educators one can sense a resistance to exposing the uninitiated to complex political issues before they were in a position to judge for themselves but midst the passionate divisions of a closed society detachment appeared to be a luxury that no one could afford.

This issue points to a third and highly complex issue confronting educators in the wake of the catastrophic war years: the undermining of basic trust, the foundation stone of both personal identity and social solidarity. The following is part of a report by the *madrichim* of *Kibbutz Ma'apilim* in Feldafing:

The *kibbutz* numbers 93 members. 35 percent girls. The age range is 15–18. Our people survived the forests and camps and some were hidden by Poles. When they were ten they left school and their parental home and since then have been on the move. These young people ... have seen life in the raw. This has had a profound impact on their character and spiritual disposition down to the present. The most troublesome and negative feature is their lack of trust. Faith in their people, in man, in the movement, in their friends is non-existent and it is not a natural and healthy skepticism. Just suspicion towards all and sundry.[78]

---

[76] Weinberg, "Hatza'ah le-tochnit avodah": 2.   [77] Ibid.: 8.

[78] Report to the Movement Leadership, Kibbutz "Ma'apilim" in memory of Zvi Brandes (17.7.1946), HHA/(2).8.13.2; see also "Survey of the Life of the *Kibbutz* in Strüth" (no date), HHA/(2).8.13.2 which describes how "The war years have left their mark on our people" and the remarks of the former Director of the JDC in Vienna in Ralph Segalman,

This spiritual disfigurement expressed itself in a variety of ways. Paul Friedman, an American psychologist who visited France and Germany in 1946, described the young camp survivors as "distrustful, defiant, cynical and refus[ing] to submit to authority."[79] Many in their early teens were heavy smokers, dishonest, rich in precocious and often tragic sexual experience and often simply unable to live up to the elementary demands of voluntary group living.[80] The impress of the past made itself felt in a wide range of situations as for example when emissaries tried in vain to dissuade the young survivors from buying high leather boots in preparation for their aliyah, recommending instead the purchase of something practical like a watch. The counter-argument was very simple: people lived for years without a watch and no watch kept anyone alive; leather boots, however, often made the difference between life and death.[81] For the same reason many demanded vocational as against agricultural training for bitter experience had taught them that a trade could be a passport to survival.

These reports are by no means limited to the first months following liberation and as late as 1947 Palestinian *shlichim* (emissaries) were often shocked by their first encounter with the young people of She'erith Hapleitah. "There is no knowing what destruction our enemies wrought in these souls," wrote an emissary, "There are times when you find yourself helpless and unable to carry out an elementary activity. May we succeed in educating towards cooperative living, brotherliness and mutual responsibility. But how do so when at every step you are faced with suspicion, distrust and a view of life that is so cruel, primitive and distorted?"[82] Or as Paul Friedman summed up his impressions of the relations between the young survivors: "There was ... hardly a trace of cohesion, of comradeship or friendship to be found among them. They were united only in their resentment and hostility to the outer world."[83] In the school of

---

"The Psychology of Jewish Displaced Persons," *Jewish Social Service Quarterly*, vol. 23, no. 4 (June 1947): 363–365.

[79] Paul Friedman, Report on a Survey of the Psychological Condition of Surviving Children in Europe, 1946: 11–12, CZA/CM 370.

[80] See the reports from the *kibbutz* in memory of the United Fighting Organization, Holzhausen (30.7.1946) and *Kibbutz "Baderech"* (On the way), Eschwege (29.10.1946) to the Movement Leadership, *HHA*/(10).8.13.2.

[81] Kliger interviews Zamir: 8.

[82] See unsigned letter from a *shaliach* to *va-adat chu"l* (the Overseas Committee) (24.9.1946), Germany/container 10/file 5. As one emissary wrote in March 1947: "Theoretically we know just about everything concerning the destructive impact of the war and camp life on the souls of the youth. However, in spite of this, what really counts is the direct encounter with these facts. I confess that in the first days I was doubtful about whether we could do the job and were fated to fail." See Bonio to Chaim (11.3.1947), *HHA*/(1)34.2.

[83] Friedman, "Report": 12.

life the children had been through, only cunning and single-mindedness would see them through and thus looking after oneself without much regard for the welfare of others – *organisierung* in camp parlance – had also become the guiding criterion of personal relations.[84]

Those who had survived the camps felt a need to tell of what they had seen and did so "Quietly, without emotion, with a kind of cynicism that chilled their audience."[85] However, this "affective anesthesia," in Friedman's view, pointed to what was only apparent indifference. The very need to rehearse past experiences and the fact that the narrator carefully avoided mentioning his fight for survival and the fate of his closest friends indicated a deep need to ventilate the searing experiences locked up within. In addition, the fact that many invented a role for themselves in resistance to the Nazis also suggested to the educator Benjamin Grinbaum that beneath the hardened exterior "churned a young soul":

All the young men have a sense of shame hidden deep, deep in their souls ... a sense of ... shame ... for the way they lived and how they were degraded is constantly eating away at them within. This is the most tragic problem that will not leave the boys in peace, it destroys their inner security and any vestige of pride in themselves.[86]

Prior to the Nazi occupation these young people had been securely ensconced in the warm bosom of their families. Suddenly, parental protection was torn asunder and the child thrust, all alone, into an endless nightmare. Many of the children now felt deep, albeit hidden hostility towards their parents who had, so to speak, let them down. The lack of trust in one's own father led to a generalized sense of distrust of the world and a feeling of being under constant threat.[87] This feeling of hostility was profoundly confusing for the youngsters were fiercely loyal to the memory of their parents and ashamed that they had not shared their fate.[88] In certain cases this ambivalence was extended to the Jewish people that bore the principal blame for what had befallen them. What other young people had suffered was perceived as the chance outcome of circumstances that was able to be set right now that the war was over – they could return home and be cared for by their families. They, however, had been the target of planned destruction that had left them abandoned and alone.[89]

---

[84] Grinbaum, "Noar palit": 8.   [85] Ibid.: 13.   [86] Ibid.: 10.   [87] Ibid.: 11.

[88] See the story "Zorgn fun a kind" (The Worries of a Child) published by Shoshana Domb in the journal of her *kibbutz* (no date or other identifying details): 33, *HHA*/(2).11.13.2. In a world in which roles are reversed she tells of a daughter taking care of her ailing mother in the unspeakable conditions of the ghetto, how she works long hours to procure food and then, with the arrival of the SS, she does everything in her power to rescue her mother.

[89] Grinbaum, "Noar palit."

These feelings of angry rejection, particularly noticeable among those who had come from assimilated families or had found refuge in Christian families, orphanages and monasteries, were, however, more general. As a young girl who had lost her parents in Auschwitz put it: "You cannot help becoming anti-Semitic when you see the lowness of the Jews and the lack of dignity which they showed in the concentration camps."[90] This barely concealed self-hatred sometimes expressed itself in a strong distaste for the study of Bible and Hebrew or contempt for the "empty superficiality" of Jewish culture. At other times it was disguised as hatred for everything non-Jewish whereby "The intellect seeking to suppress the feeling of [self] hatred comes to a chauvinistic extremism ... of a noisy and exaggerated hatred for all other peoples that [serves] to hide a sense of national inadequacy."[91]

The educators who had to deal with this debilitating ambivalence to-wards self, family and people focused their energies on helping the young people to regain their sense of trust and rebuild their inner sense of dignity. No one had a tried and tested formula for dealing with these unprece-dented problems and thus, as was to be expected, there were profound differences of opinion. Paul Friedman, for example, recommended that the children be removed from any collective framework as a first, neces-sary step towards their rehabilitation. "These boys and girls are revolting against any organized life or any regimentation. They have had enough of that and they cry to be taken out of organized homes."[92] The youth movements took an opposite view, interpreting this as an unhealthy de-sire to escape those who reminded the youth of their own past. These problems had to be worked through rather than evaded and the return to spiritual resilience led through the emotional ties of the young to their peers within a movement framework.[93] It was not ideology *per se* that was important

but the spiritual connection to a framework. The young people come to us and other movements without any sense of differentiation for they are in search of a home that promises life, food, clothing and aliyah. Only by virtue of their spiritual bond to the *madrich, kibbutz,* and movement do the children find the strength to meet the strenuous social and educational demands.[94]

The nurturing of these bonds became the key instrument of the *kibbutzim* in helping the young to restore their self-esteem, self-discipline and sense of human solidarity.

As we have seen, the central figure in the life of the *kibbutz* was the young leader, a movement member and, at times, resistance fighter who

[90] Friedman, "Report": 13.   [91] Grinbaum, "Noar palit": 12.
[92] Friedman, "Report": 13.   [93] Grinbaum, "Noar palit": 11.
[94] Weinberg, "Hatza'ah le-tochnit avodah": 2.

served as a surrogate father-figure. In many cases both UNRRA workers and the *shlichim* sought to undercut or limit the centrality of the *madrich* (youth leader) but, generally, with scant success – the need for warmth and security of family was too strong. The sense of family was often reinforced by the spread of ages in the shared framework so that in *Kibbutz Bechazit* – At the Front – in Waldstadt, for example, there were twenty-five members – one was aged 50, nineteen were 20–36 years old and five were children aged 6–16.[95] The following mourning notice sent out by *Kibbutz Ma'apilim* in Feldafing to all the *kibbutzim* of *Hashomer Hatzair* in Bavaria gives us a sense of the kind of relationships they had built up:

For the second time in one month we bring you a Jobian message. The first was Michael B. and now the death of our comrade Moshe Schwartz. Words cannot describe the sadness that overcame us with his passing. The tragedy is all the greater because we stood at his bedside, knew his fate was sealed, that there was no hope and we were helpless and lacking the strength to deal with death . . .

Standing beside his fresh grave we found comfort only in continuing our way, in realizing the dreams and aspirations of our friend, to go on until we reach our land.[96]

The inner coherence of the *kibbutzim* also found expression in their desire to continue living together upon their arrival in Palestine and as the secretariat of *Kibbutz Ma'apilim* reported: "The *kibbutz* is a healthy social body and there is a good chance that it will become a *kibbutz* in the full sense of the word if all are absorbed in one place in Palestine . . . there is concern and serious worry lest our people be dispersed among a number of settlements."[97] There were also those who sought to expand this commitment and to present Zionism as an extended family enterprise:

The six million martyrs are good teachers as to where and how to build our future. Because of this we call you Jewish children: you, who have remained without a father, without a mother, without relatives, serve as an example for us and take up your place in the ranks of the pioneers.

May you learn to be productive citizens of your land, on the soil of your people and thereby you shall retrieve that which you have lost. At this point in time only your people and land can stand for your parents who suffered such an untimely death. Your people is your father and Eretz Yisrael your mother.[98]

Beyond rhetoric the strong social ties which underpinned the *kibbutzim* were reinforced by intensive movement education. A great deal

[95] *Kibbutz "Bechazit"* in Waldstadt to the Movement Leadership (no date), *HHA*/(2).8.13.2.

[96] *Kibbutz "Ma'apilim"* in memory of Zvi Brandes, Feldafing (no date), *HHA*/(2).8.13.2.

[97] *Kibbutz Hashomer Hatzair "Ma'apilim"* in memory of Zvi Brandes.

[98] Avraham Mendrovsky, "Be-nativ" (En route), *LLT*, no. 33(45) (9.8.1946): 3; see also the *kibbutz* in memory of Yosef Kaplan in Yordenberg to the Movement Leadership (8.8.1946), *HHA*/(2).8.13.2, and "Moetzet ha-tnuah" (The movement council), *Iggereth Le-informatziah* (Information Newsletter), no. 1 (March 1946): 3.

of discussion was devoted to the movement's on-going work and achievements in Palestine and its role during the war. All the *kibbutzim* of *Hashomer Hatzair* were named after resistance fighters like Mordechai Anilewicz, Tusia Altman, Yosel Kaplan and Chaviva Reich who had laid down their lives and after the war came to serve as heroic symbols of selfless devotion; the memorial services in honor of the Warsaw Ghetto Revolt were a key event in the movement calendar and much time was devoted to a study of resistance in their educational programing.[99] The impact of this immersion emerges clearly in the following article written by the young Aryeh Gendler for his *kibbutz* journal:

Unknown you endured the onerous struggle for you fought not for freedom because that was impossible but for the honor of your people and for your own dignity you gave up your life. You still lie there with your comrades beneath the ruins of the Warsaw Ghetto and your blood calls to us and we swear to you Mordechai [Anilewicz] that the flame you lit in the hearts of hundreds of will never be extinguished and the flag of freedom you unfurled will never be lowered.[100]

There were also attempts to grapple with the problems of the hour more directly. One *kibbutz*, for example, held a mock "Trial of the Jewish Youth in the Camp" who were charged with wasting their time on playing cards and dancing while spurning more serious pursuits and remaining indifferent to both their own future and that of their people. The "witnesses" who opened the discussion were a ghetto fighter, a young boy who survived in hiding and a girl who had been in Asiatic Russia during the war.[101] Ultimately, however, what was found to be most therapeutic were the classic components of pioneering education – a life of sharing, work and simplicity lived close to nature and in this regard the *hachsharah* training farms could not be bettered.[102] As Chaim Yachil, the head of the Palestinian Mission, attested later:

The cooperative training farms played an extremely important role in those days. In terms of vocational training they were not especially valuable but the very fact that they took hundreds and thousands of young people out of the soul-destroying atmosphere of the camps, brought them together with other youth, put them in touch with nature and physical labor – all these were salutary for both body and

---

[99] See Weinberg, "Hatza'ah le-tochnit avodah": 8.
[100] Aryeh Gendler, "Mordechai", *Iton Kibbutzi* (Kibbutz Journal) (no date or identifying details): 8, *HHA*/(2).11.13.2.
[101] Trial of Jewish Youth in the Camps (no date), *HHA*/(2).13.13.2.
[102] See "Di noytvendikayt zikh umtsukern tsu der nature" (The necessity of returning to nature), *Michayei HaKibbutz: Biyulitin Informativi shel Hakkibbutz al shem Mordechai Anielewicz* (From the life of the kibbutz: information bulletin of the kibbutz in memory of Mordechai Anilewicz), Eschwege, no. 1 (Av 5706 – September 1946), *HHA*/(2).1.13.2; "Di entviklung fun undzer ferme" (The development of our farms), ibid., and *Iggereth Le-informatziah* (Information Newsletter), no. 1 (March 1946): 2.

soul. In a short space of time a new kind of person came into being very different from the general run of camp inhabitants and much closer to the kind of people found in Palestine. The *kibbutzei hachsharah* were, of course, the major source of illegal immigrants and the place where, in comparison to the camps, rich cultural activity developed. Here, too, the first *Haganah* defence units in Europe were formed.[103]

The adult *kibbutzim*, by comparison, were rather different and as Michael Deshe who was in charge of *kibbutzei hachsharah* in the Regensburg area reported: "Their social coherence is weak and unsatisfactory given that they have come together by chance. The members joined the *kibbutz* at an advanced age (over 20), some of them are married with children and, as is to be expected with this kind of human composition, there are difficulties and conflicts."[104] Similarly a report from Ziegenhain near Kassel estimated that three out of twelve *kibbutzim* in the area were worthy of the name while the rest were little more than members of the same party living in one residential block with little or no cooperation or shared cultural activity. Within this context, however, the adult cooperatives of partisans and fighters presented a very different picture and they, too, came to play a noteworthy role in the history of the survivors in Occupied Germany.

In November 1945 David Ben-Gurion convened a gathering of Jewish resistance fighters and ex-servicemen in Paris.[105] In its concluding resolution the conference called upon those who had borne arms to provide protection for their communities, to join the ranks of the international *Brit Lochamim Yehudiim* – the Covenant of Jewish Combatants – and to exercise their influence in favor of a "free Jewish Palestine."[106] *She'erith Hapleitah* was represented by Dr. Abrasha Blumovicz (Atzmon) who headed the partisan *Kibbutz Negev* in Landsberg. Upon his return he set about organizing the Union of Jewish Combatants in Germany, those who, as he put it, had played an honorable role in liberating Europe "but were unable to liberate themselves."[107] Because of this they had to see themselves as still under orders but with one difference: "Today we are fighting for ourselves, for our freedom, for our future, for justice and

---

[103] Yachil (Hoffman), "Peulot ha-mishlachat ha-eretz yisraelit," *Yalkut Moreshet*, no. 20: 29.

[104] Michael Deshe to Zeev Chaklai (11 Shvat 5077 – February 1947), CZA/S86/57, and Report to the Mission Committee, Munich, from the Zigenheim camp near Kassel (8.2.1947), CZA/S86/57.

[105] See "Der kinus fun yiddisher kemfer" (The Conference of Jewish Combatants), *Undzer Veg*, no. 10 (7.12.1945): 2.

[106] Ibid.

[107] "Erster kombatatn-konferents fun di amerikaner zone in landsberg" (First Combatants Conference in the American Zone in Landsberg), *LLT*, no. 5(17) (15.2.1946): 3.

integrity, for Eretz Yisrael."[108] The combatants were called upon to organize themselves in cooperative frameworks which would help prepare them for a productive civilian life in Palestine and affording, at the same time, a supportive environment for their disabled comrades. Following Blumovicz's lead the Union of Jewish Combatants affiliated itself with the United Zionist Organization – *Nocham* in pursuit of public backing and, hopefully, a way of preempting political divisiveness in their ranks.

The unintended outcome of this move, however, was the refusal of the left-wing *Pachach* – Partisans, Soldiers and Pioneers – to follow suit and their decision to go their own way. The movement (then called *Pach* – Partisans and Soldiers) was set up in Poland in May 1945 by Antek Zukerman, one of the leaders of the Warsaw Ghetto Revolt and Shalom Cholawski, a partisan leader in Belorussia, with the express purpose of serving the special needs of those who returned home victorious only to find themselves bereft of all. Addressing their "Brother Jewish Soldiers" Cholawski and Zukerman wrote:

For six years we have been fighting on the battlefields of Europe … we fought until we drove the enemy back to Berlin and there we strangled him. Today we return home as victors who saved the honor of their people – we, however, have lost everything. Our homes have become a pile of rubble, our fathers and mothers were murdered and asphyxiated in the crematoria of Treblinka and Belsetz. We are standing on the ruins of Jewish life, on the ruins of our own lives. We are orphaned and alone.[109]

One of the first steps taken by the movement in Poland, therefore, was the establishment of Soldiers' Homes in order to provide shelter, warmth and support for those in need. A special atmosphere permeated these homes and "people who had kept silent for years began to express themselves and to open up that which had been locked deep inside. From this point of view the homes played an extraordinary role in the lives of those who passed through until they set out, until we guided them via the *Brichah* out of Poland."[110] Here, too, special attention had to be paid to the special needs of those who had sustained severe injuries, for their decision to leave Poland placed them in a highly vulnerable situation.

---

[108] See Leon Rivkes, "Zog nit kaynmol az du gayst dem letstn veg … Oyfn kombatatn konferents in landsberg" (Never say that you go the final way … At the Combatants Conference in Landsberg), *Undzer Veg*, no. 19 (8.2.1946): 3. See also "Memorandum, tsentral-shtab fun farband fun yiddishe kemfer in daytshland tsu der ekzekutive fun der yiddisher agents un histadrut klalit shel ha-ovdim ha-ivriim be-eretz yisrael" (Memorandum, Central Bureau of the Union of Jewish Combatants in Germany to the Jewish Agency and General Labor Confederation in Palestine) (10.3.1946), CZA/S6/4685.

[109] Shalom Cholawski, Interview, OHD/145: 5–6. For background see Shalom Cholawski, *Soldiers from the Ghetto* (New York, 1980).

[110] Ibid.: 2.

Despite their great similarity the two veteran movements in Occupied Germany developed rather differently. What finally came to be called the Organization of Jewish Combatants was integrated into *Nocham* and, at least publicly, lost something of its initial prominence. *Pachach*, on the other hand, remained an independent while in Germany with an effective leadership that saw to the medical care, education and vocational training of its members, published a newspaper, set up its own Historical Commission and played an active role in the organization of illegal immigration to Palestine. By the end of 1946 the movement in Bavaria numbered approximately 4,500, in Austria 2,000 and a further 1,000 in Italy.[111] In Bavaria 40 percent of the membership had been ghetto fighters and partisans while the remainder had served in the Red Army and Polish forces. At this time the movement had thirty-two branches, six *kibbutzim* and a trade school. The relatively older age of their members together with the special esteem in which resistance fighters and soldiers were held help to account for their visible impact on the life of *She'erith Hapleitah*.

The leaders of the movement were constrained to fight for the aliyah of their people because they were not included in the party key that determined the allocation of immigration certificates.[112] The handful of certificates they procured were given to families and for the rest illegal immigration was the only alternative. The movement was an important presence in the Bad Reichenall DP camp nestling in the foothills of the Alps on the German-Austrian border and played an active role in helping to move groups of illegal immigrants into Italy. This activity reached its climax in the famous story of the "Exodus 1947." As it happened 140 *Pachach* members found themselves on the ship and, as their leader Mordechai Rosman reported, they were "the first to initiate, fight, dare and take responsibility"[113] in the clash with the British Navy. When the illegal immigrants who refused to disembark in France were sent to Hamburg, hundreds of members of the movement infiltrated the port area in order to protest and to demonstrate their solidarity with their comrades. In the final analysis 4,000 of the 7,500 members of *Pachach* in Europe made their way to Palestine including almost all of the resistance fighters who, from the outset, had constituted the backbone of the movement.

The elitist spirit of the movement flowed from the testing of the past and the acclaim of the present which, while especially noticeable midst

---

[111] All the facts and figures are taken from *Pe'iluteinu ba-kongres* (Action taken in the Congress) (7.12.1946), *Moreshet* Archive/*Pachach*/C11:5.
[112] See Cholawski, Interview: 16.
[113] See Mordechai Rosman, Interview, OHD/145:11.

the survivors in Germany, was a nigh universal phenomenon in post-war Europe.[114] At the same time the fighting talk, military terminology and nostalgia for their partisan past were also a source of worry. Both inside the movement and without people wondered how these veterans would settle down to a humdrum civilian existence, to the disciplined heroism of everyday life. In order to anticipate any undesirable reversions to their partisan past, the leaders of *Pachach* made certain that the movement would be run in accordance with democratic principles and their acceptance of the authority of the representative councils of the Zionist movement was underlined and affirmed. Another route back to everyday life led through the pioneering commitment to a life of productive labor. "Our *kibbutzim* here," stressed Antek Zukerman, "must learn to live on the basis of labor, they are obligated to preparing themselves for a productive life and not a UNRRA life."[115] In educational terms this meant going beyond vocational training and their natural attraction to questions of politics and defence and required a broadening of their horizons to include questions of settlement, agriculture, industry, soil, water, fishing and more. Only thus would they "be able to adapt the partisan experience to a totally different reality that requires ... integrating into a public that sees itself as a state in the making."[116] Happily, despite Pinson's strictures and fears, these goals were achieved in the main as the successful integration of the veterans into Israeli society during a period of upheaval, hardship and frustration clearly demonstrates.[117]

While the damage of the past was never far beneath the surface and repeatedly reawakened by the rude realities of life in Occupied Germany, the benign protection afforded by these cooperative frameworks helped their members, young and old, to start their journey back to life guided by an ethos of productive labor and public responsibility that earned them a special place in the hearts of *She'erith Hapleitah*.

[114] See Rivkes, "Zog nit kaynmol."
[115] Antek Zukerman, "*Pachach* geshikhte" (*Pachach* history), *Pachach Germaniyah Biyulitin* (Bulletin of *Pachach* in Germany), no. 9 (8.11.1946): 16.
[116] Chaim (Yachil) Hoffman, Report to the *Mapai* Secretariat (24.7.1946), Ha'avodah – Labor Archive/24/46: 13.
[117] See Yablonka, *Survivors of the Holocaust*.

8   Two voices from Landsberg: Rudolf Valsonok and Samuel Gringauz

The center of gravity of *She'erith Hapleitah* was to be found in Munich while among the large DP camps in the area, Landsberg led the way. The camp was blessed with an impressive group of leaders, who in pursuit of internal autonomy, had already set up a temporary Camp Committee in July 1945.[1] The Committee very quickly proved its mettle and by the end of September Major Irving Heymont, the camp commander, decided to grant the inhabitants administrative autonomy.[2] Internal elections followed on 21 October 1945 and a new Camp Committee was elected with Samuel Gringauz voted in, almost unanimously, as its Chairman.[3] From the outset the Committee which took a broad view of its responsibilities assumed, given the unlikelihood of an early departure from Germany, that rehabilitation was the order of the day for the survivors. What was needed was the respite to restore a semblance of order to their lives and to regain the inner strength so critical for a protracted political struggle. "We need to fight for national understanding and national discipline," wrote Gringauz, "In order to know how to prosecute the struggle for our rights and our dignity."[4] Accordingly, a wide array of institutions – representative, legal, vocational, educational and political – were set up in Landsberg in pursuit of these goals. These were the first, hesitant steps of a unique community that bore "the stamp of sovereignty . . . a deformed and sick sovereignty but one full of creativity, human endeavor, intrigues, bursting with vitality and pain."[5] Because of its *esprit des corps* Landsberg became a lodestone for newcomers who sought refuge in the American

---

[1] The members of the of Temporary Camp Committee were Jacob Oleiski, Samuel Gringauz, Rudolf Valsonok, David Treger, Dr. Nabriski, Moshe Segalson and A. Rozenzweig. For a general description of the camp and its institutions see Srole, "Why the DP's Can't Wait," and Avni, *Im ha-yehudim ba-machanot.*

[2] Heymont, *Among the Survivors of the Holocaust.*

[3] "Bakantmakhung vegn rezultat fun di valn" (Announcement regarding the results of the elections), *LLT*, no. 3 (28.10.1945): 6. Those elected to the Camp Committee were Jacob Oleiski, Dr. A. Blumovitz, Pinchas Rosenfeld, Moshe Segalson, David Treger and Yisrael Weber.

[4] Dr. Shmuel Gringauz, "Khamisho ani yodea" (Five I know), *LLT*, no. 2 (15.10.1945): 4.

[5] Dr. Shmuel Gringauz, "Di brik tsvishn nekhtn un morgn: a halb yor 'Lager Tsaytung'

Zone and a source of inspiration for *She'erith Hapleitah* as a whole. The camp was able to extend its influence through its leaders who were key members of both the Central Committee and the United Zionist Organization and by means of the *Landsberger Lager Tsaytung* which carved out a special place for itself in the life of the survivors in Bavaria.[6]

The weekly newspaper appeared for the first time on the 8 October 1945 and ran to four pages with an initial distribution of 1,000. In a short period of time it expanded from sixteen to thirty pages and eventually reached a weekly distribution figure of some 20,000. Soon after its inception, therefore, the *LLT* which eventually changed its name to the *Yiddishe Tsaytung*[7] ceased to be a purely local camp paper, and came to play a significant role in informing public opinion in Germany and abroad. Like any other newspaper, the *LLT* carried news of world affairs, of what was happening in the Jewish world in general and in Palestine in particular. A good deal of its copy, nonetheless, was devoted to reportage and critical comment on the intensive and dynamic life of *She'erith Hapleitah*. As Samuel Gringauz characterized the special role of survivor newspapers: "The broken remnants of what was a sizeable people bring to the newspapers of wherever they have fortuitously landed up the spiritual heritage of a cultivated people and, at the same time, seek, thereby, the ways and means of rebuilding its life. That [too] is the role of our paper."[8] Against this background we now turn to the writings of two men who left their indelible mark on the *Landsberger Lager Tsaytung*: Dr. Rudolf Valsonok and Dr. Samuel Gringauz.

It is no easy matter to document in detail the changes in attitude and view of survivors in the immediate aftermath of the Holocaust, especially when it comes to Bundists and Communists who returned to Eastern Europe very soon after liberation or who felt estranged from the Zionist majority in Bavaria as they awaited their opportunity to emigrate. In this context the case of Dr. Rudolf Valsonok is both rare and instructive.[9]

(The bridge between yesterday and tomorrow: six months of the camp paper), *LLT*, no. 13(25) (15.4.1946): 17.

[6] For a brief review of the paper and its history see Zemach Zemarion, *Ha-itonut shel she'erith hapleitah*: 91–93.

[7] Gringauz, "Di brik."   [8] Ibid.

[9] For biographical comments on Rudolf Valsonok see Dr. Shmuel Gringauz, "Dr. Rudolf Valsonok," *LLT*, no. 1 (13) (8.1.1946): 1; Samuel Gringauz, "Das kultur lebn in kovner geto" (Cultural life in the Kovno Ghetto), in M. Sudarsky, ed., *Lita* (Lithuania) (New York, 1951); A. Mokdony, "A yor in der litvishe melukho" (A year in the Lithuanian kingdom), in ibid.: 1093–1094; Marian Zhyd, "Litvishe yidn tsvishn der she'erith hapleitah in daytshland" (Lithuanian Jews within *She'erith Hapleitah* in Germany), in ibid.: 1921–1922; Levi Shalitan, "Rudolf Valsonok," *Undzer Veg*, no. 14 (4.1.1946): 5; Leib Garfunkel, *Kovna ha-yehudit be-churbana* (The destruction of Jewish Kovno) (Jerusalem, 1959): 169; Zvi Baron and Dov Levin, *Toldoteah shel machteret: ha-irgun ha-lochem shel*

The destruction of European Jewry was a critical turning point in Valsonok's way of looking at things and, as the founding editor of the *Landsberger Lager Tsaytung* and primary source of its reflective pieces between October and December 1945, we have a unique opportunity of tracing one man's reckoning with his past and attempt to think through his commitments anew. Rudolf Valsonok was born in 1890 in Bialystok and later moved to Kovno to complete his education. In the First World War he served in the Russian Army, having produced a number of strategic studies for the Russian General Staff. After the war he served as a staff officer in the new Polish Army but was forced to resign his commission because of antisemitic pressure. In 1920 he moved to Lithuania and was very excited by the prospects of Jewish autonomy in the newly independent state and the possibilities of cooperation between the oppressed peoples of the former Russian Empire. At this time Valsonok appeared to incline politically towards the autonomist *Folkspartei* inspired by Simon Dubnow but here, too, disappointment was not far off: an ugly wave of nationalist-inspired antisemitism washed through the country putting an end to hopes for full-blown Jewish autonomy. Valsonok, however, persisted and, having moved to the port city of Memel, worked to achieve a united Jewish–Lithuanian front that would oppose Nazi expansionist pretensions in the area. Yet again, sadly, nationalist sentiment stood in the way of solidarity and thus he abandoned political activity, returned to Kovno and devoted himself exclusively to journalism. Here he was overtaken by the German invasion in mid-1941 and shared the fate of his fellow Jews.

With the formation of the Kovno Ghetto Valsonok was employed by the *Ältestenrat* initially in the 'Airfield Department' and later as the head of the Department of Statistics. His essential work, however, was for the resistance and in view of his close contacts with the Communist underground, he sought to create a united front with the Zionist majority in the ghetto. Valsonok's greatest contribution to the underground lay in his ability to sift through and interpret any information that found its way into the ghetto from the outside. He was, as one of his colleagues put it, the "walking [living] political-military newspaper of the ghetto."[10] With the liquidation of the Kovno Ghetto in July 1944 he was among those deported via Stutthof to Dachau where his underground work continued: gathering information, working on the reconstitution of the left-wing resistance group, seeking contacts outside the camp and helping the inmates focus on the dangers and promise of liberation.

yehudei kovno be-milchemet ha-olam ha-shniyah (The history of an underground: the fighting organization of the Jews of Kovno in the Second World War) (Jerusalem 1962), passim.
[10] Gringauz, "Dr. Rudolf Valsonok."

Liberation found Valsonok close to the town of Landsberg where he opened a liaison point that assisted Jews and others who sought to return to Eastern Europe. Valsonok who apparently had hoped that the end of the war heralded the coming of a new day in inter-group understanding was profoundly distressed to hear the reports of hostility and violence from eyewitnesses who had returned home only to flee again. This was the last straw, "his final political disappointment."[11] But Valsonok, who always impressed others with his constructive vitality, refused to sink into bitter despondency. Despite a serious illness he devoted his remaining resources to the founding and editing of the *Landsberger Lager Tsaytung*. In this initial period the writing, editing and even typesetting in Latin letters was something that he did almost single-handed. It was a public statement that also embodied profoundly personal motives:

He wrote under a variety of names – Valsonok, Runicki, Breines, Tamarkin, Yisroelik and others. In a quiet, restrained act of loving memory he made our paper into a true, journalistic homage to his deceased wife and his deceased daughter. Reuven Breines was the memorial to his wife Breine. Velvele Tamarkin was the memorial to his daughter Tamara.[12]

At the same time Valsonok subjected his beliefs, ideology and political commitments to painful scrutiny. The process of clarification is formulated in general terms and laid claims to general validity but, at its heart, it remained intensely personal. "Throughout his life he carried the tragic impress of a Jewish member of the intelligentsia who sought a connection with the non-Jewish world . . . he learnt the lessons of his tragic experience – he had lived through one disappointment after another . . . he was a Jew and he drew his Jewish conclusions"[13] and it is these conclusions we now seek to uncover. His first step in rethinking his position led Valsonok to reconsider his view of the Jewish people as fitting naturally into a general human "us." One could no longer waive aside nor turn a blind eye to the profound, persistent tension between the Jews and their environment. The basic category of Jewish existence, thus, is not a universal, unifying "us" but, rather, a harsh and alienating division between "them and us."[14] After all, each time that Jews "filled with confidence in the eternal laws of a rational, truly human development" join with the progressive forces of a new era "an uninvited storm arrives, strews their path with a flood of blood and tears and forces them to retreat into a situation of unconsolable disappointment and despairing sorrow."[15]

Valsonok found the deeper cause of this unhappy dialectic in the conflict of values between Judaism and the surrounding world. This

---

[11] Ibid.   [12] Ibid.   [13] Ibid.
[14] Reuven Breines, "Mir un zey" (We and them), *LLT*, no. 3 (28.10.1945): 7.   [15] Ibid.

accounted for the clash between prophetic morality and paganism in the ancient world that ultimately led to the loss of Jewish independence and their dispersion among the nations of the world. From that moment on the Jews had been exposed to prejudice, discrimination and, at times, persecution which, it could be assumed, would have proved fatal for any other people. The Jewish people, however, found a way of preserving its moral values together with its on-going commitment to national survival. Following the guidelines laid down by Rabbi Yochanan ben Zakai at the time of the destruction of the Second Temple, they were able to develop a spiritual way of life that helped them to survive in exile without the support of either sovereignty or a physical homeland. They therefore refused positions of influence and power in the expanding world of Christianity and remained resolute even when refusal came at the price of a martyrdom that ultimately served as an inspiration for the coming generations. Having experienced persecution through the centuries the Jews entered the modern world "which heartily greeted us with [the grant of] emancipation based on liberty, fraternity and equality for all people."[16] It was difficult to resist the combined attraction of shared values and material comfort and it was not surprising that many Jews let their historically conditioned caution fall by the way and unreservedly embraced the new Europe.

We flooded all of Western Europe with a sea of bursting, energetic vitality contributing to the fruitfulness of nearly every field of material and spiritual endeavor and like the pillar of fire the great Jewish men dressed in foreign garb were in the vanguard of other peoples leading them up the way of blessed progress to the ever-white peaks of a just human society.[17]

Driven by their messianic heritage and blinded at times by material advantage, the Jews placed their faith and trust in the modern world and the promise of its future. In Eastern Europe, too, the period of emancipation opened a new and memorable chapter in Jewish history. The entrance into the broader spheres of European culture generated both social awareness and cultural ferment that gave birth to the Jewish workers' movement and Zionism. Whatever the differences between the two, and they were not negligible, they shared the goal of tearing down the barriers between Jews and their fellow men and creating a new and broader basis for Jewish equality. Internally, the precondition for this revolutionary change was to relinquish the age-long commitment to Jewish chosenness and to see themselves as a normal people, as a nation among nations.[18] In view of

[16] Ibid.   [17] Ibid.
[18] Reuven Breines, "Buntarysher trots" (Rebelliousness regardless), *LLT*, no. 2 (20.10.1945): 6.

the expectations, the sustained effort and great achievements that marked the entrance of the Jewish people into the modern world, it was not surprising, argued Valsonok, that but a handful noticed the warnings of danger that grew with every advance towards integration. In the 1880s organized antisemitism appeared for the first time and found expression in the pogroms that swept over the Jews of Russia; the devastating suffering of the Jews during the First World War and the wholesale massacre of Jews immediately after, especially in the Ukraine during the Russian Civil War, marked a new stage in the war against the Jews. These developments which were paralleled by the radicalization of antisemitism throughout Europe in the inter-war years, the perilous situation of the Jews in the Soviet Union and, in Valsonok's view, the growing difficulties of the Yishuv in the late 1930s were part and parcel of the selfsame war against the Jews that reached its climax in the Second World War:

in the physical annihilation, quantitatively and qualitatively, of European Jewry, the irreversible destruction of all Jewish cultural centers in Europe... that took place in the bloody turmoil of the Second World War under the eyes of a shamefully silent, civilized world and carried out by a nation of thinkers and poets with collaboration of all the peoples of Europe.[19]

When the pitiful few who managed to survive sought to make sense of everything that happened, there was no escaping the conclusion that Jews had been separated off from their surroundings by "a yawning chasm of estrangement and incomprehension that forces us to the view that between them and us, between us the heirs of the prophets and men of redemption and them – those who believe in and worship naked power – neither a common language nor a shared way of life is possible."[20] The handful who remained alive were called upon to examine with unremitting honesty their beliefs and expectations as Jews, the root causes of their tragedy and how best to move forward. In the first place they would have to face the well-worn truth that there is no justice in the world, at least as far as small and vulnerable peoples are concerned. This sober assessment that was widely accepted in She'erith Hapleitah led to the impatient rejection of certain romantic notions and religious beliefs that had been inherited from earlier generations. The survivor could no longer abide the weakness hiding behind certain moth-eaten truths: "He despises prayers to God offered up in a quivering-despairing call for justice and mercy"[21] and in light of the total helplessness that underlay their ghastly fate: "he completely casts off every belief in a Divine

---

[19] Ibid.   [20] Breines, "Mir un zey."
[21] Reuven Breines, "Tsvayerley mosn" (Double standards), LLT, no. 1 (8.10.1945): 3.

Presence which is not present."[22] Man is the one who reigns in this world
that rewards the strong and punishes the weak and the Jews, like the faithful lover who refuses to believe that his beloved is being unfaithful, are
repeatedly surprised by this.

This being the case, it was first of all necessary to face up to the
double standard customarily used by the world in its dealings with the
Jews. The simple proof that this continued to be the case was that even
in the wake of total destruction nothing in their situation had really
changed. In order to escape the bitter fate of oppression and persecution the Jewish people had to break out of this vicious circle of passivity and dependence, liberate its creative forces and become, once more,
the controlling subject of its history. If Jews were inwardly captive to
a long-standing cultural tradition, the primary external cause of their
tragic fate was clearly the equally long-standing tradition of European
antisemitism passed down in their "mothers' milk" from generation to
generation. In Valsonok's reading of history, furthermore, it was Christianity, precisely because it had taken over so much of the Jewish faith,
which presented a much greater threat than did paganism. The radical
turn in antisemitism which came to a head in the Second World War,
however, was far removed from its religious predecessors and had come
into being following the profound disruptions of traditional society set
in motion by the French Revolution. The erosion of the social arrangements, political frameworks and religious certainties of the old order in
which conflicts of interest were generally of limited scope erupted now
into ideological confrontations that by the twentieth century led to total war and unprecedented cruelty and destruction. In this clash of vast
movements vying for control, small nations like the Armenians and Jews
were threatened with total extinction. Germany, smarting at its defeat
in 1918 and wrenched by a series of political and economic crises in
the 1920s, provided a graphic example of how a people could lose its
sense of balance and become prey to a collective "psychosis" of suspicion and despair that could lead finally to an "uncontrollable outbreak
of hatred against the surrounding world, against whatever is foreign in
general and against the weakest embodiment of the alien in particular."[23]
In the case of Germany the outcome was the victory of the *dybbuk* (evil
spirit) of National Socialism that, in terms of structure rather than substance, could overtake other peoples in crisis. In this regard, despite
the special vulnerability of small peoples, Valsonok was persuaded that a

---

[22] Ibid.
[23] Reuven Breines, "Der dybbuk fun blindn pasasir" (The *dybbuk* [malevolent spirit] of the
blind passenger), *LLT*, no. 7 (22.11.1945): 7.

third world conflagration "would inevitably spell the irrevocable destruction of the world."[24]

What, then, emerged from this analysis? Not only had a chasm of enmity and estrangement come to divide the Jews from European culture and put an end to the process of integration but the very possibility of being able to continue living in Europe was dubious given the danger of recurrence. In view of the fact that "Splinters fly when timber is chopped and thus whomsoever has been unlucky enough to fall victim to the axe of world history"[25] should take urgent steps to remove themselves from the area of danger, especially so Jews who, given their dispersion and tendency to highlight their apartness, inevitably became a convenient target when history went off the rails. In a period where recurring crises had become endemic, the Jewish people was called upon to pay a heavy price for its very existence. The time had come to stop paying "the bill for the aberrations of others and to always have to serve as the obligatory victim for the sudden outbreak of demonism in other people."[26] The sacrifices that Jews made on the altar of humanity or in the service of their countries, in addition, did not serve them well: in the case of the former the fear of revolutionary change whipped up hatred while in the latter, many peoples were put out by the "foreign" invasion of their culture.[27] Examples of this unfortunate dynamic were legion but Valsonok fixed on the one that he found particularly distressing – the fate of Polish Jewry in the immediate aftermath of the war. After everything they had suffered and lost the pitifully few remnants were able neither to retrieve their personal property nor to bring to justice those who actively assisted in destroying their families and communities. After 700 years of shared history and suffering beyond description, the Jews had no place in the new Poland.

The Jews were but an example of the vulnerability of all ethnic minorities in Central and Eastern Europe following the war. As the national awareness of nations in Europe matured in the wake of the French Revolution it was accompanied by a persistent drive to create an overlap between people and territory. The international recognition of the principle of national self-determination together with the Minorities Clause in the guiding principles of the League of Nations had triggered off a myriad of national claims and provided a ready pretext for the larger European states to intervene in the affairs of their weaker neighbors. Nazi Germany, most noticeably, utilized this stratagem to prepare the way to conquest and expansion. Hence, a significant lesson of the war was that "People do not want foreigners in their midst. Every nation wants sole ownership

---

[24] See Reuven Breines, "Dos shtume veltgevissn" (The silent world conscience), *LLT*, no. 4 (4.11.1945): 3.
[25] Ibid.   [26] Ibid.   [27] Breines, "Der dybbuk fun blindn pasasir."

of its land and nothing to do with the protection of minorities or other half-measures. The new states rising out of the ashes of the ... Second World War do not wish to be multi-national but rather unitary in every sense."[28] The most radical step taken to achieve this goal was the expulsion of millions of Germans from western Poland, Czechoslovakia and Hungary to Germany. Valsonok vindicated these measures and saw them as both a just verdict of history and symbolic revenge for their crimes against the Jewish people.[29] But this policy did not stop with the defeated populations and even liberal Czechoslovakia had dealt harshly with its minorities[30] so that within this context of intolerance and vulnerability, the reduced Jewish minority found itself surrounded by hostile forces and at the end of its long history in Europe.

Thus the burning issue remained: in the face of these challenges, what were the Jews to do? The initial Jewish response, despite all that had happened, should echo "the proud, clarion call of our ancestors who, having survived more than one *churban* and having overcome numerous disappointments, proclaimed to the hostile world the proud assurance: '*am yisrael chai* – the Jewish people lives'."[31] To this faith in the future a further ingredient needed to be added in order to ensure the restoration of Jewish life – Zionism. Zionism provided a dignified way of terminating the tragic love affair of the Jews with European culture while affirming their determination "to insure our place under the sun shaped by the inexhaustible treasures of our own spirituality."[32] This would let the Christian European world know that the Jews, on their part, were setting aside their ambitions of integration "for if they do not wish to see us emancipated in their bit of the world it is pointless for us to continue craving and seeking it."[33]

Having a land of their own would give the Jews a roof above their heads, with the security and peace of mind that comes from being at home. Living in their own country would distance the Jews from the maddening crowd, remove them from the maelstrom of social upheaval and the center of historical transformations that always invited Jewish participation while later exacting a heavy price. The Jews who were inevitably viewed as a people apart needed to keep away from the affairs of others and to look to their own interests. They had to remember that when they were locked up in ghettos, expelled and deported to death camps, none of the Allies could be bothered to lift a finger. "Only the establishment of a Jewish

---

[28] Dr. Rudolf Valsonok, "Avu iz zeier erd?" (Where is their land?), *LLT*, no. 7 (22.11.1945): 6.
[29] Marek Ronicki, "Daytshe felkervanderung" (German folk migration), *LLT*, no. 8 (2.12.1945): 4.
[30] Valsonok, "Avu iz zeier erd?"   [31] Breines, "Buntarysher trots."   [32] Ibid.   [33] Ibid.

state in the Land of Israel will be able to transform the entire situation and create a formal base which will allow us to represent our own interests and have our own political account so putting us on the same footing as other peoples."[34] In this way Zionism would normalize relations with others, remove the immediate causes of antisemitism and provide the Jewish people with the sovereign means of dealing with any hostility from without.

A Jewish state, furthermore, would provide broad scope for the creative urge of the Jewish people and many opportunities for its prophetic heritage to find new forms of expression, a development that from Valsonok's perspective was especially important for *She'erith Hapleitah*. The Jews, like all mortals, were not immune to the deformations that historical traumas often brought in their wake. It was more than likely that the long immersion in pain and death they had suffered would call forth unfortunate responses. The bitter disappointment in European culture, for example, could give rise to "a kind of twisted sense of superiority which opens the way to being taken over by an evil spirit, by our own Jewish *dybbuk*."[35] On the other hand it could lead to the kind of response that appeared after the Cossack massacres of 1648 and conjure up "an unworldly, messianic Hasidism"[36] which according to Valsonok paralyzed large parts of the Jewish public in Eastern Europe for almost a century. Valsonok understood that it was too early to anticipate what would emerge but he did want to preempt either sick distortions or the flight into mysticism. His aim was to help the Jewish people keep its feet on the ground and the Zionist critique could be salutary in this regard:

Exile, over and above everything else, is the critical source of all our complexes, the place where our *dybbuk* lurks. This is what cripples our feel for life, awakening in us a defiant struggling under whose impress our spirits commit themselves to ephemeral fashions of cosmopolitanism and our bodies shrivel up in a rootless and landless existence parasitic on the languages of foreign civilizations. This is the parent of the Ahasver-complex and grandparent of our *dybbuk*.[37]

If history, by way of analogy, is like a train journeying through time and its passengers the nations of the world, the Jews are a people who have been on board for 2,000 years without a ticket. In the case of any other people who had lost their ticket, that is to say "their roots, their own homeland,"[38] they would climb down off the train of history. Not so the Jews: they continue their journey despite the heavy price of bribery, groveling, fear, degradation and horrific persecution. The moral of this long and tragic tale is simple:

[34] Marek Ronicki, "Polania Restituta" (Poland restored), *LLT*, no. 7 (22.11.1945): 6.
[35] Breines, "Der dybbuk."   [36] Ibid.   [37] Ibid.   [38] Ibid.

8 Elections for the Camp Committee in Landsberg DP camp. In the foreground a poster of the "Unity Bloc" No. 1 with its romantic rendition of the hope for Zion.

If one wishes to be treated with respect like everyone else, one should not come to the world with complaints about this, that and the other... [instead] one must have a ticket like other peoples, one's own identity backed up by the solidarity of one's own homeland, ultimately the only way of being assured of an equal standing in the family of nations.[39]

This, however, is not a ticket that can be bought; it has to have belonged to one all along; it cannot be concocted or manufactured synthetically. Because of this, Zionism is the only way of taking back what rightfully belongs to the Jewish people – the Land of Israel.

The acid test of this Zionist response to the tragedy of European Jewry depended on its translation into practice by *She'erith Hapleitah* and a willingness, no matter what the odds, to get on with the job "because life, following the harsh laws of unsentimental reality, has no time for mourning and moaning."[40] What needed to be done, then, was to work together so as to reshape recalcitrant reality to the extent possible. Given the urgent need to pull together Valsonok attached great importance to the internal elections held in Landsberg in late October 1945 in which the "Zionist Union" headed by Samuel Gringauz emerged victorious. This

[39] Ibid.   [40] Rudolf Valsonok, "Veilt jewish" (Vote Jewish), *LLT*, no. 2 (20.10.1945): 2.

was a resounding mandate for the creation of a true community-in-the-making that had one overriding goal:

> To shape out of a mass of slaves who were forced to languish in servitude behind the electrified fences of ghettos and concentration camps a creative and disciplined group of *olim* which . . . has to prove itself worthy of the right to speak on behalf of the forsaken Jews of Europe and to represent it midst the ingathering of the surviving remnants of this great tribe in the hills and valleys of its own land.[41]

Thus, Valsonok became a strong advocate of the cause of unity that was central to the platform of the Zionist Union. He rejected any lingering trace of Marxism by arguing that both religious and class differences counted for nothing after the destruction of European Jewry – for better and for worse they shared a community of fate which implied unity, both within and without. Internal unity was crucial for a people facing a critical moment in its history bereft of its human hinterland. From this perspective the Central Committee in Munich which had such a vital role to play left much to be desired. Instead of a resourceful and intrepid leadership, *She'erith Hapleitah* found itself burdened by "a fawning, philanthropic and flawed group of party hacks, that concealed their political nakedness with the fig-leaf of courageous resolutions for their own consumption to the accompaniment of complacent self-praise."[42]

Because Valsonok was realistic about the ability of the survivors to influence public opinion, he viewed the weakness of the *ZK* as a severe handicap when it came to talking to the outside world. The Allies, from their point of view, did not want to dwell on matters Jewish for fear that some dubious and highly compromising wartime decisions would come to light. In the Western democracies, furthermore, Jews were seen, at least formally, as a faith community and thus relating to them as a people apart would be to play into the hands of their detractors. Ironically, those who had defeated antisemitism from without were loathe to tackle it from within. *She'erith Hapleitah* was duty-bound to break this conspiracy of silence for in its battle for international support "Our strength consists solely in the moral validity of our claim upon the world, a claim grounded on the millions of victims of a folk that was sacrificed for the world in its fight for freedom and equality."[43] Despite his sober realism Valsonok remained convinced that just causes were intrinsically compelling and he was persuaded that he could discern the first signs of a pro-Jewish turn in both the American and British press. This was the time to bring the tragedy of European Jewry to the attention of the world, to insist on its responsibility for seeing that justice be done, which meant opening

---

[41] Ibid.   [42] Velvele Tamarkin, "Zieberstrasse 3 . . .," *LLT*, no. 8 (2.12.1945): 4.
[43] Rudolf Valsonok, "Unzer koakh" (Our strength), *LLT*, no. 4 (4.11.1945): 1.

the gates of Palestine to the victims of Nazism and finally allowing the Jewish people to live in dignified security. Valsonok, who concurred with Ben-Gurion's assessment that She'erith Hapleitah would have a pivotal role to play in the struggle for Jewish statehood, believed that mounting a campaign of unremitting pressure could be of great consequence.[44] Above all, he was persuaded that the militant Zionism of the survivors was as widely assented to as it was profound and truly represented "a readiness and determination to shoulder the responsibility at this critical juncture, to show the world the resolute will of the remnant of European Jewry [to fight] for a viable, independent national existence in accordance with what rightfully belonged to the Jewish people as proclaimed in the just demands of the Palestinian Yishuv."[45]

In summation it is possible to challenge the claim that it was the destruction of European Jewry that brought about the radical change in Valsonok's political commitments. As we have seen, one could easily string together a litany of failures that punctuated his public life between the two world wars. After liberation, in addition, he stuck to his guns and continued to believe that the Jews could find their place midst the peoples of Eastern Europe. According to this reading of the events, it was the renewed persecution of Jews in post-war Poland that finally broke the camel's back. Indeed, the difficulties that Valsonok encountered in the Polish Army and later in minority politics in Lithuania helped to shape his move to Zionism, but only in retrospect. Prior to the European Jewish tragedy each instance of antisemitism could be explained away as local and limited, a leftover of the past that would fade with the coming of a new day. This appears to be the way Valsonok saw things and it certainly accounts for his leftist proclivities in both the Kovno Ghetto and Kaufering and his public encouragement of repatriation on liberation.

With the disturbing reports that filtered in from Poland Valsonok had finally to come to terms with what he already knew in his heart of hearts – that the catastrophic scope of the tragedy and the depth of the failure could no longer be explained away. Germany with its high culture, Christianity, the nations of Europe and Western civilization, the dream of the Jews finding their place in a world of social justice, had all failed beyond repair. The vast killing had exposed the hidden roots of the fatal tension between Jewish uniqueness and European culture and demanded a ruthlessly honest reckoning. In taking this upon himself Valsonok emerges as a man of integrity who did not balk at reexamining his dearest beliefs

[44] For one example among many see the report in the *LLT*, no. 3 (28.10.1945): 2.
[45] Rudolf Valsonok, "Unzer entfer" (Our answer), *LLT*, no. 3 (28.10.1945): 1.

and recasting his most profound political loyalties. Clearly this was in no way a mechanical exercise of simply embracing what was once spurned and negating what was once affirmed. The process of revision was far more complex and entailed dealing with a series of tensions which he either could not or would not resolve.

On the one hand, Valsonok was unsparing in his cutting critique of European culture but, on the other, sought to prevent the Jewish people from closing in on itself and viewed Jewish statehood as a way of reshaping relations with the rest of the world. He had come to recognize the deep structure of Jewish singularity while drawing attention to the shared background of mass destruction in the twentieth century. He viewed the destruction of European Jewry as *sui generis* but insistently warned against retreating from critical reason into a world of mystical obscurantism. Valsonok learned to his sorrow that justice without power is fatally vulnerable and, at the same time, continued to embrace the idealism of prophetic morality. Despite the fact that what has come to be called the Holocaust left his previous world in a shambles, he found the vitality and strength to face up to the bitter reality and to seek out a worthy way for his people to reconstitute itself. In the wake of the privations of the ghetto, the exposure of deportation and the extremities of concentration camp life, his personal role in this process of rebuilding was cut short by a fatal illness. Rudolf Valsonok died on 2 January 1946 and was laid to rest in the Jewish cemetery of Munich.

Valsonok's closest collaborator on the *Landsberger Lager Tsaytung* was Dr. Samuel Gringauz. Gringauz was born at the turn of the century in Tilsit in Eastern Prussia and studied economics, philosophy and law at some of the better known institutions of higher education in Germany, Switzerland, Russia, Italy and France. On completion of his studies he served as scientific assistant in the Institute of Social Sciences in Heidelberg and became active in the German labor movement. In 1933 he left his post and until the outbreak of war served as a judge in the regional appellate court in Memel. He was elected to serve on the Council of the local Jewish community and it was here that he first became acquainted with Rudolf Valsonok and like him eventually found himself in the Kovno Ghetto. For a period he headed the Labor Department of the *Ältestenrat* and was among those deported to Dachau in August 1944. In Kaufering he was active in the Zionist underground, was liberated at the end of April 1945 with the group that found itself near the village of Schwabhausen and a little later moved to the DP camp that was beginning to form in Landsberg.

Gringauz participated in the Liberation Concert in St. Ottilien on 27 May and was one of the signatories of the survivors' appeal to the

World Jewish Congress a few days later.[46] These were his first steps towards the impressive role he was to play in the leadership of *She'erith Hapleitah*. Gringauz was elected three times as head of the Jewish Committee of Landsberg and twice as President of the Council of the Liberated Jews in Bavaria. In October 1947 he emigrated to America, continued his publishing career and worked for the United Restitution Organization.

Gringauz was a man of many parts but his work for the *LLT* was closest to his heart: "Of all my experiences in the two years after liberation, my work for the Landsberg paper was the deepest and the brightest. And if public service is made up of light and shadow, usually more shadow than light, the work for the paper was all light."[47] Gringauz's writing in terms of both content and style bears the clear impress of his biography. Any subject he dealt with was analyzed against a backdrop of broad human concern and on a high level of abstraction. His presentation was usually marked by objectivity and balance but his writing was clearly engaged and sought to influence and direct public opinion. This also accounts for the strongly didactic tone of his work and his constant effort, sometimes forced, to resolve his argument into a number of clearly formulated theses that would help his readers make sense of the bewildering reality in which they found themselves.

As part of the underground activity in Kaufering Gringauz presented his views, published at the time in *Nitzotz*, on "The new Jewish nationalism."[48] In his scheme of things four key movements had determined the inner course of Jewish history in the nineteenth century: "Traditionalism, liberal assimilationism, modern nationalism and Jewish socialism."[49] Except for the traditionalist option none of these movements "flowed from an internal Jewish development. They were all bound up with European-wide currents and their impact on the Jewish spirit." This argument was central to Gringauz's outlook: contemporary Jewish life could not be understood cut off from its general context and, therefore, in thinking about the future one had to resist the tendency to dismiss the outside world in order to seek solace in the narrow confines of the Jewish experience. In the wake of the ghastly suffering they had all gone through

[46] Dr. Z. Grinberg, Bericht an den Juedischen Weltkongress (31.5.1945), YIVO/DPG 21.
[47] Shmuel Gringauz, "Shalom Hermanovitz: tsu der aliyah fun unzer shef director" (Shalom Hermanovitz: marking the aliyah of our chief editor), *Yiddishe Tsaytung*, the new name of the *Landsberger Lager Tsaytung*, no. 117 (49) (4.7.1947): 3.
[48] Shamgar (S. Gringauz), "Ha-leumiut ha-yehudit hachadasha" (The new Jewish nationalism), *Nitzotz*, no. 5 (40) (Purim 4705 – February 1945): 6–8; for a description of the conditions under which the lecture was given and its translation into Yiddish see Dr. Shmuel Gringauz, "Der moderner yiddisher natsionalizm" (Modern Jewish nationalism), *LLT*, no. 5 (11.11.1945): 4.
[49] Shamgar (Gringauz), "Ha-leumiut ha-yehudit ha-chadasha": 6.

and the many setbacks they had suffered since liberation this was no mean task. Gringauz himself vacillated in this regard and there were times when he wondered if Western civilization would survive the blows it had sustained during the war. In time, however, he sought to regain his equilibrium and to return to a nuanced and realistic appraisal of the Jewish future.

What Gringauz hoped for in the wake of the war was a new and worthier humanistic culture that would help "overcome the clash between nationalism and socialism."[50] In his mind's eye he envisaged a synthesis between national freedom, social justice and a respect for individual rights that would be based on the recoil from the horrors of National Socialism and the wartime spirit of cooperation that seemed to characterize relations between the Allies. In short, the vision presented by Gringauz in Kaufering was of a new world order based on an ideal mix of American freedom and Soviet equality. In this context the Jewish people had to reorder its priorities and move its fight for individual rights to a concerted effort on behalf of both national equality and international recognition, with the Zionist movement taking the lead. When this underground piece was republished in Yiddish in November 1945 Gringauz felt it necessary to qualify his earlier views as "too optimistic" but at the same time continued to hold that the context, orientation and hurdles accompanying the achievement of Jewish national aspirations remained essentially the same.[51]

Gringauz accounted for the lack of realism in his earlier prognosis as a function of survivor utopianism on the eve of liberation. The tiny remnant that remained alive after years of murder and torture "had but one feeling in their bloodied hearts ... 'liberation.' Liberation became a heavenly dream, the embodiment of an ideal situation."[52] The reality they met when finally set free, however, was far from what they had expected and they were soon forced to face up to some harsh facts: the Jewish people had not moved heaven and earth to bring them comfort and help; the Allies refused to recognize the Jewish people as a partner to the war effort with all that meant in both Europe and the Middle East; it also had become apparent that the survivors themselves had been deeply scarred by their years of enslavement and loss and that their rehabilitation would be longer and more complex than had been expected.[53] A further victim of this awakening to reality was their yearning for a world of truth, justice and national dignity that had been supplanted by a seeming return to "the old world as it had been before the war with all of its deficiencies, shackles,

---

[50] Ibid: 8.   [51] Gringauz, "Der moderner yiddisher natsionalizm."
[52] Gringauz, "Khamisho ani yodea."   [53] Ibid.

outrages and conflicts, with its old respect for might and its inattention to right."[54]

This general sense of let down became more extreme after the decision of the Labour Government in November 1945 to persist in the White Paper policy. Gringauz viewed this as a nefarious betrayal of both social democracy and the whole purpose of the war[55] which had not been waged for territorial gain or economic gain but in order to repulse "the barbarism that trampled underfoot all the principles of humanity and morality."[56] Averting one's gaze from the war's primary victim, cordoning off Palestine and asking the survivors to reintegrate into European life were not exclusively Jewish concerns. The opposite was true: this was the critical test of an entire culture because "The fate of the Jews embodied the fate of civilization."[57] If the world paid an horrendous price to be rid of a regime that based itself on hatred of the Jews then neglecting the welfare of the survivors or worse indicated "a deep moral disease."[58] A culture that openly belittled all it held dear was a culture that would lose its credibility and ability to call forth dedication. The continued torture of the Jews, prophesied Gringauz, would be the undoing of an entire civilization.[59] It would not happen all at once but would be slow and cumulative, the sinking in of a sense of failure that would end in the erosion of the fundamental belief system at the heart of any human society.

When he set about summing up the historical significance of 1945, Gringauz did not hide his bitter disappointment – instead of constructive rapprochement the great powers had redivided the world into spheres of influence, the United Nations had not succeeded in moving beyond what had been achieved by the League of Nations while the atomic bomb cast its deathly pall near and wide. The outlook at the beginning of 1946 was grim for it threatened to become the year in which Western civilization would begin to unravel and a unique opportunity for profound historical change would have been lost.[60] At the same time the people of *She'erith Hapleitah* began to grasp that for many in Europe they continued to be an undesirable nuisance and that few genuinely regretted the annihilation of an entire people. At the heart of this huge failure, furthermore, stood Germany which for so many Jews, especially in Eastern Europe, had historically represented the great promise of Western progress. In his

---

[54] Ibid.
[55] Dr. Shmuel Gringauz, "Finfakhike begido" (The fivefold betrayal), *LLT*, no. 7 (11.1945): 3.
[56] Ibid.   [57] Ibid.   [58] Ibid.   [59] Ibid.
[60] Dr. Shmuel Gringauz, "1945 in der welt-geshikhte" (1945 in world history), *LLT*, no. 12 (13.12.1945): 3.

first public lecture in Landsberg Gringauz gave passionate expression to this mood of revulsion and radical perplexity:

in the hearts of Jews this question will never cease to be asked – how was it possible? How was it possible after two thousand years of Occidental and Christian culture, after Michelangelo, and Leonardo da Vinci, after Molière and Victor Hugo, after William Shakespeare and Lord Byron, after Alexander von Humboldt and Immanuel Kant? How was it possible that professors and writers, priests and philosophers, artists and judges – how was it possible that almost the entire intellectual elite of Germany rapturously cheered on the blood-drunk murderers?[61]

Towards the middle of 1946 one can detect a definite shift in his position, an attempt to achieve a more balanced perspective marked by a retreat from sweeping judgments, dire prophecies and a moralistic view of international politics. It is not clear what motivated this move to moderate realism and, occasionally, cautious optimism. It was certainly connected to the perspective that comes with the passing of time and, we may surmise, the need for a leader to think more concretely about the future and to offer hope when spirits were low and tempers quick to flare. In relating to this on the eve of the first anniversary of liberation Gringauz noted that: "Many of us over this last year have lost our perspective on what is happening and have been brought to [the verge of] psychological aberration."[62] The source of this distortion was to be found in the hunger of concentration camp survivors for a world of saintliness and idealism[63] which brought them to liberation with a series of false hopes: they looked forward to a new day of "mercy and justice," they assumed that the world of Nazism would be totally obliterated and, in a way, they fell victim to the Nazi claim that the war was, in essence, a Jewish war and thus "We convinced ourselves that those conducting this ghastly and fateful war were doing so either for us or because of us."[64]

After liberation it became abundantly clear that these expectations were hopelessly out of touch with reality for the Hitlerite poison had not lost its potency and the Allies had gone to war, first and foremost, in service of their own interests. That led the survivors to the bitter and hurtful understanding that their martyrdom and heroism were largely an internal matter and that their role in the war, as far as others were concerned, did not amount to much. Gringauz who believed that this mood of angry

---

[61] The article is quoted in Gringauz, "Jewish Destiny as the DP's See It": 505.

[62] Dr. Shmuel Gringauz, "Das Kulturverbrechen am Judentum: Ansprache gehalten am Tage der Opfer des Faschismus in Stadttheater von Landsberg," *LTT*, no. 10 (22) (15.3.1946): 7.

[63] Dr. Shmuel Gringauz, "Tsum yortag fun nitsakhon" (The anniversary of victory), *LLT*, no. 16 (28) (10.5.1946): 3.

[64] Ibid.

despair could be harmful to the well being of *She'erith Hapleitah* worked hard to encourage a more balanced view of the Allied victory and to restore "a fair assessment of the situation and the required psychological balance."[65]

According to Gringauz, the Second World War, at its heart, was an attack by all the forces of darkness against the world of human freedom and progress which carried the stamp of the French and Russian Revolutions. As such, it was equally an attack on the emancipationist forces that had sought to liberate the Jews from the degradation of ghetto life. Because of the dramatic change for the better in their situation, Jews were perceived as the chief beneficiaries of these revolutionary movements and, in consequence, "all the anti-freedom movements are always more or less anti-Jewish and for this reason the counter-revolution turned anti-Semitic."[66] Initially this approach largely characterized conservative groups but after the First World War right-wing movements underwent a process of radicalization and began to seek mass support in a style that had, until then, remained a preserve of the left. This process that began in fascist Italy climaxed in the Nazi rise to power in Germany. One should not forget, warned Gringauz, the remarkable successes of fascist regimes in the inter-war years and Hitler's stunning achievements on all fronts until 1941. The victory of the Allies should not be taken lightly for everything could have ended very differently and then

Before long the world would have turned into a spiritual desert caught in the claws of the SS criminals! If not for what happened – the entire earth would be covered by a network of concentration camps . . . and if things had not turned out as they did – then throughout the world, including Palestine, not a single, solitary Jew would have survived.[67]

The cardinal values that had protected civilization for 2,000 years faced a real danger of extinction and therefore, despite their bitter sense of disappointment, it was imperative that the survivors see things in their correct historical perspective and come to understand the Jewish and universal significance of the Allied victory. They, like everyone else in the free world, should bow their heads before the millions who gave their lives in order to make this possible.

This move to moderation also became evident in Gringauz's shift to a more pragmatic interpretation of the international scene, including the very sensitive issue of British policies in the Middle East. It was wrong to argue that the English people hated Jews or that the Labour party had turned antisemitic. British policies in Palestine had to be seen, in the first place, as a function of the imperial crisis brought about by the

[65] Ibid.   [66] Ibid.   [67] Ibid.

Second World War. Britain emerged from the war with an empty treasury, huge debts, economic difficulties and a promise to leave India by 1948. Her great fear was that the vacuum that would inevitably be created by the retreat from empire would be rapidly filled by the Soviet Union and thus to take a pro-Zionist stand would be to push the Arabs into the waiting arms of Russia. *She'erith Hapleitah* should take careful note of underlying historical realities and, thus, instead of premature despair, given the growing vulnerability of the British position, they should focus their energies on the struggle for Jewish statehood driven by their history, suffering and will to be free.[68]

The angry condemnation of Western culture that Gringauz had expressed so powerfully also underwent a process of reformulation. The *cri de cœur* to depart from Europe forthwith remained in place but the overwhelming abhorrence of the earlier period was now placed in a broader historical context and given a more constructive turn. The point of departure for this revised approach stemmed from the realization that the European period in Jewish history had come to an end and, given the continued isolation of Soviet Jewry, the Jewish future would focus on two new centers – the United States of America and Jewish Palestine. The survivors of European Jewry would carry their glorious heritage to these new centers where it would become part of the building materials out of which the Jewish future would be shaped. And this is where a new theme and tone can be heard:

the renunciation of Europe in no way signifies for us the renunciation of European culture. Quite the contrary. Our resolve to quit Europe is based precisely on the conviction that Europe itself has betrayed the legacy of European culture, and that European culture must be carried forward outside of Europe. We have been too much part of European culture to abandon it now. As we once expressed it: "We leave Europe because Europe has injured us in our very quality as Europeans."[69]

The Jewish presence in Europe from the Hellenistic period to the twentieth century led to a long and profound cultural exchange between the two. The tension between Jewish culture and Western civilization should not be seen, therefore, as a confrontation between two separate entities; it was better described as an internal clash played out in shared context. The exodus from Europe aimed to sever geographic ties but not the tradition and values that had been built in concert. As Gringauz expressed it in the summer of 1946:

---

[68] Dr. Shmuel Gringauz, "Dos yiddishe problem oyfn plonter veg fun der impiryaler dekadenz" (The Jewish problem in the muddle of imperial decadence), *Bafrayung*, no. 11 (6.6.1946): 3.
[69] Gringauz, "Jewish Destiny as the DP's See It": 505.

We, who are the victims of this civilization, have been called upon to discover the positive basis on which we can unite with it. We have a bill of indictment to prefer against this civilization. At the same time we know that we are part of it and must therefore bear a responsibility for it. We cannot and will not turn away from it. Our experience must serve to redirect the Jewish people. Our tragedy must become part of a new humanism.[70]

The realization of the "new humanism" was, as we shall see, integral to Gringauz's vision of Zionism. What needs to be stressed at this juncture is that despite these shifts in his relationship to European civilization one element remained constant and firm – his profound conviction that antisemitism was deeply embedded in European culture, that the destruction of the European Jews had not changed anything and that it continued to pose a threat to the Jewish people. *She'erith Hapleitah*, claimed Gringauz, had quite understandably developed a special, at times not altogether healthy, sensitivity to antisemitism. They had personally experienced how groups that were in every sense marginal had become the dynamic center of an implacable machine of destruction and now felt it their duty to warn communities untouched by murderous hatred of the possible dangers they faced. Over the generations, it was true, antisemitism doffed one garb and donned another but at its core it was constant in its determination to end Jewish existence.[71] The deep, historical embeddedness of antisemitism was reflected in the fact that the very approximation of the Jews to European culture and their strong desire to be integrated into it called forth a fierce reaction: "Assimilation was the prime cause, the chief author of modern antisemitism. Nothing helped, not patriotism and neither contributions nor sacrifices. As assimilation advanced apace so the Jewish question became increasingly acute."[72] The radical antisemites of the late nineteenth century came primarily from those social classes that were casualties of modernization and had come to view the Jews as the initiators of these unwanted changes and those that benefited most from them. Because of this identification of the Jewish people with revolutionary change "the counter-revolution became antisemitic."[73] After the First World War, as previously indicated, what had been the preserve of conservatives and monarchists was taken over and radicalized

[70] Dr. Shmuel Gringauz, "Über die Aufgaben der europaischen Judenreste", *Jüdische Rundschau*, vol. 1, no. 6 (July 1946): 5.

[71] Dr. Shmuel Gringauz, " 'Beilis protses' un freilecher purim in deggendorf" (The Beilis trial and a festive Purim in Deggendorf), *YT*, no. 21 (89) (14.2.1947): 3.

[72] Dr. Shmuel Gringauz, "Herzl: di novi fun auschwitz, der moshe rabeinu fun 20-tn yorhundert, der shefer fun der yiddisher natsionale politik, der legendarer melekh yeshurun" (Herzl: the prophet of Auschwitz, our twentieth-century Moses, the author of Jewish national politics, the legendary king of Israel), *YT*, no. 15 (119) (11.7.1947): 3.

[73] Gringauz, "Tsum yortag fun nitsakhon."

by fascist movements in search of mass support. As this turned into an organized campaign against the progressive world Nazi Germany took the lead "and transformed Jew-hatred into a religion . . . The sciences and arts, the radio and press, schools and the courts, the diplomatic service and bureaucracy – all of these were mobilized in a murderous campaign of hatred and deception with the single purpose of making it impossible for Jews to live among others."[74]

The upshot was that there was no way of comparing, either quantitatively or qualitatively, the fate of the Jews during the war with that of other peoples who had also sustained heavy losses. Their suffering was painful and tragic but, at the end of the day, they were severely wounded rather than destroyed. The uniqueness of the Jewish situation emerged from the fact that the European nations "were able, following the downfall of fascism, to more or less heal and restore their national and political existence. There was but one, single people in the countries under German rule that was . . . not just injured by German fascism but done to death without the possibility of recovery or reconstituting its existence and those were the Jews."[75] This was not a fortuitous outcome but the direct result of a differential Nazi intention with respect to their various enemies. The Nazis did not call to slaughter the French, neither did they sing about massacring the Poles nor incite an entire nation to wipe out the Norwegians. Only the Jews were the target of a sustained campaign of hatred that sowed the seeds of an hostility that would not be easily uprooted. The domestic opponents of Nazism had also suffered a different fate: labor leaders were tortured and put to death but the working class remained, a number of outspoken religious leaders were martyred but their churches remained intact. When it came to the Jewish people, however, the sentence handed down was of: "Total destruction, total dispossession and total condemnation. In the case of a handful of Jews flight, false papers or chance circumstances kept them alive but the Jewish people as a whole was done to death."[76]

According to Gringauz's estimate, of the roughly 8,250,000 Jews who were under Nazi occupation about 6,250,000, that is 75 percent, were murdered. By comparison, of the approximately 380 million people living in the same area something like 6,000,000, that is 1.5 percent, met the same fate. This meant that Jewish losses were fifty times larger than those suffered by non-Jewish civilians.[77] These colossal losses of life and

---

[74] Dr. Shmuel Gringauz, "Pesakh – 5706" (Passover – 1946), *LLT*, no. 13 (25) (19.4.1946): 19.

[75] Gringauz, "Das Kulturverbrechen": 7.   [76] Ibid.

[77] In all likelihood Gringauz took his figures from the material prepared by the World Jewish Congress and the Jewish Agency for the Anglo-American Committee of Inquiry. While

property threw the singular situation of *She'erith Hapleitah* into sharp relief and explained why it was pointless to seek rehabilitation in Europe, especially in view of the fact that while the Nazis had been defeated the poison they had disseminated lingered on.[78] This conclusion was forced upon the survivors by what they felt to be a general indifference to their fate. The Allies were not exerting themselves to track down war criminals implicated in the "Final Solution", Britain was showing her true colors in Palestine while in Europe itself antisemitism had lifted its head once again and in the East often proved to be murderous. In the light of the above Gringauz concluded that the devastation of war and mass death had engendered "a new social disease – the new antisemitism."[79] At first he believed it was a transitory phenomenon but in time it began to appear as something that would require close monitoring. It obviously bore a strong resemblance to its predecessors but the key element that set it apart was its psychological underpinning.[80] It had its root cause in the centrality of the Jewish ingredient in both Nazi policy and propaganda. Even prior to the Nazi rise to power the Jewish question had been prominent in international affairs and it had become customary for many to identify the Jews with the undesirable and problematic. With the defeat of the Nazis not only did this tendency not dissipate – in point of fact it grew stronger.

The peoples of Europe felt compelled to explain away both their indifference to the fate of the Jews and their active collaboration in their dispossession and persecution. Now that the crimes of the Nazis had been brought into full view and had been universally condemned it was necessary to find fault with the Jews and so justify their own sins of omission and commission. Whether this was done consciously or unconsciously mattered little for either way post-war European antisemitism continued to be remarkably influential. If the need for self-vindication was powerful in Europe generally, how much more so was this the case in Germany. Gringauz had no doubt that the German people was fully aware of its culpability: how willingly and easily the denial of Jewish rights, the expropriation of their property, their exclusion from German society and

---

the absolute numbers are not always completely accurate the order of the estimates are not far from what later research has established. In this regard see Lucy S. Dawidowicz, "Thinking about the Six Million: Facts, Figures, Perspectives," in *The Holocaust and the Historians* (Cambridge, Mass., 1981): 4–21.

[78] Dr. Shmuel Gringauz, "Undzer geshterter yom tov" (Our spoiled [disrupted] holiday), *LLT*, no. 14 (26) (26.4.1946): 3.

[79] Dr. Shmuel Gringauz "Di psikhologishe wurtslen fun neo-antisemitizm: naye vintn alte mitln" (The psychological roots of neo-antisemitism: new winds old means), *YT*, no. 38 (106) (23.5.1947): 5.

[80] Ibid.

deportation to the East had been accepted and supported in the hope that victory would retroactively legalize all.[81] While it was true that thinkers, artists and men of faith earnestly discussed the collective guilt of a people who did not hear, see or know,

> In their hearts they knew the truth and sought to protect their souls by fabricating an alibi for their people ... and finding that they had no arguments in defence of the murderer, they defended themselves by turning against the victim telling themselves and the occupation forces that they were crooked, thieves, underhand, black-marketeers and filthy – in one word the kind of person one should be rid off.[82]

This was the psychological wellspring of the new antisemitism being quietly but effectively diffused through the length and breadth of Occupied Germany. Moreover, the smarting defeat of Germany, the destruction of its cities and economy and, most particularly, the need to resettle more than 10 million ethnic Germans further sharpened the hatred of the Jewish survivors who were perceived as foreign, defiant and pampered.

Sadly enough, there was not one European government or significant political movement ready to pick up the cudgels and to take on the good fight for the Jewish people and against antisemitism. Thus, he concluded, if Europe was not able to take the initiative in the face of both what had happened to the Jews and the horrendous price its own peoples had to pay, there was little hope that this would happen sometime in the future. The present was grim, the outlook gloomy and the conclusion but one:

> Life in the Diaspora, for the Jewish DPs is synonymous with the danger of recurrence. No sociological argument can obliterate from their minds what experience has stamped on it. For they have seen not only Germany. Eastern Europe and Central Europe are part of their experience. And they have seen the countries of Western Europe ... and they had watched these different nations *after* the end of the war, especially those who found their number of surviving Jews too high, and also those who met the influx of Jews with cold antipathy. And they have seen the growth of a new anti-Semitism in Germany, in Europe, and among the occupation troops.
>
> The Sherit Hapleita therefore undertakes the prophetic mission of warning the Jews of the unaffected countries. Neither equality of rights, not a constitution, nor patriotism is security against persecution ... One cannot escape one's Jewishness – either by assimilation, baptism or mixed marriage ... And they say to the Jews of the countries untouched by the catastrophe: It can happen again. And therefore we demand of you to build up Palestine not only for us, but as an ultimate place of refuge in general (*ir miklat*).[83]

Through the centuries the possibility of migration had provided the critical means of evading danger. In a world of nation states wracked by

[81] Ibid.   [82] Ibid.   [83] Gringauz, "Jewish Destiny as the DP's See It": 503–504.

economic crises the opportunities for geographic mobility had been reduced to a minimum and thus, in the face of the Nazi threat, the Jewish
people tragically found itself trapped in Europe. Now, in the aftermath
of the catastrophic war years, the dangers of immobility persisted and
Gringauz, sensing that the survival of his people hung by a slender thread,
embraced the Zionist endeavor as a solution to the fateful problems of
the present and as the best promise of a vibrant future.[84] The Nazi onslaught had dealt a death blow to what for centuries had served as both
the demographic hinterland of the Jewish people and the seedbed of its
spiritual creativity. The Jews of Europe had been destroyed and with them
a vast array of cultural and religious institutions informed in the West by
Jewish "intellectualism" and in the East by Hasidism that stood at the
very core of "Jewish folk-feeling."[85] With the obliteration of the *shtetl*
(traditional small town communities) the Nazis choked the wellspring of
all European Jewish culture and with it the linguistic dualism that gave this
culture its essential flavor. Most of the Yiddish-speakers in the world had
been killed, *She'erith Hapleitah* as a community in transit would not reach
the stage of cultural production, the Yishuv was shaping a new Hebrew
culture and Yiddish in America could not be expected to fare well for it
had always depended on new waves of immigration from Europe. As had
been the case in Germany in the previous century, so in the largest Jewish
community in the world "The Yiddish language will be, in precisely the
same way, condemned to death."[86] Gringauz also predicted a profound
religious crisis because he feared that *Yiddishkeit*, the spirit of Jewishness
that had shaped the life of East European Jewry, was not something that
could be moved and transplanted elsewhere. All of these represented a
serious threat to Jewish continuity.

   Within this disturbing inventory of cultural resources Grinhauz was
able to identify two countervailing forces: the budding primacy of the
Yishuv and "the intensification of a general Jewish national awareness
as a result of what happened these last six years and the real sense of a
Jewish interdependence of fate."[87] One of the critical questions for the
Jewish future was how these trends would influence American Jewry. At
first blush it did not seem that they would be adequate to the heavy responsibility that had fallen on them. Gringauz viewed the melting pot
as doing its work only too well: the overall involvement in things Jewish
was dropping, Yiddish was fading, intermarriage growing and with the

---

[84] Dr. Shmuel Gringauz, "Di goraldike vendung" (The fateful turning-point), *LLT*, no. 2
   (14) (18.1.1946): 7.
[85] Dr. Shmuel Gringauz, "Di tsukunft fun der yiddisher kultur" (The future of Jewish
   culture), *LLT*, no. 19 (31) (4.6.1946): 6–7.
[86] Ibid.   [87] Ibid.

move of many to large urban centers this erosion of their historical identity could only be hastened.[88] On the other hand the Jewish catastrophe in Europe, the plight of *She'erith Hapleitah* and the fight for Jewish independence in Palestine had together generated a powerful and widely shared sense of Jewish togetherness and solidarity. These forces would not bring about immediate change but they could create a new climate that would slowly percolate down into personal attitudes and community organization. Gringauz noted the attack on the ideal of the melting pot, affirmed its rejection of uniformity (which for him carried totalitarian overtones) and welcomed the competing ideal of cultural pluralism that could open the way to a Jewish renaissance. He took heart from the fact that many on the margins of Jewish life had been drawn into the battle to open the doors of Palestine to free immigration, that organizations like the American Jewish Committee and Jewish Labor Committee had shifted from a consistent anti-Zionist position to a more moderate non-Zionism that included extending aid to the Yishuv politically, supporting its efforts to take in *She'erith Hapleitah* and aligning itself with the assertive Zionist line of the American Jewish Conference, the most representative body in American Jewry. This coming forward to play an active role in determining the Jewish future represented a highly significant departure in American Jewish life, the move from being the object of American history to taking a leading role in attempting to shape the fate of its own people.[89]

Gringauz, however, warned against unrealistic expectations. American Jewry for profound structural reasons would not be able to supplant the Jews of Eastern Europe. These communities had drawn their sustenance from a separate and organic Jewish existence. In America, by comparison, Jewish life was largely shaped in shared frameworks and its singularity was to be found more in awareness than substance. If it is true, suggested Gringauz, that "what is specifically Jewish in America is expressed more in intellectual content than in patterns of living"[90] then it would be reasonable to expect that it would be able to fill the vacuum created by the destruction of the Jews of Central and Western Europe while only Palestinian Jewry might, in the long run, be able to provide a partial answer to the deafening absence of East European Jewry. If this was to be the shape of things to come, the fate of the Jewish people would be largely shaped by the ties that would come to bind these two communities together.

---

[88] Dr. Shmuel Gringauz, "Dos amerikaner yidntum" (American Jewry), *YT*, no. 54 (66) (20.12.1946): 3.

[89] Gringauz, "Di goraldike vendung": 7.

[90] Gringauz, "Jewish Destiny as the DP's See It": 508.

For the present it was *She'erith Hapleitah* that had created an initial platform for cooperation as the living embodiment of Jewish homelessness,
a prominent argument in international politics, the promise of the future
for the Yishuv and the key factor in the effective mobilization of Diaspora
Jewry for the upbuilding of Palestine. All this placed a heavy burden of
public responsibility on the shoulders of *She'erith Hapleitah* and gave
cause for concern for he was well aware that there was "a deep discrep-
ancy... between our human strengths and our tragic-fateful charge."[91]
This was not simply a function of objectively degrading conditions – it
went *tifer* – deeper. The survivors, said Gringauz on many occasions,
survived by virtue of a process of negative selection.[92] When they were
overtaken by the murderous reality of mass destruction, the good, the
worthy and the innocent went under first and those who survived then
underwent a further series of experiences that could not but mark them
for life:

Year in and year out we lived in a situation of moral crippling... all principles of
basic decency, of duty and discipline were stamped out by the naked struggle for
physical survival, by staying alive at the expense of those closest to us, by a life
based on theft, bribery... vile deeds and a total lack of concern for others.[93]

They had hoped and believed that after the liberation the scars of the
past would disappear and they would be able to return to a life of integrity,
honest work and mutual trust. "Instead, we found that the black devil
had insinuated himself deep into our souls; that the process of inner
purification and moral recovery was both difficult and slow."[94] Thus, the
attempt to deal with this complex reality via productive work, education,
vocational and agricultural training, this urgent and "colossal task" was
the decisive testing ground of the survivors. There was no guarantee of
success but the dead who served as a goad to their conscience and their
renewed commitment to a life of dignity would not allow them to desist.[95]
From the outset this dedication to moral rehabilitation had been on the
agenda of *She'erith Hapleitah* without, however, enjoying high priority. In
the first months of liberation all their efforts were devoted to a stubborn
fight for basic living conditions; at the beginning of 1946 they focused

---

[91] Dr. Shmuel Gringauz, "In tsaykhn fun martirertum hofnung un arbet" (Under the sign
of martyrdom hope and work), *LLT*, no. 2 (14) (18 January 1946): 1.

[92] For example, following the First Congress of *She'erith Hapleitah* Gringauz wrote: "But
people are no longer as people should be and concentration camp people are even less
so for somewhere deep in the soul, a camp-like – *kapo*-like worm insinuates itself." See
"Dos wos der kongres hot nit geton" (That which the Congress did not do), *LLT*, no. 4
(16) (15.2.1946): 2.

[93] Gringauz "Khamisho ani yodea": 4.   [94]Gringauz "In tsaykhn fun martirertum": 1.

[95] Ibid.

on the overriding goals of the political struggle of the Jewish people, a priority that accompanied them until the Anglo-American Committee of Inquiry had come and gone and they impatiently waited for the doors of Palestine to be opened.

The first real shift in the priorities of She'erith Hapleitah began to be felt in the second half of 1946. The fight for free immigration to Palestine remained a cardinal concern for the growing number of DPs impatiently awaiting the first opportunity to leave Germany but the public focus of the campaign had now shifted to Palestine, London, Washington, Cyprus and the embarkation ports of illegal immigration. "We have used up and exhausted all our ammunition," was how Gringauz summed up the situation, "While our position is clear our demonstrations have become clichéd and work no more . . . today we are no more than an argument in the great debate that is raging and even if for us, it is without us."[96] This, then, was an opportune moment to reinforce all of the rehabilitation programs in the various centers of She'erith Hapleitah, especially in view of the morally corrosive effects of a life lived in limbo that offered few opportunities for real work and almost no possibility of making a significant contribution to one's own future. In the light of what the survivors had already been through the prolongation of the enforced stay in the DP camps began to look like "a slow form of genocide . . . exactly the same crime for which people were put on trial by the International Tribunal in Nuremberg."[97] In point of fact, Gringauz had been led by his own experience in running rehabilitation programs to conclude that they were nothing more than palliatives and that only one thing could make a real difference: aliyah and emigration.

Aliyah (going up to settle in the land of Israel), in addition to its intrinsic value and promise of healing would also help to overcome the extreme factionalism which had come to plague and demoralize She'erith Hapleitah. In the name of narrow group interest people were ready to lie and deceive without regard for democratic principle or broader solidarity. A mass aliyah might shake this survivor community out of its lethargy, and, in view of the greatness of the hour, return it to an ethos of unity and sharing.[98] Ironically, observed Gringauz, what finally tilted the scales towards a large-scale exodus had little to do with the legitimate claims of She'erith Hapleitah. On the one hand, the Labour Party, given

---

[96] Dr. Shmuel Gringauz, "Der ruf tsu moralisher konsolidatsia: tsum 2-tn kongres fun di yidn in der amerikaner zone" (The call for moral consolidation: towards the 2nd Congress of the Jews in the American Zone), YT, no. 13 (81) (14.2.1947): 3.

[97] Ibid.

[98] Gringauz, "Dos wos der kongres": 2. Gringauz presented a principled position in favor of unity but there is no denying that these developments eroded his standing as a nonpolitical figure.

its ambitious program of social reform and empty coffers, began to tire of the mounting expenses of ruling Palestine. The foreign ministers of the great powers, on the other, began to discuss the future of *She'erith Hapleitah* "not so as to find a way of ridding us of the Germans but, rather, to find a way of freeing the Germans of us."[99] The German expellees from Eastern Europe needed to be absorbed and Germany put back on its feet given the crucial role it had come to play in the cooling relations between the great powers. Morally, it was not easy to swallow the cold indifference towards the survivors as opposed to the concern for their tormentors but politically, if it opened the way to emigration, it was to be welcomed. Numerous countries began to scout the DP camps in search of immigrants who could serve their economic needs but not many Jewish DPs had the particular skills they were looking for. Thus by mid-1947, reported Gringauz, an increasing number of Jews in Germany, young and old, single and married, affiliated and unaffiliated began to see aliyah as their only real option.[100]

Gringauz hoped that those returning home to Zion would also see themselves as fulfilling a universal mission, bringing the world the message of neo-humanism. The critical underpinning of this response to Nazi inhumanity was Jewish monotheism, "The idea of the value of the individual person"[101] which was the foundation stone of the belief in the sanctity of life, personal freedom and human dignity. In the light of the centrality of this idea in Western civilization, reasoned Gringauz, the source of Nazism was not to be found in the substance of European culture; it resided, instead, in the chasm that opened up between its general moral level and its technological development. The moral development of the West had been slow and by the twentieth century was yet to spread beyond a narrow range of social classes. Technological development in the wake of the industrial revolution, by comparison, had been rapid and in the process liberated many from the protective bonds of tradition and custom. Democratization, therefore, put control into the hands of those who were yet to internalize the habits of moral autonomy. Because of this disparity "the moral underworld and even unabashed criminals were able to win control over the masses and the technical apparatus of society and defile European civilization with blood and shame."[102] This analysis pointed up the convergence of the Jewish ideal of *tikkun*

---

[99] Dr. Shmuel Gringauz, "Pesakh 5707: yetsiat lagern – yetsiat daytshland" (Pesach 1947: exodus from the camps, exodus from Germany), *YT*, no. 26 (94) (4.4.1947): 4.

[100] Ibid.

[101] Dr. Shmuel Gringauz "Di kultur badeitung fun shavuot" (The cultural meaning of Shavuoth [Pentecost]), *YT*, no. 19 (31) (6.4.1946): 18.

[102] Gringauz, "Jewish Destiny as the DP's See It": 506.

olam – mending the world – and the values of humanism embraced by *She'erith Hapleitah*. Gringauz hoped that the Surviving Remnant would embrace

neo-humanism as its cultural ideal – the ideal of the moral and social perfection of humanity, the perfection of the broadest possible mass of the population in its daily activities, which would create a community that would resist the pressure of the instincts as well as the oppression of the state and follow its conscience only.[103]

The trauma of destruction, furthermore, had not appeared to have persuaded many to a return to faith and tradition. The observant among the survivors, according to Gringauz's impression, had brought their commitment from their pre-war lives. He did not find the absence of a religious resurgence, a recoil from man and a turning to God, in any way surprising: when survival depended on blind chance, or the whim of a Nazi murderer or the surrender of one's moral sensibilities, it did not leave much room for faith in either miracles or a compassionate God. The opposite was the case – in the kingdom of death, those who did not compromise themselves, who maintained their humanity and sense of solidarity intact elicited a respect for the man of integrity which almost had "the character of religious awe."[104] Moreover, the survivors had learnt the transient value of property as opposed to the infinite value of true friendship and a helping hand. This was the existential underpinning of their attraction to neo-humanism, their search for a synthesis of social justice and personal freedom.

The testing ground of neo-humanism, however, was less in its formulation than in its realization in life. Gringauz believed that this was only possible in the context of a fully rounded Jewish life such as could be found in Palestine after the war. Only people sure of themselves, living in the freedom of an organic Jewish society and with a rich tradition of cooperation and sharing would make this possible. The most profound response of the Jewish people to its destruction would emerge from the exemplary society that was in the making in the Land of Israel.

In September of 1947 Gringauz emigrated to the United States of America and played an active, professional role in various organizations that took care of reparations and compensation for survivors from West Germany. Despite his strong Zionist convictions, from the very outset Gringauz consistently refused to take on any official position in the Zionist

---

[103] Ibid: 507.   [104] Ibid.

movement.[105] In point of fact, a strange, inexplicable silence envelops his departure – no speeches, no thanks, no good wishes. The only noticeable change is that his name was removed from the editorial board of his great love, the *Landsberger Lager Tsaytung* which had matured into the *Yiddishe Tsaytung*.

[105] Zvi Shiloah, somewhat presumptuously, tells the following "I also had to see to the Chairman of the Zionist Organization. (We are talking about August 1945.) I approached someone who was introduced to me and his name was Gringauz. I was told that within *She'erith Hapleitah* he was the most educated. And, in truth, this was the case. But he was totally a-political and quite uninterested in public life . . . he took no interest in anything except books and his own rehabilitation . . . he turned me down . . . everyone indicated that he was the right person to head the Zionist organization and that were he to accept the position he would wield great influence." Interview, OHD/64(4): 22–23.

9 Destruction and remembrance

The remembrance of what had befallen the Jews of Europe was of urgent concern to *She'erith Hapleitah*. On one level it expressed an elementary sense of family responsibility sharpened by the lonely guilt of surviving, on another it was a conscious attempt to foil the Nazi attempt to cover up their crimes and obliterate the identity of their victims. For some, remembering was essential to learning the lessons of the past, for others it was an attempt to frustrate the inevitable inroads of human forgetfulness. "The history of humanity is rich in horror," stated Samuel Gringauz in early 1946,

And if the annihilation of the Jewish people belongs among the most horrible events of history, still, we know – this too will be forgotten. Grass will grow where inexhaustible suffering and martyrdom were earlier enacted. Where once the mass graves were, children will play their games and the fathers will pursue their occupations. But in the hearts of Jews this question will never cease to be asked – how was it possible?[1]

The first attempts to think comprehensively about the commemoration of the European Jewish catastrophe appeared among the surviving remnant in Germany as the first anniversary of liberation approached. The passage of time, the growing presence of repatriates who had gone through different experiences and the felt need to order commemoration brought about the first formalization of remembrance and mourning. In the first months of freedom the shadow of death was everywhere and innumerable ceremonies marked personal loss and community commemoration. Zalman Grinberg gave voice to this mood at the Liberation Concert in St. Ottilien in May 1945:

Millions of the members of these communities ... have been annihilated. What is the logic of fate to let us then live. We belong into [*sic*] the common graves of those shot in Kharkov, Lublin and Kovno, we belong to the millions

---

[1] Gringauz, "Jewish Destiny as the DP's See It": 505.

gassed and burnt in Auschwitz and Birkenau, we belong to those tormented by milliards of lice, the starvation, the cold ... we are not alive – we are still dead.[2]

Samuel Gringauz reverted to the same theme when, on *Yom Kippur* – the Day of Atonement – he addressed the congregants during the *Yizkor* memorial prayer: "We, who feel ourselves closer to the dead than to the living do not really require a special memorial service. We say *Yizkor* in the morning and in the evening, we say *Yizkor* while awake and also in our dreams ... we do not really require a special memorial service."[3] In this early period the past found diverse forms of public expression: *Landsmanshaften* commemorated their communities,[4] personal testimonies and memoirs were a regular feature of the survivor press, *Undzer Veg* opened its first number with a Memorial Declaration[5] and in many DP camps memorial plaques were put up in places of public assembly.[6] All of the above were but a pale reflection of the traumatic personal memories that, as Dr. Leo Srole summed up his clinical observations, manifested themselves in a series of psychosomatic disorders: disturbed sleep, exaggerated sensitivity, flawed recall, great difficulty in remaining focused, wildly fluctuating moods, excessive sweating, depression and apathy.[7] These disorders, in his opinion, did not indicate mental breakdown; they were to be understood, instead, as neurotic symptoms that were to be expected in the case of people exposed for so long to unprecedented deprivation, torture and loss.

Coping with the past, therefore, was no simple matter: some inured themselves to all feeling[8] and others sought to escape into nihilistic abandon.[9] This, in turn, renders the attempts to make memory serve humanity all the more remarkable. The following was spoken at a memorial meeting in a makeshift camp near Stuttgart not long after liberation.

[2] Speech given by Z. Grinberg, MD Head Doctor of the Hospital for Political Ex-prisoners in Germany at the Liberation Concert.

[3] Dr. Shmuel Gringauz, " 'Zakhor': rede, gehaltn yom kippur, dem 17 september in beyt tfila fun lager landsberg" ('Remember': speech delivered on Yom Kippur, 17 September in the synagogue of the Landsberg camp), *LLT*, no. 1 (8.10.1945): 3.

[4] See for example, Ostry, *After the Holocaust*: 41–44.

[5] "Yizkor" (Prayer for the dead), *Undzer Veg*, no. 1 (12.10.1945): 1; it was reprinted in May 1946 to mark the first anniversary of liberation: see *Undzer Veg*, no. 11 (10.5.1946): 1.

[6] See the description of H. Leivik, *Mit der she'erit hapleitah* (With She'erith Hapleitah) (Toronto, 1947): 7.

[7] Leo Srole to the Anglo-American Commission [*sic*] for Palestine (February 1946), AJDC/DP's Germany 1946.

[8] See for example, Theodore Frankel, "My Friend Paul: One Who Survived," *Commentary*, vol. 23, no. 2 (February 1957): 147–160.

[9] See for example Samuel Pisar, *Of Blood and Hope* (London, 1980): 86–116.

The chairman of the local DP Committee who had lost his wife, children and entire family described how death came in Radom and concluded his speech with the following:

They used ... every brutality to wipe us out physically ... to still forever our hopes and aspirations, our heritage. Those of us who survive are bleeding still ...

There are some among us who say it is too late now for redemption. It is true, it is impossible to bring back our dead. But those of us who remain, those who are the last remnant of our people, must once more have hope ... for the revival of all those moral, ethical and cultural values which we hold so dear, and without which the world would plunge into barbarism ...

We must struggle ... we must strive to rise again. We owe that to the memory of our dearly beloved dead ... who had the same yearnings. We owe it to them to spend our remaining days in creating ... a worthy life once more.[10]

In the first third of 1946 this complex picture of remembering and remembrance began to change. As the days went by the wounds of the past began to heal, albeit superficially, to the accompaniment of feverish activity which changed little but was not without significance: "I mentioned ... that I found our brothers full of vigor and cheerful," reported Dr. Ignacy Schwartzbart,

It seems to me, nevertheless, that in this cheerfulness ... the main element is a hectic desire to deafen the past, the urge not to admit to oneself one's own memories ... because otherwise, if one would constantly look into the abyss which the Deity filled up with the ashes of our brothers, the only way out would be suicide.[11]

But, more prosaically, life did go on and, inevitably, made its own demands. Despite the bitter fate of the Jewish people "The world has not stopped in its tracks and we, therefore, cannot set aside an entire year in order symbolically to mark [our] deep tragedy and national catastrophe."[12] In purely practical terms, furthermore, any attempt publicly to commemorate the destruction of individual communities would lead to a situation where "One would, undoubtedly, come out of one mourning ceremony and go into the next."[13] Thus, as the first anniversary of liberation grew closer, what had become an unbearable round of remembrance together with the pressing need to set an agreed day of

---

[10] Ostry, *After the Holocaust*: 42–43.

[11] Dr. Ignacy Schwartzbart, Report on the Visit to the American Zone in Germany (January 1946), CZA/S25/5232: 5.

[12] Dr. Zalman Grinberg, "14-tn iyar: gedenk tog un bazinungs tog" (14th *Iyar*: a day or remembrance, a day of celebration), *Undzer Veg*, no. 32 (10.5.1946): 2.

[13] Yosef Gar, "14-ter iyar – a vikhtike yid. date" (14th *Iyar* – an important Jewish date), *LLT*, no. 17(29) (17.5.1946): 2.

mourning for those who knew not when their near-ones had perished pushed the leaders of *She'erith Hapleitah* to determine an official day of memorial.[14]

On 5 May 1946 the Central Committee devoted its weekly meeting to setting up a "Unified Day of Remembrance and Liberation."[15] In addition to its regular members, the following also participated: Levi Shalitan, the editor of *Undzer Veg*, Ernst Frank, representing the Palestinian Mission, Leo Schwarz and Sylvia Weinberg on behalf of the JDC together with the representatives of the Cultural Mission of the World Jewish Congress to *She'erith Hapleitah* – the renowned poet H. Leivik, the author Israel Efros and the well-known singer Emma Shaver. This was a first attempt to give commemorative form to the European Jewish catastrophe and a special atmosphere hung over the protracted deliberations: "for the entire year there had never been a session so sad," wrote Levi Shalitan, "People kept silent rather than speak. And when they did speak it was hesitatingly, nervously accompanied by an inner shudder. In order to capture the thoughts of those speaking one had but to look at their faces."[16] The Chairman, Zalman Grinberg, who had initiated the discussion saw the commemoration as bearing a double imprint: "The day should bring together the destruction of the past with the rebuilding of the future. Hurt, pain, suffering and, simultaneously, hope, courage and faith should be the mark of the day."[17] The Surviving Remnant as the living bridge between destruction and rebirth would have a crucial role to play in effecting this fragile fusion – "The profound logic of fate kept us alive as witnesses of the annihilation so that we could give voice to the call for [a life of] security and well being that our brothers gave up with their souls – and to carry it forward to the day of victory."[18] There were those who doubted the authority of the representatives of *She'erith Hapleitah* to lay down a day of remembrance for the Jewish people as a whole and suggested that the decision be handed over to rabbis and Torah scholars. Israel Efros and his colleagues vigorously opposed this position and thought it but natural and right that the survivors who had been directly implicated in the tragedy would be those to decide.[19] The majority of those present

---

[14] See Levi Shalitan, "Ve-ha'alitem et atzmotai mi-zeh..." (And ye shall carry up my bones from hence...), *Undzer Veg*, no. 16 (15.1.1946): 2.

[15] See Protokoll nr. 42 des *ZK* (5.5.1946).

[16] Levi Shalitan, "Fun undzer seder-yom: frayd oder troyer – haynt u-le-dorot" (From our agenda: joy or sorrow – today and for the generations to come), *Undzer Veg*, no. 32 (10.5.1946): 2.

[17] Grinberg, "14-tn iyar": 2.   [18] Ibid.

[19] Israel Efros, "Nesiyah le-machanot yisrael be-germaniyah" (A journey to the Jewish camps in Germany), *Hadoar*, no. 4 (22.11.1946): 94.

agreed with this approach and Grinberg's assessment that in this instance "For the first time *She'erith Hapleitah* had decided to take an active role in shaping Jewish symbolic forms."[20]

The key issue in the discussion focused on the shape of the day, on which elements would dominate: mourning or thanksgiving? Martyrdom or the miracle of survival? Agonizing suffering or inspiring heroism? Some suggested that Purim with its shades of Haman, planned annihilation and deliverance would serve best. Others saw the overwhelming mourning of the Fast of the 9th of Av as more appropriate while yet a third view thought that Passover with its narrative of destruction and redemption was best suited to creating a new day of remembrance and hope. In this debate Leivik took a firm stand: this was no time for celebration or even a pretence of celebration for "Joy lies paralyzed in Jewish hearts and all or our words are saturated with sorrow."[21] A day of remembrance could not but highlight the tragedy of the victims while casting into sharp relief the cruel truth that survivors were seen as a nuisance, the murderers were being courted by the Allies and, to boot, "the unbelievable and scandalous fact that one year after the war tens of thousands of Jews, the direct victims of Hitler ... are stuck in camps on the accursed soil of Germany while tens of thousands continue a nightmarish existence on Polish soil."[22] On the afternoon of the same day Leivik found further confirmation of his view in a visit to 500 tuberculosis patients in the Gauting Sanatorium. These people lying unwanted, vulnerable and afraid in a German sanatorium symbolized a tragedy yet unresolved.[23] Rejoicing was premature.

Samuel Gringauz agreed that the survivors were approaching Liberation Day "with a feeling of sad bitterness"[24] but, as opposed to Leivik, he warned against a loss of historical perspective. Indeed, a new day was yet to dawn, antisemitism had still to be reckoned with and their suffering remained unredeemed. Nonetheless, he argued, "we must and ought not obscure the great historical truth relating to the awful battle waged against the hydra of human oppression, against spiritual and moral darkness."[25] The Allies paid a devastating price for their victory over Nazism and without it the civilized world would have gone under and with it any hope of Jewish survival. Despite their profound regard

---

[20] Grinberg, "14-tn iyar."

[21] H. Leivik, "Tsum yor-tog fun bafrayung" (Regarding the anniversary of liberation), *Undzer Veg*, no. 32 (10.5.1946): 3.

[22] Ibid.   [23] Ibid.

[24] Dr. Samuel Gringauz, "Undzer geshterter yom tov" (Our spoiled [disrupted] holiday), *LLT*, no. 14 (26) (26.4.1946): 3.

[25] Dr. S. Gringauz, "Tsum yor-tog fun nitsakhon" (Concerning the anniversary of victory), *LLT*, no. 16 (28) (10.5.1946): 3.

for Leivik, the members of the *ZK* opted for the approach Grinberg and Gringauz shared. This is how Leo Schwarz accounted for what he witnessed:

One of the central questions was whether the liberation should be commemorated as a day of mourning or a day of thanksgiving. About the remembrance of the martyred dead there was little difference of opinion. As for the celebration of the liberation a marked difference of emphasis between the delegates and the survivors was expressed. But the representatives of the Sheerith Hapletah ... whose psychology was then already inspired by a positive dialectic of the future prevailed.[26]

The majority supported the official announcement declaration of "A Unified Day of Remembrance and Liberation which will emphasize both our sadness and bitterness in the face of the great tragedy that consumed European Jewry and as a commemoration symbolizing national rebirth, underlining that '*Am Yisrael Chai*' – the Jewish people lives."[27] It was further decided to fix the 14th day of the month of *Iyar* (which fell on 15 May in 1946) as the Day of Remembrance and Victory and Zalman Grinberg was assigned the task of formulating an official declaration which would be sent to Jewish communities worldwide with the request that they too mark the day.[28] The Declaration that opened with a brief historical narrative went on to declare in the name of *She'erith Hapleitah* that "the 14th of *Iyar* had been designated as the shared, official Day of Remembrance, a solemn day both now and for the generations to come ... This day [too] will forever be inscribed in Jewish history as the symbolic date of the liberation from the Hitlerite yoke."[29]

The 14th of *Iyar* was declared a day of rest and the Surviving Remnant joined together to remember and to give thanks. While this was largely done locally a survey of the events of the Day indicate a number of recurring motifs: the assemblies opened or closed with the singing of *Hatikvah*, the intoning of the memorial *Yizkor* and *El malei rachamim* prayers, standing in silence in honor of the *kedoshim* – martyrs, public addresses, victory marches and community singing. In camps close to where their inhabitants were liberated mass graves were visited, parts of the death marches were symbolically reenacted and wreaths were laid on memorial tablets they had erected. The décor generally included memorial candles, the black borders of mourning notices, the Zionist and American flag

---

[26] Leo W. Schwarz, "Memorial in Munich", *Congress Weekly*, vol. 22, no. 15 (1955): 6.
[27] Protokoll nr. 42. des *ZK* (5.5.1946).   [28] Ibid.
[29] "Dekleratsie fun *ZK* fun di bafayte yidn in der amerikaner bezatsungs zone, daytshland, tsum yor-tog fun der bafrayung" (Declaration of the Central Committee of the Liberated Jews in the American Occupation Zone, Germany, concerning the anniversary of liberation), *Der Nayer Moment*, no. 3 (7.5.1946): 1.

and the inscription, usually large and bold, *Am Yisrael Chai!*[30] Those invited to these memorial assemblies included US Army officers and UNRRA officials and, on occasion, representatives of the local German administration.

In most cases the ceremonies wove together the contrary themes of remembrance and thanksgiving. In Munich, for example, the first half of the program was dedicated to the victims of Nazism while in the second half some 2,000 participants filled the "Aula" of the University of Munich and joined Emma Shaver in a moving evening of song.[31] In Landsberg, by way of comparison, the evening program which was held on the sportsfield opened with a few remarks from the distinguished guests after which a series of campfires were lit followed by a march past and, finally, community singing.[32] On the following morning, a memorial service was held and at its center a lesson taught by Rabbi Horowitz, the Augsburger *Rebbe*. The day ended with a series of programatic speeches followed by an appearance of the camp choir accompanied by the St. Ottilien Orchestra. The very real tension between mourning and affirmation which had divided opinions in the Central Committee was also addressed by the Augsburger *Rebbe*, this time within a religious idiom.[33] The difference in emphasis could be seen as stemming from a generational difference as was the case in the time of Ezra the Scribe: when the rebuilding of the Temple got underway the elderly burst out in tears while the young, who had not known the First Temple, were overjoyed. And that, suggested the *Rebbe*, is what transpired after the "Catastrophe": the young fixed their gaze on liberation and the promise of the future while their elders who had been deeply embedded in the life of East European Jewry could not tear themselves away from the past. The Jewish tradition commands the person saved from danger to offer up a prayer of thanksgiving – how much the more so when an entire people has experienced an act of deliverance. The Nazis, like all those who had hated the Jewish people down through the generations, "sought to destroy and kill off all the Jews and when we see the Remnant before us it is no less than a miracle from Heaven."[34] The overwhelming sorrow and pain should therefore be accompanied by the affirmation of miraculous survival and the hope born of deliverance.

---

[30] For just two examples from many see "Der 23 april 1945: tsum ershtn yor-tog nokh der bafrayung" (23 April 1945: towards the first anniversary following the liberation), *Der Nayer Moment*, no. 3 (7.5.1946): 1; "Yetziat katsetn fayerungen" (Celebrating the release from the concentration camps), *Undzer Vort*, no. 11–12 (4.6.1946): 11.

[31] David Kova'i, "Yud-daled iyar – yizkor farzamlung in minkhen" (14th *Iyar* – memorial assembly in Munich), *Undzer Veg*, no. 34 (24.5.1946): 3–4.

[32] See "Di fayerlekhkayten fun yud-daled iyar yom tov in landsberg" (The 14 *Iyar* festival celebrations in Landsberg), *LLT*, no. 17 (29) (17.5.1946): 2.

[33] Ibid.   [34] Ibid.

Basing himself on Ecclesiastes, Rabbi Horowitz sought further to illuminate the dilemma felt by all. When King Solomon laid down that
"There is a time for everything and a season for every purpose under heaven" (Ecclesiastes 3 : 1–8) in the twenty-eight times mentioned,
special attention is given to "A time for mourning and a time for dancing." All the other pairs appear in the infinitive "A time to be born and
a time to die" suggesting independent times, a divide that prevents in-
terpenetration – "In no case is the time to be born, the time to die."[35]
When, in comparison, it comes to "A time for mourning and a time for
dancing" it would indeed be possible for the two to exist side by side or
even to run into one another, as has always been the case in the Jewish
calendar. In the new day of remembrance which is part and parcel of the
long history of Jewish martyrdom, therefore, "Joyfulness must be accompanied by our obligation to remember our martyrs who were privileged
to die for *Kiddush Hashem* – the sanctification of God's name – for no
other reason than they were Jewish and to their last breath refused to
disavow their people."[36] In this fashion the *Rebbe* sought to integrate the
Jewish tragedy into a more traditional understanding and to show a way
to remembrance that kept painful complexity at its center. Indeed, "until
the Redeemer will come unto Zion" human reality would continue to be
flawed "and no Jewish celebration could be whole."[37]

Most of those who addressed the public on the Day of Remembrance
spoke little of entitlement and much more of the obligations resting on
She'erith Hapleitah: their duties to the dead, the need to revitalize the
Jewish heritage and, above all, to achieve Jewish independence in the
Land of Israel. What came to the fore with respect to the victims of
Nazism was the need to afford them a dignified burial and, where this
was no longer possible, at least to create a symbolic grave and to allot them
a place of honor in the memory of the Jewish people.[38] Thus the survivors
in Regensburg retraced the path of their final death march, set up a monument at the site of the mass graves between Neuenberg and Stamsrid
and vowed not leave until the dead had been properly laid to rest.[39]
In Landsberg, too, Dr. Akabas emphasized the importance of seeing to
Jewish mass graves in Germany which was "a holy duty of respect for the
martyred dead and something, therefore, that Jews alone would take care

---

[35] Ibid.   [36] Ibid.   [37] Ibid.

[38] In January 1946 Levi Shalitan bemoaned the fact that "still today our martyrs lie in
nameless graves in nameless places ... how did we become so inured to elementary human feelings?" Shalitan, "Ve-ha'alitem et atzmotai mi-zeh." For a psychological reading
of the phenomenon of "homeless dead" see Lifton, *Death in Life*: 492–494.

[39] "Der 23 april 1945."

of."[40] In Leipheim the final act of the day involved decorating thirty cars and buses in blue and white, carrying aloft a banner which proclaimed "Despite it all the Jewish people lives!" and traveling to Ichenhauzen in order both to restore the old cemetery and to unveil a monument to the victims of Nazism.[41]

Many sought to articulate their profound sense of responsibility to the dead, of being worthy enough to speak in their name and to serve as their living monument.[42] This was no easy task where liberation was not synonymous with victory but many, nevertheless, chose to celebrate a deeply rooted vitality the Nazis were unable to extinguish.[43] Some saw the messianic movements that frequently emerged after a period of persecution as indicative of this "call to life" while Rabbi Shmuel Snieg who had taught at the famous Slobodka Yeshiva, served as the Chief Chaplain in the Lithuanian Army and was in charge of Religious Affairs in the ZK, refused to view "the historical responsibility" of She'erith Hapleitah in messianic terms. His appeal to those who gathered in Munich was simple and straightforward: to utilize the unique opportunity given to them as survivors "to reshape and rebuild Jewishness and Judaism."[44] Israel Efros took a similar tack in his address to the memorial assembly in Munich: "Each of us is obligated to live to the full thousands of lives that have been lost if there is to be enough strength to see through the Jewish battle for survival."[45] He was especially disturbed by the sore lack of culture he found in the DP camps where life appeared to be more biological than spiritual. Therefore, despite the objective limitations of which he was well aware, Efros urged the survivors to reappropriate their culture for without this immersion whence would emerge the contemporary Job "who would call down the voice from the storm and make sense of our agony?"[46]

It was, however, the call for statehood and independence that dominated all the remembrance day ceremonies. In Munich Shmuel Reisman, one of the few survivors of the Treblinka revolt, called for "a secure home for our coming generation and that can only be in Eretz Yisrael";[47]

---

[40] "Di fayerlekhkayten fun yud-daled iyar yom tov in landsberg": 2. See also Shalom Hershkopf, "In tog fun bafrayung" (On liberation day), Dos Fraye Vort, no. 29–30 (3.5.1946): 7–8.

[41] See "Der bafrayung yom-tov yud"daled iyar bey unz" (Our 14th Iyar liberation festival), Dos Fraye Vort, no. 29–30 (3.5.1946): 7–8.

[42] See S. Gringauz's speech reported in "Di fayerlekhkayten fun yud-daled iyar yom tov in landsberg": 2, and C. Galperin, "Bafrayte one frayhayt" (Liberated without freedom), Dos Fraye Vort, no. 29–30 (3.5.1946): 4.

[43] See the speech of B. Kagan, Chairman of the United Zionist Organization in Landsberg in "Di fayerlekhkayten fun yud-daled iyar yom tov in landsberg": 2.

[44] Kova'i, "Yud-daled iyar": 4.

[45] Israel Efros, "Nesiyah le-machanot ysrael be-germaniyah" (A journey to the Jewish camps in Germany), Hadoar, no. 12 (17.1.1947): 291.

[46] Ibid.   [47] Kova'i, "Yud-daled iyar."

in Landsberg, Gringauz reiterated his view that "All the while the Jewish people does not have its own home, catastrophes of this kind are unavoidable."[48] Others called for unity in order better to conduct the campaign for independence which was the only viable solution to the Jewish problem.[49] The yearning for a national home was everywhere accompanied by a dismissive rejection of Europe and a desire to begin anew far from the continent where so much blood was shed.[50] As Israel Efros wrote after conducting a seminar in Landsberg: "The conversation was shot through with disappointment in Europe and the pull of Palestine and sometimes a causal connection was made between the two. They are going to the land of Israel not by virtue of love of the country but because of their hatred of Europe."[51]

Yosef Gar in Landsberg, on the other hand, adopted a more balanced position. For the Surviving Remnant the pain of remembrance was deeply personal but the more joyful aspects of the day were public and related, primarily, to the significance, general and Jewish, of the defeat of Nazism. "This victory, setting aside the many disappointments that came with liberation, "is for us Jews, much more than for any other people in the world, of crucial significance. Given that Hitlerism sought to realize its program of *total destruction of the Jewish people* without exception this is not something of which we need to be persuaded."[52] Given the critical challenges the Jewish people would have to meet now that its historic center had been destroyed, it was in desperate need of all the help it could get. Setting the Day of Remembrance on the anniversary of the liberation, was, therefore, a move in the right direction, a building of bridges that could only be beneficial. Thus the universal aspect of the Nazi threat needed to be thrown into sharp relief – Hitler set out to destroy every expression of human progress and it was not by chance that he fixed on the people who from early in its history elevated the sanctity of all human life to a central value.[53] Because of this the Jewish people and all those committed to human advancement paid a ghastly price. As Gringauz expressed it, "our Day of Remembrance is also a way of allying ourselves with the better part of humanity."[54]

As this far from comprehensive survey shows the Day of Remembrance was almost universally observed in *She'erith Hapleitah*, in large camps

---

[48] "Di fayerlekhkayten fun yud-daled iyar yom tov in landsberg."

[49] See "Groyser katset fayerungen" (Great camp celebrations), *Undzer Vort*, no. 10 (24.5.1946): 7.

[50] See "Fayerung fun yetsiat katset in muenchberg" (Celebration of the exodus from the concentration camps in Muenchberg), *Undzer Vort*, no. 10 (24.5.1946): 6.

[51] Israel Efros, "Nesiyah le-machanot ysrael be-germaniyah" (A journey to the Jewish camps in Germany), *Hadoar*, no. 38 (4.10.1946): 965.

[52] Gar, "14-ter iyar."   [53] Ibid.

[54] "Di fayerlekhkayten fun yud-daled iyar yom tov in landsberg."

and small, by religious and secular alike. For many of the participants this was accompanied by a warm feeling of Jewish solidarity, a sense that the entire Jewish people had united with them in honoring the memory of the dead and celebrating the end of the war. Zalman Grinberg was proud that for the first time *She'erith Hapleitah* had, indeed, become a player on the stage of Jewish history,[55] the *Nayer Moment* was persuaded that "From this year the coming generations will think of this day as the Exodus from the Camps."[56] Yosef Gar assumed that what they had initiated "would certainly receive the necessary consent from all parts of the Jewish people throughout its dispersion."[57] In Yisrael Efros' assessment if

Esther and Mordechai declared the festival of Purim and Jews all over took it upon themselves and marked the day it was certain that with respect to the 14th of *Iyar* those who had survived destruction had the right to enter it into the Jewish calendar and Jews, wherever they dwelled, would observe it, take it upon themselves and their offspring."[58]

And as Leo Schwarz testified: "I was deeply conscious that I was witnessing the birth of a holiday which would probably be engraved on the heart and calendar of the Jewish people."[59]

In point of fact, however, neither the day nor its dual purpose was embraced by the Jewish world. With one exception, there is no mention of the 14th of *Iyar* in public debate, books, newspapers and journals throughout the Jewish world.[60] The exception is Dr. Shimon Federbush, the head of the Culture Department of the World Jewish Congress in New York who received the announcement of the Central Committee on 8 May 1946. Two days later after consulting with rabbis, educators and community leaders he wired back a negative response. He explained that the notification had arrived very late and in addition had been set for a month after Passover, a date traditionally put aside for those who

---

[55] Grinberg, "14-tn iyar."

[56] "Yud-daled iyar: tog fun der bafrayung – groyser fayerlekhkaytn in der yidishe velt", *Der Nayer Moment*, no. 3 (7.5.1946): 1.

[57] Gar, "14-ter iyar."

[58] Efros, "Nesiyah le-machanot ysrael," *Hadoar*, no. 12 (17.1.1947): 286.

[59] Schwarz, "Memorial in Munich": 6.

[60] The 14th of *Iyar* is not mentioned, for example, in any of the comprehensive Yad Vashem bibliographies. See M. Piecacz, ed., "Azkarah ve-hantzachah: yemei zikaron" (Memorialization and commemoration: remembrance days), in both *Ha-shoah ve-ha-gevurah be-aspeklaria shel ha-itonut ha-ivrit* (The Holocaust and heroism as reflected in the Hebrew press) (Jerusalem, 1966), and also in *Ha-shoah ve-sficheah be-aspeklariat ha-itonut ha-ivrit* (The Holocaust and its aftermath in the Hebrew press and journals), ed. M. Piecacz (Jerusalem, 1978), in addition to the section on "Reflections, Interpretations, Responsibilities, Commemoration, and Teaching of the Holocaust," in Jacob Robinson, ed., *The Holocaust and After: Sources and Literature in English* (Jerusalem, 1973).

were not able to observe the festival at its appointed time and therefore a date on which mourning was customarily forbidden. Federbush, accordingly, requested a postponement which would enable him to engage in a process of consultation in both the US and Palestine for this was, indeed, a question of great consequence.[61]

On the morrow of the Day of Remembrance Federbush wrote that, as he feared, no one appeared to have responded in any shape or form to the impassioned plea of the survivors in Germany. Neither did the initiative of *She'erith Hapleitah* leave its mark in Palestine.[62] In the public debate that later accompanied the various attempts to lay down the official form of Holocaust commemoration, what had been set in motion in Germany simply did not figure.[63] What ultimately determined the order of events was the decision to make the 5th of *Iyar* the Day of Independence of the newly declared state. If Jewish statehood was to be seen as a symbolic response to the tragedy of European Jewry then the day of Holocaust remembrance would have to be set before, as a lead up to independence and not on the 14th of *Iyar* after the event. It appears that the survivors in Germany were essentially a community in transit and thus not long enough on the stage of history in order to become a recognized focus of cultural authority. The sharp awareness of the Catastrophe midst *She'erith Hapleitah*, in addition, was not yet the common property of the Jewish people worldwide so that the survivors in Germany were responding to questions that the rest of the Jewish world had not yet begun to ask.

The questions of memory that in varying degrees exercised, dogged and haunted the survivors in Germany went far beyond the architecture of commemoration. What should be broadcast and what muted? What was central and what peripheral? What could be said and what was best left unsaid? The concern with memory raised a series of sensitive personal and public issues that were impossible to forget and difficult to deal with. Every Jewish household in Nazi-dominated Europe was marked with the blood of the innocent and the Angel of Death passed over none. Much could be told about the infinite cruelty of the perpetrators, and the active indifference of the bystanders but somewhere along the line the story of the victims came to the fore and could not be evaded. When it came

---

[61] Unfortunately I have not managed to recover the archival source of the exchange with Federbush which I recorded a number of years ago.

[62] See for example, "Yom zikaron" (A day of remembrance), *Ha-aretz* (11.1.1949): 2.

[63] See "Hachlatah bi-dvar kviat yom shoah u-mered ha-getaot" (Decision regarding the determination of a [remembrance] day for the Holocaust and ghetto revolts), The *Knesseth* Records, vol. 9 (1951): 1655–1657, 1708; "Chok yom ha-zikaron la-shoah ve-la-gvurah, tikun" (The day of remembrance for the Holocaust and heroism law, amended), The *Knesseth* Records, vol. 31 (1961): 1504–1506.

to armed resistance, the telling was easy and welcome. When it came to narratives of survival, by comparison, one entered a minefield that claimed many casualties.

For the people of *She'erith Hapleitah* survival *in extremis* came down to one critical concern: how did I stay alive when so many, including those nearest and dearest to me, perished? For this very reason, claimed Yosef Gar, the celebration of liberation focused on the general and steered away from the particular fate of the individual. Every survivor knew that it was chance that had ultimately saved them from death. "In no way was it a function of his own cleverness or bravery"[64] and, moreover, "How can the consciences of many surviving Jews rest in peaceful repose when they remember that in the fateful days of Hitler their ability to arrange things so as to remain alive came – in a greater or lesser degree – at the expense of their own brothers and sisters?"[65] Gar's thoughts and agony reveal the dark, inner Jewish side of life in hell: How did people remain alive? What was the price of survival and what did it do to their humanity? How should one relate to those who cooperated with the Nazis to escape death? As a survivor wrote in March 1946: "This is a subject we former concentration camp inmates have long sought to clarify but which, for a variety of reasons has not been brought out into the open."[66] For the historian, probing this area is, therefore, a sensitive and complex undertaking.

The interpretation of survival most widely accepted saw it exclusively as a matter of "chance, blind chance".[67] When the people of *She'erith Hapleitah* spoke of these matters the terms they employed generally contained the phrase *al pi nes* – by a miracle as in "the few who survived miraculously" or "those who miraculously remained alive"[68] – but used generally in the very prosaic sense of accidental, totally unexpected, unplanned and chance survival without any religious overtones. A second interpretation pointed to collaboration with the oppressor as the key to survival. Some of these erstwhile servants of the Nazis who had developed a taste for authority and power sought positions of influence in the institutions of *She'erith Hapleitah* as well. In Feldafing, for example, the temporary Camp Committee in the last months of 1945

---

[64] Gar, "14-ter iyar."   [65] Ibid.

[66] A. Akselrod, "Mir torn nit farshvekhn undzere kedoshim: a entfer h. leivik" (We ought not to dishonor our martyred dead: an answer to H. Leivik), *A Haym*, no. 6 (28.3.1946): 4.

[67] Agr. Yaakov Oleiski, "Fun farknekhtung tsu oysleizung" (From enslavement to redemption), *LLT*, no. 16(28) (10.5.1946): 4.

[68] Yosef Sperling, "Di metsuraim mi-chuts la-machane" (The lepers - beyond the pale), *A Haym*, no. 9 (11.4.1946): 10, and Levi Shalitan, "Fun undzer seder yom: di she'erith hapleitah hat dos vort – kol hamon kol shaddai" (On our agenda: *She'erith Hapleitah* has its say – *vox populi vox dei*), *Undzer Veg*, no. 17 (25.1.1946): 2.

consisted of "a group of strong men who had, for the most part, ruled in the concentration camps as well, and were physically in much better shape to take over."[69] And Levi Shalitan who was not surprised by the continuing power of the camp experience pointed to the "camp-elders, block-wardens and camp police of the old school"[70] in the midst of survivor life in Germany.

When these cases came to light, they whipped up angry responses in the DP camps leading to direct action and a refusal to hide or obfuscate the ugly and the unpalatable. Local newspapers carried occasional reports on *Kapos* (prisoner chief orderlies in concentration camps) who were identified, beaten up and then handed over to the Military Government while the "Judicial Department of the Central Committee" published details about Jewish collaborators in the hope that they would be captured and brought to trial.[71] In the last months of 1945, in point of fact, a number of cases of collaboration were tried before the "Jewish Court" in Landsberg. In the first such case Meir Rubin who had served as a foreman in the Skazisko camp was accused of cruelty and abuse of the prisoners. He was found guilty, sentenced to four months' imprisonment "and the lifelong loss of all his civil rights, full disclosure of the case in the press, in the DP camps in Germany and in Jewish communities willing to cooperate throughout the world."[72] In a similar fashion collaborators from Kaufering, Krakow, Plasow, Chelmno and Salonika were put on trial. During this period when feelings ran high in Landsberg and led to numerous attacks on those who came under suspicion the Camp Committee had to come out strongly against the prevailing "lynch" mood and demand that justice be left to the courts alone.[73]

Past memories also intruded on the initial attempts to set up a Jewish police force in the DP camps for, as *Undzer Vort* in Bamberg put it, "The

---

[69] Dr. Henri and Ruth C. Heitan, Critical Report and Summary, January 1946, in Bauer, ed., *Machanot ha-akurim be-germania*: 43–44.

[70] Levi Shalitan, "Fun undzer seder-hayom: demokratizatsie" (On our agenda: democratization), *Undzer Veg*, no. 15 (11.1.1946): 2.

[71] For example the description of the *kapo* George Gruner in *Undzer Vort*, no. 11–12 (4.6.1946): 11.

[72] "Di erst(molik) gerikht-farhandlung" (The first trial proceedings), *LLT*, no. 1 (8.10.1945): 4; B. Abelski, "Kapos un blok-elteste farn yidishn gericht in landsberg" (Kapos and block-elders before the Jewish court in Landsberg), *LLT*, no. 13 (25) (15.4.1946): 2; over six months sixteen *kapos* from various camps were brought to trial and sentenced. See also C. Sukholitsky, "Tsvei problemen" (Two problems), *Undzer Vort*, no. 4 (5.4.1946): 1–2. Sukholitsky demanded that a total ban be placed on collaborators: "He must be cut off from the Jewish community so that wherever he goes or turns, in every land he will find people ready to impose the sentence of banishment, of not being able to be counted as one of our people."

[73] See "Harbere shtrof far kapos" (Harsh punishment for *kapos*), *LLT*, no. 5 (12.11.1945): 6; Dr. Samuel Gringauz, "Fal barzion" (The barzion case), *LLT*, no. 8 (2.12.1945): 7; "Fun gerichts-zal" (From the courtroom), *LLT*, no. 12 (31.12.1945): 8.

Jewish Ghetto-Police inscribed a sad chapter in the history of the Jewish people."[74] In Landsberg the camp administration tried to soothe public hostility by opening the key positions in the police force to democratic elections.[75] Elsewhere those who wished to promote the idea resorted to persuasion: the purpose of the Jewish police was to avoid degrading contact with German authorities and to move towards independence. The police were to serve as a key element in Jewish self-defence and, by virtue of their training, would also be able to be more effective in the fight for statehood for "the times have made it abundantly clear that not with the spirit but only with force will we be able to fight for our rights."[76]

Beyond the argument of chance or that of intentional cooperation there was a third version that could be termed "survival by adaptation." Following their numerous conversations with survivors a few months after liberation, the representatives of the Jewish Brigade, Chaim Ben-Asher and Aryeh Simon, formulated this approach as follows: "In the camp men were faced with the alternative of either to perish or of adapting themselves to the conditions which meant casting aside of all moral scruples."[77] At a later date Jacob Oleiski of Landsberg spelt out what this meant:

In the ghettos and concentration camps moral conduct and the basic principles of inter-personal relations were shred to bits. As a result of life in those horrible surroundings and in such shocking and depraved living conditions, the human feel for notions of beauty and spirituality, decency and honesty totally dissipated ... the human personality was ruled by animal instincts.[78]

Most remarkable in this regard are the comments of Chaim Rosenberg, a member of *Nocham* who had the good fortune to be part of the *Kibbutz Buchenwald* group that immigrated to Palestine in August 1945. In an article for *Nitzotz* marking the first anniversary of liberation Rosenberg reflected on his first nine months of *kibbutz* life:

Physically and economically one can recover with relative ease, but the spiritual contamination is the most dangerous part of what was left to us by life in the ghetto and concentration camps ... a new kind of person came into being, one deprived of faith in himself and the world, without ideals, lacking in genuine

[74] "Fayerlekher banket bei lager-politsei in bamberg" (A festive dinner hosted by the camp police in Bamberg), *Undzer Vort*, no. 9 (17.5.1946): 7.

[75] Dr. S. Gringauz, "Di yiddishe politsei in landsberg" (The Jewish police in Landsberg), *LLT*, no. 9 (9.12.1945): 5.

[76] "Fayerlekher banket."

[77] Report on the Position of the Jewish Refugees in Southern Germany: From a Tour of the Camps 6–14 July 1945, the Spektor Collection, *Haganah* Archives.

[78] Yaakov Oleiski, "Problemen fun she'erith hapleitah" (Problems of *She'erith Hapleitah*), *LLT*, no. 2 (14) (18.1.1946): 2.

feeling, without the capacity for an inner experience ... Only now, a year after our liberation, can we see more clearly what has become of us.[79]

Within this general approach there were a number of nuances. There were those who made do with the assessment of "moral crippling"; others went further arguing that survival entailed a process of negative selection whereby "the best, the most sensitive, the most honest" perished while "those of weak character, the worst, the least worthy" came through.[80] In short: not only the inhuman conditions created by the Nazis counted; the moral fibre of the victims also played its part. A kinder version spoke of avoidance of action, of "the unwillingness to sacrifice themselves – though many did sacrifice themselves – for their parents and children, to accompany them 'on their last way' and because of this they are beset by a sense of sin and stricken by conscience."[81] At the end of the spectrum there were those who concurred with Yosef Gar that "the people who survived, survived at the cost of the lives of others."[82]

This engagement with the terrors of an impossible world frequently spilt over into the present and, beyond soul-searching, drove many to seek the restoration of Jewish honor that had been trampled underfoot. This connection between the dark side of destruction and the shared memories of the Jewish people became public and explicit following the publication of an article by H. Leivik in March 1946.[83] What prompted the article were the reports of two survivors, Yaakov Twersky and Yosef Rosenzaft – Chairman of the Jewish Committee in Bergen Belsen and of the Central Committee of Liberated Jews in the British Zone – who, while touring America, told of Jews who had cooperated with the Nazis in order to save themselves and their families. Their disclosures were found shocking and sparked off a widespread debate in the Jewish press. Leivik, who wished "to keep the picture of Jewish martyrdom unblemished,"[84] feared the unwanted consequences of an open debate. Practically speaking he suggested recording these testimonies "in a special corner of our terror-filled national journal, to register it and then relinquish it to a corner"[85] so as categorically to mark off an unprecedented tragedy in

---

[79] Chaim Rosenberg, "Hirhurim li-mlot shanah le-shichrur machanot ha-rikuz" (Reflections on the anniversary of the liberation of the concentration camps), *Nitzotz*, no. 20 (65) (9.8.1946): 10.

[80] Dr. Shmuel Gringauz, "In tsaykhn fun martirertum hofnung un arbet" (Under the sign of martyrdom hope and work), *LLT*, no. 2 (14) (18 January 1946); see also Abraham Klausner's comments in this regard in his interview OHD/4(4): 9–10.

[81] Efros, "Nesiyah le-machanot ysrael," *Hadoar*, no. 12.   [82] Gar, "14-ter iyar."

[83] H. Leivik, "Mir torn nit farschvekhn undzere kedoshim" (We ought not to dishonor our martyred dead), *Undzer Veg*, no. 25 (22.3.1946): 10.

[84] Ibid.   [85] Ibid.

human history from the misdoings of a few individuals. Leivik was primarily concerned about non-Jewish reactions to these disclosures and the discussion it might engender. He sensed that world opinion was desperately seeking to avoid coming to grips with the destruction of European Jewry and having the victims discredited by their own brothers offered an elegant way out of the dilemma: "this would help it wash its hands [of the entire affair] and allow many unattended 'episodes' of the world war to be forgotten all the quicker."[86] Dabbling in this sad business might also be of aid to the murderers who now sought to evade responsibility for their deeds. It was, therefore, advisable to bury the unfortunate question of Jewish collaboration with the Nazis until such time "that we feel it is opportune to take it out of its wraps. We – the victim, and not them – the victimizer."[87]

Leivik restricted his views to those who had not suffered directly at the hands of the Nazis and expressly did not presume to talk in the name of those "who had been there." There were those in *She'erith Hapleitah*, who, nevertheless, construed what he said to be of general application and thus took issue with his position. A. Akselrod from St. Ottilien agreed that the sanctity of the dead had to be protected and the responsibility of the murderers in no way diminished. On the other hand, he rejected Leivik's desire to downplay, albeit temporarily, "all the sins, treachery, filth and murderous acts carried out by those who, for the sake of a little food, tortured their own brothers."[88] Those who lost everything cannot fence off a section of their hearts, in truth they do not wish to turn a blind eye to the harmful presence of *Kapos*, informers and despicable traitors. Firm and decisive action taken against these elements would be salutary for the Jewish people and would serve to strengthen its international standing. Any half-measures in this regard would "dishonor our martyred dead even more."[89] Yosef Sperling from Weilheim was surprised by Leivik's intuitive grasp of a wound so painful deep in the hearts of the survivors.[90] Leivik, nevertheless, had failed to understand that the dignity of the dead was inextricably bound up with the dignity of the survivors – how could any self-respecting man stand aside when those who had served the Nazis had yet to be punished and, in the meanwhile, filled positions of public trust in *She'erith Hapleitah*? Despite the poet's misgivings, it was necessary to open the wounds of the past and to take action against those who turned rotten because "our inner sense of Jewish honor warns and exclaims, calls out and demands justice."[91]

[86] Ibid.   [87] Ibid.
[88] Akselrod, "Mir torn nit farshvekhn undzere kedoshim: a entfer h. leivik": 4.
[89] Ibid.   [90] Sperling, "Di metsuraim mi-chuts la-machane."   [91] Ibid.

All told, it appears that in important ways the survivors in Germany were less cautious than Leivik when it came to dealing with the shades of the past. Perhaps it stemmed from their personal involvement and it may have reflected the strong group spirit that had grown up in the camps, a spirit that thought little of Europe and less of the Germans. If, indeed, the subject was neither investigated nor much discussed it resulted from their own closeness to the subject. "The question 'For what reason do I deserve to live?'," testified Israel Efros on the basis of numerous conversations in the DP camps, "occupies and disturbs them greatly and whatever solution is opted for, it inevitably sinks into a spiritual morass of unexplained guilt."[92]

Armed resistance and its central symbol, the Warsaw Ghetto Revolt, enjoyed an uncomplicated place of honor in the memory of *She'erith Hapleitah*. At every opportunity the valor of the "ghetto fighters, the dedication of the underground movements and the heroism of the partisans"[93] was raised on high together with the tribute paid to the Jewish soldiers in the Allied forces and, most especially, the soldiers of the Jewish Brigade. The reasons for this on-going, almost ritualistic engagement with armed resistance were diverse but one is left with the strong impression that for many it served to lighten the crushing burden of victimhood, the torment of helplessness. In this regard it is worth repeating what Levi Shalitan said at a meeting to commemorate the Warsaw Ghetto Revolt: "a people cannot live off Treblinkas and Maidaneks – only thanks to Warsaw can this people live on."[94] There were those who detected an element of apologetics in the glorification of resistance especially when survivors had to contend with the superior airs of young Palestinians. As Chaim Rosenberg wrote to his friends in Germany about settling down to life in Palestine: "Our people have shut themselves off ... and because they lack self-respect many in *She'erith Hapleitah* seek to prove that they were once partisans."[95]

These concerns, however, were not only a response to pressure, real and imagined, from without. They had flowed from within as the events were unfolding[96] and continued to demand a reckoning once the war was over. As Gringauz expressed it:

[92] Efros, "Nesiyah le-machanot ysrael," *Hadoar*, no. 12.
[93] "Zakhor," *Undzer Veg*, no. 32 (10.5.1946): 1.
[94] Levi Shalitan, "Varshe als symbol: troyer akademye tsum 3-tn yortzayt fun varshever oyfshtand" (Warsaw as a symbol: a memorial assembly on the 3rd anniversary of the Warsaw uprising), *Dos Fraye Vort*, no. 29–30 (3.5.1946): 7.
[95] Rosenberg, "Hirhurim."
[96] See, for example, Emmanuel Ringelblum, *Polish Jewish Relations during the Second World War* (Jerusalem, 1974): 156–161.

It is not unusual for Jews to look back with a deep sense of shame and feelings of guilt at the years of the great catastrophe when millions of their people helplessly clung to life and went unresistingly to their deaths. As a young man said in a poem he sent me in the concentration camp just before his death:

> Cowards, we hang on to life
> As sheep we go to the slaughter.[97]

Mark Dvorjetski, the doctor and resistance fighter from Vilna asked the same, probing questions in *Undzer Veg*. "Why did things turn out the way they did? And what ought we to have done?"[98] What would have happened if Jews had resisted the Nazis every inch of the way? There would have been massive losses but would the number have reached 6 million? What would have happened if the revolt had broken out in Warsaw earlier, when there were nearly half a million inhabitants rather than in April 1943 when the ghetto had been emptied out? What if the Jews of Europe had taken Hitler seriously, had thrown off the comfortable approach of business as usual, had not anesthetized themselves with the magic words: "The Eternity of Israel will not fail us"? For Dworjetzki the existential source of these questions were the children in the Vilna Ghetto who wished to know "When will they come to take us to Ponar?" Not only did they know what awaited them, they equally knew "that their father would not protect them because he did not know how to protect and did not have with what to protect."[99] And the fate of the children was shared by the women-folk and the elderly – they, too, went to their death "unprotected and helpless."

What gnawed at the survivors was their inability to help, to save, to make a difference and it was this reality that lent the heroism of the ghetto fighters its special quality. For the most part when soldiers go out to do battle they hope to return victorious. No such hope was available to those who took up arms in Warsaw and elsewhere: they could neither push back the invader nor liberate their country or just save lives. Perhaps things might have been different if aid from the Poles or the Allies had been forthcoming but, in actual fact, the help revived from the Polish underground was marginal while "the world, for its part was unfortunately blind, deaf and dumb."[100] They, too, were fully aware of their tragic situation. "From

[97] Shmuel Gringauz, "Varshever oyfshtand: a ring fun dorot'diker heldish-yidisher kayt" (The Warsaw uprising: a link in the generations-long chain of Jewish heroism", *YT*, no. 29(97) (8.4.1947): 4.

[98] M. Dvorjetski, "Wos mir habn undzere kinder nit gelernt" (What we did not teach our children), *Undzer Veg*, no. 32 (10.5.1946): 5.

[99] Ibid.

[100] Moshe Kaspi, "Varshever vidershtand: zikhronos fun an antaylnemer" (Resistance in Warsaw: memories of a participant), *Dos Fraye Vort*, no. 29–30 (3.5.1946): 7.

the outset the fighting was hopeless," said Jacob Oleiski at the Landsberg memorial assembly for the Warsaw Ghetto Revolt, "The Jewish heroes were not fighting for their lives . . . they did not sacrifice their lives in order to protect their property that had already been destroyed. They fought for Jewish honor, for the honor of the Jewish people and in this battle they achieved an historic victory."[101]

The revolt, as many survivors emphasized, was not an act of despair. Despair could lead to paralysis or wildly improbable deeds; it would not have generated the inner reserves to sustain training, the purchase and manufacture of weapons, trial runs, planning and unending pressure over a period of months.[102] In truth, physical resistance depended on the moral reserves that the fighters could draw on to overcome hunger, disease, fear and guilt.[103] Or, as Baruch Wind from Leipheim put it, "They did not believe in their victory but, despite this, they were far from despair. Despair is the opposite of heroism. Could their final appeal to the Yishuv and the freedom-loving world be seen as an act of despair?"[104] Thus, it was the love of man and the love of the Jewish people, the twin foundations of the pioneering movement, that motivated those who took up arms in the ghetto. Others, without gainsaying Wind's observations, chose to stress the broad participation in resistance: "Rabbis and free-thinkers, Agudists and Communists, Zionists and Bundists – all bound by one burning desire joined together to take up arms."[105] The ghetto fighters were in no way an extraordinary group for "they were cut from the same cloth as millions of other Jews who, owing to different objective conditions, were unable to mount open resistance."[106] In other localities the critical mass of the capital's Jewish population was missing, there was no support from without as was the case in Warsaw which could also boast a long tradition of social activism.

In other words, because at heart Warsaw was not exceptional, the revolt came to express and symbolize that which many other Jews had

---

[101] Yaakov Oleiski, "Grandiezer troyer akademye likhvod dem 3-tn yortog fun yidn oyfshtand in varshe" (Impressive memorial ceremony in honor of the 3rd anniversary of the Jewish uprising in Warsaw), *LLT*, no. 15 (27) (3.5.1946): 8.

[102] See Fayge Miedrzycki (Vladka), "A mit-bataylikte dertsaylt un fodert" (One who participated tells and demands), *Undzer Veg*, no. 29 (19.4.1946): 3.

[103] Dr. Zalman Grinberg, "Gaystiker un fizisher vidershtand" (Spiritual and physical resistance), *Undzer Veg*, no. 29 (19.4.1946): 2.

[104] Baruch Wind, "Di nonte gefalene khaverim: oyfshtand in geto – paradoks fun khalutsyshn heroizm" (The fallen, our close friends: uprising in the ghetto – the paradox of pioneering heroism), *A Haym*, no. 8 (11.4.1946): 6.

[105] Moshe Lestny, "Grandiezer troyer akademye likhvod dem 3-tn yortog fun yidn oyfshtand in varshe" (Impressive memorial assembly in honor of the Warsaw uprising), *LLT*, no. 15 (27) (3.5.1946): 8.

[106] Gringauz, "Varshever oyfshtand."

wanted but, given their objective conditions, were unable to achieve. The revolt was symbolic in a further sense: the resistance fighters hoped and wished that their deeds would serve as a beacon and example for those who, after the war, would take responsibility for the Jewish future. Many of the leaders of She'erith Hapleitah were persuaded that this was indeed the case. "They rescued Jewish honor and with it they also rescued ... the Jewish people," wrote Levi Shalitan, because their deeds generated "a surge of spiritual strength and national resilience for all the survivors and the generations to come."[107] As the embattled Jews of Massadah were able to infuse their brothers, nearly 2,000 years later, with strength and determination so the heroes of Warsaw would surely touch posterity.[108]

It became part of the shared wisdom of the Jewish displaced persons in Germany that the battle begun in Warsaw was as yet unfinished. The Jewish people which held out against the might of the German Army for no less time than the French Army in 1940 was entitled to its share in the fruits of victory. From this point of view the French had regained full sovereignty while the Jewish people were still denied any form of statehood. The battle, in Zalman Grinberg's words, was not yet over and both She'erith Hapleitah and the Yishuv had to be prepared to answer the fateful question: "would the Warsaw Revolt emerge victorious or not?"[109] In this fashion the fight for Jewish independence in Palestine was seen as the direct continuation of what had begun in Warsaw – the revolt had opened a new era in the history of the Jewish people that would determine its fate for many generations to come.

According to the narrative embraced by many survivors in Germany, the guiding ethos of this historical turning point was essentially Zionist.[110] There were those who highlighted the role of the Bund in the ghetto fighting and the social activism that lent it remarkable strength but in terms of She'erith Hapleitah as a whole this perception did not enjoy the currency it perhaps deserved.[111] As the story was now told, between the Bar Kochbah revolt and the appearance of the Zionist movement "the

---

[107] Levi Shalitan, "Fun undzer seder-hayom: fun masada biz varshe – od lo nutka ha-shalshelet" (On our agenda: from Masada to Warsaw – yet is the chain unbroken), Undzer Veg, no. 29 (19.4.1946): 2.
[108] Ibid.   [109] Grinberg, "Gaystiker un fizisher vidershtand."
[110] See, for example, "Groyser un impozanter tsuzamenfal fun partizaner un geto-kemfer: anthilt a denkmal farn umbakantn yidishn held" (A large and imposing gathering of partisans and ghetto fighters: unveiling of a monument to the unknown Jewish hero), A Haym, no. 10 (16.5.1946): 9.
[111] For example Gringauz, "Varshever oyfshtand." Levi Shalitan during an address in Feldafing, a Bundist stronghold, criticized the fact that the Bund had taken so long to join forces with others in the Warsaw Ghetto uprising. In this regard see his "Varshe als symbol."

Jewish people had been frozen in a long, lethargic sleep."[112] The Zionist youth movements that had repeatedly demonstrated their profound dedication to the needs of their people were viewed as the heirs to the committed minority that through the ages had always kept the Jewish people alive. But with one difference: their heroic spirit was primarily this-worldly and thus was translated into action in the here and now. "What came to the fore was the determination to sacrifice themselves for life rather than death. *Kiddush Hashem* – the sanctification of God's name – was transformed into the sanctification of people and land."[113] The fact that this activist ethos made its most impressive showing in Warsaw was attributed to the size of the Jewish population, even in its reduced state, as opposed to the level of militant motivation elsewhere. The thrust of the Zionist argument in favor of a large concentration of Jews in the Land of Israel was sadly borne out by the fate of Jewish resistance during the catastrophic war years: quantity at a certain level became qualitatively significant[114] but only up to a certain point. There was no way to break out of the debilitating isolation of exilic life, especially when the world was at war. The "symbolic significance" of Jewish abandonment when solidarity was so desperately needed was inescapable: it pointed to the critical need for Jewish independence at the hub of the Jewish future.[115]

There were those, however, who felt that the importance of armed resistance had been exaggerated beyond its true proportions. Dr. Wiederman of Feldafing, for example, felt uncomfortable with the way in which "an heroic myth had been built around the 6 million Jewish victims"[116] of the Nazis. Anyone who wished to learn from the past was duty-bound to be true to the facts however unpleasant and had to steer clear of this self-serving "cult of heroism."[117] The young people who decided to exact a heavy price for their lives, fully deserved the place of honor granted to them in popular memory. This in no way justified covering up the bitter truth that most Jews had been led to their death "like sheep to the slaughter." The picture of an entire people locked in armed combat with superior forces was ridiculous and misguided; objective conditions rendered this impossible. The true Jewish heroism in the days of darkness was not primarily of the fighter but of the mother who refused to abandon her children "and voluntarily accompanied ... [them] until death came. This was Jewish heroism."[118] Levi Shalitan felt the same way: if so many

---

[112] Shalom Hershkopf, "Batrakhtungen vegn varshever oyfshtand" (Thoughts on the Warsaw uprising), *Dos Fraye Vort*, no. 28 (26.4.1946): 2.

[113] Wind, "Di nonte gefalene khaverim."

[114] See contribution of Aryeh Retter in Shalitan, "Varshe als symbol."

[115] See Adv. Friedheim's remarks reported by Oleiski in "Grandiezer troyer akademye."

[116] Dr. Wiederman, "Der kult fun heroizm" (The cult of heroism), *Dos Fraye Vort*, no. 45–50 (29.9.1946): 7.

[117] Ibid.   [118] Ibid.

had fled, resisted and fought there would be far fewer victims and the people of *She'erith Hapleitah* would not be agonizing over a calamitous, historic failure.[119] For sure there were weighty reasons that prevented mass resistance – the refusal to believe that they faced total annihilation, the desire to avoid a head-on confrontation with the murderers, the scarcity of weapons and trained personnel, the indifference of the nations of Europe in the face of destruction. Only those who saw things as they were would be able to learn from the past. And for Shalitan the lesson was clear: a sovereign state alone would provide the Jewish people with the indispensable conditions to take care of themselves and protect their vital interests.

The immersion of the survivors in the difficult questions of their recent past found a more structured and detached expression with the establishment of the Central Historical Commission created under the auspices of the Central Committee in December 1945. Viewed in a broader context this should be seen as a local continuation of a program of documentation that had begun before the outbreak of war and that persisted as a clandestine, often daring endeavor as the destruction of European Jewry unfolded.[120] At the end of the war this documentary work was resumed with renewed energy – so much more was now at stake – and historical committees were set up in Poland, France, Hungary, Slovakia, Italy, Austria and in Germany too. The shared purpose of these groups was "documentation *per se*, documentation to embrace all historical features during the Nazi regime, including the internal life of the Jewish community at that time, its social, cultural, religious, artistic and literary activities etc."[121] As early as the St. Ottilien Conference in July 1945 a resolution was passed with reference to "Documentation in the countries of Exile" pleading that survivors, wherever they be found, dedicate themselves to:

1. Collecting the names of all the Jews who were done to death and
2. Given the disappearance of all signs of Jewish life in Europe our cultural institutions devoted to the past must be moved to Palestine and with them all the documents pertaining to Jewish communities on the European continent.[122]

As things turned out, it was only a few months later that a small group of devotees began to think about documentation in a more organized

---

[119] Levi Shalitan, "Der nayer yid" (The new Jew), *Undzer Veg*, no. 27 (3.4.1946): 6.

[120] Phillip Friedman, "Problems of Research on the European Jewish Catastrophe," *Yad Vashem Studies*, vol. 3 (1959): 25–40.

[121] Ibid.: 27.

[122] Resolutionen und Beschlüsse der Konferenz der überlebenden Juden auf dem deutschen u. österreichishen Territorium, St. Ottilien (25–26 July 1945), CZA/ S6/4360.

and planful fashion. In November 1945 Yisrael Kaplan who was to play a central role in the *Tsentraler Historisher Komisye* (*THK*) appealed the public to set about "Documenting and Recording."[123] Not only had the Nazis destroyed both the Jews of Europe and their historical treasures, they had come close to successfully concealing what they had perpetrated under the cover of war. There were many localities where not a single witness lived to tell the tale and no one was left to lead investigators to the testimonies they had almost certainly recorded and hidden. It was the sacred duty of the survivors to save whatever could be dredged up from the past for the sake of the future. Each of them was, without exception, a font of knowledge about the past that could be critical in preparing the foundations of the historical edifice yet to be erected.[124]

Kaplan pressed to get started immediately while memories were still fresh and *She'erith Hapleitah* had not begun to leave Germany *en masse*. The presence of a large concentration of survivors in one geographic zone made it possible to check reports, verify dates, names and places and, thus, "any delay in moving this work forward would be an unforgivable sin."[125] Kaplan was not deterred by the argument that in the main, the survivors would neither be able to undertake disciplined writing nor suffer sustained questioning. He pointed to the enormous volume of mail being sent overseas daily and the veritable flood of articles reaching their own press. These private letters that told of the fate of family and friends by-passed the historian while the articles which steered clear of the past and focused on issues of the hour were similarly of limited documentary value. Kaplan turned to both these populations and pleaded with them to become active partners in erecting what could be the most significant memorial to European Jewry: a comprehensive history of the most devastating *churban* (catastrophic destruction) in the annals of the Jewish people. In terms of priorities Kaplan believed that the recording of personal testimonies was of primary importance and should be granted the lion's share of their limited resources. He suggested paying special attention, in addition, to the popular culture that had grown up under Nazi terror, the "songs, anecdotes, jokes, sayings, phrases, quotes, nicknames, passwords, curses, greetings etc."[126] and proposed, furthermore, the systematic collection of the artifacts of destruction for the museums of the

---

[123] Yisrael Kaplan, "Zamlen un fartsaykhenen" (Collect and record), *Undzer Veg*, no. 5 (9.11.1945): 3.
[124] Ibid.   [125] Ibid.
[126] Kaplan published two articles dealing with this in the first two numbers of *Fun Letstn Khurbn* and then as a separate monograph. See Yisrael Kaplan, *Dos folks-moyl in nazi klem: reydenishn in geto un katset* (Folk expression under Nazi occupation: sayings in the ghetto and concentration camp), The Central Historical Commission (Munich, 1949).

future – concentration camp clothing, the wooden clogs, eating utensils, all the trivia that were often a question of life or death. Finally, given that they were living in Germany, documents, books, posters and any other paraphernalia connected to their persecution and the "Final Solution" should also be collected and catalogued.

In actual fact, the key figure in the work of the *THK* from start to finish was M.Y. Feigenbaum and it was he who conducted the initial consultations that lead to the creation of the Central Historical Commission attached to the Central Committee of the Liberated Jews in the American Zone of Germany.[127] Feigenbaum who had grown up in Biale Podlaska and had escaped the Nazis by hiding in an underground bunker[128] came to realize after the war that without a systematic and concerted effort, not a single trace of the Nazi destruction of European Jewry would survive. At the height of the murder when it appeared that no one would live to tell the tale, many hoped that what so many had witnessed would be remembered and made known by the nations of Europe. But since liberation it had become increasingly clear that these peoples had little desire to pay Jewish suffering any special attention. If their neighbors did anything it "was to take the trouble to minimize the Jewish tragedy, to cover it up and where possible, to cast aspersions."[129]

The sizeable amount of material collected and collated in preparation for the Nuremberg trials, furthermore, did not mean that someone else had done the work. Part of the material remained classified and those guiding the work had no special interest in things Jewish. Thus, this vast collection of material that focused on getting war criminals sentenced "was fragmentary when it came to our tragedy ... and it only showed how the murderers related to us, treated us and, ultimately, what they did to us. Did our lives in those nightmarish days only consist of these fragments?"[130] How could the historian, restricted only to this material, describe what happened in the ghettos, how the Jewish people contended with a collective death sentence, how they heroically sought to frustrate Nazi designs? The devastation left behind by the Nazis had largely wiped out the sources generally used by historians to reconstruct the past. Only if *She'erith Hapleitah* set its mind to it, could part of the damage be undone. While Feigenbaum wanted to save the past for the Jewish future,

---

[127] See the report of M. Feigenbaum to the Congress of *She'erith Hapleitah* in the American Zone (23.2.1947), Yad Vashem Archives/MI/B/File 11.

[128] M. Feigenbaum, "In der bafrayte biale" (In the liberated biale), in M.Y. Feigenbaum, *Sefer biale podlaska* (The Biale Podlaska [memorial] book) (Tel Aviv 1960): 464–469.

[129] M.Y. Feigenbaum, "Tsu vos historisher komisyes" (To what end historical commissions), *Fun Letstn Khurbn*, no. 1 (August 1946): 2.

[130] Ibid.

he also understood their work to have a political purpose. In this regard
he hoped that the *THK* would be "an instrument that would be used
by ... Jewish organizations who are fighting for our tomorrow in the
international arena."[131]

The goals of the Commission were ambitious but the means at its disposal less than scanty so that when Feigenbaum and S. Glover, the Chief
Archivist-to-be, opened the doors in December 1945, their total posses-
sions amounted to a small table in the *ZK*'s Department of Culture,
and, not surprisingly, a chronic lack of trained professionals. But it was
not only a question of human and other resources for, whereas their colleagues elsewhere in Europe had access to material concealed during the
war, they found themselves isolated in a foreign land where the Allies had
already confiscated most of the official material of Jewish relevance.[132]
Finally, as Yisrael Kaplan commented wryly: in a period of such dramatic
impermanence, it was much easier to make history than to write it.[133]

Midst these unportentous beginnings Feigenbaum's most urgent assignment was to set up a comprehensive network of regional and local
committees that would carry the actual work of the Central Historical
Commission forward. It was a long and arduous task of recruiting workers, mobilizing local support – moral, political and financial – and creating an effective organization. Many local committees began to operate
in the first half of 1946 but there were large camps like Föhrenwald[134]
where operations only began in August 1946 and newer communities that
joined the network as late as 1947.[135] The regional committees became
the executive arm of the *THK*, recording personal testimonies, circulating
questionnaires from Munich, seeking to locate the cultural property of
nearby communities that had been destroyed, gathering archival material
of Jewish interest[136] and mediating between their local committees and
the central office.[137] At a conference of activists in May 1947 Feigenbaum
was able to report to the seventy participants that the regional committees

[131] Ibid.   [132] Ibid.   [133] Kaplan, "Zamlen un fartzaykhenen": 5.
[134] See the Protocol of the Meeting of the Culture Department in Foehrenwald
(18.8.1946), Yad Vashem Archives, MI/B/File 1.
[135] See the Jewish Committee in Bensheim to *THK* (27.2.1947), YSA/M-1/B/File 1.
[136] The reference is to Torah scrolls, ritual objects and community property. The Committee in Franken, for example, gained possession of the archives of twenty-two communities that had once lived in the area. See the Report of the Regional Historical
Commission in Franken (no date) YSA/M-1/B/File 2.
[137] See Yeshayahu Eiger, Garmisch Partenkirchen, to the *THK* (24.2.1946); Wolf
Gliksman, Gauting, to the Historical Commission attached to the Central Committee
(8.3.1946), telling of fifty-three documents of historical worth discovered in the local
police; Historical Department, Frankfurt, to the *THK* (14.8.1946), telling of archival
material acquired through the intervention of the Military Government. The above
three letters are found in YSA, MI/B/File 1.

in Bamberg, Frankfurt, Regensburg, Stuttgart, Munich and Berlin were coordinating the activities of some fifty-nine local branches.[138]

A large part of Feigenbaum's time was devoted to watching over the entire operation, pushing all and sundry to speed up the work and to be diligent in maintaining professional standards. Throughout this period a large volume of letters and circulars containing instructions, guidance, criticism and encouragement was sent from his office to the regional committees.[139] On the administrative front the Commission had to promote its interests within the Central Committee while maintaining an on-going correspondence with research institutions in Europe, America and Palestine and, in this regard, representatives of the *THK* participated in international research conferences on the destruction of European Jewry that were held in Jerusalem in mid-1947 and in Paris at the end of the year.

Those guiding the work of the Commission understood that within a community of survivors soon to disperse, the recording of personal testimonies had to be their first priority.[140] Appeals to come forward were repeatedly published in the press, notices were put up on bulletin boards and children and youth were encouraged to participate in an essay contest on the subject of "My War Experiences" which proved to be successful.[141] The appearance of the journal of the *THK*, *Fun Letstn Khurbn: tsaytshrift far geshikhte fun yidishn lebn beysn natsi rezhim* – From the Recent Destruction: A Journal for the History of Jewish Life under Nazi Rule – also served to encourage others to tell their personal story. In this fashion by May 1947, 1,022 testimonies were recorded running from two to twenty pages, for the most part in Yiddish and on occasion in Polish, Hungarian, German, Russian and Hebrew. In order to supplement the data gathered with regard to the stages of the destruction process a statistical questionnaire was distributed and 466 were returned by July 1947. At the same time a more detailed historical questionnaire "About Destroyed Jewish Communities and Deceased Jewish Personalities" was prepared.[142] A special form was designed to help pupils and

---

[138] See Circular no. H/5 (17.1.1947), Historical Department of the Regional Committee in Frankfurt to the Historical Commissions, YSA/M-1/B/File 2, and Activity Report of Benjamin Orenstein, Head of the *THK* in Franken (7.2.1946–1.6.1946), YSA/M-1/B/File 1.

[139] M.Y. Feigenbaum, Report to the First Convention of the Delegated Co-workers of the Historical Commissions in the American Zone in Germany (11–12.5.1947), YSA/M-1/B/File 11.

[140] The full correspondence of the *THK* is to be found in YSA/M-1/B/Files 1–14.

[141] *THK* to all Regional Commissions (27.1.1947), YSA/M-1/B/File 11; in the same vein see *THK* to the Historical Commission in Neu Freiman (14.6.1946), YSA/M-1/B/File 1.

[142] See Historical Commission Stuttgart to the *THK* (10.2.1947), YSA/M-1/B/File 2.

young members of *kibbutzim* document their wartime experiences. In the main the response to this initiative was disappointing except for the case of Foehrenwald where UNRRA workers assisted 345 young people in writing their responses which, as it turned out, contained important historical material.[143]

The Commission also sought to document the inner life of Jewish communities under Nazi rule.[144] This went beyond the expression of national assertiveness and, as Yisrael Kaplan saw it, was an attempt to see the historical reality in all of its complexity. The Nazis, in his reading, had failed in one of their central goals: they had not succeeded in undermining the *élan vital* of the Jews of Europe. "One of the life-giving extracts relished by almost every Jewish community was the eternal 'voice of Jacob' – the sayings, witticisms, anecdotes ... they were the soothing balsam for the broken hearts and sorely pressed, wounded souls."[145] Already in December 1945 Kaplan had published "A Questionnaire for the Collection of Materials relating to Folklore" which was aimed at using linguistic-ethnological tools to penetrate the inner recesses of Jewish life under Nazi rule. In this fashion Kaplan sought to uncover the speech patterns used by Jews with regard to the Germans and their local auxiliaries, their feelings about the *Judenrat*, the Jewish Police and other privileged Jews in the ghetto. Kaplan was in search of descriptions of starvation, forced labor, disease and the desperate fight to survive; the most comforting prayers, what was hoped for, what people dreamed about, which stories, past and present, were in demand, which songs were popular, what was written, drawn, photographed and the games children invented. These and more were the themes Kaplan's questions sought to capture for fear that the inner story of how Jews had attempted to fend off the corrosive power of Nazi dehumanization would be lost forever.

A further questionnaire attempted to illuminate Jewish resistance by documenting the history of underground movements in the ghetto, their decision to leave for the forest and subsequent partisan activity, relations within the unit, relations with the surrounding population, the role of women, the fate of the family camps, the names of the units, their commanders and those wounded or killed. In both these endeavors – folklore and resistance – the yield was rather disappointing. One successful endeavour, however, was the collection of popular songs from the war years – hundreds of songs were musically transcribed and audio recorded but for the rest the results were rather meager. With respect to the poor yield as regards resistance the reason was that veteran partisans organized in

[143] See YSA/M-1/B/File 11.   [144] Feigenbaum, Report to the First Convention": 8.
[145] Yisrael Kaplan, *Dos folks-moyl in natsi klem, Fun Letsn Khurbn*, no. 1 (August 1946): 22.

Pachach had set up an historical committee of their own and recorded their own testimonies. As far as museum-worthy objects were concerned the achievements fell short of the objectives set except for a valuable collection of some 700 wartime photographs. It was going to be many years before the realities that Kaplan's ethnography sought to uncover moved into the center of Holocaust research.

As regards Nazi documents of destruction, the major card-file of Dachau came into the possession of the *THK* as did thousands of additional documents collected locally by the historical committees. Tens of thousands of additional documents were within reach but because of the unavailability of duplicating facilities had to be forfeited. The Commission built up an impressive collection of antisemitic publications and acquired a large library that included many books confiscated from Jewish collections. In addition, with the permission of the Military Government, a questionnaire relating to prison camps and the fate of the local Jewish population was circulated among mayors and regional administrators. The response was surprisingly good and, according to Feigenbaum, some new and important facts were uncovered.[146] In the middle of 1947 a similar attempt to circulate the questionnaire in the Russian Zone was blocked by the Soviet authorities.

In terms of documentation, finally, the *THK* assiduously collected all the newspapers, journals, publications, posters and printed material of *She'erith Hapleitah* itself. It also commissioned the writing of 195 short histories of the new settlements that had grown up in the American Zone of Occupation.[147] Much of the former has been gratefully used in the writing of this history.

At the outset those running the new Central Historical Commission refused to contemplate the publication of the material they had begun to gather. They did not see it as a priority, they had neither the technical nor the financial means to do so and, in Feigenbaum's opinion, "there is too great a paucity of intellectual resources for us to allow ourselves to put out publications."[148] As the work progressed, however, it became increasingly clear that a literary platform was necessary "in order to come into direct contact with the society and to inspire them to join us in our labors."[149] It was only when the historian Yisrael Kaplan joined the Commission team, however, that the idea became practicable. The first number of *Fun Letsn Khurbn* appeared in August 1946 and two more were to follow before the

---

[146] YSA/M-1/B/File 11.   [147] Ibid.
[148] Feigenbaum, Report to the First Convention: 7.
[149] M.Y. Feigenbaum, "Peuloteha shel ha-va'adh ha-historit be-minchen" (The activities of the Historical Commission in Munich), *Dapim Le-cheker Ha-shoah Ve-ha-mered*, no. 1 (April 1951): 109.

year was out.[150] The journal was well received in *She'erith Hapleitah* and abroad and reached a distribution of 12,000 copies.[151] It succeeded in persuasively demonstrating the importance of historical documentation and in the months that followed the publication of the first number, a further 700 survivors gave testimony.[152]

In its first year *Fun Letstn Khurbn* reflected the work initiated by the *THK* with most of the material relating to the Nazi war against the Jews based on personal testimonies: the liquidation of communities, transports, forced labor, concentration and death camps.[153] Generally speaking, even though the descriptions were presented in a balanced, matter-of-fact tone, it is not difficult to detect the pain and to see the testimonies as an act of identification with those who did not survive. In their more intimate moments the testimonies appear to be part of an internal conversation in *She'erith Hapleitah* rather than an attempt to address a broader audience. On the one hand, they focused on the systematic killing, the atrocities carried out by the Nazis and their accomplices and, on the other, the vulnerability of the elderly, of mothers and children facing a terrible fate alone. These descriptions, for the most part, avoid being judgmental and, in view of the impossible odds against survival, seek to protect the dignity of the dead. Another, smaller group of articles discussed armed resistance to the Nazis in both ghetto and forest and aspects of what could be termed spiritual resistance.[154] Each number included a selection of photographs and poems from the war years and a few Nazi documents accompanied by a translation and commentary.

When *Fun Letstn Khurbn* first appeared Yosef Gar, the future historian of the Jews of Kovno, related to the goals of the Commission in general and the journal in particular:

We ought to carry forward this holy work for our people for the following reasons: 1) To honor the memory of our millions of martyrs ... 2) Out of a sense of obligation to the coming generations who will certainly seek an authentic account of our horrific experiences; 3) Because we cannot and should not allow this to be

---

[150] Feigenbaum, Report to the First Convention: 9.   [151] Ibid.

[152] All told by 1948 ten volumes were published.

[153] See, for example, Yaakov Waldman, "Di khelmner tragedye" (The Chelm tragedy), *Fun Letstn Khurbn*, no. 1 (August 1946): 8–12, and Moshe Weisberg, "Leben un umkum fun di yidn in dubne" (The life and death of the Jews in Dubno), *FLK*, no. 2 (September 1946): 1–11.

[154] Yisrael Segal, "Der ershte kontsert in vilner geto" (The first concert in the Vilna Ghetto), *FLK*, no. 1 (August 1946): 12–13; Aaron Shwarin, Chaim Shakliar, Avraham Feinberg, "Lachwa," *FLK*, no. 3 (October–November 1946): 1–11; Y. Rosenbaum, "Vertelekh fun lodsher geto" (Sayings from the Lodz Ghetto), *FLK*, no. 3 (October–November 1946): 68–71.

done for us ... by those who are not Jewish and 4) Because of the lessons to be learnt by Jews throughout the entire world about the Hitler phenomenon.[155]

It could be said that the *THK* fulfilled the first three goals laid down by Gar but consciously avoided any attempt to learn lessons and draw conclusions. This was best left to individuals and movements that sought to put their particular impress on the Jewish future.

The past flooded the consciousness of the survivors in Germany. "All of us here live with the shadows of yesterday. It is enough just to overhear the conversations in *She'erith Hapleitah* which start out with the word crematorium and end with memories of the camp. These too are the themes in speeches at weddings, celebrations, meetings and funerals."[156] This involvement with the past also features prominently in the reports of visitors who noticed how very quickly conversations spilt over into stories of personal tragedy. Leivik, for example, told of his first meeting with survivors in Garmisch on the second day of Passover. Sitting at the table of the Rabbi who was also the leader of the community

for hours on end, deep into the night we heard stories of the exodus from the ghetto, the exodus from the *katzet*, the exodus from Dachau, the exodus from Treblinka ... One after the other. Each was unable to wait for the previous speaker to finish. Often they would interrupt one another to take up the thread of *their own* story.[157]

This impulse, the need to tell, was equally evident in the survivor press. Over the period of a year some 120 articles told of communities that had been destroyed and the systematic killing in the death camps; some commemorated remarkable people who had not survived and others told the bitter tale of Jewish collaborators who had lost their humanity; many articles reported on ghetto revolts, partisan activity and resistance in the concentration camps.[158] The shared, underlying message at the heart

---

[155] Yosef Gar, "Fun letstn khurbn numer 1" (From the last destruction volume 1), *Undzer Veg*, no. 50 (25.9.1946): 14.
[156] S. Halevi (Levi Shalitan), "Yizkor," *Undzer Veg*, no. 44 (9.8.1946): 4.
[157] Leivik, *Mit der she'erit hapleitah*: 68.
[158] See the following examples: "Troyer akademye tsum 3 yortog fun likvidatsye fun bialystoker geto in bamberg" (Solemn memorial for the the 3rd anniversary of the liquidation of the Bialystok Ghetto in Bamberg), *Undzer Vort*, no. 25 (13.9.1946): 10; Elimelech Garfinkel, "Fun tomashever pinkas hakhurbn 1939–1942: tsu der 4-ter yortsayt fun di yidn likvidatsye" (From the Tomashow book of destruction 1939–1942: for the 4th memorial day of the liquidation of the Jews), *YT*, no. 47 (59) (15.11.1946): 7; Dr. G. Nower, "Zichronos vegn yanush korczak: tsum 3-yeriken yortsayt fun zayn tragishn umkum" (Memories of Janush Korczak: on the 3rd annual memorial of his tragic end), *Dos Fraye Vort*, no. 5 (11.12.1945): 3; Gustavo Schiller, "Yidishe kamfs-grupe in buchenwald" (Jewish combat-groups in Buchenwald), *LLT*, no. 21 (33) (13.6.1946): 6; A. Gelbart, "Tsestochover oyfshtand" (The Czestochowa uprising), *Undzer Veg*, no. 39 (28.6.1946): 3; Yitzchak Soutin, "A hitleryshe shtat-komandant, a yid, an anfirer

of all of these contributions to the press was *Zachor* – the imperative to remember. In time the survivors in Germany had also come to learn that forgetfulness was a constant temptation and remembrance "a heavy burden."[159] The real challenge was to embody memory in life, to continue the dreams and aspirations that had been nipped in the bud. As Shalom Kotler from Leipheim proclaimed in his salute to resistance fighters: "By your grave and in the light of your heroic deeds we swear to you that we shall live and fight and gather together the remnants of our orphaned people with both plow and gun in hand. This will be the great monument that we shall erect for you."[160] *Zachor* also meant making certain that the crimes of the Nazis would be engraved in the history of humankind and making every effort to ensure that the criminals had received their just punishment – the biblical injunction "To extinguish the memory of Amalek from beneath the heavens, do not forget" (Deuteronomy 25:19) served *She'erith Hapleitah* well. In truth, many of these calls for revenge were rhetorical flourishes that concealed a sinking feeling that despite the sentences handed down in Nuremberg, most of the murderers in Germany and elsewhere would not ultimately pay for their crimes.[161]

The anger and frustration to which this gave rise led some to point an accusing finger at the God who had chosen His people and then failed to intervene on their behalf.[162] As Leib Garfunkel gave expression to his anguish and pain: "You want to scream out, raising your hand to Heaven [saying] that we can exalt the Sovereign of the Universe for everything except the suffering of the little children, these unflawed little ones with their pure souls, for this we cannot forgive you, not today, not tomorrow and not in even a hundred years."[163] These accusations were not only

fun yiddishe partizanen: zikhronos fun a partisan" (A Hitlerite town commander, a Jew, a leader of Jewish partisans: memories of a partisan), *LLT*, no. 19 (31) (4.6.1946): 9; Tuviah Blatt, "Der oyfshtand in sobibor: a kurts bild fun oyfshtand fun di yidn in farnikhtungs lager sobibor dem 14.10.1943" (The uprising in Sobibor: a brief sketch of the uprising of the Jews in the extermination camp Sobibor on the 14.10.1943), *A Haym*, no. 19 (30.8.1946): 4.

[159] Dr. Fayvel Wiederman, "Nit fargesn" (Do not forget), *LLT*, no. 13 (25) (15.4.1946): 7.

[160] Shalom Kotler, "Interesante fragmentn fun oyfshtand" (Interesting fragments relating to the uprising), *A Haym*, no. 10 (2.5.1946): 10.

[161] M. Shuster, "In dermonungs tog" (On the day of remembrance), *A Haym*, no. 17 (16.8.1946): 4, and Dr. Fayvel Wiederman, "Der kult fun heroizm" who called for revenge equal to the crime.

[162] See G. Avigeto, "Far tsvei-yorn in kovner geto: tsum yortsayt fun der aktsye iber kinder, alte un invalidn" (For two years in the Kovno ghetto: on the memorial day of the action against children, the elderly and invalids), *LLT*, no. 12 (24) (2.4.1946): 13. See also Yaakov Oleiski, "Di likvidatsye fun kovner geto" (The liquidation of the Kovno Ghetto), *LLT*, no. 41 (53) (9.10.1946): 11–12.

[163] L. Garfunkel, "Di kinder-aktsye in kovner geto" (The children's "action" in the Kovno Ghetto), *Undzer Veg*, no. 11 (14.12.1945): 4.

directed at others – they implicitly included the survivors themselves as well. Thus, the printed accounts highlighted the fate of those who could not save themselves.[164] Leib Garfunkel who wrote about the *Kinder-Aktsie* in the Kovno Ghetto described the agonizing dilemmas parents faced with regard to the rescue of their children.[165] In the light of reports regarding the fate of children received from other ghettos, many parents weighed the possibility of handing their children over to non-Jewish families. At the end of March 1944 when most of the adults were at their places of work, the Germans rounded up all the children they could find and murdered them. The parents who had not been able to bear the separation or, as happened elsewhere, had to watch helplessly as their children were driven to their death could not forgive themselves.

This unspeakable grief and pain was everywhere just beneath the surface of life in *She'erith Hapleitah* but rarely spoken about publicly. One such moment came when Gutman spoke at the end of a seminar run by Leivik with the leadership of the Landsberg camp:

By what right do we continue to live when those closest to us have have perished in the crematoria? By what right have we remained untouched by the flames? By what right have we come to terms with the thought of going on with our lives and saying to ourselves that we, so to speak, are not guilty that we remained alive?

When I see any Jewish children amongst us I think to myself: It is possible that tomorrow they will fuel additional crematoria!

And us – it's as if nothing has happened. We have lost everything, we have lost everyone and – we lie down to sleep, we get up, we argue among ourselves, we hold discussions, we rejoin parties and – we talk of ourselves as martyrs!

I tell you again: we are not martyrs but cast-offs! We are not worth the earth on which we stand.

This is exactly what sticks in my hearts as I sit here and hear everyone speaking. I must scream it out. I must, I must![166]

After Gutman spoke, reported Leivik, all those present fell silent. He had touched on a hidden truth that rendered further discussion pointless.

For *She'erith Hapleitah*, as we have seen, remembering was a complex undertaking shot through with contradiction. Commemoration answered a deeply felt need to honor the dead; it was a way of galvanizing the survivors in preparation for the hard road ahead and bringing unfulfilled dreams to fruition. The very act of remembrance, on the other hand, could reawaken a paralyzing guilt that engendered remorse and despair. This danger was ever-present for no one had succeeded in providing a persuasive account for what had befallen them. The impossible questions

---

[164] For example, Y.K. (Yisrael Kaplan), "Gedenk dem tog! Riga di ir ha-harega" (Remember the day! Riga the city of slaughter), *Undzer Veg*, no. 10 (7.12.1945): 4.
[165] Garfunkel, "Di kinder-akstye."   [166] Leivik, *Mit der she'erit hapleitah*: 99.

about the meaning of the catastrophe remained unanswered. "Why," agonized Leon Neiberg, "did they die such strange and horrific deaths? What were they guilty of in the eyes of the world?"[167] Or as K. Shabtai formulated it as he witnessed the opening of the Nuremberg trials: "I felt as if I was participating in the terrible, colossal funeral of all our fathers and children, mothers and wives and I had this strong feeling that the spirits of our martyrs were floating around in the hall and had come in order to demand an answer to their terrible question: Why?"[168]

In his study of the survivors of the atomic bomb dropped on Hiroshima Robert Lifton identified a psychological connection between the contradictory aspects of memory we have been describing:

> In studying the Hiroshima experience I have been impressed by the relationship of death–guilt to the process of identification – to the survivor's tendency to incorporate within himself an image of the dead, and then to think, feel and act as he imagines they did or would. He feels impelled, in other words, to place himself in the position of the person or persons maximally wronged – or else to castigate himself for falling short of such identification. The same is true of the concentration camp survivors.[169]

In the contest between these contradictory tendencies it could be argued that the positive identification came out on top. Not always, not everywhere. The dark side of sustained terror and destruction demanded a reckoning and yet, the fact that memory did not surrender to despair, that life was chosen in response to death was one of the more significant achievements of *She'erith Hapleitah*.

---

[167] Leon Neiberg, "Zikhronos vegn oyfshtand in varshe" (Memories of the uprising in Warsaw), *Undzer Veg*, no. 28 (15.4.1946): 7.
[168] K. Shabtai, "Makom haresha – sham hamishpat" (In the place of evil – there justice be done), *Undzer Veg*, no. 9 (30.11.1945): 4.
[169] Lifton, *Death in Life*: 495–496.

10   The survivors confront Germany

The survivors who remained in Germany after liberation, together with the tens of thousands who were drawn to the American Zone of Occupation over the next two years, sought to escape the hostility of their neighbors, the fear of being trapped behind sealed borders and ever-present reminders of the past. In Occupied Germany, the US Army and UNRRA afforded protection and the provision of basic needs, *She'erith Hapleitah* offered community and care while both the Jewish Agency and JDC could serve as potential bridges to the future. In their first months on German soil the survivors were persuaded that deliverance could not be long in coming – surely, given what they had been through, the enlightened world would recognize their elementary right to start anew in a land of their own. Labour's adherence to the White Paper policy was a rude shock but hopes soared again when the Anglo-American Committee of Inquiry recommended allowing 100,000 survivors to enter Palestine forthwith. With the understanding that nothing was going to change just yet, the pendulum swung again and deep disappointment set in. They were stuck in Germany with no way out.

The people of *She'erith Hapleitah* were keenly aware of the bitter irony of their situation, of being forced to prolong their stay in the heartland of Hitler's Germany. When this was seen as a temporary measure and Germany as nothing more than a way station, the bitterness and anger could be kept in check. But, as the months dragged by and the policies of the Military Government became less accommodating, frustration grew and with it the tensions of their anomalous situation came to the fore. From the outset the disparity between the poor living conditions of *She'erith Hapleitah* and what they perceived as the relative well being of the German population was a constant source of tension and anger. Those who had been stripped of their property saw this as a burning insult and, starting with its founding conference in St. Ottilien in July 1945, the Surviving Remnant insistently demanded material compensation for what had been stolen or lost: "We, the survivors of 7 million murdered Jews, as War Allies demand compensation for Jewish property that was either plundered or destroyed in the framework of reparations from Germany which will assist us in rebuilding our homes in our land."[1]

It should be noted, at the outset, that while in Germany, no survivor voices were raised in principled opposition to the acceptance of compensation. H. Leivik spoke for himself when he argued that the affirmative response of survivors to the General Claims law passed by the German Government in 1949 set a dangerous precedent.[2] The arguments behind his passionate cry "Do not take bloodmoney from the Germans" had not guided the Surviving Remnant who believed that it was possible to make a firm distinction between property and those things to which a price could not be attached. As Zalman Grinberg put it, there could be "no compensation for the horrific pain and suffering, for the tears shed by mothers and children. Which earthly power can reawaken the dead to life?"[3] It was so obvious it hardly needed to be justified – this was simply the return of stolen property[4] for the benefit of those who survived, an elementary act of justice the victims of Nazism would surely have welcomed.[5]

In the short run these monies could help the survivors achieve a modicum of independence and limit their undignified dependence on outside help. The funds referred to were enormous for in Germany alone they would have to include private and public property confiscated by the Nazis, the emigration tax, the fine imposed on the Jewish community after Krystallnacht and additional forms of state-sanctioned robbery. If the core budgets of *She'erith Hapleitah* were to come from stolen Jewish property, as Ernst Landau suggested, it would be necessary to set up a public body to represent Jewish claims on Germany to the Allies. In the first instance the demands of the *ZK* focused on the transfer of communal property and heirless private property to shared guardianship with the public body that needed to be set up.[6] This demand, that remained central to the agenda of the Central Committee for many months, was

---

[1] Resolutionen und Beschluesse der Konferenz der ueberlebenden Juden auf dem deutschen u. oesterrichischen Territorium, St. Ottilien (25–26 July 1945), CZA/S6/4360.

[2] See H. Leivik, "No Blood-Money from the Germans," *Jewish Frontier* (May 1950): 14. For detailed background see Nicholas Balabkins, *West German Reparations to Israel* (New Brunswick, 1971).

[3] Dr. Z. Grinberg, "In dervartung" (In expectation), *Undzer Veg*, no. 7 (20.11.1945): 2.

[4] Y. D. Sheinson, "Mitn ponim tsum lebn: vidergutmakhung" (Facing life: reparations), *Dos Vort*, no. 8 (11.12.1946): 3; see also "Krigs-reparatsies far yidn" (War reparations for Jews), *A Haym*, no. 23 (9.10.1946): 1.

[5] Grinberg, "In dervartung."

[6] Ernst Landau, "Falshe yidishe finants-politik" (Misguided Jewish finance politics), *Dos Fraye Vort*, no. 13 (3.12.1946): 2.

underscored by two further developments. The German population, first of all, had begun to return to economic stability[7] and, at the same time, remained seemingly oblivious to the crimes they had committed or that were committed in their name. There was "no trace of regret"[8] and, equally, no attempt to make good crimes that suffered compensation: "It was not yet self-understood that the victims of political and, indeed, economic terror from 1933 to 1945 have to be compensated."[9] Instead of sympathetic concern for their needs, they were met everywhere with hostility and constant complaints about the amount of food they consumed and the number of houses they required for billeting. There was a minority that favored compensatory action, some for reasons of conscience, others because they believed it would serve to neutralize the opprobrium of the past and help to hasten Germany's return to the comity of nations. When some of their initiatives finally came to fruition they provided a small but useful supplement to the chronically strained budget of the Central Committee.

It was not the Germans only, however, who adopted dilatory tactics. In time, the leaders of *She'erith Hapleitah* came to appreciate that the realization of their claims was part of a complex international undertaking that would be moved forward by negotiation rather than public pressure. Direct pressure was of little avail because all major economic decisions went through the Military Government that received its directions from Washington. Jewish property, private and communal, that remained behind in Germany was valued at £800,000,000 without taking into account claims for physical disability, loss of income and earning power. This was a vast sum especially in view of the Military Government's first priority of rebuilding the German economy so as to reduce the heavy cost of the occupation. This accounted for its consistent objection to transferring either hard currency or industrial equipment abroad so leaving the thousands of potential claimants high and dry. This situation necessitated close cooperation between the office of the Special Adviser on Jewish Affairs, the *ZK*, the Jewish Agency, JDC and World Jewish Congress so as to ensure that in any overall settlement with Germany the legitimate demands of the Jewish people would be dealt with fairly.[10]

---

[7] Chaim Rosenbaum, "Blimelekh fun neo-natsishn gartn" (Flowers from the neo-Nazi garden), *LLT*, no. 17 (29) (17.5.1946): 3.

[8] Ernst Landau, "Vos hert zikh mit der widergutmachung" (What's happening about reparations), *Dos Fraye Vort*, no. 51 (4.10.1946): 5.

[9] Ibid.

[10] Ernst Landau, "Vos iz nit in ordnung in bayern" (What is not right in Bavaria), *Dos Fraye Vort*, no. 46 (30.8.1946): 3.

The representatives of Jewish organizations distinguished between individual claims for the return of property and compensation as opposed to the collective claims of the Jewish people.[11] This general claim flowed from the fact that the Germans "destroyed entire communities in Europe and saddled the Jewish people with the obligation to help those uprooted and rendered homeless to start anew."[12] By their calculations the resettlement of 100,000 Jews in Palestine would cost £50 million. This time, however, it was a formal, legal obstacle that stood in the way of the realization of their claim: there were doubts about the validity of a collective claim made by a group that lacked internationally recognized collective status. As an interim step, not contingent on the settlement of the larger claims, the Conference on Reparations in Paris decided at the end of 1945 and then again in the summer of 1946 that $2,500,000 of German funds captured outside of the country be made available to the survivors in Germany through the good offices of the JDC and the Jewish Agency.

What remained to be done in Germany proper was to keep track of German legislation with respect to compensation and amends. It should be noted that as late as the beginning of 1947, with the exception of Thuringia, no laws arranging the return of property had been passed. In the American Occupation Zone only two relevant laws were operative: Military Directive 52 that placed property that had been confiscated or acquired by pressure under the supervision of the Military Government and a law that provided for monthly assistance to victims of Nazism in need.[13] A law had been proposed to the *Länderrat* – the coordinating body of the states in the American Zone – with regard to the direct return of property. In the seventy clauses of the proposed law (in which the word "Jew" was not mentioned even once), there were, nonetheless, two determinations of cardinal importance to Jewish survivors: the annulment of sales sealed under pressure and a reference to private and communal property left without legal heirs. In this regard the Military Government accepted the suggestion of the Jewish Agency that this property not revert to the German states but, throughout 1946, refused to rule on the next part of the proposal which was to transfer the legal rights of title to an international Jewish body. In the absence of any real legislation, the Central Committee, Jewish Agency and JDC decided, at the beginning

---

[11] See Dr. Nussbaum, "Ha-tviot shel ha-yehudim neged ha-am ha-germani ve-neged germanim bodedim" (Jewish claims against the German people and individual Germans), Minutes of the Conference of *Shlichim* (Emissaries) in Germany, January 1947, CZA/S6/4685. For the general background to these developments see Nana Sagi, *German Reparations: A History of the Negotiations* (Jerusalem, 1980): 31–40.
[12] Nussbaum, "Ha-tviot shel ha-yehudim."   [13] Ibid.

of 1947, quietly to set in motion a number of private claims so as to set legal precedents in anticipation of new legislation.[14]

When it became apparent that the battle for just compensation would be long and hard, the public debate began to shift from material to moral claims.[15] The journalist Ernst Landau, himself Austrian born, sought to persuade the German public that "reparations were not only a concern of Jews and political perscutees, but should also be an inner, deeply personal opportunity to return to democracy, justice and decency."[16] The conduct towards the Jews, in his estimate, would come to serve as the touchstone of German democracy. Others and most especially survivors from Eastern Europe saw things in a very different light.[17] What Germany would ultimately have to pay to its primary victims would symbolize both its collective guilt and responsibility for what had been perpetrated by the Nazi regime. As Samuel Gringauz formulated the issue at a later date:

Punishment can be meted out only to individuals on the basis of individual proven guilt. Even moral condemnation can be applied only where there is individual guilt. But material responsibility for criminal deeds can be placed on an aggregate of humanity in the form of financial reparations for crimes committed by the institutions, agents and representatives of that collective. This is, in fact, the meaning of restitution. *It is the criminal-material responsibility of the German people for the misdeeds of its agents and representatives ... One might look upon it as a symbolic demonstration of German guilt expressed in financial terms.*[18]

The assumption of German collective responsibility for the crimes of the Nazi regime was a critical commonplace in the survivor community.[19] It was fed by a widely shared sense that in their darkest hour the Jewish people had been faced by undifferentiated hostility so that every German, man, woman and even child, awakened foreboding and fear. It was hard to forget how German civilians had walked past heaps of corpses in railroad stations without batting an eyelid. As Jean Amery who was liberated in Bergen Belsen put it: "It seemed to me as if I had experienced their

---

[14] See Dr. A. Blumowicz, Barikht fun der tetikayt fun tsentral komitet farn kadents yor 1946 (Report of the activity of the Central Committee for 1946): 7, YIVO/DPG 658. For *She'erith Hapleitah* this did not entail surrendering their demand for full reparation; it represented, instead, a tactical decision to work with international Jewish organizations towards this end - see the opening address of David Treger at the Second Congress of *She'erith Hapleitah*, Bad Reichenhall, 10–12 February 1947, YIVO/DPG 658.

[15] See, for example, Mendel Mann, "Dos ponim fun hayntikn Daytschland" (The face of contemporary Germany), *Der Nayer Moment*, no. 16 (29.11.1946): 4.

[16] Landau, "Vos hert zikh."   [17] Rosenbaum, "Blimelekh."

[18] Samuel Gringauz, "Germans Should Pay: A Reply to Leivik," *Jewish Frontier* (May 1950): 17.

[19] See, for example, C. Berger, "Gemaynzamer akhrayut" (Collective responsibility), *Oyf der Fray*, no. 1 (December 1945): 1.

atrocities as collective ones."[20] The German populace who were aware of these feelings feared a night of long daggers following liberation. When the threat did not materialize, however, there was a widespread attempt to distance themselves from the crimes committed in their name.[21] The survivors were shocked and angered by the degree of denial and the repeated attempts to cast doubt on what they knew in their bones. Thus, anyone who followed the German press, as Yosef Sperling observed, "could easily discern the gigantic task undertaken by the Germans to wash away any connection between their people and these murderous deeds and killings."[22] Suddenly the legendary unity of the German people fell apart, and it appeared to break into tiny factions that saw not, knew not or had tenaciously fought Nazi tyranny. "None of us would have believed . . . what we are experiencing today while locked up in the *katzet*. We were very understandably unable to grasp that there were quite so many anti-fascists, Communists, socialists, democrats and liberals of every description in Germany."[23] In the same vein Gringauz wrote a satirical piece on the unsuccessful attempt to track down three Nazis in all of Germany.[24]

Furthermore: after the war the country was flooded by pamphlets seeking to contend with questions of conscience. Many of the essays were written by Catholics and proposed one, common thesis: "the guilt for the evil deeds performed these last years rests with Satan or the Devil who unfortunately invaded the person of the Fuehrer [*sic*] and led him to sinfulness."[25] Shulevitz suggested, therefore, that the Devil also be put on trial in Nuremberg. Others used the metaphor of a slave ship in the hands of a mad captain and sadistic crew where liberation and independent action would only become possible if the ship went down."[26]

The people of the Surviving Remnant were bitterly opposed to what they saw as the attempt to sidestep and blur German collective responsibility for Nazi crimes. As part of their attempt to block these evasive tactics there were those who underlined the deep historical roots

---

[20] Jean Amery, *At the Mind's Limits: Contemplations by a Survivor on Auschwitz and its Realities* (Bloomington, 1980): 65.

[21] Mendel Mann, "Zei kumen tsu zikh" (They are recovering), *Der Nayer Moment*, no. 14 (10.11.1946): 2.

[22] Yosef Sperling, "Mit efene oygn" (With open eyes), *A Haym*, no. 4 (14.3.1946): 7.

[23] Echad, "Az ikh bin shvarts un du bist vays" (If I am black then you are white), *Undzer Veg*, no. 5 (9.11.1945): 6.

[24] Elmar Digrin (S. Gringauz), "Purim 5706" (Purim 1946), *LLT*, no. 10 (22) (15.3. 1946): 1.

[25] Avraham Shulevitz, "Shuldik iz der tayvel" (The devil is to blame), *LLT*, no. 31 (43) (2.8.1946): 3.

[26] Dr. Rudolf Valsonok, "Ikh bet a vort: tsu der diskusie iber dem kol-kore fun franz werfel tsum daytshn folk" (May I have a word: on the discussion of Franz Werfel's manifesto to the German people), *LLT*, no. 2 (20.10.1945): 4.

of Nazism and, in line with this approach, Adv. Aldak of Foehrenwald argued that Hitler's singularity lay less in the originality of his ideas and more in their translation into reality.[27] As he saw it, the three pillars of Nazism – racial superiority, expansion to the East and total war – had shaped German policy since Bismarck. What was revolutionary about Hitler was his consistent actualization of the guiding motifs of German political culture. Others posited the existence of a German soul or personality "with its chauvinistic posturing, its superiority complex, its mania for mastery, lust for war and disregard for all non-Germans."[28] If these were shared characteristics, it made little sense to suggest a deep divide between a handful of criminals and an essentially peace-loving people. In this sense, "the whole German people, including those in opposition, should be seen as sharing in the guilt for the destruction of Europe. In fact and in deed, the majority of the people served the ideal of murder."[29]

It was the German people, moreover, who put the reins of government in Hitler's hands and continued to support him to the bitter end.[30] In this regard, it was crucial to draw a clear line between the public reservations expressed after Hitler's fall as opposed to the blind obedience he was able to command when things looked better. Who was jubilant, asked C. Berger, when Hitler moved his troops into the Rhineland, annexed Austria and the Sudetenland and carved up Czechoslovakia? Who welcomed the conquest of France, pushed to force Russia into submission and saluted Rommel in Africa? Who was it that supplanted Jesus with Hitler and called him the Savior? Thus in the victorious phase "there was no difference of opinion whatsoever between Hitlerism and the German people".[31] For twelve years there had been no sign of opposition to Hitler or his policies and, as Rudolf Valsonok commented on Franz Werfel's call to the German people: "not one single person throughout the Germanic lands took a stand against the tyranny, thereby publicly demonstrating that in Germany (with the exception of the famous Pastor Niemoeller) no one was to be found that feared God more than he feared the Gestapo."[32] The survivors were highly skeptical, therefore, of the reports of widespread German resistance that began to do the rounds after the war. There were those who courageously swam against the current but they were few and far between. The stories

---

[27] Adv. D. Aldak, "Der Kayser iz avek – di generaln zaynen geblibn" (The emperor has departed – the generals have remained), *Bamidbar*, no. 7 (4.6.1946): 4.

[28] Menes, "Di 'hydra' hat asakh kep" (The "hydra" has numerous heads), *A Haym*, no. 9 (2.5.1946): 6.

[29] Ibid.   [30] Grinberg, "In derwartung."   [31] Berger, "Gemaynzamer akhrayut."

[32] Valsonok, "Ikh bet a vort."

of a student revolt in Munich in 1943 were wildly exaggerated as were the tales of widespread clerical resistance. The relatively large number of men of the cloth imprisoned in Dachau, surmised Valsonok, was more indicative of the anti-Christian bent of the regime than of active church opposition to the Nazis. But most incriminating of all was the remarkable fact "that never and nowhere did it happen that a raid, a pogrom, a deportation, a slaughter was avoided because of the resistance of the German perpetrators who had decided to disobey the order."[33]

In the eyes of the Surviving Remnant, not only did the German people support Hitler, significant sections of the public, in addition, played an active role in the murder of millions of Jews, Gypsies, Russians, Poles and others. This was a huge killing machine that required the sustained cooperation of all of its parts: the SS, the Nazi Party, the Army, the government service, big industries and others.[34] The murder of millions

could only be carried out by a broad, extended organization of hundreds and thousands of criminals backed up by industry in the construction of the crematoria, in partnership with firms that produced the required poison gas, with the assistance of science to process new raw material, with the aid of the Reichsbank to dispose of the valuables stolen from the victims. In short, a murder-organization in which all sections of the population participated ... an entire people – a gang of murderers.[35]

The death industry in all of its ramifications also made a mockery of the plaint so commonly heard after the war: we did not see, we did not hear, we did not know.[36] *She'erith Hapleitah* refused to believe that there was anyone in Germany who did not know directly or indirectly what was happening in the East and later on their doorstep. Whence, inquired the survivors, did the strange trains loaded with hair, spectacles and clothing stained with blood come from?[37] Soldiers sent home the photographs they took of mass murders, 15 million families received parcels of stolen Jewish goods and the *Kraft durch Freude* organization turned to the administration of Maidanek with a request for perambulators, children's

---

[33] Ibid.

[34] Moshe Gershenovitz, "Das 'herren' folk oyf der bashuldikungs bank" (The "herrenvolk" in the seat of the accused), *Untervegs* (4.4.1946): 4; and, in addition, Echad, "Di khayot in di oygn" (To look the animals in the eye), *Undzer Veg*, no. 6 (16.11.1945): 4.

[35] Dr. Tuli, "Letste teg in nirenberg" (Last day in Nuremberg), *Undzer Velt*, no. 17(25) (29.9.1946): 7.

[36] Menes, "Di offensive fun tiranishe neo-hitlerizm: oyfn margines fun nirenberger protses" (The offensive of tyrannical neo-Hitlerism: from the margins of the Nuremberg trial), *A Haym*, no. 9 (2.5.1946): 6.

[37] Berger, "Gemaynzamer akhrayut."

clothing and toys.[38] All told, if the German claims were taken at face value one might reach "the tragic-comic suspicion: that it was the Jews and non-Jews that gassed and cremated themselves, that, in fact, this was not mass murder but mass suicide and that's why nobody except for themselves was aware of their death."[39] Many survivors had vivid recollections of their reception by the local German population towards the end of the war – the indifference, the cold lack of concern, the cruel laughter. "I remember well," recalled a survivor of the death marches, "how on the return march to the Tyrol nobody brought out a drop of water for those dying of thirst."[40]

What happened after liberation also served to reinforce the conviction of many survivors that the German people were collectively responsible for what had happened to the Jewish people. Only rarely did anyone come across shame, regret and basic humanity – for the most part they met up with hostility, barely concealed hatred and a lack of humanity.[41] In this regard Rudolf Valsonok wrote a short story about the inhabitants of a small village that spent their time "drinking beer and having babies"[42] and in this way succeeded in cutting themselves off from the storm that raged without. Moreover, "their private consciences were kept inviolate from any contingencies by bowing to the categorical imperative of corpse-like obedience in carrying out the commands of their divinely ordained leader."[43] One day they caught sight of some strange looking people harnessed to a wagon and they tried hard not to notice what they had seen. And then the big change came – the great leader turned into a corpse and the dream of ruling the world had, unfortunately, to be set aside. And then the strange people came back, unguarded, and the village folk feared for their lives. They therefore received their unwanted guests warmly and, after a while, wanted to know when they would be moving on. When they heard the sad news of homes destroyed and families shot "their hearts darkened and their thoughts clouded over."[44] How were they to be rid of these people? They prayed for an answer throughout the night and the next day their prayers were answered. Soldiers came, put the visitors in a camp and fenced them in. The villagers could breathe easy again. And what of the strangers? In the long and bloody years of their slavery they had become accustomed to living in hovels and narrow

---

[38] Chaim Goldzamd, "Shvaygt" (They keep silent), *Undzer Vort*, no. 19 (26.7.1946): 6; see, in addition, Jonas Turkow, "Mir veln zei kaynmol nit fargesn" (We shall never forget them), *Undzer Veg*, no. 28 (15.4.1946): 12.
[39] Menes, "Di offensive."   [40] Echad, "Az ikh bin shvarts."   [41] Ibid.
[42] Velvele Tomarkin (Rudolf Valsonok), "Der beyzer gewissen: a maysele" (The bad conscience: a tale), *LLT*, no. 2 (20.10.1945): 6.
[43] Ibid.   [44] Ibid.

confines behind barbed wire so that they neither murmured nor complained and accepted their fate with "submissive grace."[45]

Within the Surviving Remnant there was a small group that would neither bow to their fate with "submissive grace" nor would they make do with material compensation. The Germans had certainly to bear the full cost of their crimes but this did not in any way diminish their right to take revenge and redeem the blood of the victims of Nazism.[46] This was the will and testimony they brought from the valley of death for, as M. Besserglik expressed it: "In those nightmarish days each one of us had one request, one desire: a passion for life but only so as to take revenge."[47] After the liberation Besserglik was able to capture an SS man who had served in the Czestochowa Ghetto and handed him over to the Occupation authorities. As a result, he testified, "I went through the most powerful experience in my life. I was drunk with my lucky break. I have come to see it as the event which to a certain extent helped me put my life together after the terrible storm. Revenge is sweet."[48] The words of Mordechai Gebirtig, the poet from Krakow, spoke powerfully to many survivors:

> And I tell you, brother, remember what I say!
> The only consolation and comfort –
> Will come, do you hear? A day will come
> On which it will be ours to take revenge.[49]

However, beyond sporadic acts of revenge carried out in the first flush of victory, the survivors in Germany did not, for the most part, take active steps to exact retribution. The small group that made vengeance their primary goal cut themselves off from other survivors, operated underground and, in consequence, their thoughts, plans and deeds remained unknown and did not leave their mark on the life of *She'erith Hapleitah*. Today, even though many details remain undisclosed, a good part of the story in all its complexity has been researched and made public. *Hanakam* – the Revenge group – consisted of partisans and ghetto fighters who made up the inner core of the Division of East European Survivors. It should be noted that the critical role played by the Division in laying the foundations of the *Brichah* and setting it in motion was fed by a number of

---

[45] Ibid.

[46] Yosel Holzer, "Haylike nekome" (Holy revenge), *Undzer Veg*, no. 13 (28.12.1945): 4.

[47] M. Besserglik, "Nekome iz zis" (Revenge is sweet), *LLT*, no. 8 (20) (1.3.1946): 3. In this regard see also the poem of Sonia Sorzsher, "Mir viln nisht mer shenkn" (We no longer wish to forgive), *Untervegs* (4.4.1946): 3.

[48] Besserglik, "Nekome iz zis."

[49] Mordechai Gebirtig, "A tog fun nekome" (A day of revenge), *LLT*, no. 9 (21) (8.3.1946): 3.

motivations, some clear and others less obvious. The profound sense of solidarity with the bereaved survivors, the fear that the danger of persecution had not yet passed and the hope that the routes they were opening would lead from Eastern Europe to Palestine were there for all to see. But there was more to it. It also gave expression to a sharp rejection of any attempt to rebuild Jewish life on the ruins of the Nazi devastation for to do so would of necessity be based on an unfortunate attempt to either repress or domesticate the past. As Abba Kovner, the leader of the group, testified: "We said to ourselves that if we were privileged to live, the privilege had been granted to us so that we would take steps to ensure that this life would no longer follow its usual course" and what was required, therefore, "Was to shock the world by a deed that would signify that what had been done did not allow for repentance, could not be made good. That was how the idea of the *Hanakam* group was born."[50] The world would have to be taught that the murder of an entire people would call forth terrible retribution.

From the second half of 1944 those committed to revenge began to separate out from the rest of the Division and increasingly focused on the unprecedented task that lay ahead: were they convinced that they could morally sustain an act of revenge that would literally follow the biblical model of "an eye for an eye and a tooth for a tooth"? What should they do, to whom, when and where? What needed to be done in preparation? Who could be turned to for help and who could be trusted with their secret? In the first third of 1945 the group became committed to two operative goals: first and foremost, to inflict massive harm on the German civilian population and, secondly, to target SS and Gestapo prisoners of war for large-scale retribution. This conspiratorial preoccupation with revenge and its implications put a strain on relations with those who saw the exodus from Europe and illegal immigration to Palestine as their essential concern. The decision, in mid-1945, to seek out the Jewish Brigade in Northern Italy provided both sides with a useful way of avoiding open confrontation: those committed to the *Brichah* saw themselves cooperating with Palestinian soldiers in the promotion of aliyah, whereas the others who were looking to get closer to Germany hoped to find helpful allies within the ranks of the Jewish Brigade. As it turned out, while

---

[50] See combined Interview with Abba Kovner, Vitke Kovner and Ruz'ka Korczak, OHD/ 2(4)a: 26. See also " Reishita shel 'habrichah' ketnuat hamonim be'eduyotav shel abba kovner" (The beginnings of the 'brichah' as a popular movement in the testimonies of Abba Kovner), *Yalkut Moreshet*, no. 37 (June 1984), and no. 38 (December 1984). The present discussion owes a great deal to the first comprehensive discussion of this important chapter of history by Levi Aryeh Sarid, "Irgun hanakam – korotav, d'muto, ma'asav" (The "Hanakam" organization – its history, character and deeds), *Yalkut Moreshet*, no. 52 (April 1992): 35–106.

some of the people they took into their confidence were supportive, many were strenuously opposed and in balance the *Hanakam* group did not gain much.[51] In August 1944 Kovner left for Palestine in order both to promote the project and to procure the wherewithal for its execution, some of the group remained in Italy as *Brichah* activists while the rest of the group, who felt Kovner's absence keenly, infiltrated Germany in order to prepare the way for what they had in mind. A logistic center was set up in Munich and smaller teams established themselves in Hamburg, Frankfurt, Nuremberg and Dachau.

Kovner returned to Europe in December 1945 having achieved some of the tasks he set himself. All of the people he took into his confidence supported the attacks on the SS and Gestapo prisoner of war camps; almost none responded affirmatively when it came to the plans to harm hundreds of thousands if not many more civilians. When the ship got close to France, Kovner, suspected of being an anti-British terrorist, was arrested and jailed in Egypt for many months. Deprived of its leader, financial support and the critical means of putting their plan into action, the group in Germany found itself in dire circumstances and Kovner, writing from jail, advised them to rethink their plans. At this time Shaul Avigur, the head of the *Mossad* for Illegal Immigration met with Pasha Reichman (Yitzchak Avidov), Kovner's deputy, in Paris and let it be understood that the leadership of the Yishuv was opposed to any large-scale action that would threaten the *Brichah*, the continued presence of the Jewish Brigade in Europe, the purchase of arms and illegal immigration which, when taken together, were seen as crucial components in the fight for statehood. When it came to more defined targets of revenge, on the other hand, logistic support would be forthcoming. Nachum Kremer (Shadmi) who was sent in February 1946 to coordinate *Haganah* activities in *She'erith Hapleitah* stuck to this line in his dealings with the *Hanakam* group while seeking to persuade them to accept his operational authority.[52] No one could act in the name of the Jewish people, especially when so much was at stake, without the authorization of a representative body. The group was loathe to compromise its freedom of action but given the pressing need for both financial assistance and institutional backing, they finally relented and began to plan smaller scale revenge against the SS prisoners. Some members of the group gained access to the bakery of Stalag 13 near

---

[51] On the encounter with the Jewish Brigade see Yehudah Toubin, "Mifgash anshei ha-brigada im rishonei ha-nitzolim – edut ishit u-mabat le-achor" (The meeting of the Brigade members with the first survivors – a personal testimony and retrospective view), *Yalkut Moreshet*, no. 39 (May 1985).

[52] See Sarid, "Irgun hanakam": 78–79; for a different perspective see Yehuda Slutzki, *Sefer toldot ha-haganah: mi-ma'avak le-milchamah – [3]* (A history of the *Haganah*: from struggle to war – [vol. 3]) (Tel Aviv, 1978): 1072–1704.

Nuremberg while others were taken on as kitchen workers in the SS prisoner camp set up in Dachau.[53] On 13 April 1946 an attempt was made in Nuremberg to poison the prisoners' bread but, because of unforeseen circumstances, the team was unable to complete its task. According to the report of an American Jewish officer 2,800 SS men were poisoned and 900 subsequently died. On 24 April the *Süddeutsche Zeitung* reported that 2,283 SS prisoners had suffered arsenic poisoning and 207 had been hospitalized. Yulek C. who led the Nuremberg team believed the former estimate and argued that US military censorship prevented further disclosures as to what had really transpired.[54] The attempt to poison the prisoners' food in Dachau was scuttled for reasons unknown as the plan was about to go into action.[55]

The group, numbering some forty members, immediately redeployed, desperately sought out new avenues of activity but finally heeded the call of both Kovner and the *Haganah* and set sail for Palestine in the middle of 1946. Having settled on Kibbutz Ein Hachoresh the group almost immediately began a round of discussions about returning to Europe to complete what had been left undone.[56] They could not settle down to their new lives – so some of them felt – before they had done their duty and thus in late 1947 and early 1948 a small group returned to Europe. Over the next two years they carried out a series of attacks against ex-Nazis and neo-Nazi organizations and returned to Israel in 1950.[57]

The *Hanakam* group, as we indicated, was exceptional for but few survivors translated their thirst for revenge into concrete action. Some accounted for this in terms of an exilic, minority mentality that, despite the provocation, avoided answering force with force.[58] Some of the obstacles in the way of vengeance, however, were far more prosaic and immediate. Planned revenge required military training, an organized framework, financial assistance and great daring. It meant going underground and consciously surrendering that which the survivors wanted more than anything else: to reach the safety of home and to begin building a normal life again. It also required both moral conviction and group support for there was always the danger that innocent people would get hurt. Thus Moshe Smolar who reached Germany in the ranks of the Red Army towards the end of 1944 discovered that for him taking revenge was no simple matter:

[53] See the anonymous testimony of a member of the *Hanakam* group in the *Moreshet* Archive/A-587.2.
[54] Ibid., and Kovner, Interview: 8–10. See, in addition, Sarid, "Irgun hanakam": 81–86.
[55] Ibid.: 86–87, and, also, the anonymous testimony, *Moreshet* Archive/A-587.2.
[56] Kovner, Interview: 16–17.
[57] For details of tensions within the group and the return of a breakaway group to Europe see Sarid, "Irgun ha-nakam": 92–95.
[58] Besserglik, "Nekome iz zis."

I looked into myself and behold, the sweet revenge, so sought after had turned bitter and depressed me deeply. A huge battle raged inside of me – between the logic which commanded: avenge yourself! and the humane feeling that had survived in this mad world. You who have been granted the possibility, almost unlimited, of wiping out these beasts in human form; you, whose aim throughout the catastrophic years was to have the historic chance of settling accounts with the murderers of your people and dear family – and now the hour has struck – rise up and do what has to be done! But... on the other hand – who are you – a man or a wild beast? Will you, because of your thirst for revenge descend to the level of the Germans, the greatest criminals in the history of humankind?[59]

In addition, compared to the period immediately following liberation, the political climate that had developed in Germany a few months later was no longer conducive to acts of vengeance. In the shadow of the growing tension between the two super-powers, their efforts were directed more at rebuilding Germany and ensuring that they had a powerful and faithful ally in Central Europe than in undoing the legacy of Nazism.[60] Any widespread acts of revenge would almost certainly have both shaken the standing of *She'erith Hapleitah* in Germany and endangered the continued flow of refugees from Eastern Europe.

For all of the above reasons, most of the survivors in Germany opted, in one or another measure, for symbolic rather than real revenge. The term "symbolic revenge" seeks to describe a wide array of actions – economic, judicial, political, educational and spiritual – that had a dual aim: to inflict punitive harm on the German people without resorting to the use of force and, secondly, making certain that the war waged against the Jewish people would ultimately end in defeat. Shlomo Frenkel articulated this idea very aptly at the end of 1945:

Of course we were not considering revenge proper: an eye for an eye and a tooth for a tooth. We sought to take revenge on our enemies through disparagement, rejection, banning and keeping our distance rather than in acts of vengeance that could only bring gross instinctual satisfaction to the individual. Only by setting ourselves apart from these murderers completely... will we be able to satisfy our desire for vengeance which in essence means: doing away with the European exile and building our homeland in the Land of Israel.[61]

As in so many other aspects of the life of *She'erith Hapleitah*, symbolic revenge was perceived as a holy duty imposed by the dead.[62] This is how Pesa Mayevska expressed it in her poem "To my murdered brother":

[59] Moshe Smolar, *Ne'evakti al chayai* (I fought for my life) (Tel Aviv, 1978): 159–160.
[60] Dr. Rudolf Valsonok, "Farbrekhn un shuld" (Crime and guilt), *LLT*, no. 4 (4.11. 1945): 4.
[61] Ivri (Shlomo Frenkel), "Hatzatzah min ha-tzad" (A glimpse from the sidelines), *Nitzotz*, no. 6 (51) (17.12.1945).
[62] Dr. Sarina, "Di masn merder fun mizrakh eiropeyishn yidntum" (The mass murderer of East European Jewry), *LLT*, no. 3(15) (30.1.1946): 4.

> Here he stands my loved one,
> With burning eyes
> I gather the pain
> Of his last moments
> He is insistent and calls out
> "Do not forget me my sister!
> Forget not my death
> My blood that was shed!"[63]

The forms of symbolic revenge were many and diverse and there were constant debates in an attempt to stake out the boundaries of the permissible and the unacceptable. Many, for example, celebrated their delight in Germany's defeat and made it their business to visit the historic symbols of the Nazi regime.[64] The *LLT* carried a festive report on the special session of the Council of the *ZK* in Berchtesgaden, "the den of impurity in the past – a meeting of Jewish delegates."[65] Similarly a demonstration of thousands of Jews in the streets of Landsberg "was no small revenge on one of our bloodiest enemies"[66] and, equally, the fact that *Kibbutz Nili* was situated in Julius Streicher's estate was taken as a divinely inspired example of "poetic justice."[67] "There, where until very recently hatred and poison was spoken against the Jews – there one can now hear Jewish songs of hope and faith. There where 'Enemy Number One' of the Jewish people was ensconced, now reside and work the sons and daughters of the remnants of the Jewish people who were not consumed by the flames."[68]

There were also forms of action that were more direct and far less delicate. M. Gavronsky, the editor of *Dos Fraye Vort* took issue with those "who do 'bad things' like pilfering, stealing, making a row, molesting passengers on the train" and believe that by so doing "they are taking revenge for our suffering and for our dead."[69] Yitzchak Nementsik was also critical of the unbecoming behavior of some survivors in public places

---

[63] Pesa Mayevska, "Tsu mayn umgekumene bruder" (To my murdered brother), *LLT*, no. 4 (16) (5.2.1946): 14.

[64] See, for example, Avraham Shulevitz, "Oyf der khurvot fun broynem hoyz in minkhen" (On the ruins of the brown house in Munich), *A Haym*, no. 5 (21.3.1946): 5.

[65] "Berchtesgaden – nest fun greste tum'ah in avar – farzamlungs-ort far yid. forshtayer" (Berchtesgaden – den of the greatest impurity in past: meeting place of Jewish representatives), *LLT*, no. 40 (52) (25.9.1946): 14.

[66] B.H., "Hasne" (The burning bush), *LLT*, no. 8 (2.12.1945): 7; for a similar response in different circumstances see Shmuel Gringauz, " 'Beiliss protses' un freylikher purin in deggendorf" ("The Beilis trial" and a merry purim in Deggendorf), *YT*, no. 21 (89) (14.3.1947): 3.

[67] Marian Zhyd, "A tog mit a nacht oyf streichers farm" (A day and a night at Streicher's Farm), *LLT*, no. 6 (18) (19.2.1946): 3.

[68] Ibid.

[69] M. Gavronsky, "Mir darfn vert zayn di frayhayt" (We must be worthy of freedom), *Dos Fraye Vort*, no. 2 (14.10.1945): 2.

including forms of trickery that were dressed up as vengeance. He told the story of someone who took some onions from a German tradesman and then refused to pay. When the tradesman objected the response was: "You dare speak about a few onions whereas you Germans murdered my Father and my Mother. I ask you, is this revenge for a father and mother?"[70] Those who opposed this kind of behavior were against compromising Jewish honor for the sake of dishonest gain.[71]

The more traditional survivors had their own versions of symbolic revenge. In October 1945 the *LLT* printed a picture of Nazis evicting Jews from their homes in the Kovno Ghetto in January 1942 and accompanied it with a picture of Germans surrendering their homes to survivors. The caption told of the Divine will that abhors injustice and balances the wrong with right.[72] Rabbi Eliezer Burstein was not willing to make do with Divine retribution and sought a more active form of symbolic revenge. The surviving remnants wished to give violent expression to their pain but because they were Jewish they were simply unable to repay the Nazis in their own coin. The very fact that they were alive, suggested the Rabbi, could be seen as "material" revenge which they should strive to convert into "spiritual" revenge.[73] In his interpretation, the destruction of the Jews was aimed at the destruction of Judaism and thus the revitalization of their spiritual heritage was the most appropriate response to their persecutors. Similarly, Avraham Shulevitz who witnessed the printing of the Babylonian Talmud initiated by Rabbi Snieg noted that this was done in a German press, using German paper, on German soil: "The immortal *Gemara Baba Mezia* greets Julius Streicher and other Streichers with: *Am Yisrael Chai.*"[74] Others sought out an appropriate response to the Germans in Jewish history. Mendel Mann of Regensburg saw the ban believed to have been imposed on Spain as the most telling precedent to follow. The ban did not limit itself to the inquisitors but was said to encompass the entire Spanish people down to the last generation. In consequence Jews refused to tread on Spanish soil and the name of

---

[70] Yitzchak Nementsik, "A shlekht farshtonene nekome" (A wrongly understood revenge), *A Haym*, no. 4 (14.3.1946): 7.

[71] Yaakov Katz, "Mayn ruf" (My call), *Oyf der Fray*, no. 1 (December 1945): 3.

[72] "Tsaytn baytn zikh" (The times change), *LLT*, no. 2 (15.10.1945): 4.

[73] Harav Eliezer Burstein, "Undzer lebens oyfgabe" (Our life's goal), *Dos Fraye Vort*, no. 9 (30.11.1945): 3; see also Harav Mordechai Gladstein, "Der mythos fun der yiddisher froy: tsu der shafung fun bnot agudos yisroel" (The myth of the Jewish woman: regarding the education of the daughters of Agudat Yisrael), *Dos Fraye Vort*, no. 11 (14.12.1945): 3.

[74] Avraham Shulevitz, "A gris far julius streicher fun der gemara 'baba metsia' " (A greeting for Julius Streicher from the Talmud tractate 'Baba Mezia'), *A Haym*, no. 2 (28.2.1946): 1. The editors of *Dos Fraye Vort* took a similar line, this time cultural, at the opening of the People's University in Feldafing – this was yet another way to foil the intentions of the Nazis. See *Dos Fraye Vort*, no. 10 (11.12.1945): 1.

Torquemada became a symbol of repulsive evil for centuries to come. "In this fashion the *cherem* – ban – on Spain became a significant educational force for our people giving us the moral backbone of scorn and unlimited hatred for those who wanted and willed us destroyed."[75] Mann hoped that a religious leader would take the initiative of integrating the call of the victims to avenge their blood into the daily prayers. This revenge would not take the form of "wild destruction" of the Nazi variety but rather of a long-term historical retribution that would remove the Germans from the comity of nations. In practice, despite the difficulties it entailed, this meant avoiding any unnecessary contact with the German population and striving to make sure that the ban on Germany would be as effective as the *cherem* on Spain.[76]

In reality, however, things were not quite so straightforward. There were cases, and not a few, where Jews and Germans became involved with one another so giving rise to anger and disappointment. As Shlomo Frenkel commented in late 1945:

When you accompany this *She'erith Hapleitah* that just a half a year ago was miraculously saved from destruction, you are shocked by their indifference to the Germans. For six years of suffering they shouted for and demanded revenge, but since liberation came and they went out of the camps into [a world of freedom], the survivors have forgotten their demands and the voice of revenge has been silenced.[77]

In point of fact, the survivors were caught in a difficult situation. Each person carried a burden of pain, loss and hostility but, given their daily and unavoidable encounters with the larger society, they had to devise "a modus vivendi: in order to continue living sanely under...present circumstances."[78] At this point it is important to distinguish between institutional as opposed to personal relations. Institutional relations, given their formal nature, were generally less problematic and justified in terms of the objective needs of a community in transit. As early as November 1945 a delegation of the Central Committee paid a formal visit to the President of the Bavarian Landesrat and, in the light of their assumption that their stay in Germany would be short and their strong aversion to asking for help, they desisted from any substantive discussion of their urgent needs.[79] When the leadership of the *ZK* understood that their forecast had been too optimistic they were "forced to revise

---

[75] Mendel Mann, "Shedlekhe tendentsn" (Harmful tendencies), *Der Nayer Moment*, no. 13 (31.10.1946): 4.
[76] Ibid.   [77] Ivri, "Hatzatzah min ha-tzad."   [78] Shochet, *Feldafing*: 159.
[79] See Protkoll nr. 15 des *ZK* (4.11.1945): 7, YIVO/DPG 94.

[their] position with respect to utilizing the German economy to improve local living conditions as well taking action with respect to restitution and reparations."[80] Dr. Phillip Auerbach, the State Commissioner for the victims of Nazi persecution, played an active and formative role in building these ties with special reference to welfare, compensation, work and cultural activity. In order to place these activities on a sound footing Dr. Auerbach set up a Committee on Jewish Affairs and held regular meetings with the Central Committee.[81]

Personal relations were more complex by far. As Simon Shochet remembered it, "How to behave with a German citizen in a given situation is a daily dilemma with which we have to grapple and which is resolved according to the specific situation and based on its own merits."[82] Nonetheless, over time certain general patterns of behavior appeared. Business relations were conducted on a formal level while studiously avoiding anything to do with the past and keeping one's feelings hidden.[83] In this regard there is little doubt that the black market was the king's highway to a wide range of instrumental relations with German society. In the context of our discussion, the big dealers and high-flying speculators are less significant than the run of the mill people of *She'erith Hapleitah* who used the black market to satisfy their most elementary needs. Whoever wished to buy milk, eggs, vegetables or an item of clothing after years of deprivation and hunger could only do so on what many called the grey market. In Occupied Germany the local currency was worthless and the economy had essentially become one of barter. On one side was the American Army that lacked for nothing, on the other the German population, especially the town dwellers, who initially had little or nothing and between them the DPs. Within this reality the Jews used part of their allowance from UNRRA, the JDC and Red Cross to acquire what they needed. Furthermore, the goods used to pay for work in the DP camps also found their way, in part, to this sector of the economy.[84]

The black market, in short, was an integral part of the German economy in the aftermath of the war with prices fixed by supply and demand and not a few of the on-going activities of the Central Committee and even the Joint were discreetly financed by transactions of this kind.[85] German antisemites portrayed this activity as a uniquely Jewish preserve

---

[80] Blumowicz, Barikht: 7.   [81] Protokoll nr. 15 des *ZK*.   [82] Shochet, *Feldafing*: 160.
[83] Agr. Y. Oleiski, "5706 in yidishn lebn in daytshland" (1946 in Jewish life in Germany), *LLT*, no. 40 (52) (25.9.1946): 27.
[84] See Report by E. Rock (8.11.1945), AJDC/DP's Germany 1945/1946 and see also Avni, *Im ha-yehudim be-machanot*: 14.
[85] In this regard see Klausner's testimony in OHD/4(4).

and, as far as the Military Government was concerned, got some of the tar to stick. Black market raids on the DP camps became a common occurrence and a serious source of friction with the authorities.[86] But there was also a psychological cost that accompanied this activity – it was both illegal and created relations of dependence on the local population which many survivors found to be unsettling and compromising.[87]

Far more sensitive and complex in this interplay between the private and the public were the relationships that developed in certain cases between Jewish men and German women. This was an area of intimacy that in various ways invited the deeply felt intrusion of the past. As Simon Shochet reported, the relatively few Jewish women who managed to survive "are treated only with the utmost respect and awe accompanied by strong feelings of attraction and love, and are approached with only the serious intention of matrimony in mind."[88] The relationship to German women, on the other hand, appeared to be motivated by both natural drives and the psychological need to topple the untouchable Aryan female of Nazi propaganda from her pedestal. Thus, "these men, filled with a mixture of revenge and the desire to taste the forbidden fruit, seem to want to possess the entire garden. They jump from one affair to another and keep long lines of girlfriends in tow."[89] Some of these concerns came to the fore in *Kibbutz Buchenwald* already in late June 1945. At a *kibbutz* meeting Chaim Meir Gottlieb wanted formally to prohibit intimate relations with German women. In terms of their pioneering ethos it was both wrong and profoundly dishonorable and in the ensuing discussion Gottlieb used an argument that came up repeatedly in *She'erith Hapleitah*: "When our beloved Jewish girls burned in the crematoria their clothes were brought to Germany and these very girls might be wearing their dresses, their rings."[90] The decision reached was that any member who became intimate with a German woman would be asked to leave the group.[91]

This phenomenon, that was not all that common, elicited angry criticism especially where romance was involved and, in a few cases, the question of marriage. This was a shameful stain on the memory of the dead, a mockery of all the blood that had been shed and made people ask:

[86] See Robert Murphy, United States Political Adviser for Germany to the Secretary of State (3.6.1946), NA/800/4016DP/6-346.

[87] Shochet, *Feldafing*: 160.   [88] Ibid.: 161.   [89] Ibid.: 162.

[90] Leo W. Schwarz, "*Kibbutz* Buchenwald," in Schwarz, ed., *The Root and the Bough*: 315. In the same vein M. Even-Chalak asks: "how can you be in the vicinity of those who are wearing the clothes of your poor sister and mother?" in "Tsu hot ir shoyn fargesn?" (Have you really forgotten already?), *Dos Fraye Vort*, no. 21 (9.11.1945): 3.

[91] For an actual case where this happened see C.G., "A vayle bei undzere khalutsim" (An interlude with our *chalutzim*), *Undzer Vort*, no. 21 (9.8.1946): 7.

"Did our suffering have no meaning?"[92] There was no way of bridging the chasm that had opened between the two peoples and each person had to decide where they ultimately stood: either with his brothers "or on the side of our hangmen and murderers."[93] The editor of the *Yidishe Tsaytung* went so far as to suggest that in a Jewish state this blot on Jewish honor would merit severe punishment.[94] There were those who suggested that these people be excommunicated in the manner of those engaged in "white slavery" at the time of the great emigration to the New World – for the deeper impact of these relationships, which were happily few and far between, would be morally to disarm the Jewish people and blacken their name that, in a time of uprooting, disorientation and desperate need, was to be prevented. Given what was at stake, therefore, these men should be excluded from all forms of community life, their children should not be permitted to marry within the faith and they should be denied a Jewish burial.[95] Religious leaders took an active role in this campaign and imposed a blanket refusal on requests for conversion except when it related to Jews of mixed parentage whom the Nazis had marked off as "Mischlinge," people of mixed blood. In these cases alone, conversion according to Jewish law was not automatically ruled out.[96]

With respect to the more general question of Jewish–German relations there were also differences between Jews of German origin and the East European majority in *She'erith Hapleitah*. Ernst Landau, by way of example, claimed that Jews had a moral responsibility to take an active role in the attempt to shape a new German democracy. In reality the German people was already seeking a way to normalize relations with the West and it stood to reason that the traditional Jewish bearers of the flag of humanism would play their part in this process.[97] Reuven Rubinstein, who replaced Levi Shalitan as the editor of *Undzer Veg* towards the end of 1946, was strongly opposed to this line of argument. He saw it as belated attempt to reinstate the conception of a Jewish "mission" favored by assimilationists who could not abide the notion "that a Jew can just live in the world without a why or a wherefore, enjoying himself with other

---

[92] Even-Chalak, "Tsu hot ir shoyn fargesn?"   [93] Ibid.

[94] See S.B., "Dos yidishe lebn in neuenberg" (Jewish life in Neuenberg), *YT*, no. 43(55) (25.10.1946): 8, that reports on a number of mixed marriages among the 180 Jews living there. See also the editorial response to this report – Baruch Hermanovitz, "Oyfn yidishn seder-hayom" (On the Jewish agenda), *YT*, ibid.: 7.

[95] Yechezkiel Keitelman, "Tmey'im" (The impure), *Der Nayer Moment*, no. 14 (22.11.1946): 3.

[96] "Daytshn viln zikh megayer zayn" (Germans seek to be converted), gesprakh mitn forzitser fun agudat harabanim, hagaon r' shmuel abba snieg (a conversation with the chairman of the rabbinical council, hagaon rabbi shmuel abba snieg), *Undzer Veg*, no. 51 (15.11.1946): 6.

[97] See Landau, "Vos iz nit in ordnung."

people simply because he is a fellow human."[98] But this was really not to the point because it failed to take into account those Jews who were planning to start anew in Germany, and for them the question of democracy's future was of great consequence. These considerations, moreover, were also relevant in a more limited sense for those who only perceived Germany as a way station. The fact that over 100,000 Jews had found temporary asylum in Germany effectively foreclosed the option of placing a ban on the country.[99] "We cannot place Germany under religious ban," claimed Samuel Gringauz,

Even our rabbis have not done so. We live amongst them and the German people exists and will return to being a player in world politics. Today it is too early for us to set aside our moral reservations about the German people but it is clear that we wish to cooperate with the German administration, which, by the way, is behaving correctly towards us.[100]

Not everyone, however, could afford to adopt such a philosophical attitude. There were those who felt a deep, inner need to maintain a degree of symmetry between the dimensions of the catastrophe and the responses it called forth. As a friend who confided in Levi Shalitan put it: "In the *katzet* I fought against death through my drive to wreak vengeance for my family... and now, having remained alive I see just how much senselessness one encounters in one's life. So why did I survive? What is the point of it all?"[101] For Shalitan all the compromises and surrender of principle that stemmed from their basic helplessness had served to embitter the survivors and led them to the indignity of forgetfulness.[102] What then was to be done? In the long run the anger and frustration could help create a new Jewish reality, a life of dignity where a fate of this kind would be a thing of the past. In the short run very little, although many comforted themselves with the hope that the forthcoming trial of the major war criminals in Nuremberg would inform the world about the Jewish tragedy and help it better understand their desperate desire to be finally free and independent in their own

---

[98] Reuven Rubinstein, "Katzetnikes zoln zikh farshtendikn mit... daytshland" (Camp survivors should reach an understanding with... Germany), *Undzer Veg*, no. 51 (15.11.1946): 3.

[99] "We have not imposed a ban on Germany because in the meanwhile Germany has become the 'fortunate' refuge for more than one hundred thousand Jews." S. Levi (Levi Shalitan), "Yizkor" (Prayer for the dead), *Undzer Veg*, no. 44 (9.8.1946): 4.

[100] Dr. Shmuel Gringauz, "In tsaykhn fun martirertum hofnung un arbet" (Under the sign of martyrdom hope and work), *LLT*, no. 2 (14) (18 January 1946): 1.

[101] S. Levi (Levi Shalitan), "Zayn oder nit zayn – zin oder umzin" (To be or not to be – meaning or meaninglessness), *Undzer Veg*, no. 46 (23.8.1946): 3.

[102] Ibid.

land.[103] In October 1945 David Wolpe wrote the following in his poem "Nuremberg":

> I know you not and do not wish to recall you
> Like a curse you lie on my lips –
> You are the deepest depths of human depravity
> For you inscribed hatred and murder on your tablets
>
> . . .
>
> They return to you – the missionaries of your faith
> With raven-black squalid and dark souls
> From deep mass graves I hear the scream of the deaf
> My voice quivers, and join them in crying out: revenge![104]

What was to unfold in Nuremberg for many survivors was an act of elementary justice and, hopefully, a vehicle of their burning desire to see the Nazi leaders shamed, humiliated and hung. In this regard it is interesting to note that in the estimate of the historian Bradley F. Smith, the International Military Tribunal was looked to by others, as well, as an instrument of symbolic revenge.

Considering the atmosphere of the time, the deliberations associated with the trial may well have forestalled a bloodbath. The summer of 1945 was not a time for calm consideration by much of the European population, and only the prospect that the Great Powers would take care of the major task through legal process served as a barrier to direct action.[105]

In July 1945 the delegates to the St. Ottilien Conference resolved to request formal Jewish representation at the International Commission for War Crimes and active participation in the trials of these criminals. Their declared aim was to inform world opinion of the nature and extent of the destruction of the Jewish people and to ensure that these crimes received the hearing they deserved.[106] Levi Shalitan was dubious that Jewish expectations of the Nuremberg trials could be fulfilled because what was needed, so that justice be done, was to hold separate trials for those responsible for crimes against the Jewish people. The Second World War in his reading was comprised of two parts: a conventional war in which Jews also participated and a separate, singular war against the Jews which began long before September 1939 and ended in "total

---

[103] See Valsonok, "Farbrekhn un shuld." On Nuremberg as a form of symbolic revenge see Leon Rivkes, "Fun streicher–farm tsum nirenberger protses" (From Streicher's Farm to the Nuremberg trial), *Undzer Veg* no. 22 (1.3.1946): 3.
[104] David Wolpe, "Nirenberg," *Undzer Veg*, no. 3 (16.10.1945): 3.
[105] Bradley F. Smith, *Reaching Judgment at Nuremberg* (New York, 1977): 303.
[106] Resolutionen und Beschluesse . . . St. Ottilien.

destruction and extermination."[107] It was therefore necessary to judge the accused as criminals in the general tribunal and as murderers in the court trying crimes against the Jewish people. Shalitan was afraid that this fundamental distinction would first be blurred at Nuremberg and then lost sight of altogether. Zalman Grinberg was also skeptical as to the outcome – in his view an entire nation had been party to the murder, but, because a whole people could not be put in the dock it would turn out that where all were guilty none were to blame. The Jewish people, secondly, had no representation at the trial and this, too, made it less likely that justice would be done.[108]

In the same fashion K. Shabtai, the special correspondent of *Undzer Veg* in Nuremberg approached the forthcoming trials with "mixed feelings."[109] On one level it was hard to swallow that these "arch-devils" incarnate deserved a trial whereas the millions of their innocent victims had met a very different end.[110] It was also difficult to accept that masses were part of the killing machine, millions stood by and benefited from the spoils and so very few, ultimately, were brought to trial. Despite all these reservations there was another, profoundly symbolic aspect to the trial that Shabtai, paraphrasing Ecclesiastes, felt keenly. "I sense that I am standing before one of the greatest mysteries of world history, before the most monumental nemesis of all time ... in Nuremberg, in the place of evil, there where the snake developed and grew, that is to be the place of justice."[111] However, the day-by-day reality of the trial was less dramatic and far more complicated. The manner in which the prosecutor, Justice Jackson, addressed the fate of the Jews in his opening statement was remarkable.[112] Immediately after his presentation, however, an American film documenting the liberation of the concentration camps was screened and as it ended the narrator detailed the nations and peoples who had suffered at the hands of the Nazis. The list was long with the Jews bringing up the rear and that for the observers of *She'erith Hapleitah* became the interpretive key of the trial as a whole.[113] The fate of the Jews was averred to in many different contexts but never in a coherent and systematic fashion. "The entire 'Jewish section' of the trial,"

---

[107] Levi Shalitan, "Mir klagn an" (We accuse), *Undzer Veg*, no. 1 (12.10.1945): 1.

[108] Grinberg, "In dervartung": 2.

[109] K. Yupiter (Shabtai), "Makom ha-resha – sham ha-mishpat" (In the place of evil – there will be justice), *Undzer Veg*, no. 7 (20.11.1945): 3.

[110] K. Shabtai, "Makom ha-resha," *Undzer Veg*, no. 9 (30.11.1945): 4.   [111] Ibid.

[112] "Rede fun rikhter Jackson" (The speech of Judge Jackson), *Undzer Veg*, no. 9 (30.11.1945): 6. See also "Bashuldikungs-akt fun nirenberger protses" (The charge sheet at the Nuremberg trial), *Undzer Veg*, no. 3 (16.10.1945): 2.

[113] K. Shabtai, "Makom ha-resha," *Undzer Veg*, no. 16 (18.1.1946): 2.

as Shabtai summed it up, "was handled like a step-child, cast about by everyone and claimed by none."[114]

Many also found the detached impersonality of the discussions to be troublesome, especially when they related to events quite unprecedented in human history. In this rhetoric of disassociation words lost their edge and deeds their horror so that atrocities emerged as somehow sterile and unreal. As one survivor put it – "In Nuremberg one hears the figures but does not see the pictures."[115] Some accounted for this by pointing to the distance from the scene of the crime,[116] others emphasized the inability of the mind to grasp deeds so monstrous while yet a third argued that familiarity did not necessarily breed contempt: "In the first week the gang were called gangsters, in the second – criminals, in the third – the accused. Today we call them by their names: Hess, Goering and the like. By the time the trial ends and the gang are hung we will be somewhat put out trying to manage without them."[117] K. Shabtai attributed it to the differing backgrounds of the prosecution team – the English and Americans who were new to Europe were consistently low-key while the French prosecutor who had fought in the Resistance was passionate and involved. He was also the first to raise the question of the death sentence and the only one to talk about the collective responsibility of the German people for the crimes of the Nazis. In this regard the appearance of the Russian delegation to the International Military Tribunal (IMT) raised survivor hopes for a more forceful presentation of the Jewish tragedy by a country that had paid so dearly for victory. The Russians, however, had little patience for the niceties of differentiation and, in pursuit of true equality, made all the victims of the Nazis into Soviet citizens.[118] In this fashion the victims of Riga, Kovno, Ponar, Babi Yar, Krakow and so many other sites of slaughter lost their identity. A Russian journalist explained the educational logic behind this policy – they did not want the German populace to think that such terrible things happened only to Jews.[119]

The observers from *She'erith Hapleitah* were also disappointed that with regard to Germany Justice Jackson insisted on differentiating "between the party and the people and drawing a demarcation line between 'guilty' and 'innocent', between 'good' and 'bad' Germans."[120]

---

[114] K. Shabtai, "Makom ha-resha," *Undzer Veg*, no. 11 (14.12.1945): 5.
[115] M.D. Olihav, "Di simbolik fun nirenberg" (The symbolism of Nuremberg), *Bamidbar*, no. 12 (23.7.1946): 4.
[116] See Dr. Yosef S., "Ayner fun yene: der masn merder, dr' frank, der henker fun poylisher yidntum un polakn" (One of those: the mass murderer, Dr. Frank, the hangman of Polish Jewry and Poles), *Bamidbar*, no. 1 (12.12.1945): 5–6.
[117] K. Shabtai, "Makom ha-resha," *Undzer Veg*, no. 21 (26.2.1946): 6.   [118] Ibid.
[119] Ibid.   [120] K. Shabtai, "Makom ha-resha," *Undzer Veg*, no. 19 (13.2.1946): 6.

Given their premise of collective guilt, the survivors were angered by the approach of the prosecution to criminal organizations like the SS, SA, SD, Gestapo and Nazi Party. By putting their fate into the hands of German courts tens of thousands of mass murderers were, to all intents and purposes, granted a pardon.[121] Despite these disappointments, a constant stream of survivors traveled to Nuremberg, sat in on the trial and derived great satisfaction from seeing the prisoners in the dock and watching them squirm, lie and pretend under cross-examination. Witnessing the grovelling indignity of the leaders of Nazi Germany proved to be of great therapeutic value to many who, because of what they had endured, had begun to doubt themselves.[122] The death sentences handed down met with widespread approval in *She'erith Hapleitah* while the lighter sentences called forth caustic comment as in the *Undzer Velt* editorial that asked: "How many Jews must one actually send to Auschwitz in order for the International Tribunal to find that somebody should be sent down the same road as Kaltenbrunner?"[123]

When the trial ended, estimates as to its usefulness and historical value differed greatly. The German people feigned disinterest and, as is always the case with news, whereas the trial initially attracted a lot of attention as the months went by, it lost its prominence to other headlines. The people of *She'erith Hapleitah* were disappointed that not one of their number was called to give testimony; in some quarters the inadequacy of the Central Committee was blamed but it was generally understood that the real answer lay elsewhere, most pointedly in the policies of the four powers that "acted in accordance with their own interests. For them our misfortune is an episode which had once been part of their goals."[124] For that reason there had been no call to present a comprehensive picture of the Jewish tragedy or properly to utilize the rich documentary evidence that had been amassed. The Jewish catastrophe figured in Nuremberg but, as Dr. Tuli put it, "only as an example and never as something in its own

---

[121] Dr. Tuli, "Der nirenberger protses," (The Nuremberg trial) *Undzer Velt*, no. 10 (18) (9.8.1946): 5; see, in addition, Moshe Zilberberg, "Der nirenberger protses" (The nuremberg trial), *Dos Fraye Vort*, no. 9 (30.11.1945): 1 and K. Shabtai, "Makom ha-resha," *Undzer Veg*, no. 47 (30.8.1946): 6.

[122] Dr. Moshe Feinberg, "3 teg oyfn nirenberger protses" (Three days at the Nuremberg trial), *LLT*, no. 17(29) (17.5.1946): 3; also Leon Rivkes, "Fun streicher-farm" (From the Streicher farm), and "Goering, ribbentrop and keitel – yidn-fraynt?" (Goering, Ribbentrop and Keitel - friends of the Jews?), *Der Nayer Moment*, no. 3 (15.4.1946): 5. Moshe Zilberberg, in "Tsvey protsesn" (Two trials), *Dos Fraye Vort*, no. 49 (25.9.1946): 12, compared the underground fighters in Palestine facing trial with the defendants in Nuremberg as did C. Sucholowsky in "Nirenberg," *Undzer Vort*, no. 25 (13.9.1946): 9.

[123] Dr. Tuli, "Der nirenberger protses: der internatsyonaler bet din" (The Nuremberg trial: the international tribunal), *Undzer Velt*, no. 11(19) (16.8.1946): 5.

[124] Ibid.

right."[125] Furthermore, if the Tribunal had adopted Raphael Lemkin's neologism "genocide" as a valid legal concept in international law, it would have helped prepare the ground for decisive international intervention whenever the need would arise. As things now stood, not even mentioning the crime of genocide could be seen as an "indirect invitation to a new Treblinka."[126]

Dr. Samuel Gringauz took issue with the skeptical voices in the survivor community and argued that the International Tribunal had made an important contribution to fighting antisemitism and represented an historic contribution to the advancement of human rights.[127] The trial had been a model of civilized behavior and the closely argued sentence would serve as an important foundation stone in the emerging world order. Declaring every war of aggression a crime was an innovation in international law for it denied war its automatic legitimacy, as did the principled decision to hold both politicians and those who carried out their policies criminally responsible for their actions. For the first time the leaders of a state were judged not by a military tribunal dealing with the defeated but by a civilian court that tried them as criminals. This set an important precedent: "For the first time the principle that the state is not answerable for its deeds was overturned."[128] And to this should be added the new concept of "criminal organizations" whereby voluntary affiliation with an organization of this kind was punishable by law.

The Tribunal had also made a significant contribution to the fight against antisemitism. Hatred of Jews had figured prominently in the clause of "Crimes against Humanity" and had been underscored in the sentencing of Streicher, Goering, Ribbentrop, Kaltenbrunner, Rosenberg, Seyss-Inquart, Funk, von Schirach and Borman in absentia. "Antisemitism had been declared a crime against international society, a crime against humanity,"[129] and, in so doing, a blow had been struck against the easy legitimacy and respectability it had long enjoyed. Gringauz was well aware that the trial had not satisfied the desire of many of his fellow survivors for revenge but in view of the fact that retribution of "measure for measure" was inconceivable, he put this out of his mind

---

[125] Ibid. See also his "Letste teg in Nirenberg" (The last day in Nuremberg), *Undzer Velt*, no. 17(25) (25.9.1946): 7. In the same vein see M. Shuster, "Menuvalim oyfn rand fun nirenberger protses" (Blackguards on the margins of the Nuremberg trial), *A Haym*, no. 21 (3.9.1946): 3.

[126] "Der tragisher sakh ha-kol: tsum urtayl in nirenberger protses" (The tragic summation: regarding the judgment in the Nuremberg trial), *Dos Vort*, no. 1 (9.10.1946): 1; on the role of Raphael Lemkin in the proceedings see "Nirenberger protses" (The Nuremberg trial), *Undzer Veg*, no. 39 (28.6.1946): 1.

[127] Dr. Shmuel Gringauz, "Fuit justitia," *LLT*, no. 41 (53) (9.10.1946): 6–7.

[128] Ibid.: 6.   [129] Ibid.: 7.

and focused on the way the trial would help shape humane sensibility in the post-war world. From this perspective he saw it as one of the great achievements of modern times.[130]

Many others were not persuaded because they found it hard to measure their extreme experiences against what to them often sounded like empty legalisms and high-sounding nothings. Rita Vasanowitz of Bad Nauheim concluded that irrespective of what was achieved in Nuremberg the question of vengeance did not allow of a satisfactory answer for it was somehow bound up with the mysterious nature of what had befallen them. Even in the concentration camp, she recalled,

Our hearts were silenced by deep grief and pain . . . This was the silence of conscience and feeling in the face of something that went beyond our understanding and grasp . . . This was the passive surrender of the matter to a higher spiritual authority which must surely exist in one or another form . . . (and the categories which transcend our thought awaken this kind of reflection even in the case of an atheist . . .).[131]

The Nuremberg trial awakened thoughts on what visitors felt to be the mysterious fate of the Jewish people but, as they well understood, could not resolve them. Where ultimate meaning was elusive Rita Vasanovitz chose the way of response – to act in such a way so as to ensure that the Jewish people would never again be caught in a situation where it was totally at the mercy of an enemy bent on its destruction. As she put it: if the killing was not to bring forth a new cadre of murderers "we have to be committed to the one place on earth that belongs to us, we have to put a stop to our accursed, homeless wandering and our being the victims of the hate of strangers."[132]

She'erith Hapleitah also took an active part in the attempt to bring Nazi criminals to justice. In February 1946 the Central Committee established a Judicial Department headed by Adv. V. Friedheim, the leader of Polish Jewry in Germany.[133] The Department advised the *ZK* on legal matters, extended legal assistance to Jewish DPs who ran afoul of the law and opened a division for Nazi and War Criminals. The work of the division was divided into two: exposing war criminals who had managed to evade arrest and helping the authorities successfully to prosecute those who had already been apprehended. The division got off to a hesitant start in 1946 and expanded its activities in 1947 when it collected incriminating

[130] Ibid.
[131] Rita Vasanovitz, "Der nirenberger protses iz farendikt" (The Nuremberg trial is over), *A Haym*, no. 24 (25.10.1946): 7. In this context it is worth noting Peter Berger's response to the Eichmann trial – see *A Rumor of Angels* (Harmondsworth, 1984): 84–87.
[132] Vasanovitz, "Der nirenberger protses."
[133] For a general description see Blumowicz, Baricht:17–18.

material against 254 suspected war criminals. They cooperated with the American Military Tribunal in Dachau that tried the Nazi personnel employed in Buchenwald, Nordhausen and Flossenbürg by providing 125 witnesses and over 200 sworn testimonies; in Nuremberg they worked hand in glove with the prosecution in the cases of I.G. Farben and Otto Ohlendorf and 154 dossiers on war criminals were handed over to the Polish Military Mission and were instrumental in transferring over 100 criminals to Poland where they were put on trial.[134]

The division ran a campaign called "Help Punish the Murderers" which entailed the posting of a list of 501 war criminals with the following explanation attached:

It is the sacred duty of She'erith Hapleitah to our martyred dead that we should spare neither time nor effort in ferreting out and punishing the torturers and murderers of our fallen ones. This high and important goal we can do something about only while we are here. Time is short! We hereby turn to the whole of She'erith Hapleitah with the following appeal: Jews! Get your committees immediately to make announcements about known war criminals and, wherever possible, to publish it in the press! Publish whatever is known about war criminals still at large.[135]

For the sake of greater efficiency the division set up a network of regional offices that were greatly assisted by the local historical committees.[136] In the nature of things the survivors were most effective when it came to tracking down East European collaborators who had sought asylum in Germany disguised as DPs. "It is high time," wrote A. Krosny at the beginning of 1946, "that our representatives should, for once and for all, interest themselves in these so-called 'displaced people' and unmask the murderers UNRRA is cultivating."[137] A great amount of energy was expended on flushing out these collaborators, a good number of whom were apprehended and handed over to the military authorities.[138] The division also cooperated with the German authorities who dealt with war

---

[134] Yuridishe aptaylung farn yor 1947 (Judicial Department (activities) 1947, YSA/M-1/P-71: 8–9; for the voluminous correspondence with the Polish Delegation for War Crimes see YSA/M21/3: 9–10.

[135] See YSA/M-1/P-72 and M-1/P-73.

[136] See Di historishe komisye bei yid. komitet in neu–freimann tsu der yuridishe referat (The Historical Commission at the Jewish Committee in Neu-Freimann to the Judicial Section) (2.4.1947), YSA/M-1/P-72-1.

[137] A. Krosny, "Gekhapt a litvishn blut-hunt" (Captured – a Lithuanian blood-hound), Undzer Veg, no. 16 (18.1.1946): 1.

[138] See for example Nadich, Eisenhower and the Jews: 169–171; "Lager freimann unter terror" (The Freimann camp terrorized), Undzer Veg, no. 22 (29.2.1946): 8; Dr. Sarina, "Di masn merder"; and M. Rabinovitz, "Der emes un di litviner" (The truth and the Lithuanians), Undzer Veg, no. 19 (8.2.1946): 3.

criminals and denazification.[139] But, as many had foreseen, the results were disappointing and it became increasingly clear that their German counterparts were interested in burying the past and, where this was not possible, to hand down token punishments.[140]

The survivors were disturbed but hardly surprised. From their point of view this was a country covering up for tens of thousands of SS men guilty of the most heinous of crimes; the large companies that had shamelessly exploited slave laborers to the point of death continued operating as if nothing had happened, and what they termed "reactionary elements" were angling to return to power.[141] They could point to the obsessive interest of the German press in things Jewish, their accusations regarding the leading role of Jews in the black market and its destructive influence on the German economy and, during 1946, a series of violent clashes between Jewish DPs and the local population and German police.[142] This reading of reality by She'erith Hapleitah is significant in and of itself but it would be instructive to compare it with parallel social research conducted at the time. One such study that was carried out by the Military Government sought to uncover German attitudes to the Jews in the wake of reports on increasing antagonism. According to the report which was based on a sample of 3,415 respondents

about four in ten people in the Zone (39%) can be said to be very seriously disposed to exhibit racial prejudice. Another fifth of the population (22%) easily go along with the more extreme positions and cannot be expected to counter any expressions of anti-semitism. Thus about six in ten (61%) of the Germans are deeply imbued with racist feeling. Opponents of race hatred in any positive sense form a very small fraction (of the order of 20%) of the population.[143]

A survey of public opinion carried out in October 1945 showed that 20 percent of the population supported Hitler's treatment of the Jewish question and about 19 percent agreed that something had to be done but felt that Hitler had gone too far. In April 1946 and then again in December the indicators rose pointing to 61 percent of the population who could be

---

[139] See, for example, the Judicial Referat to the Polizeipraesidium, Stuttgart (22.2.1947), YSA/M-1/P-72, and, in the same location, Criminal Over-Secretary Valer on the investigation of SS officers who served in Buchenwald. See Yuridishe aptaylung: 8.

[140] Ernst Landau, "Vert bayern endlikh denatsifirt?" (Will Bavaria be finally denazified?), Dos Fraye Vort, no. 43 (30.8.1946): 3; Agr. Yaakov Oleiski, "Der partsuf fun hayntikn Daytshland" (The face of contemporary Germany), LLT, no. 11 (23) (22.3.1946): 3; and Landau, "Vos iz nit in ordnung": 3.

[141] Landau, "Vert bayern."

[142] Oleiski, "Der partsuf," and "Ratevet: di hitler-mageifa fershprayt zikh alts mer" (Help: the Hitler plague is spreading more than ever), Der Nayer Moment, no. 2 (15.4.1946): 3.

[143] Antisemitism in the American Zone: ODIC Opinion Surveys Headquarters, Report Number 49 (3.3.1947), UNRRA Archive/RG-17/66,516.

described as antisemitic. The researchers who did not see those who were opposed to antisemitism as having much influence concluded that "The elimination of of antisemitism in Germany is a very long-range problem, likely to take generations. A concerted program could offer some hope of reduction."[144]

While the leaders of *She'erith Hapleitah*, for their part, did not believe that the Military Government would take radical measures against German antisemitism, they did hope that it would act to limit its impact and spread. A memo from the Executive Staff of UNRRA from the middle of 1946 suggested that even this was unlikely.[145] What worried them was the fact that the Jewish DP's "are held in the greatest contempt by the Germans who lose no opportunity to discredit them in the eyes of the American Military Authorities. The effect of the derogatory influence has been strong and widespread to the point where it has seeped up from the operating levels to even the highest military echelons."[146] In the same vein, Chaplain Emmanuel Rackman, the Assistant to the Special Adviser on Jewish Affairs, said of the prevailing atmosphere of G-5 that had charge of DP affairs "basically, from top to bottom, you will find that the whole problem [is] just one grand nuisance so far as the Army is concerned."[147] And the problem grew worse during 1946 as fresh troops began arriving – troops that had not been adequately trained, that did not begin to understand the complex problems confronting them, and with attitudes towards the German population very different from those who had fought and liberated the camps. Following their exposure to the prevailing currents in Germany it became apparent that with respect to the Surviving Remnant "there is even less human sympathy and consideration than there is understanding."[148]

The following were some of the disturbing patterns of behavior that the UNRRA workers began to notice: recurrent accusations of the leading role of Jews in black market activities, the increased use of German police in raids on Jewish installations, the sealing off of installations without prior warning, the arbitrary transfer of DPs from one camp to another "so that they should not become, argue high officers, too 'settled' in their living conditions."[149] To which had to be added the chronic difficulties of

---

[144] Ibid.: 17. For the follow-up see Rabbi Phillip S. Bernstein to the Commander in Chief European Command, "A Program to Deal with Anti-Semitism in Germany" (16.7.1947), YIVO/DPG 161.

[145] Statement of the Executive Staff of UNRRA US Zone Headquarters (May 1946), UNRRA Archive/RG-17/66,516.

[146] Ibid.: 1.

[147] Chaplain Rackman's Report to the Interim Committee (20.9.1946), American Jewish Conference Interim Minutes: 1, American Jewish Conference Archives.

[148] Ibid.   [149] Statement of the Executive Staff of UNRRA: 3.

the DPs throughout: overcrowded living conditions, a monotonous diet, degrading clothing and a clear preference for Germans when it came to the allocation of work by the military. This behavior also served as a negative example to the German authorities who were gradually regaining control of their own affairs. The DPs found themselves in an increasingly vulnerable situation – on the one hand, less protected by the army and, on the other, "giving everything back to the Germans means that the status of the Jewish DP becomes a desperate one. Whatever he wants he must acquire from an ungracious and very antagonistic German population."[150]

The UNRRA officials were caught in an unenviable bind: their job was to care for the DPs but they were nothing more than an executive arm of the army that blocked many of their attempts to be of help. They felt, and with good reason, that they were losing the respect and trust of their wards. Levi Shalitan voiced the opinions of many when he attacked, perhaps unfairly, the UNRRA "bureaucrats" who knew how to take care of themselves while living out in reverse the biblical story of the prophet Balaam: "They came to assist us and ended by cursing us."[151] The reading of the situation reported on by the UNRRA officials and other observers was confirmed by an army study that examined the relationship of 1,790 soldiers to Germans, antisemitism and racism.[152] Of the respondents, 51 percent believed that there were positive sides to Hitler's rule, 22 percent believed that the Germans had justifiable cause for the Final Solution while 19 percent believed that there were good reasons for Germany's going to war.[153] The researchers accounted for these disturbing findings in terms of basic ignorance, the complete lack of any educational and information work with the troops, the conscious attempt by certain circles to infect the new troops with antisemitism and the influence of German women who had soldier boyfriends.[154]

A number of attempts were made to address the problem. In Regensburg Chaplain Eugene Lipman brought survivors and officers together in order to clarify their differences.[155] Dr. Gringauz participated in military

---

[150] Chaplain Rackman's Report: 2. For further examples see Leah Freiburg, "Tsurik in di katzetn: es fehlen unz noch 4 khodashim tsu 6 fule yor" (Back into the camps: we lack another four months to make up six full years), *Der Nayer Moment*, no. 8 (9.8.1946): 5; and Hamamesh, "Burgermeister Krempel vil ptor vern fun yidn" (Mayor Krempel wants to be rid of the Jews), *Der Nayer Moment*, no. 11 (20.9.1946): 7.

[151] Levi Shalitan, "Fun undzer seder-hayom: farvos numer tsvey?" (From our agenda: why number two?), *Undzer Veg*, no. 35 (31.5.1946): 2.

[152] "Antisemitizm tsvishn amerikanishe soldatn" (Antisemitism amongst American soldiers), *Undzer Veg*, no. 23 (8.3.1946): 4.

[153] Ibid.

[154] Ibid. In addition see "Antisemitizm unter di shtern un shtrayfn in Daytshland" (Antisemitism under Stars and Stripes in Germany), *Undzer Vort*, no. 17 (12.7.1946): 4.

[155] Eng. Stefan Schwartz, "Tsi iz be-emet nishta kayn eytsa?" (Is there truly nothing to be done?), *Der Nayer Moment*, no. 4 (3.5.1946): 7.

study days that focused on the DPs and their problems. From within an
account of his own story Gringauz sought to account for their deep antagonism to the Germans and their almost instinctual distaste for uniforms,
discipline and regulations: "for six years the laws and commands meant
being hung or robbed and if one remained alive it was only because he
found a way of disobeying these laws."[156] The army from its side came
out with a number of publications and, in one of them, asked the soldiers
to remember "that the D.P.s are human despite everything the Nazis did
to them and that they are the product of conditions over which they had
little control."[157] Beyond the satisfaction of their basic needs, therefore,
they were in need of the army's encouragement and understanding.

These initiatives, despite their good intentions, could not cope with the
complex realities of life in Germany. A direct encounter with *She'erith
Hapleitah*, claimed A. Piotrkovski of Feldafing, would very quickly undo
what had been learnt in the classroom. "They meet up with wild people
who are tactless, lacking in basic manners and the elementary [rules of]
conduct... And when they meet Jews of this kind all the explanations
that spoke to them earlier are undone and burst like soap bubbles."[158] In
addition, the reports on the Jewish DPs in the army magazine *Stars and
Stripes* were consistently hostile and one sided.[159] Some observers felt
that this was the case because the higher command was not setting the
tone and their reticence was a function of American grand policy in what
was shaping up to be the Cold War. Given Germany's strategic position in
Europe, its reserves of trained manpower and industrial infrastructure,
argued Yaakov Oleiski, it was quite clear why both the Russians and
Americans were investing in Germany and laying the groundwork for
a long-term, strategic partnership.[160] Or, as an American officer put it
candidly: "We have to take the Germans out of the cellars and put them in
decent houses; when we fight the Russians we want them on our side."[161]

Thus, taking all these factors together, we can better understand why,
throughout 1946, the people of *She'erith Hapleitah* felt increasingly abandoned, isolated and under threat. It also explains why their responses
to a series of German provocations were quite so extreme. As early as

---

[156] "A tat vos iz vert tsu bagrisn: d.p.'s dertsayln g.i.'s" (A deed worth applauding: DPs tell
it to GIs), *LLT*, no. 41(53) (9.10.1946): 8.

[157] Army Talk: 151, War Dept., Washington (30.11.1946), reproduced in Dinnerstein,
America and the Survivors: 307–313.

[158] A. Piotrovski, "Vegn di oyfklerungs referatn far di amerikaner zelner" (Concerning the
information talks for the American soldiers), *YT*, no. 46 (58) (8.11.1946): 8.

[159] Report of Chaplain Abraham J. Klausner (20.3.1947), American Jewish Conference
Archives, Filebox 7.

[160] Yaakov Oleiski, "Der partsuf fun der velt demokratye" (The face of the democratic
world), *LLT*, no. 13 (25) (15.4.1946): 3.

[161] Chaplain Rackman's Report: 3.

February 1946 reports began to reach Munich about recurring incidents in Lampertheim.[162] The German police began unauthorized patrols in the camp, houses were searched, passers-by were accosted in public places and all this seemed to be happening with the tacit consent of the American forces. In late February a Jew was murdered in Munich and *Undzer Veg* reported a month later that "another victim", Yaakov Greenblatt had been killed in Grünwald near Munich.[163] For the survivors the moral of the story was clear: "The Germans have become *chutzpedik* and disposed to becoming murderous again. They see that they have not been punished for setting Europe alight and then killing it off."[164]

On 29 March 1946 a far more dramatic incident shocked the survivor community in Germany. In the early morning German soliders, unaccompanied by American troops, raided some Jewish homes in Stuttgart. The screams of "raus," the kicking in of doors and willful destruction of property led to determined resistance. In the clashes a number of young Jews were arrested but soon freed by their friends. In the course of the incident Shmuel Danziger was killed and a number of others wounded. Danziger who had been convalescing in France had just met his wife and children, also Auschwitz survivors, the evening before for the first time since their deportation.[165] The traumas of the recent past sprung to life and "Once more each and everyone of us experienced and relived the horrific six year long drama"[166] leading to suggestions that the survivors arm themselves and prepare to follow in the footsteps of the ghetto fighters.[167] There were angry demonstrations in all of the DP camps, newspapers put out special editions and the Central Committee met in extraordinary session and demanded that German police be denied access to Jewish installations, that the Jewish police be issued with arms and that no Jews be moved without prior coordination with the ZK.[168]

This last point came in response to attempts made in Bamberg and Fuerth forcefully to transfer Jews from one place to another without prior warning. Abraham Klausner was led to believe that these incidents were

[162] Irving Kwasnik, Report on Lampertheim (no date), YIVO/DPG 215.

[163] "Noch a korbn"(Another victim), *Undzer Veg*, no. 26 (29.3.1946): 1.

[164] "Stuttgart: di luft iz vayter farzamt" (Stuttgart: the air has been poisoned again), *Bamidbar*, no. 5 (15.4.1946): 4.

[165] "Aktsye in Stuttgart" ("Aktion" in Stuttgart), *Dos Fraye Vort*, no. 25 (5.4.1946): 1, 4.

[166] "Stuttgart: di luft."

[167] Shlomo Leit, "Vos lernen undz di letste geshe'enishn" (What do the latest events teach us), *Undzer Vort*, no. 6 (26.4.1946): 5.

[168] See, for example, *Undzer Veg*, ekstra oysgabe (special edition) (2.4.1946); *Oyf der Fray*, ekstra oysgabe (8.4.1946); *A Haym*, no. 7 (4.4.1946): 1; and *Der Nayer Moment*, no. 2 (15.4.1946).

indicative of a change of policy at a time when Judge Rifkind, the Adviser for Jewish Affairs, had left and his successor was yet to arrive. "It is my feeling that we face our most serious problem at this time. The great tragedy is that we have no one to bat for us."[169] The JDC office also reported "Situation in Germany becoming increasingly tense and explosive necessitating immediate replacement of Judge Rifkind... Incidents occurring almost daily... in past weeks our Munich office has been raided twice and our staff subjected to indignities."[170] The UNRRA Council on Jewish Affairs met in extraordinary session, expressed its dismay at the deterioration of relations between the army and the DPs and recommended that the local UNRRA director be informed of raids and be present when carried out, that German policemen be banned from Jewish installations, that Jewish policemen be granted greater authority and that new recruits be both taken on a tour of concentration camps and introduced to the problems and achievements of the Jewish DPs.[171]

Following the Stuttgart affair General McNarney prohibited the entrance of German police into Jewish installations but little else changed.[172] In April a fourteen-year-old boy was killed in Regensburg and at the end of the month there were serious disturbances in Landsberg. On the morning of 27 April 1946 when the news – later discredited – spread that the guards in a nearby *kibbutz* had been kidnapped and murdered, an angry crowd attacked German passers-by and set a bus alight.[173] About twenty Germans were injured and the American troops that arrived quickly sealed off the camp.[174] The situation was on the verge of explosion and it required all the talents of the local leadership to calm everyone down and prevent a bloody clash. There were many arrests and finally twenty young people stood trial. Dr. Gringauz appeared for the defense and, beyond his factual presentation and legal arguments, sought to impress upon the Military Tribunal the psychological background

---

[169] Abraham J. Klausner, 'The First Jew Officially Killed in Germany' (29.4.1946), AJDC/DP's Germany 1946.

[170] Greenleigh to Leavitt (9.4.1946), AJDC/DP's Germany General,1945/1946.G.

[171] UNRRA US Zone: Council on Jewish Affairs, Passing (3.4.1946), UNRRA Archive/RG –17/66,483.

[172] *Dos Fraye Vort*, no. 25 (5.4.1946): 1.

[173] For a dramatic description of what transpired in Landsberg see the interview with Eli Zamir in *Sefer ha-shlichut* (The book of missions abroad), Archive of *Bet Lochanei Hagetaot*, Container 2, file 7: 1–5. For the UNRRA account of the same events see J. H. Whiting to Lt. General Sir Frederick Morgan (23.5.1946), UNRRA Archives/RG-17/66,652.

[174] See "Farshvundn 2 yidishe yunglayt in diesen: oysnam tsushtand in landsberg un umgent" (Two Jewish youth in Diesen have disappeared: state of emergency in Landsberg and surroundings), *LLT*, no. 15 (27) (3.5.1946): 2. In addition UNRRA Daily Press Clippings, USA, no. 86 (30.4.1946), UNRRA Archive/RG-17/66,652.

that helped lead up to the outburst.[175] The crowded conditions in the DP camps generated a nervousness that often led to disproportionate responses to the irritations of daily life. This exacerbated the deep scarring of life in extremity which, in turn, activated a third factor:

Over the last years these people have been haunted by the suppressed concern over "Why people went like sheep to the slaughter." After liberation this suppressed complex was opened up and transformed into a flood of ideas about resistance and self-defence. That has become the law of life, our constitutional right which overrides all other laws.[176]

Gringauz's plea was to no avail and on 22 May 1946, six of the accused were sentenced to two years' imprisonment, twelve to a year, one to three months and one was released.[177] For the survivors these were unreasonable punishments and in response some residents of Landsberg declared a hunger strike while She'erith Hapleitah under the guidance of the ZK began a campaign for clemency and a reversal of the tribunal's ruling.[178] None of the protests helped and it was only a few months later when Rabbi Bernstein, the new Adviser for Jewish Affairs, appealed to General Adcock that the sentences were somewhat reduced.[179]

The military commanders were unconvinced that any radical revision of policy was required and there was little surprise in the survivor community when troubled brewed up at the end of May in Foehrenwald. In the wake of rumors about the murder of Jews in nearby Wolfrathshausen the camp residents took to the streets and vented their anger on the German population.[180] This opened the way for the German police to answer in kind and in an incident in July, Yitzchak Feldberg was shot to death and someone else wounded.[181] At the funeral the following day there were clashes with the American forces and six residents of the camp were wounded. The committee of inquiry set up by the army stuck to the specifics of the Foehrenwald incident and refused to look into the larger

---

[175] See "Sharfer urtayl in in protses kegn di 20 landsberger yidn" (Harsh sentence in the trial against twenty Landsberg Jews), *LLT*, no. 18 (30) (24.5.1946): 7.

[176] Ibid.   [177] Ibid.

[178] See "Oyfruf tsu der yidishe bafelkerung in landsberger tsenter!" (Call to the Jewish population of the Landsberg center), *LLT*, no. 16 (28) (10.5.1946): 2; "Vaytogdik – groyzamer urtayl" (Painful – cruel sentence), *Undzer Veg*, no. 34 (24.5.1946): 1; A. Valtikh, "Nokhn landsberger urtayl" (After the Landsberg judgment), *Bamidbar*, no. 7 (4.6.1946): 2; and "Der ZK vegn urteil in landsberger protses" (The Central Committee on the judgment in the Landsberg trial), *A Haym*, no. 13 (4.6.1946): 1.

[179] See "Farklenert di shtrof fun di 19 farmishpete landsberger yidn" (Sentence of the nineteen Landsberg Jewish defendants reduced), *A Haym*, no. 17 (16.8.1946): 2.

[180] Address by Henry Cohen, former UNRRA Director, Camp Foehrenwald, Germany (7.11.1947), YIVO/DPG 61.

[181] "Daytshe politsay dershosn a yid in foehrenwald" (German police shoot a Jew in Foehrenwald), *LLT*, no. 29 (41) (26.7.1946): 2.

issues.[182] At the end of May 1946 Levi Shalitan attempted to sum up the causes behind the dangerous restiveness of *She'erith Hapleitah*:

How long can people just go on talking, warning, begging, and longing and all of these under one heading: Why? Why are we still sitting here in Germany? Why are we being kept in camps? Why does UNRRA relate to us as step-children? Why are these underhand Germans better off than their victims? Why is the world so deaf to our pain? Why this coolness (so as not to use another term) of the Military Government towards us?[183]

Beverly Diamond, a consultant to UNRRA on Jewish affairs, also began to pick up signs of crisis and discouragement in the survivor community – receding interest in public activity, extreme political divisiveness, an increased movement from camp to town, a greater prevalence of black market activity, pregnant mothers who were depressed at the thought that their new born had nowhere to go and ugly pressure on those who had given up on Palestine and were seeking their fortunes elsewhere.[184]

By mid-1946, in short, the remnants of European Jewry began to feel themselves trapped on German soil. What was supposed to have been a way station and staging ground for mass aliyah was beginning to look like a *cul-de-sac*. It was as if the warning issued by the veteran leader of Polish Zionism, Yitzchak Gruenbaum, was beginning to come true. At the beginning of 1946 he had registered his strenuous objection to the risky bet of concentrating Jews in Germany when in a private conversation he warned Chaim Hoffman, "You are going to bring disaster down on us. There will not be mass immigration, the American army will leave and these Jews will be exposed to danger and their blood will be on our heads."[185] As the journalist Victor Bernstein reported, the question of mass immigration to Palestine had again moved into center stage: "I found a remarkable unanimity in the opinion of thoughtful observers that the answer to the Landsberg riots is not 20 prison sentences but 100,000 certificates for Palestine."[186]

This also accounts for the supreme importance the people of *She'erith Hapleitah* attached to the work of the Anglo-American Committee of

[182] "Vos iz be'emet geshen in foehrenwald" (What really happened in Foehrenwald), *Bamidbar*, no. 13 (14.8.1946): 3–4; see, too, M.D. Olihav, "Aspektn fun foehrenwalder blut" (Aspects of the bloodshed in Foehrenwald), *Undzer Veg*, no. 43 (2.8.1946): 8.

[183] Levi Shalitan, "Fun undzer seder-hayom: farvos?" (From our agenda: why?), *Undzer Veg*, no. 35 (31.5.1946): 2.

[184] Beverly Diamond to C.J. Taylor, Deputy Director, UNRRA US Zone (16.7.1946): 1–3, UNRRA Archive/RG-17/66,652.

[185] Report of Chaim (Yachil) Hoffman, *Mapai* Secretariat (24.7.1946), *Ha'avodah* – Labor Archive/24/46.

[186] Victor H. Bernstein, "Cure for DP 'Itch to Riot': Get Jews out of Reich," *PM* (6.5.1946), UNRRA Daily Press Clippings.

Inquiry and the unbearable tension as its findings and recommendations were awaited. In the estimate of Jack Whiting, the director of UNRRA in the American Zone:

the recently announced findings of the Anglo-American Commission may do much to ease the situation, for under the policy that the commission urges approximately 30,000 of the 60,000 Jewish DPs in Bavaria would receive certificates authorizing their admission into Palestine; if, however, the findings of the commission are not accepted, then it is the prediction of Dr. Aumer, the Land Commissioner for Jewish Welfare, that further outbreaks of violence will occur because "the future looks so hopeless and black for them and because the findings of this commission are the one thing upon which they have pinned their hopes."[187]

And so it was. When the hopes pinned on the Anglo-American Committee began to fade, the leadership of *She'erith Hapleitah* faced the most difficult challenge of its short history.

---

[187] Whiting to Morgan: 3.

11 *She'erith Hapleitah* towards 1947

As the tension mounted and dissatisfaction grew during 1946 the leaders of *She'erith Hapleitah* were painfully reminded of their basic impotence and, in response, renewed their efforts to be recognized by the US Army as the legitimate representative of the "liberated Jews" in the Occupation Zone. At the end of February 1946 they had turned to General Truscott with a request for the formal recognition of the Central Committee as the authorized representative of the Jews in Germany.[1] The problem of the *ZK*, as they wrote to the General, was not with the overall policy of the Supreme Command but with its implementation on the ground. Beyond the immediate damage caused by the disparaging attitudes and dilatory tactics they often encountered, these actions of the lower ranks were closely observed by the local German population who saw them as legitimizing their own deeply rooted hostility to the Jewish people. Many of these difficulties could be avoided if the Supreme Command would issue a directive informing its officers that "The Central Committee of Liberated Jews... and... [its] branches should be considered as representing the interest of the Liberated Jews. This should be the base line for policy on the local level."[2]

The leaders of the Central Committee hoped, in addition, that legalization would open the way to unmediated access to the military authorities and would thus allow them to dispense with what they saw as the dubious role of UNRRA. Those who were there to aid them did not strenuously oppose German police raids on Jewish facilities, failed to prevent Jewish DPs from being arbitrarily pushed around and lacked the initiative and drive effectively to help newcomers from Poland settle in. Zalman Grinberg addressed this issue in a letter written to General Morgan in late March: "It has been the policy of the Central Committee to approach U.N.R.R.A. on all these problems. The Central Committee has

---

[1] Protokoll nr. 36 des *ZK* (Protocol no. 36 of the *ZK*) (21.2.1946), YIVO/DPG 95.
[2] Memorandum of the Central Committee to General Truscott (26.3.1946), YIVO/DPG 113.

the feeling that even though it is received with practiced politeness there is very little effort being exerted on behalf of these people."[3]

The response of the army to these proposals was not, to put it mildly, enthusiastic. The commander of the Third Army who was consulted suggested a simple letter of recognition that would in no way augment the authority of the Central Committee while appointing a liaison officer to improve communications without the headache of direct access. In the formulation of his opinion General Schmidt based himself on an intelligence report that raised doubts as to both the credibility of the ZK and the results of the elections to the First Congress. "USFET errs in referring to this organization as a 'representative elected agency.' German Jews disclaim the committee as representing them, as do non-Zionist Jews. Many thousands of refugees have arrived since the elections and could not have taken part in them."[4] Acceding to the request of the committee, argued Lt. Edwin Clarke, the author of the report, would serve as an unfortunate precedent for other DP groups who would seek to follow suit and would be seen as a slap in the face by their British allies. The ZK far from being a responsible body was a collection of opportunistic trouble-makers led by a sly, dishonest man – "Dr. Zalman Grinberg (alias Greenhouse, alias Greenberg, alias Gringauz,) a Lithuanian Jew."[5] The confusion between Grinberg and Gringauz and the hostile innuendo is an important indicator of how the middle and lower echelons of the army related to *She'erith Hapleitah* and its leadership. The report ends by saying that "Dr. Grinberg is ambitious and no matter what concessions he gets he asks for more. He now has in mind recognition by the United Nations as 'the destroyed Jewish nation.' This charter is a rung in his ladder."[6]

The leaders of the ZK who were fully aware of the hostility encountered by survivors on the local level but unaware of what was happening behind the scenes, persisted in their efforts to reach an accommodation with the upper echelons of the army and by mid-1946 could point to some progress.[7] In July they received the first draft of a letter of recognition, responded with comments of their own and most of the remaining difficulties were ironed out at the end of August when, together

---

[3] Dr. Zalman Grinberg to General Frederick Morgan, UNRRA Director European Theater (26.3.1946), YIVO/DPG 113; see also Zitsung fun rat fun di bafrayte yidn in amerikaner bazetsungs zone in daytshland (Meeting of the Council of the Liberated Jews in the American Occupation Zone of Germany) (31.3.1946–1.4.1946), YIVO/DPG 105.

[4] Secret Report of Lt. Edwin Clarke (no date) in W.R. Schmidt, Chief of Staff, Third United States Army to Commanding General USFET (27.6.1946), YIVO/DPG 113.

[5] Ibid.   [6] Ibid.

[7] See the Protokoll fun der zitsung fun rat fun ZK (Protocol of the Council of the ZK) (9.6.1946), YIVO/DPG 105, and see, also, Major General H.R. Bull, C.O.S. USFET to Central Committee of Liberated Jews in the US Zone (July 1946), YIVO/DPG 113.

with Nachum Goldman and Rabbi Stephen Wise, they met with General Joseph T. McNarney who had replaced General Eisenhower.[8] On 5 September 1946 Major General Huebner sent a memorandum[9] to the Central Committee spelling out the US Army's reading of the general formulations in the Letter of Recognition which was duly signed by General McNarney two days later recognizing the Central Committee "as a representative, elected agency of an association of Jewish Displaced Persons in this Zone."[10] The army granted the *ZK* executive, consultative and representative powers in concert with those enjoyed by itself, UNRRA and the voluntary agencies. All of its activities would be subject to the supervision of a military liaison officer, the Committee undertook to refrain from political activity and both sides had the right to rescind the agreement unilaterally. In view of earlier requests of the Central Committee to gain control of heirless Jewish community property, the army stressed that the agreement in no way compromised their exclusive ownership of these assets.[11]

Did the Letter of Recognition significantly change the standing and executive capacity of the Central Committee? It very certainly contributed to the confidence and morale of the Committee members and generated widespread expectation of change for the better. They soon learnt, however, that their repeated efforts to develop independent initiatives were generally thwarted. Thus, even though David Treger told the delegates to the Second Congress of *She'erith Hapleitah* in early 1947 that in the wake of official recognition the Central Committee "had entered a new period of activity"[12] and had direct access to the upper command of the army through the person of Colonel Scithers, the new liaison officer, these laudatory remarks were primarily an exercise in public relations. In the closed meetings of the *ZK*, by comparison, all the old frustrations resurfaced including the well-worn threat of turning to the American press in order to expose the failings of the Military Government.[13]

Relations with UNRRA, in addition, did not significantly change. The initial assumption of the *ZK* was they had achieved a status of parity with the international organization allowing them to act directly without

---

[8] Protokoll nr. 57 des *ZK* (26.8.1946), YIVO/DPG 97.

[9] Major General Huebner to the Central Committee of the Liberated Jews in the US Zone (5.9.1946), YIVO/DPG 113.

[10] Joseph T. McNarney, Commanding General, USFET, to the Central Committee of the Liberated Jews (7.9.1946), YIVO,DPG 113.

[11] Ibid.

[12] David Treger, 2-ter kongres fun she'erith hapleitah (2nd Congress of *She'erith Hapleitah*), Bad Reichenhall (10–12.2.1947), YIVO/DPG 658.

[13] See for example Protokoll nr. 71 des plenum fun *ZK* (Protocol no. 71 of the plenum of the *ZK*) (12.3.1946), YIVO/DPG/97.

having to negotiate its cumbersome bureaucracy. In accordance with this assumption a permanent representative was sent to Heidelberg so as to liaise with UNRRA headquarters.[14] The directors of UNRRA refused to accept these new arrangements and complained to the army command that "the Central Committee appears to be exceeding its terms of reference in that members of the committee, or sections thereof, are not only dealing directly with UNRRA and displaced persons personnel in assembly centers throughout the Zone, but are also giving them instructions which relate to camp procedures and operations."[15] The angry responses of UNRRA personnel in the field threatened to undermine the work of the ZK and very quickly forced them to moderate their independent line.[16]

As part of this overall thrust for greater independence there was also an effort to reshape the working relations of the ZK with the JDC but here too the results were disappointing. The discussion with the Joint turned on two matters: the conversion of the monthly budgetary allocations received by the Central Committee into a long-term commitment that would allow them to develop some of their own initiatives and, secondly, the long-standing request to hand over the distribution of supplementary supplies to the ZK which would mean dismantling the parallel framework set up by the JDC and provide additional employment for the survivors themselves.[17] In theory this was an approach that the Joint embraced and, as Leo Schwarz put it: "The professional objective of the AJDC is to help develop the Central Committee and all its constituents to the point where the people may attain the maximum degree of self-government and self-sustenance."[18] But in practice things looked rather different. Schwarz proudly reported that within one year the JDC in Germany had moved from 20 to 300 employees and these figures told their own story. Those in charge of the JDC operation appeared to assume that She'erith Hapleitah, given its human composition and transient character, should not run its own affairs. Long-term planning was out of the question and in terms of public accountability neither the leaders

[14] Protokoll nr. 64 des ZK (23.10.1946), YIVO/DPG/97.
[15] J.H. Whiting to G-5 Division Headquarters, Third US Army (20.12.1946), UNRRA Archive/R.G.17/66,484.
[16] See Protokoll der beratung fun rat (Protocol of the Council session) (15.1.1947), YIVO/DPG 105.
[17] See Protokoll fun der zitsung fun rat fun ZK (9.6.1946), YIVO/DPG 105, Protokoll no. 52 fun der zitsung fun ZK mit dem director fun joint, mister schwarz (3.8.1946), YIVO/DPG 97 and Protokoll fun der gemaynzamer zitsung fun ZK mit dem joint (Protocol of the joint session of the ZK with the Joint) (6.8.1946), YIVO/DPG 97. For an illustration of the complexity of cooperation even when it came to education and culture see Proyekt Minkhen (Project Munich) (24.12.1946), YIVO/DPG 19.
[18] Leo W. Schwarz, Summary Analysis of the AJDC Program in the US Zone of Occupation, Germany (13.1.1947), YIVO/DPG 9.

nor their provisional institutions could be implicitly trusted. The heads of the *ZK* found this to be both insulting and humiliating and said as much in a letter to Edward Warburg, the President of the JDC, in July 1946: "It is our feeling that the Directors of the American Joint look upon us as DP's. The use of the term DP in this sense connotes an individual not only displaced in terms of a home but also in terms of vision and responsibility."[19]

The attempt to recast the relationship between the JDC and the Central Committee reached its climax during the visit of Dr. Boris Pliskin, Aryeh Retter and Shmuel Shlomovitz to the United States at the beginning of 1947. In the harsh report that they brought with them – An Evaluation of the AJDC Program in the American Occupied Zone of Germany from its Inception to January 1947 – they laid out their long-standing grievances against their American benefactors.[20] The Joint workers arrived on the scene only after a long delay, came empty-handed, were often second-rate, developed a paternalistic attitude towards the survivors, generated opposition and by virtue of their chronic, "legalistic" caution, which they called being "apolitical", they condemned themselves to futility. Taking effective action on every issue that was of vital concern to the community of survivors – recognition of their national identity, tracing family and relatives, absorbing refugees from Eastern Europe and immigration to Palestine –

implied an infringement upon some political directive. Either the directive had to be changed or circumvented. The Joint was always subservient to the period in the directive. So much so that when a Joint worker snubbed that period, he or she was up for dismissal. In ... political work it is impossible to be effective and apolitical at the same time.[21]

The representatives of *She'erith Hapleitah* extended their stay in America and turned to other Jewish organizations in their attempt to win support for their basic demands: long-term finance, the distribution of supplemental rations, dismantling the dual organizational setup and bringing the remuneration of *ZK* workers up to a par with that of Joint employees.[22] The three returned to Germany with a sense of achievement and if, initially, the JDC was accommodating on the margins, in

---

[19] Dr. Zalman Grinberg and David Treger to Edward W. Warburg (5.7.1946), YIVO/DPG 694; see also, for example, Chaplain Klausner to Leo Schwarz (10.7.1946), AJDC/DP's Germany 1946.

[20] An Evaluation of the AJDC Program in the American Occupied Zone of Germany from its Inception to January 1947, AJDC/DP's Germany 1947.

[21] Ibid.: 9.

[22] Memorandum from the American Jewish Conference to the AJDC (5.2.1947), AJDC/DP's Germany 1947.

time it became clear that they would not budge on issues that really mattered.[23] Thus the stage was set for another round in the ritual dance of ambivalence that had characterized the relations between the two bodies from the outset. There were periodic threats from the *ZK* to break off ties with the Joint but this was never a real option. Only few of the growing Jewish population in the American Occupation Zone were aware of these power struggles behind the scenes and would not have been willing to forgo the small but significant JDC supplement to their meager earnings, if any. Thus the leaders of the *ZK* who sought a degree of control after so many years of powerlessness found themselves caught up in a tangle of dependence from which they could not extricate themselves.

The Central Committee, nonetheless, did succeed in chalking up some commendable successes in the latter half of 1946. They persuaded the Bavarian Government to channel its limited support for *She'erith Hapleitah* via their good offices[24] and, internally, managed to induce the "Ort" network to accept its guidelines for its vocational work in the Zone.[25] The Committee, in addition, was widely praised for its varied accomplishments in helping to deal with the continuing influx of refugees from Eastern Europe. Its efforts which focused on material aid and guidance in setting up new camps worked because it was an internal matter that depended on volunteer work. When it came to fateful questions like keeping the borders of Germany open to the constant flow of refugees the *ZK* had little clout and it was the pressure of American Jewry that counted for more.

As we saw earlier, the dramatic growth of the Jewish population in the American Zone came from two sources – first, the *Brichah* and, secondly, the sharp increase of the birthrate within *She'erith Hapleitah*. According to the estimates of the JDC, the population that had grown to 40,000 by the end of 1945 had reached 142,000 a year later[26] and it did not take long for the budgetary implications of the growth to reach those footing the bill in Washington. By the end of April some officials were weighing the possibility of cutting off access to Germany and Austria for fear that the findings of the Anglo-American Committee of Inquiry

---

[23] Paris Office to Joint New York (22.1.1947), AJDC/DP's Germany General, 1947/1948. See also Joseph Schwartz to AJDC New York (12.2.1947), AJDC/DP's Germany 1947.

[24] Protokoll nr. 61 des *ZK* (28.9.1946) and also Protokoll nr. 62 des *ZK* (2.10.1946), YIVO/DPG 97.

[25] Ibid. See, also, Protokoll nr. 60 des *ZK* (9.9.1946) and Protokoll nr. 64 des *ZK* (23.10.1946), YIVO/DPG 97.

[26] Jewish Population in the US Zone of Germany, Effective December 31, 1946, Prepared by AJDC US Zone Hq. – Heidelberg in the private papers of Chaim Yachil (Hoffman).

would trigger off an even larger flow of infiltrees.[27] The Department of War was in favor of closure or severely limiting the influx while the State Department was more cautious and feared sparking off an embarrassing public outcry. The administration decided to embark on a series of consultations with the Jewish community and then to leave the final decision to the President. These decisions were communicated to General McNarney and General Clark in Austria together with a clear directive: the flow of refugees was not to be stopped until Washington gave the sign. Hints of these discussions were divulged to members of the *ZK* who met at the beginning of May in order to think through the options and to plan their response.[28] All of those present concurred with Grinberg's assessment that "antisemitism in Poland was on the upswing and that no laws and no prohibitions would be able to staunch the massive flow of refugees. The Jews from Poland would have to be allowed into the Zone and every means and possibility had to be galvanized to lighten the heavy burden [this entailed]."[29] The operative decision was to conduct a survey of the absorptive capacity of all the camps and communities, consult with the Jewish directors of UNRRA camps and coordinate with the JDC the supply of vital necessities for those who would arrive with all of their worldly property in a suitcase.

At the same time the five large Jewish organizations in America launched a campaign against any attempt to close off the Occupation Zone to Jews fleeing persecution.[30] This was a key issue raised by Rabbi Stephen Wise, Nachum Goldman and representatives of the Central Committee in their meeting with General McNarney in August 1946. The General, as it was reported back to the *ZK*, presented the group with one of his major dilemmas: "Either to improve the living conditions of the Jews already in the Zone or to allow in newcomers. As was obvious, the Jewish representatives chose the second option."[31] In September after coordinating strategy with the Jewish Agency and the JDC, the Committee announced a "Mobilization for Absorption" campaign.[32] They turned to local committees to suggest people who could help the new camps get organized, they began collecting contributions of food and clothing and decided to divert some supplies from the established camps to those just

---

[27] Howard Petersen, Assistant Secretary of War to Dean Acheson, Acting Secretary of State, NA/RG 165/Records of the War Department and Special Staffs/P&O 000.7/Sect.1/Case 1.

[28] Protokoll nr. 42 fun presidium fun der *ZK* (Protocol no. 42 of the Presidium of the *ZK*) (5.5.1946), YIVO/DPG 97.

[29] Ibid.

[30] See J.C. Hyman to J.H. Levy (25.7.1946) and David Wohl to Meir Grossman (23.7.1946), AJDC/DP's Germany 1946.

[31] Protokoll nr. 57 des *ZK*.   [32] Protokoll nr. 59 des *ZK* (4.9.1946), YIVO/DPG 97.

starting out.[33] Rabbi Phillip Bernstein, the Special Adviser, requested that the JDC significantly increase its commitments to the absorption of newcomers. The rabbi had persuaded General Clark to increase the number of Jews in Austria, which until then had served primarily as a way station[34] to Germany, from 5,000 to 30,000 while General McNarney was willing to persist in his liberal "open borders" policy if the Joint would share in the burden of helping these refugees settle in. In Bernstein's view it was crucial that the Jewish people demonstrate its willingness to take responsibility and actively help for "the U.S. Army is the only friend the Jews have in Europe, that if the Army should close down on its Jewish program the...situation would immediately become desperate and hopeless."[35]

The *Brichah* and the feverish activity surrounding it created the feeling of an entire people on the move – "Jews are fleeing," wrote the editor of the *Landsberger Lager Tsaytung*, "They flee from East and from West, from North and from South, all are fleeing in the direction of one destination, even though it is so far and so difficult to reach."[36] Or, as Chaim Hoffman expressed it at a gathering of *shlichim* in Germany:

Herein lies the Zionist, historical significance of the *Brichah* which has become the central event in Diaspora life since the liberation for it removes the Jews from holding on to something temporary, thrusts them into a vacuum from which there is no way out except to surge forward. This is its meaning – the burning of bridges, the formation of a determined, driving force that will not allow itself or the world bypass our claim for life.[37]

As 1947 approached, therefore, the persistent limitations and humiliation of DP life together with dramatic impact of the *Brichah* refocused public attention on the question of immigration to Palestine.

In its early days the *ZK* did not think systematically about the question of aliyah. Once the dimensions of the Jewish tragedy became known, it was assumed, the civilized world would immediately open the Land of Israel to the few who had survived.[38] Many months were to pass before the survivors could come to terms with the fact that nothing had

---

[33] Protokoll nr. 72 des *ZK*, YIVO/DPG 97.

[34] See Thomas Albrich, "Way Station of Exodus: Jewish Displaced Persons and Refugees in Post War Austria," in Berenbaum and Peck, eds., *The Holocaust and History*: 716–732.

[35] Adviser to the Theater Commander on Jewish Affairs to Joseph Hyman (8.9.1946), AJDC/DP's Germany 1946.

[36] Barukh Hermanovitz, "Kibbutz galuyot" (The ingathering of the exiles), *LLT*, no. 34 (46) (16.8.1946): 3.

[37] Chaim (Yachil) Hoffman, Kinus ha-shlichim be-germaniyah (The conference of emissaries in Germany), CZA/S6/4685.

[38] See Yachil (Hoffman), "Peulot ha-mishlachat ha-eretz yisraelit," *Yalkut Moreshet*, no. 30: 26–28.

9 A common sight in Occupied Germany: DPs protesting against camp life and the British refusal to allow free immigration into Palestine.

changed and that their petitions and demonstrations counted for little. It was only in April 1946 that a mere 566 immigration certificates were placed at the disposal of the Jewish Agency for *She'erith Hapleitah*. There was general agreement with Chaim Yachil's proposal to allocate them to children and their departure, as the recommendations of the Anglo-American Committee were tensely awaited, generated great excitement in the DP camps. The flames of hope were further fanned when 1,200 members of Zionist youth movements left at this time for Italy in order to board illegal immigrant ships. Thus the recommendation of the Anglo-American Committee to allow 100,000 survivors to enter Palestine came at a propitious time and led many to believe that the great exodus from Europe was at hand. At the end of May thirty-five additional *shlichim* arrived and the now seventy strong Palestinian Mission began actively to prepare for mass immigration. This required close coordination with the US Army and UNRRA, joint planning with the *ZK* and local committees and the need to generate a broad consensus on the criteria that would determine the allocation of certificates. In the end the following priorities were agreed upon: the first to go would be children followed by families being reunited, veteran Zionists and then special cases.

However, the expectations were premature and the harsh truth was that until the end of the Mandate but 984 Jews immigrated legally to Palestine. Thus, once Britain had effectively derailed the recommendations of the Anglo-American Committee the only option that remained was illegal immigration. Here, too, difficulties were encountered as the British sought to block the routes leading from Southern Germany to Italy. In response the *Mossad Le-Aliyah Bet* began the complex task of setting up new routes to ports in the south of France and it took a few months before they became fully operational. Most of the 9,500 *ma'apilim* – illegal immigrants – who departed from Germany during 1946 were members of *kibbutzim* who received their quota according to the size of their movements. Unaffiliated *ma'apilim* who made up about a third of those departing were selected by the Palestinian emissary and aliyah committee in each locality. Despite the fact that the whole movement was semi-clandestine and focused primarily on youth movement members, it left a clear impress on the life and morale of *She'erith Hapleitah* – "A significant exodus involved everyone, even those staying behind while a slowdown in the flow of immigrants generated despair . . . and pushed the survivors to seek alternative ways of leaving Germany or at least the DP camps."[39] Or, in the words of David Treger, the Chairman of the Central Committee, after the departure of Zalman Grinberg aliyah meant the future and thus for those sitting on their suitcases was "the problem of all problems."[40] Treger's formulation was perhaps too sweeping. As 1947 began the survivors continued to seek ways out of Europe but, to the chagrin of the Zionists, many more were prepared to consider emigration as opposed to aliyah. As Baruch Hermanovitz had written in mid-1946:

Aliyah is the opposite of "emigration." Aliyah means a goal, emigration does not. Aliyah means concern for the entire people, emigration does not. Aliyah means rebuilding in the wake of destruction, emigration does not. Aliyah means taking steps to prevent this kind of tragedy from repeating itself, emigration does not. Aliyah means independence, emigration means exile.[41]

Hermanovitz found the contemplation of emigration in *She'erith Hapleitah* to be especially disturbing. Survivors, more than anyone else, had the Jewish tragedy imprinted on their minds and souls – they understood how much the Jewish people needed a country of its own and they also knew that the destruction of European Jewry had brought about

---

[39] Moshe Kliger interview with Gershon Gal (9.4.1974), *Sefer ha-shlichut* (The book of missions abroad), Archive of the *Bet Lochamei Hagetaot*, Container 2/file 5: 23.

[40] Treger, 2-ter kongres.

[41] Barukh Hermanovitz, "Aliyah oder emigratsie" (Aliyah or emigration), *LLT*, no. 15 (27) (3.5.1946): 3.

the destruction of the human hinterland of the Zionist movement. Any survivor who despite this knowledge turned away from aliyah to emigration was acting in a way he could only describe as criminal.

May 1946, when the above was written, was a time of great hope for large-scale immigration and Hermanovitz must have felt that he was speaking for the majority of Jews in Occupied Germany. Indeed, for the most part, the surveys, observations and educated guesses from liberation to mid-1946 appear to bear him out. Members of the *ZK*, JDC workers, the Special Adviser for Jewish Affairs, numerous visitors from abroad and the Anglo-American Committee of Inquiry all agreed that at least 70 percent of the survivors sought to settle in the Land of Israel.[42] The noticeable change in this trend first comes to light in the second half of 1946 when the people of *She'erith Hapleitah* realized that the British government was not going to honor the recommendations of the Anglo-American Commission. Chaim Hoffman captured this mood in a letter to Giora Yoseftal in June 1946:

I confess to you that over these last few days I have been very depressed. Bevin's speech at the Labour Conference was not a surprise but his brutality and cynicism really hurt... How are we going to hold on? Here we are for the third month without certificates – and despair is upon the public and us.[43]

At this time the United States opened a number of consular offices in German cities and began to receive applications for immigration. By the end of 1946, according to the Immigration Bureau of the JDC, 4,135 Jews had immigrated to the United States, 1,217 to various destinations in South America, 82 to Australia and 310 to European countries and elsewhere and some 10,000 to Palestine.[44] Taken together we see that over 11 percent of the Surviving Remnant managed to depart from Germany in 1946. The growing interest in immigration to the United States of America embarrassed the Zionist camp and generated a lot of tension in the DP camps. Beyond accusations of submission, a few altercations and an intensive propaganda campaign the Zionist response focused on broadening the circle of illegal immigration, a policy that was fully consonant with an important change in the overall priorities of the Zionist movement.

---

[42] For some estimates of the percentage of survivors seeking to immigrate to Palestine in the earlier period see Nadich, *Eisenhower and the Jews*: 79; Phillip Struchan, Landsberg Report AJDC Staff Conference; Paris Memo No. 114 to AJDC New York; Dr. Ignacy Schwartzbart, Report on the Visit to the American Zone in Germany (January 1946), CZA/S25/5232.

[43] Chaim (Yachil) Hoffman to Giora Yoseftal (18.6.1946), CZA/S6/4676.

[44] Countries of Destination of Jewish Emigrants from the US Zone in Germany Effective 31 December 1946, AJDC, CZA/S6/4676.

Following the Black Sabbath (29 June 1946) during which the British raided the offices of the Jewish Agency and arrested many of its leaders and then the disastrous bombing of the King David Hotel on 22 July 1946, most of the Zionist leadership were persuaded that the policy of rebellion had exhausted itself and was no longer serving the cause of independence. At the meeting of the Jewish Agency Executive in Paris in August 1946 an historic decision was taken to enter into negotiations regarding the partition of Western Palestine.[45] This radical departure in Zionist politics was adopted in the hope of winning over President Truman to the Zionist cause at a time when illegal immigration was moving into center stage and the British had begun to expel the *ma'apilim* they intercepted to Cyprus. Rabbi Stephen Wise and Rabbi Yehudah L. Maimon (Fishman) forcefully argued, in addition, that it was morally wrong to allow the survivors to continue stagnating in the DP camps without making every effort to break the Palestinian deadlock so as to open the way to mass immigration. They recalled the heavy price the Zionist movement paid for rejecting the British partition plan of 1937 – even a small state would have provided a safe refuge for masses of Jews and the same mistake, so they argued, should not be made twice. If there was no hope of aliyah, furthermore, the people of *She'erith Hapleitah* would seek other solutions and the Zionist movement would begin to lose the little that was left of its historic, European hinterland.[46]

The measures adopted by the British in Palestine elicited an immediate response in *She'erith Hapleitah*. At the beginning of July the Council of the Liberated Jews in Germany met in extraordinary session in order to plan and coordinate the protest against British policy. The guiding assumption of those present was that the British were seeking to forestall the creation of a Jewish state and, therefore, threatening their own future. When it came to deciding on the appropriate response, however, opinions were divided. Gustav Lachman of Feldafing took an extreme position: "Our protest should be the last [of its kind] ... people should abandon the camps and join a crusade to Eretz Yisrael. We don't have anything to lose."[47] This idea of setting out *en masse* to the Mediterranean surfaced in Germany whenever British policy appeared to threaten the Zionist endeavor. The idea that bore a family resemblance to some of Ben-Gurion's more radical thinking on the matter was mooted at the Second Congress of *She'erith Hapleitah* by Rabbi Klausner and supporters of the Revisionist Bergson group in America which was known for

---

[45] See Heller, *Be-maavak le-medinah*: 436.

[46] Yehuda Bauer, *The Jewish Emergence from Powerlessness* (London, 1980): 72–75.

[47] Protokoll fun der oyserordentlikher zitsung fun rat (Protocol of the extraordinary session of the council) (2.7.1946), YIVO/DPG 105.

its imaginative campaigning and again claimed public attention a few months later when Yitzchak Tabenkin, the activist labor leader, spent some time in Germany.[48] The Council, however, refused to countenance Lachman's proposal lest it awaken a mass hysteria that could only end with a tragic whimper. Neither were the majority willing to accept the comparison Lachman drew between the helplessness of Jews under Nazi rule and the vulnerability of Palestinian Jewry – the Yishuv was a coherent, national community living on its own soil that had grown into a force to be reckoned with in the Middle East. For the opponents of the march to Palestine, invidious comparisons with Jewish victimhood during the war were not only invalid but could generate widespread paralysis and despair.

The Council opted for a more moderate course of action declaring 3 July 1946 as a day of protest and the start of a hunger strike. The response to the call of the Council was almost universally affirmative and throughout the American Zone of Occupation total opposition to British policy was demonstrated in a way that was both forceful and resonant. The Jewish Committee in Olching, for example, handed the following resolutions to the Military Governor in the nearby town:

1. *We demand* the immediate liberation of our brothers arrested by the English in Palestine.
2. *We demand* the ultimate redemption of the promise given by the Anglo-American Commission on Palestine *approved by President Truman* providing permit of a [*sic*] entry for 100,000 Jews into Palestine.
3. *We demand* the immediate permission for all Jews to leave Germany, this bloody soil, which has become the common grave of our brothers and sisters.[49]

The widespread participation of the general public in the protests underscored something that even the most radical Zionists knew deep down: potential emigrants also participated actively because in most cases the choice between Palestine and other destinations was personal or practical but rarely a question of principle. Even Baruch Hermanovitz toned down his virulent views on emigration "For all Jews, I am certain, Eretz Yisrael

---

[48] See Gelber, *Toldot ha-hitnadvut*: 495–497. For additional comments on the idea of "the march on the borders" see Report from Chaplain Abraham J. Klausner, Heidelberg (20.3.1947), American Jewish Conference Archives, Filebox/Germany/4; Copy of telegrams from NY to Pelcor, Jerusalem (1.4.1947), CZA/S25/5232; Chaim (Yachil) Hoffman's letter from Munich (6.4.1947), CZA/S6/4676; Rabbi Phillip S. Bernstein, Report on the Jewish Displaced Persons in the US Zone, Germany and Austria to the Five Organizations (12.5.1947): 7, YIVO/DPG 61; Moshe Kliger interviews Gershon Gal: 17; Moshe Kliger interviews Avraham Gevelber, ibid.: 13–18; Moshe Kliger interviews Eli Zamir, ibid.: 18.

[49] UNRRA Archive/RG17/66,652.

remains their mother – and, as with mothers there can only be but one – so all the other lands remain step-mothers."[50]

The feeling of many leaders that events were overtaking them and leaving Zionism behind made it imperative to go beyond banners and speeches. In July a delegation from the Central Committee set out for Paris in order to confer with David Ben-Gurion and representatives of the Jewish Agency.[51] Their key proposal was to establish a special department for the affairs of *She'erith Hapleitah* in the Jewish Agency run by people close to them with two main aims in mind: to avoid the creation of new camps in Palestine when mass aliyah finally came and to ensure productive employment so long denied to their people. Ben-Gurion accepted the idea in principle and suggested that a delegation of experts be sent to Palestine to prepare the ground for the aliyah that would get underway when the conditions were ripe. His offer was enthusiastically taken up and in August Zalman Grinberg, David Treger and Abraham Blumowicz set out for Palestine. After nearly a month of meetings, site trips and planning Blumowicz and Treger returned to Germany while Grinberg stayed on with his young son who was diagnosed as suffering from a malignant disease. On their return they were happy to report that the absorption authorities had accepted the principle that *She'erith Hapleitah* should be treated with dignity and consideration and a special department and bank would be set up to ensure this; their job, in turn, was to make sure that the survivors arrived as an organized group rather than a unruly mass.[52] Blumowicz set aside his many responsibilities in the *ZK* and set out to visit all the major survivor concentrations in order personally to communicate what had transpired in their trip to Palestine and what it meant for the survivors in Germany.

In preparation for immigration, and this was central to Blumowicz's message, it was critical that as many people as possible become engaged in productive work and vocational training. But this was easier said than done. For many, work was associated with the horrors of the past while in the present they resisted being integrated into the local economy and helping to put Germany back on its feet. Isaac Neiman asked of those who entered into business deals with Germans if this is what "revenge" was supposed to look like: "have we in fact fallen so low that for the sake of money we are ready to forget everything?"[53] To these misgivings a

---

[50] Barukh Hermanovitz, "Oyfn yidishn seder-hayom: khesed leumim khatat" (On the Jewish agenda: charity begins at home), *YT*, no. 48 (60) (20.11.1946): 6.

[51] See Protokoll nr. 45 fun der plener zitsung fun rat (Protocol no. 45 of the plenary session of the Council) (30.6.1946), YIVO/DPG 105.

[52] See Protokoll nr. 60 des *ZK*.

[53] Isaac Neiman, "Der goldener kalb vert tsu geferlekh" (The cost of the golden calf is too high), *Undzer Veg*, no. 32 (10.5.1946): 8. See also Hoda ben Ish Wieden, "Der nayer egel hazahav" (The new golden calf), *Der Nayer Moment*, no. 5 (20.6.1946): 5.

10 Learning a new trade in preparation for emigration. The Zeilsheim
DP camp.

further factor needs to be added: workers did not receive a proper wage.
Service workers in the DP camps, for example, received an additional
ration of cigarettes, soap, chocolate and other commodities in lieu of
payment. This created a rankling sense of dissatisfaction while rendering
daily dealings on the black market unavoidable for there was no other way
to purchase fresh food, clothing and other necessities these people sorely
lacked. In consequence, as Simon Shochet described it, the rations in demand on the black market were rarely consumed: "no one can of coffee
is ever opened, nor one American cigarette smoked. Smokers use an inferior type of tobacco available cheaply from the Germans . . . Chocolates
are eaten only by the children, and then only on special occasions."[54]
Many and varied suggestions were put forward to deal with this situation
including transferring hard currency to the worker's country of destination or, alternatively, the distribution of coupons for special canteens. In
the final analysis, none of these suggestions got off the ground and the
basic payment for services rendered continued to be in the hard currency
of Germany at the time – cigarettes.

Within *She'erith Hapleitah* there was a clear distinction between dealings on the grey market to satisfy personal needs as opposed to large-
scale dealings on the black market in pursuit of easy profits. The former
was an integral part of a barter economy with desperate shortages and an

[54] Shochet, *Feldafing*: 123.

unreliable official currency.[55] The ZK and even the Joint discreetly traded in cigarettes in order to procure vital necessities and services. Leo Srole argued that this illicit trade with its unavoidable association with Germans took its psychological toll but this appears to be overstated: what was in fact a universal norm could not be experienced as truly criminal.[56] On the other hand, wholesale operations on the black market was something undertaken by individuals, perceived as criminal and found to be undesirable by many. As we saw, German antisemites portrayed the black market as a potentially destructive Jewish preserve, German police raided Jewish facilities in order to put an end to these illicit dealings and many of the Occupation forces were ready to believe that this was how things stood. The Central Committee that was constrained to deal with this injurious image of the Jew highlighted the leading role of the Germans themselves in the black market and how the classic ploys of antisemitism were used to shift blame from the guilty to the innocent.[57] Internally there was an on-going effort to push large-scale dealings on the black market beyond the pale and the honor courts in the DP camps punished those who were caught and found guilty.[58] The major thrust, however, was devoted to opening up additional avenues of vocational training and the creation of new jobs and a brief glance at the discussions of the ZK shows just how much this topic riveted their attention.[59] UNRRA was a junior partner in these endeavors and even the army that had previously feared that training would delay the departure of many from Germany decided to be of help on the employment front.[60]

The Central Committee, on its part, devised an ambitious scheme for the employment of 36,000 workers but both the lack of funds and a sufficiently large infrastructure rendered it impractical. The JDC started out supporting this initiative but when it failed to come up with the requisite

[55] Report from Klausner (20.3.1947).
[56] Leo Srole, Report to the Anglo-American Commission [sic] for Palestine (February 1946), AJDC/DP's Germany 1946.
[57] See, for example, Yaakov Oleiski, "Shvarts-handel" (The black market), YT, no. 49 (61) (21.11.1946): 3 and Reuven Rubinstein, "Oyf undzer front: shvarts-handel" (On our front: the black market), Undzer Veg, no. 58 (22.11.1946): 3.
[58] See, for example, Barikht fun gerikht beym dem adminstrativn shtrof aptaylung (Report of the court in the administrative penalties division), Landsberg (29.7.1946), YSA/M-1/P-17, and Barikht fun shnel-gerikht beym administrativn shtrof aptaylung (Report of the summary court in the administrative penalties division), Landsberg (15.10.1946), ibid.
[59] For the various discussions of productivization see Protokoll nr. 43 des ZK (14.5.1946), YIVO/DPG 97; Protokoll nr. 57 (26.8.1946), ibid.; Protokoll nr. 65 (26.10.1946), ibid.; Plenum Protokoll nr. 71 (3.12.1946), ibid.; Protokoll nr. 72 (10.12.1946), ibid.; Protokoll nr. 73 (16.12.1946), ibid.; Protokoll nr. 79 fun der zitstung fun presidium.
[60] Dr. Joseph Schwartz to Moses A. Leavitt (9.11.1946), AJDC/DP's Germany 1946.

funds, it continued to focus its attention on service workers in the DP camps. The Jewish Agency that favored a more modest plan of action encouraged the opening of workshops and assisted cooperatives and *kibbutzim* to purchase machinery and tools. All of these activities helped expand the circle of those gainfully employed and engaged in learning a trade but, looking at the larger picture, the change was incremental rather than transformative. Even the establishment of the Employment Council that brought together the *ZK*, Joint and Jewish Agency in early 1947 was not able to bring about significant change at a time when many were actively seeking to prepare themselves for the future.[61] As Chaim Yachil saw it "Only people imbued with a very strong drive to start anew, and only some of these knew how to impose a severe regimen of serious study and hard work on themselves."[62] As time went by, in addition, it became apparent that the call to clandestine aliyah was in tension with the programs of productivization for "We learned that Ort students and those working in schemes set up by the Employment Council were less likely to respond to the call to set out for Palestine or to begin military training in preparation for aliyah."[63]

In short: for a variety of reasons the employment programs were unable significantly to improve the predicament of survivors who remained trapped in Germany. As the months went by the question of aliyah and emigration became increasingly urgent and towards the end of 1946 the people of *She'erith Hapleitah* began to hope that the 22nd Zionist Congress that was due to convene in Basel in November would bring an answer to their prayers. In the October elections to determine the composition of the survivors' delegation to the Congress 47,110 valid votes were cast with the following results:[64]

Party – List	Votes	Mandates
The UZO (*Mapai, Mizrachi*, General Zionists)	15,374	4
The Labor Bloc (*Poalei Zion, Hashomer Hatzair, Dror, Pachach, Haoved*)	15,060	4
The United Revisionist Party	12,350	3
General Zionists and ex-Revisionists	3,724	1

---

[61] For a summation of the question of employment see Luva Lak to Eliyahu Dobkin (6.3.1947), CZA/S25/5226.

[62] Yachil (Hoffman), "Peulot ha-mishlachat ha-eretz yisraelit," *Yalkut Moreshet*, no. 31: 139.

[63] Ibid.

[64] "Val rezultatn tsum tsiyonistishn kongres" (Election results for the Zionist Congress), *Under Veg*, no. 51 (15.11.1946): 10.

The impressive results of the Labor Bloc are somewhat surprising for these were ideological movements guided by a highly differentiated vision of Zionist fulfillment. Their success may be attributed to two factors: the central role they played in *kibbutzim*, training farms, children's homes and other educational endeavors and, secondly, the fact that, as compared to the predominantly Palestinian leadership of the other lists, they had placed heroes of Jewish resistance at the head of their Bloc. Even more remarkable was the public support for the Revisionists who were now able to claim that they were the single largest movement in *She'erith Hapleitah*. Initially the members of *Betar*, the Revisionist youth movement, joined forces with *Nocham* but as the unitary framework began to weaken in early 1946, they broke away and set up an independent movement. Their initial request for official recognition and financial support was turned down because, in consonance with Revisionist policy, they refused to recognize the authority of the World Zionist Organization.[65] With the growing influx of repatriates in 1946 the movement grew by leaps and bounds and it was Levi Shalitan, the editor of *Undzer Veg*, that came to serve as its spokesman. This turn of events angered many in the *ZK* who felt that their official organ had ceased to be representative of the rich fabric of the survivor community[66] and at the end of June an editorial board was appointed to oversee publishing policy.[67]

At the end of July 1946 Chaim Yachil informed the *Mapai* Secretariat of the tangible advances of the Revisionist movement in *She'erith Hapleitah* and accounted for this growth of "Zionist extremism" in terms of the frustration and despair so rife in the DP camps. The elections to the Zionist Congress confirmed this assessment as did the movement conference held in Pöcking in November 1946. 300 delegates participated representing 15,000 members in over 100 locations.[68] The conference proceedings and particularly the opening address of Dr. Zvi Kantor, the General Secretary of the movement, make it clear that the major themes of survivor Zionism – the catastrophic price of life in Exile, the abandonment of the Jewish people in their darkest hour, the imperative of unity and the call to leave perfidious Europe and return home – made an attractive mix with Revisionist opposition to the partition of Palestine,

---

[65] Protokoll nr. 35 des *ZK* (7.2.1946), YIVO/DPG 95.

[66] Protokoll fun der zitsung fun der rat fun *ZK*; and Protokoll nr. 45 des *ZK* (27.6.1946), YIVO/DPG 97. On the background to these events see Levi Shalitan to Leo Schwarz (1952), YIVO/DPG 167.

[67] Chaim (Yachil) Hofmann to the *Mapai* Secretariat (24.7.1946), *Ha'avodah* – Labor Archive/24/46: 14.

[68] "1-te konferents fun der farayniker tsyonistish-revizionistisher bavegung in daytshland" (1st Conference of the United Zionist–Revisionist movement in Germany), *YT*, no. 49 (61) (29.11.1946): 7.

support for the underground activities of the *Etzel* and a liberal, right-wing approach to politics.[69]

Those who hoped that the activity surrounding the Zionist Congress would raise the spirits of *She'erith Hapleitah* pointed to the impressive turnout for the elections. Others pointing to the half-empty glass were quick to note that of 81,600 registered voters 49,278 – i.e. 61 percent – actually went to the polls.[70] From their point of view this did not reflect poor organization – it was a direct function of the despondency which had overtaken the Jews waiting to leave Germany.[71] Opinions were also divided as to the degree to which *She'erith Hapleitah* was central to the proceedings in Basel: the pessimists argued that most of the delegates were removed from the European Jewish experience and unable fully to comprehend the breadth and depth of their tragedy, and the confusing disunity of their own delegation did not help matters. Reuven Rubinstein, the newly appointed editor of *Undzer Veg*, was able to point to the rhetorical resonance of the survivors in the discussions and speeches but he too had to admit that their practical concerns were barely addressed.[72] Instead the various factions in the Zionist movement sought to annex *She'erith Hapleitah* to a vindication of their particular policies. Those who sought to avoid any territorial concessions in Palestine emphasized the inner resilience of the survivors and their ability to continuing living in uncertainty. The moderate voices expressed their fears of breakdown and disintegration in the DP camps and recommended political compromise because it would also afford a solution to the unwarranted pain of those who had suffered enough.

The concerns of *She'erith Hapleitah* were dealt with comprehensively and in depth in the survey of Rabbi Phillip Bernstein[73] and in the moving address of David Treger. The principal lesson of the European Jewish catastrophe was shared by all survivors – "Already then in the presence of those we lost," said Treger,

we understood and swore in our hearts, before God and before the whole world, that if we come out of this alive, we shall raise our voices and declare to our brethren living in comfort in the lands of freedom, to our brothers throughout the world, that our people can no longer live and has no right to live, without a home of its own, without a land of its own.[74]

---

[69] Ibid.   [70] S.H., "Dos Vort" (The word), *Dos Vort*, no. 9 (24.12.1946): 1.

[71] R. Kovner, "Oysfirn" (Achievements), *Undzer Veg*, no. 51 (15.11.1946): 11.

[72] Reuven Rubinstein, "Problemn un strkihn: oyfn tsyonistishn kongres" (Problems and features of the Zionist Congress), *Undzer Veg*, no. 61 (20.12.1946): 2.

[73] "Harav bernstein oyfn kongres" (Rabbi Bernstein at the Congress), *Undzer Veg*, no. 62 (24.12.1946): 1.

[74] *Hakongres ha-zioni ha-kaf-bet* (The 22nd Congress), Basel (24–29 December 1946), a stenographic report (Jerusalem, no date): 125.

The reasons of the survivors were clear: their compatriots, their neighbors of long-standing cooperated with the Nazis while the civilized world stood by, or as in the case of England, actively prevented Jews from leaving Europe. However, neither the murder nor the bitter disappointment broke the spirit of *She'erith Hapleitah* which retained a remarkable vitality. Treger also described some of the immediate concerns of the Jews in Germany: the imminent disbandment of UNRRA, the reawakening of German antisemitism, the difficulties in providing productive employment and, above all, the future of their children. Despite the acute problems they faced, Treger did not demand that Zionist policy be dictated by urgent needs of *She'erith Hapleitah* and promised that they would find a way of accommodating themselves to the imperatives of the hour.

She'erith Hapleitah figured prominently in many of the resolutions of the Congress but no operative plan to deal with its problems was forthcoming. Those returning to Germany, therefore, were not bearers of good tidings and could only offer the consolation of moral support.[75] In Reuven Rubinstein's assessment, the meeting in Basel had been, all told, a "tragic Congress": the thunderous silence marking the absence of European Jewry, the deep cleavages in the movement, the personal tragedy of Chaim Weizmann who was not reelected as President and the fundamental fact that the Zionist movement had been unable to overcome the stumbling blocks strewing the road to Jewish independence.[76] Because of objective limitations the 22nd Zionist Congress was not the harbinger of the much awaited historical breakthrough.

As the Second Congress of *She'erith Hapleitah* in February 1947 drew closer, Samuel Gringauz sought to sum up the critical trends of the previous year and, on the basis of this, proposed a plan of action. The Jews in Germany found themselves caught on the horns of a dilemma. The Surviving Remnant, on the one hand, was now recognized by many as the representative voice of European Jewry. World opinion paid scant attention to what was happening to the Jews of Hungary, Romania and Poland and for it the problem of all surviving communities focused on "the problems of the Jews in Germany."[77] *She'erith Hapleitah*, on the other hand, had lost its primacy in the struggle to realize the goals of Zionism. The focus of their first Congress had been primarily political and they were happy to set aside their internal concerns for the sake of the larger struggle. That had also been the case during the visit of the

[75] "Dos vort: in shayn fun bazler *bashlushn*" (In the glow of the Basel resolutions), *Das Vort*, no. 10 (1.1.1947): 1.

[76] R.R., "Tragisher kongres" (Tragic congress), *Undzer Veg*, no. 63 (31.12.1946): 1.

[77] Dr. Shmuel Gringauz, "Der ruf tsu moralisher konsolidatsye" (The call for moral consolidation), *YT*, no. 13 (18) (14.2.1947): 3.

Anglo-American Committee but now things had changed. The focus of the Zionist campaign had now moved to Palestine itself, Western capitals, Mediterranean ports and Cyprus leaving *She'erith Hapleitah* with but a minor role. "We have used up and exhausted all of our weapons. Our position is clear, our demonstrations have become a cliché and are no longer effective. Today we are no more than an argument in the grand debate which is prosecuted on our behalf but without us."[78]

In the light of this analysis Gringauz suggested that the Second Congress should devote itself to their internal problems in an attempt to stave off the process of moral decline that was spreading throughout the survivor community. The first step in this direction was to deal with the anti-democratic norms that had crept into their leadership. Those elected to public positions questioned the legitimacy of criticism, the opposition engaged in venomous personal attacks while the focus on factional interests to the detriment of larger shared concerns threatened to undermine the democratic ethos which, of necessity was founded on a basic consensus of interest and value. A second danger, no less severe, was a function of the economic abnormality of the survivor community in Germany. Living off charity and dubious deals in the grey and black markets could not but leave its moral mark in the public realm. Thus Gringauz highlighted the political importance of the programs seeking to promote economic health. UNRRA was due to be disbanded in mid-1947 and its successor – the International Refugee Organization – only existed on paper. The only one able to look after the affairs of *She'erith Hapleitah* was the US Army which was suffering from a chronic shortage of trained manpower. If the army would find itself dealing with a consolidated and responsible leadership in the DP camps there was a good chance that they would be left in office and, indeed, granted additional responsibilities. These should be the guiding considerations when the electorate came to choose their local and regional representatives.

At the same time, Gringauz was well aware that his recommendations were not very much more than "palliatives" and that what really counted were opportunities for aliyah and emigration. He therefore addressed some of his remarks to the wartime Allies who still held the key to the future: "We must proclaim that keeping the camps going is a slow form of genocide . . . the selfsame crime which the International Military Tribunal in Nuremberg tried. The camps are destroying our readiness to return to life in the same way as the concentration camps destroyed our lives."[79] This line of reasoning reflected the difficulties facing *She'erith Hapleitah* in early 1947 with, perhaps, one reservation: Gringauz represented the

[78] Ibid. [79] Ibid.

direct survivors of the Holocaust who had been living, waiting and hoping in DP camps for twenty months. From this point of view he did not necessarily represent the energetic group of repatriates who had started arriving in 1946 and by now made up the majority of the Surviving Remnant. They became a critical resource for the survivor community in its hour of need, until such time as the dramatic events in the second half of 1947 breathed new life into *She'erith Hapleitah* as a whole.

Concluding remarks

In August 1945 UNRRA distributed a report compiled by a team of experts on the psychological problems their field workers were likely to encounter in their dealings with displaced persons.[1] The anticipated response of those who had been exposed to deprivation, extreme danger, suffering and loss was of regression to infantile patterns of behavior characterized by a lack of restraint, neglect of cleanliness, a weakened sense of shame and little patience with tradition and form. The people they were to administer and counsel would often be marked by restlessness, an attenuated sense of communal responsibility, apathy, passivity, a loss of initiative, sullen suspicion of authority and an impaired sense of trust. This process of demoralization combined with an infantile sense of unworthiness – "I was cast out and suffered because I was unworthy" – represented a resounding blow to self-respect that could lead to a generalized hostility to the world without or, when turned inwards, to withdrawal, depression and, in extreme cases, suicidal tendencies. Thus, the primary goal of their work in relief and rehabilitation was to help the displaced persons regain "a sense of value and of purpose, [the] restoration of self-respect and social status."[2]

These projected responses can easily be identified, singly or together, in the brief history of *She'erith Hapleitah* but never became its defining feature. Instead, the creation of a community of fate imbued with a sense of purpose was a critical factor in deflecting, mitigating and transmuting the destructive impact of massive psychic trauma. Indeed, the UNRRA report underscored the vital importance of the displaced person becoming an active, participating member of "a hopeful and integrated community. The growth of participation and the sense of 'belonging' to a community is clearly related to the delegation of responsibility and the development of graded self-government; while the hopefulness of the community will

[1] United Nations Relief and Rehabilitation Administration, Subcommittee on Welfare in Europe, *Psychological Problems of Displaced Persons* (11.8.1945), YIVO/DP 2201.
[2] Ibid.: 31.

285

depend to some extent on its capacity to relate its tasks and its atmosphere to the future of its members."[3]

What distinguished the Surviving Remnant in Germany was the articulated group awareness that their singular situation prompted. As compared to West European Jews and other groups of DPs, they had, sometimes reluctantly, turned their backs on their previous lives; they sought to limit their interaction with the German population to a functional minimum so that within the crowded confines of DP life, Jewish concerns continued to dominate their lives. Thus, whereas the term *She'erith Hapleitah* in its broader connotation referred to all European Jews who had survived the Nazi onslaught a second, more circumscribed sense of the term referred most particularly to those who had created a transient community of survivors in Germany, Italy and Austria. Indeed, it was in Occupied Germany alone that the Jews referred to themselves collectively as *She'erith Hapleitah* and thereby gave expression to their unique identity accompanied by the potent sense that they represented the dynamic center of European Jewish life. Because they had cut themselves loose from their previous lives, enjoyed the benign protection of the American Occupation forces and, as their numbers grew, became the activating focus of both Jewish and international attention, they were able to speak and act with a degree of openness and freedom denied to those who chose to readapt to life in post-war Europe.

This remarkable sense of community rested on two proximate foundation stones: the experience of the European Jewish catastrophe and their identification with the goals of Zionism – they envisaged themselves as the living bridge between destruction and rebirth, the last remnants of a world destroyed and the active agents of its return to life. Their self-declared role helped the survivors regain a sense of value and purpose and certainly was a salutary step in their return to life. Nevertheless, even though this role and self-understanding realized in the public realm was a source of hope and provided a way of coping with loss, we can assume that it left the submerged experience of each survivor, so rarely expressed, largely untouched. Facing up to the deep psychic wounds of a long immersion in the extremities of Nazi terror was often a lifelong burden that the rigors and excitement of heroic times could initially allay but never undo. What Primo Levi called "survivor's disease" now clinically termed posttraumatic stress disorder (PTSD) is described by Cathy Caruth as: "a response, sometimes delayed, to an overwhelming event or events, which takes the form of repeated, intrusive hallucinations, dreams, thoughts or behaviors stemming from the event, along with numbing that may have

---

[3] Ibid.

begun during or after the experience, and possibly also arousal to [and avoidance of] stimuli recalling the event."[4] Caruth, happily avoiding the temptation of reductionism, locates the enigmatic core of the trauma in "the delay or incompletion in knowing, or even seeing an overwhelming occurrence that then remains, in its insistent return, absolutely *true* to the event... The traumatized, we might say, carry an impossible history within them."[5]

Prolonged exposure to arbitrary, anonymous violence, being treated as a subhuman thing by a criminal state that had transformed ideological murder into an ideal created an impossible reality that compromised the integrity of all those who fought to remain alive. In no way do we seek to evoke the mechanisms of regression and identification with the aggressor that stand at the center of Bruno Bettelheim's flawed account of survival, one that singularly fails in illuminating the remarkable story that unfolded in Kaufering and Buchenwald in the last stages of the war.[6] What I have in mind is much closer to Primo Levi's reading of humanity *in extremis*: "We do not believe... that man is fundamentally brutal, egoistic and stupid in his conduct once every civilized institution is taken away... We believe, rather, that the only conclusion to be drawn is that in the face of driving necessity and physical disabilities many social habits and instincts are reduced to silence."[7] Social instincts were silenced by driving necessity – silenced but not destroyed and, thus, a brief respite from the camp regime could bring old sensibilities to the surface in the same way that liberation opened the way for a fuller return to civilized life. Nonetheless, the "memory of the offense"[8] and all it brought in its wake cast its unspoken, nagging pall over the survivor community in *She'erith Hapleitah* and persisted long and deep into the hidden loneliness of their lives beyond.

Throughout their brief moment in Occupied Germany the survivors struggled to make sense of what they termed the *katastrofe* or the *khurban*. The resort to a general term like catastrophe that lacked any specificity or *khurban* that evoked the destruction of the First and Second Temples understandably demonstrated the proximity of the event and the absence of the perspective and conceptualization that comes with time. Indeed, the feeling of many was that the gas chambers had been the culmination

---

[4] Cathy Caruth, ed., *Trauma: Explorations in Memory* (Baltimore, 1995): 4.

[5] Ibid.: 5.

[6] See Bruno Bettelheim, *Surviving and Other Essays* (New York, 1979).

[7] Primo Levi, *Survival in Auschwitz* (New York, 1961): 79.

[8] Primo Levi, "The Memory of the Offense," in *The Drowned and the Saved* (New York, 1986): 23–35; in this regard see also the telling insights of David Weiss Halivni in *The Book and the Sword: A Life of Learning in the Shadow of Destruction* (New York, 1996): 123–136.

of a long history of rejection as amply demonstrated by the help the Nazis received in their war against the Jews, even from their bitterest enemies. Those who defied the Nazis and endangered themselves to rescue Jews were remembered and honored but, as most survivors agreed, they were sadly few and far between, for the dream of a world without Jews was a seductively enduring strand in European civilization. For many, the Zionist narrative of a people apart, a landless minority with nowhere to go and no one to protect them provided an explanation of the historical context within which the Holocaust was possible but the persistent attempts to go further and probe the purpose and meaning of what had happened invariably ended in a sense of defeat and left the agonizing question *farvos?* – to what end? – unanswered.

Against this background we can better understand the unseen dimensions of the very real struggle to cope with the bitter disappointment and frustration that soon supplanted the utopian exhilaration of liberation. Here were a group of people who had been exposed to unspeakable suffering and having lost everything that was dear to them, now found themselves living on handouts, in DP camps, with no way out, a nuisance to all and championed by few. The leaders of *She'erith Hapleitah* who feared the corrosive potential of self-pity this situation might engender enjoyed broad, public support in their attempt to root out demoralization, be it in the form of idleness, rowdiness, a lack of consideration for others, petty dishonesty or the failure to maintain good order and cleanliness in the DP camps. They equally feared the threat of moral breakdown and nihilistic abandon especially among the young. Keeping DP life on an even keel, most particularly when hopes of early emigration had receded, was a constant battle in which the affirmation of life, despite many reversals, came out on top. On the one hand, this basic drive to start anew, to take hold of life and work for the future was integral to the guiding ethos of the Surviving Remnant; on the other hand, those attracted to a life of crime were few and far between and, perhaps most significantly, suicides were relatively rare. The horrors of the past imposed a terrible burden on the survivors but did not lead them to question the ultimate worth of their own lives. As compared to many West European survivors who ofttimes had to find their way back to life on their own, a life shared with others in the same boat could be burdensome but was equally a source of comfort and strength.

This vigor and resourcefulness came as something of a surprise to the numerous emissaries who, *en route* to Germany, rehearsed what they would say to those who survived in order to persuade them that there was something worth living for. But, as one *shaliach* indicated,

I could not say that they were necessarily in need of phrases of this kind. Perhaps the most surprising thing that accompanied me . . . throughout my period of service was that the people I met, mainly young but also grown-up – they had been caught up in the war and catastrophe – manifested an extraordinary vitality, an extraordinary will to live.

This was even more surprising in view of the fact that the pre-war leadership of East European Jewry had, in large measure, been wiped out by the Nazis. Thus, it bears repeating that *She'erith Hapleitah* was largely made up of ordinary folk who were neither angels nor saints, and who, despite many failings that were all too human, did not succumb to the deformities of suffering: they got on with their lives to the degree circumstances allowed, planned for the future and, in the main, preserved their humanity intact.

Any attempt to account for what many contemporaries found remarkable should begin with one basic historical fact: the East European survivors were born and bred into a millennial tradition of community that had its roots in the self-understanding of a people covenanted to God. In its long history of exile and dispersion, it was believed that the return of the Jewish people to the Holy Land would come with divinely ordained Redemption and, in the long interim, the erstwhile "kingdom of priests and holy nation" was recast into a faith-community that, despite local variation, maintained important structural continuities: a significant measure of autonomous self-government, judicial independence, a separate system of education and a wide variety of socio-religious institutions. Over the centuries, changing political fortunes and the degree of autonomy these afforded led to the emergence of preeminent centers that made their spiritual authority and influence felt throughout the Jewish world. In this fashion the Palestinian center gave way to Babylon, later shifted to Spain whence it moved northwards to Ashkenaz and so on to Eastern Europe that for many centuries served as the dominant center of the Jewish world. The end of the European era in Jewish life prefigured in Stalin's anti-Jewish policies reached its denouement in the unprecedented war of annihilation unleashed by Hitler.

The cultural reflexes of *She'erith Hapleitah* were profoundly conditioned by this long tradition of community but, more immediately, it was ghetto life under Nazi occupation to which they turned for inspiration and guidance. As the survivors remembered it, those crowded into the ghettos of Eastern Europe succumbed neither to the selfish disregard of all social responsibility nor to the bewildered paralysis of total despair. Instead, they worked together in order to stave off the threat of hunger, cold and disease, set up makeshift institutions to succor those who could no longer fend for themselves, sought to resist the dubious temptations of criminality and betrayal and created a rich cultural life that expressed their pain and protected their humanity. The following characterization by Samuel Gringauz in a paper delivered in New York in 1948 reflects a view widely shared in *She'erith Hapleitah*:

> Nevertheless, and this is the most amazing and most interesting sociological fact, there was no suppression of cultural values in the ghetto. Important group decisions were made not under the pressure of pure self-preservation but because of definite religious, national and political considerations. Individual decisions in not too infrequent instances rose above the pressure of the instinct of self-preservation. The level of social and moral values did indeed decline but never to the extent warranted by such living conditions.[9]

This was held up as an ideal standard of conduct for *She'erith Hapleitah*: if in the depth of darkness their people sought to remain true to themselves there could be no justification, *a fortiori*, not to do the same in the infinitely easier circumstances of liberation. Group solidarity was also identified as a critical factor in staving off dehumanization midst the impossible pressures of concentration camp life. On the basis of hundreds of interviews with survivors, Leo Eitinger has suggested that

> prisoners who were completely isolated from their families, deprived of all contact with groups to whom they were related before the war, people who were completely overwhelmed by the notion that they had nobody and nothing to struggle or live for, were those who most readily succumbed. Prisoners able to stay with members of their prewar peer groups, to help others, and to get help, resisted best.[10]

Similarly, Dori Laub has written that for survivors who experienced the massive failure of empathy built into the Nazi genocidal system "life appears only as an endless dying or as a long struggle to rid oneself of the image created by the perpetrator – *not a negative self-image but an image of the self as non-human and hence with no links to humanity.*"[11] What our study shows is that those able to retain these "links to humanity" were better equipped to cope with the ravages of life *in extremis*.

This conscious tie between the vigor of the Surviving Remnant and spiritual resilience during the Holocaust appears to confirm the view of historians who see the sanctification of life as a key dimension of Jewish behavior in the face of disaster. From this point of view *She'erith Hapleitah*

---

[9] Samuel Gringauz, "The Ghetto as an Experiment of Jewish Social Organization: Three Years of the Kovno Ghetto," *Jewish Social Studies*, vol. 11, no. 1 (January 1949): 6.

[10] Leo Eitinger, "Holocaust Survivors in Past and Present," in Berenbaum and Peck, eds., *The Holocaust and History*: 773.

[11] Dori Laub with Marjorie Allard, "History, Memory and Truth: Defining the Place of the Survivor", in ibid.: 803.

can serve as a unique control group in comparing behavior during and after the Nazi Occupation and, in this context, the fact that the survivors in Germany became an important voice in European Jewry so soon after liberation raises some interesting questions. It appears to refute, for example, the characterizations of Jewish responses to the Holocaust because of the distortions of what one group of scholars have variously termed a "ghetto mentality," an exilic "mindset" and a rather abstract, diasporic "unworldliness." Conditioned passivity of this kind that was assumed to have permeated Jewish minority existence over nearly two millennia could surely not be undone by an act of will in such a short space of time, especially given the important lines of continuity that began during the Holocaust and persisted into liberation beyond. The initial organization of *She'erith Hapleitah* started, as we saw, many months before liberation and in itself was the product of clandestine activity that had begun two or three years before. The critical variable appears to be the presence or absence of Nazi terror rather than the deformities of minority life. Many arguments have been marshaled against the way Raul Hilberg, Bruno Bettelheim and Hannah Arendt, each in their own idiom, characterized and accounted for Jewish behavior in the face of the Nazi onslaught – the historically rooted activism of the survivor community in Occupied Germany is another.

In the interest of a balanced assessment of the resilience of *She'erith Hapleitah*, there are two things worth bearing in mind: by 1947, first, some two-thirds of the Jews in Occupied Germany were Polish repatriates who had spent the deadliest years of the war in the Asiatic steppes of the Soviet Union. They had fled from their homes or had been forcibly exiled, they had been exposed to harsh conditions and chronic scarcity, most of the family members they left behind died at the hands of the Nazis, their property had been appropriated by others and, on returning, they had to contend with hostility, homelessness and destitution midst the ruins of what had once been one of the great centers of Jewish life. They were not strangers to suffering. Nonetheless, their fate had been very different from those who had been at the center of the storm. They still had families to care and provide for, work skills they had acquired and, most importantly, they had been spared the physical damage and psychological scarring of the direct survivors. These differences, however, did not translate into a power struggle between the two groups. There was a lot they shared in common and, as a rule, the repatriates who bore their own freight of guilt for those they had left behind when they fled eastwards accepted the moral leadership of those "who had been there." What we wish to stress in the context of our present discussion is that their energy, resourcefulness and strength became increasingly important as life in Germany became insufferably claustrophobic, the gates of Palestine and other preferred destinations remained closed and the patience of the original nucleus of *She'erith Hapleitah* began to wear thin.

The Surviving Remnant, despite its remarkable achievements, was hemmed in, secondly, by the objective limitations of DP dependency and could not have operated effectively without the advocacy of the Special Adviser, the political guidance of the Palestinian Delegation and educational input of its emissaries, the financial aid and social services of the JDC and, unbeknownst to most, its critical role in the clandestine funding of both the *Brichah* and illegal immigration. After the fatal impotence of the war years, those who had survived worked hard at regaining a modicum of control over their lives and welcomed the idea of cooperative ventures and partnership. The slightest hint of patronization and condescension, however, elicited a response of frustrated anger expressed most prominently in the crises that periodically marred the relations between the Central Committee and the JDC. A greater forbearance was generally shown to Palestinians, even when they overstepped the mark, for they seemed to enjoy the aura of being official representatives of the Jewish state-in-the-making.

From early in its history the Zionist movement addressed itself to both the threat and indignity of antisemitism and to the challenge of translating a religious civilization into the idiom of a secular, scientific world. Not surprisingly, what spoke most powerfully to the East European survivors in the aftermath of the war was the Zionist response to the indignities of powerlessness, its answer to "wounded pride and a sense of humiliation... which in due course produce anger and self-assertion."[12] Many commentators have assumed a simple, causal relationship between the level of antisemitism and popular support for the Zionist cause. In the light of his reading of the past, by contrast, Jacob Katz has suggested that this simplified formulation may conceal the workings of a subtler dialectic. Violent antisemitism can unsettle and, ultimately, uproot a community but the crisis it engenders, and this is the heart of the argument, can call forth a variety of responses: some could decide to surrender their identity, others to place their faith in liberal reform or revolutionary change; emigration might be the answer for many and some could opt for settling in Palestine. Thus, by way of illustration, between 1880 and 1914 of the roughly two-and-a-half million Jews who emigrated from Russia and Rumania, but 70,000 made their way to Palestine. Persecution and harsh conditions uprooted many but it was the secularized messianism embraced by Zionism that led the return of a small minority to

---

[12] Isaiah Berlin, "Nationalism", in *Against the Current* (Oxford, 1981): 346.

Palestine.[13] In the very different circumstances of the post-war world responses to the destruction wrought by the Nazis also varied between different communities. West European survivors liberated in Germany generally chose to go home, Hungarian and Romanian Jews were ambivalent about the future but when it came to East European Jews, most of the historical responses to persecution had ceased to be relevant and Zionism moved into center stage.

From the outset a commitment to Zionism was the defining feature of those who chose to remain temporarily in Occupied Germany. The bitter fate of the Jewish people during the war was understood in terms of the Zionist critique of the vulnerabilities of life in Exile; Jewish resistance to the Nazis was seen as a primarily Zionist enterprise, while the creation of a Jewish state was taken to be the last will and testament bequeathed by the victims to the survivors. Furthermore, the institutions set up by the survivors – local and regional committees, the Central Committee of the Liberated Jews in Bavaria, the press, political parties, youth movements, children's homes, schools and training farms – were informed by a spirited Zionist ethos. The traditional opponents of Zionism from left and right, we should add, had either departed or had undergone a change of heart. Those with decidedly left-wing proclivities returned, by and large, to Poland after liberation. On the other hand, the repatriates who had experienced the callous cruelty and anti-Jewish animus of the Soviet system at close quarters returned to Poland disabused of any illusions they might have had regarding the blessings of Communism. They, like most of those who had survived the war in Poland, initially sought to start their lives afresh in familiar surroundings despite the dark shadows cast by the recent past. Some remained in the larger cities, others returned to the villages of their birth and many others were attracted by the promise of a new start in the newly annexed territories in Western Poland previously populated by ethnic Germans. However, dogged by impoverishment and fear wherever they went, increasing numbers turned to the *Brichah* for help in leaving Poland. In the process they were impressed by the selfless dedication of the young Zionists who guided them across Europe, their ability to extend real, meaningful assistance and, most especially, the warm, familial atmosphere of the groups they temporarily joined. In this fashion many of those who reached Occupied Germany arrived with a positive disposition to the idea of settling in Palestine.[14] The relatively small right-wing Orthodox groups on the other side of the political

---

[13] See Jacob Katz, "The Jewish National Movement: A Sociological Analysis," in *Jewish Emancipation and Self-Emancipation* (Philadelphia, 1986): 100–103.

[14] See the invaluable study by Engel, *Bein shichrur le-brichah*: 117–152.

spectrum while retaining their primary commitment to the study of Torah were also interested in settling in the Holy Land and, thus, moderated their traditional opposition to Zionism while seeking a *modus vivendi* with prevailing opinion in the DP camps.

This is not to suggest that all the survivors were ideological Zionists – some opted for Palestine in order to join family and friends, those pessimistic about the chances of getting elsewhere chose it by default and yet others were driven by religious conviction. On the other hand, many of those who were weary of war and sought a safe haven far from the dangers of a country threatened by upheaval retained their deep, instinctive sympathy for the idea of a national Jewish home in Palestine. In our estimate the majority of survivors, whatever their personal plans for the future, were touched by the spirit of Zionism and gave their support to the achievement of its goals. The committed Zionists who were the predominant group midst the founding fathers of *She'erith Hapleitah* went further. They were firmly wedded to the ideal of Jewish independence, believed that Palestine held out the most realistic hope for the rescue and rehabilitation of the remnant of European Jewry and that this desperately needed demographic boost, in turn, would help the Yishuv fulfill its historic role as the promise of the Jewish future.

Almost from the outset there has been a lively debate as to the extent and depth of the survivor Zionism, a debate that has generally revolved around varying responses to a series of hypothetical questions like: where would the Surviving Remnant have chosen to go if the doors to the United States had been open while the gates of Palestine remained shut and vice versa? How would things have turned out if both were simultaneously open? Any historian courageous or foolhardy enough to enter the fray has to juggle with any number of variables and imponderables: what period in the brief but volatile history of *She'erith Hapleitah* is being referred to? Which estimates, internal and external, does one depend on? Does one follow the logic of common sense or heed the passion of deeper stirrings? How does one evaluate the inevitable gap between what people recognized as valid and what they actually did? In the same way as the smoker lighting a cigarette might be in full agreement with the dire warnings of the Surgeon General, so there may very well have been survivors who genuinely identified with the need for a Jewish state but personally sought to meet up with their family elsewhere. Any fair-minded attempt to answer these "what if" questions, therefore, could not claim to be very much more than an educated guess. If the doors of Palestine alone had been opened, for example, there would have been a wholesale exodus from the DP camps but, we can safely assume, a fair number of those proceeding to Palestine would have gone with the intention of moving on when

11 1947: Mr. Griebler, who served as a marine officer in the First World War puts the final touches to the 6 × 2.5 meter boat built in Zeilsheim in preparation for its maiden voyage to Palestine.

circumstances allowed. If the reverse happened we can equally assume that a sizeable group who were not deterred by the British blockade on Palestine or the threat of another round of incarceration or internment in Cyprus would have held their ground and refused to surrender their dream of aliyah.

The argument takes on a different hue, however, when in service of a political agenda it is argued that the Zionism of *She'erith Hapleitah* was, by and large, a foreign import imposed on it by the unfair pressure and unfeeling machinations of the leadership of the Yishuv and its emissaries. Sometimes the starting point of the argument is commonsensical rather than historical: why after the extreme suffering of the Holocaust would it not be more than surprising for survivors actively to seek out the uncertainties and palpable dangers of a country on the brink of war as opposed to the safety of quieter shores? In her challenging history of clandestine immigration to Palestine in the aftermath of the war Idith Zertal seeks to expose what she views as the dubious Zionist exploitation of the

European Jewish tragedy. Her narrative focuses on David Ben-Gurion who was driven by the overriding goal of achieving Jewish statehood and rather callously used the plight of the survivors to discredit British policies in Palestine and to win international sympathy for the Zionist cause. Because he, like many others in the Yishuv, tended to view exilic Jews in general and the Surviving Remnant in particular as passive objects of history, he felt few reservations about harnessing them to the larger goals of Zionist fulfillment. In order to bolster her argument Zertal portrays the survivors, who only appear as shadowy background figures in her narrative, as victims of their circumstances: they were, to all intents and purposes, trapped in Germany and, given the heavy toll of their past suffering, lacked the inner resources to stake out their own future. "These were people who had lost their footing during the war, whose families were murdered and their lives totally destroyed. Two years after the termination of the war they were still in camps, shut up behind fences in Germany. A history of this kind does not necessarily make for 'free people'."[15]

Her reading of the events, however, disregards the hard-earned achievements of *She'erith Hapleitah* and diminishes their human stature. After all, in both Eastern Europe and Germany the struggle for the future began long before any Palestinians had appeared on the scene led by people steeled in adversity who had survived against all odds. Nothing came easily and in the uninviting conditions of Occupied Germany, many were fired by the comforting dream of starting afresh in a land of their own. In this regard Yisrael Gutman has suggested another way of testing the intentions of *She'erith Hapleitah*. Why, he inquires, did so few survivors attempt to make their way to the countries of Western Europe that had traditionally served as a refuge and way station for East European Jews seeking their fortunes elsewhere? For those that way inclined, it offered a way to escape the Zionist majority of the DP camps and to find a more promising staging ground for emigrating from Europe.[16] Given the resourcefulness and experience of the survivors in crossing international borders, Gutman is not persuaded by the counterclaim that the entry points to the West were sealed. What this suggests, rather, is a cohesive consensus around the declared Zionist goals of *She'erith Hapleitah*,

---

[15] Idith Zertal, "Ha-meunim ve-ha-kedoshim: kinuna shel martirologiya leumit" (The tortured and the martyrs: the constitution of a national martyrology), *Zemanim*, no. 48 (1994): 44, and her important study of clandestine immigration to Palestine – *From Catastrophe to Power.*

[16] See the contribution of Yisrael Gutman to the symposium on "She'erith hapleitah ve-hakamat hamedinah" (*She'erith Hapleitah* and the establishment of the State [of Israel]), in *Yalkut Moreshet*, no. 65: 26–31.

a willingness to wait and, for a fair number, a fluctuating, ambivalent interest in actively seeking alternatives to Palestine.

When viewed in this light, illegal immigration takes on the aspect of a shared enterprise, a partnership founded on a meeting of hearts and minds. Certainly the roles played by each – survivors on the one hand and *shlichim* or *Mossad* operatives on the other – differed but there was neither a clear-cut division of labor between leaders and led nor an instrumental imposition from above. Indeed, without willing cooperation and a sharing of the burden, without the interlocking of urgent individual needs with the profound political imperatives of the day, the whole project would have foundered. Thus, any portrayal of the Surviving Remnant as helpless objects of history is both misleading and unfortunate. Unfortunate since it flies in the face of the facts and misleading because patronizing interpretations of this kind hinder our ability to see that in some important ways the people of *She'erith Hapleitah* were, in fact, ahead of their time.

The survivors who had gravitated towards the extra-territorial enclave in Germany worked at piecing together a coherent picture of what they had personally been through while seeking to find out what had become of their family and friends. Why had the Nazis embarked upon the unprecedented murder of an entire people? What prompted some of their countrymen to become partners to genocide and how did their neighbors stand by and watch with equanimity as they were marched off to their death? What had now to change in the wake of what had happened? These issues were worried over and clarified in a myriad of discussions, public and private, about the facts of the past and its meaning for the future. The people of *She'erith Hapleitah* found themselves grappling with issues that only began to exercise the Jewish world and other concerned observers twenty years later and more. Thus, by way of illustration, when Samuel Gringauz formulated his understanding of the retributive mission imposed upon the Surviving Remnant by the dead, he saw it as taking "the form of a defiant affirmation of life and national rebirth. Nothing must permit Hitler a final triumph by the destruction of the Jews through the circumstances of the post-war world or through inner disintegration."[17] Those who read Gringauz at the time may very well have been impressed but his words did not cause a public stir.[18] By comparison, when Emil Fackenheim spoke in 1967 of Jews being commanded "not to offer Hitler a posthumous victory" his words and

---

[17] Gringauz, "Jewish Destiny as the DP's See It": 503.
[18] In this regard it is instructive to compare the level of involvement in *She'erith Hapleitah* with the early post-war reception of the Holocaust in America as portrayed by Peter Novick in *The Holocaust in American Life* (Boston, 1999): 63–123.

commentary aroused considerable interest and came to play an important role in shaping the broader Jewish awareness of the Holocaust.

The leaders of *She'erith Hapleitah*, to take the argument further, were quick to grasp and internalize the larger implications of the destruction of European Jewry for the Jewish future. When Shlomo Shafir wrote in late 1944 that Hitler had "solved" the Jewish problem he was among the first to initiate a public discussion of the future of Zionism now that its human hinterland and its historic *raison d'être* had been destroyed. On the basis of this understanding the Zionists liberated in Germany mounted a single-minded campaign against American and Soviet pressure for the repatriation of the liberated Jews to the countries of Eastern Europe and were the first to advocate and promote the creation of a temporary enclave under the protection of the American Occupation. If Jewish independence in Palestine was to have any hope of success, every last survivor had to be saved and won over to the cause of Eretz Yisrael. The campaign to create a unified Zionist movement, similarly, came in response to all that had been lost. Neither time nor energy should be expended on political squabbles in a time of dire emergency, when everything they believed in rested precariously in the balance. Decades were to pass before this strategic reading of the post-war situation was appropriated by broad sections of the Jewish people.

Beyond its immediate and practical purpose, the quest for unity also represented a search for both a new politics and a reconstituted framework of values. After everything they had been through, so many survivors felt, life just could not simply go on as before. In his address to the soldiers of the Jewish Brigade in July 1945 Abba Kovner addressed this issue and managed to articulate what many survivors sensed in a more inchoate fashion. The troubling implications of total destruction could not be sidestepped by attributing the murder of the Jewish people to a minority of demented criminals – "Only a handful of sadistic S.S. men were needed to hit a Jew, or cut off his beard, but millions had to participate in the murder of millions. There had to be masses of murderers, thousands of looters, millions of spectators."[19] How was one to make sense of the fact that among those directly implicated in the unspeakable torture there were doctors, lawyers and people of learning who "on the eve of the slaughter spoke of labor, law, philosophy, art, and Christian love." Many Jews in Eastern Europe who had supreme confidence in the redeeming culture and conscience of the West were initially disarmed by their faith in human solidarity and their belief that deeds of this kind went beyond the reach of human possibility. What then was

---

[19] Kovner, "The Mission of the Survivors": 675.

left, on whom could they depend given the devastating bankruptcy of so much they had believed in? The search for a new politics, therefore, was but one expression of a crisis of faith and trust whose enormity began to shake the confidence of people of conscience in the West, thirty to forty years later. At the time, however, many found these early adumbrations of post-modernity to be outlandish and disturbing. Indeed, the leaders of the Yishuv who were intent on normalizing the Jewish people and nurturing its commitment to a broad human solidarity were strongly opposed to these tendencies that they found both subversive and threatening.

She'erith Hapleitah, to adduce one last example, were the first to institute a day of remembrance to mark the destruction of European Jewry. In their daring move to join remembrance to liberation they were able to evoke the inner dialectic of many Jewish festivals, tempered the particular with the universal and created a unique day of memory and hope. They were of course disappointed that their initiative failed to arouse greater interest and that their desire to show the way came to naught. However, given the great disparity between the historical experience of those "who were in Treblinka" as compared to those "who only read about Treblinka" this might have been expected. What emerges from our discussion is that the people of the Surviving Remnant were compelled to negotiate a multilayered reality of isolation: orphaned and living in limbo, they developed an historical awareness that further separated them from many of their contemporaries outside Europe.

This isolation that accounts in part for the overlong neglect of *She'erith Hapleitah* should not be overdrawn, however, for the large majority who opted for Palestine were very quickly drawn into the harsh realities of the struggle for national independence. What we do need to clarify at this juncture is the impact of the Surviving Remnant on the processes that culminated in the achievement of Jewish statehood. In order to answer this question it would be analytically helpful to distinguish between the two major, interrelated phases in the attainment of sovereignty: the retreat of Britain from the Mandate and the victory of Israel in the 1948–1949 War of Independence. We turn first to a consideration of the former.

With the intial organization of *She'erith Hapleitah* on the morrow of liberation, one of their first priorities, as mentioned, was to campaign against too hasty a return to Eastern Europe for fear that there would be no way back. This meant resisting the insistent military pressure, American and Russian, to return home without delay and led to the first adumbration of the idea that Occupied Germany might serve as a staging ground for those who wished to make their way to Palestine. Indeed, with the aid and assistance of the first Palestinian soldiers to reach Bavaria, some 15,000 survivors moved south into Italy where they were taken care of by the Jewish Brigade until such time as transportation to Palestine became available. A few months later when, in response, the British Army tightened its control of the entry points into Italy and redeployed the Jewish Brigade in Western Europe, the movement south was reduced to a trickle. Thus, from October 1945 Bavaria, because of its organized Jewish presence and the protection and support afforded by the American forces, became the primary destination for the groups the *Brichah* was moving out of Poland.

When David Ben-Gurion visited *She'erith Hapleitah* in October 1945 and gauged for himself the passionate and formative Zionist presence among the survivors, he very quickly grasped the political potential of a large, restive concentration of Jews under the benign protection of the American occupation forces in Germany. Thus, the understanding he arrived at with the Supreme Command of the US Army according to which Jewish refugees from Eastern Europe would be allowed to enter the American Occupation Zone unhindered and would be granted the benefits of DP status set the stage for the key role the Surviving Remnant was to play in Zionist diplomacy. The costly, vociferous and volatile presence of a large Zionist-inspired community in Occupied Germany was a strong incentive for Truman's administration to keep urging the British government to open the way for the admission of the 100,000 victims of Nazism into Palestine forthwith. On the diplomatic front, the encounter with the survivors in Germany left its clear impress on the Harrison report and, later, the recommendations of the Anglo-American Commission of Inquiry, both of which proved to be important milestones on the uncertain path leading up to the United Nations decision to partition Palestine on 29 November 1947. At the same time *She'erith Hapleitah* became the focal symbol of the Jewish tragedy and an effective force in winning over American Jewry to the cause of Palestine as a refuge and home for those who survived the Nazi onslaught: anti-Zionists moderated their opposition to Jewish national aspirations, former non-Zionists began publicly to affirm the urgent need for a Jewish homeland in Palestine and in the Zionist camp itself, the more militant voices came to the fore. In consequence, the pressure exerted by the Surviving Remnant in Germany was now paralleled by the effective political organization of the major Jewish organizations in America and their careful monitoring of both administration policies on the Palestinian front and the performance of the military in Occupied Germany.

Equally, if not more important, was the willingness of tens of thousands of survivors to vote for Palestine with their feet. The journey which began with the trek across Europe and was followed by a spell in the DP camps continued on to a variety of embarkation points in Italy and France where the frail vessels of the *Mossad Le-Aliyah Bet* were boarded. While hoping to evade the naval blockade on Palestine, those who braved the rigors of the trip understood full well that they, in all likelihood, faced the prospect of a lengthy internment in Cyprus or elsewhere. In various ways these waves of clandestine immigrants helped to loosen the British hold on Palestine: in a period when the Soviet Union was increasing its pressure on Greece, Turkey and Iran, the British Navy was forced to neglect important aspects of its own strategic priorities; the harsh treatment of the victims of Nazism symbolized most dramatically by the return of the immigrants aboard the *Exodus* to German soil embarrassed the Labour Government and subjected it to a barrage of adverse public opinion; with each interception of an immigrant boat, the Yishuv was enflamed anew so assuring the resistance movements of widespread public support; and, finally, once the internment camps in Cyprus were filled to capacity and the German option sealed by the *Exodus* debacle, no one knew what to do with the thousands of illegal immigrants still making their way to Palestine.

In terms of the larger picture, the escalation of terror in Palestine itself was also an important factor in sapping the British resolve to hold on to the Mandate not least because the vicious circle of terror and repression rendered the idea of using the country as a strategic base for the British forces in the Middle East increasingly untenable. For the sake of balance it is important to point out, however, that neither the pressure, direct and oblique, exerted by survivors of the Holocaust nor the thankless task of maintaining law and order as violence spiraled in mandatory Palestine were ultimately decisive in the retreat from the Mandate. The critical variable was Britain's imperial decline that had its roots in the gradual growth of anti-colonialist movements that were quick to take advantage of both the havoc wreaked by Japanese conquests in the Far East and British exhaustion in the wake of the war. The British were not pushed out of Palestine; they decided to leave and in so doing the role of both *She'erith Hapleitah* and the underground movements was significant but not crucial.

With the British withdrawal from Palestine in 1948 and the ensuing escalation of Jewish–Arab hostilities, the burden of full-scale war naturally fell on the Yishuv, straining the socio-economic, political and military infrastructure built up over seventy years of settlement almost beyond endurance. The sensitive and controversial question of the role of Holocaust survivors in the fledgling state's battle for survival that for many years was clouded over by hearsay and denial can now be better assessed in the light of recent research. While a clarification of the disturbing attitudes and difficult moral questions of the time go beyond our brief, some of the facts and figures adduced in the pioneering research of Hanna Yablonka serve to round out the picture: "of all overseas recruits into the IDF [Israel Defence Forces] during the War of Independence, the number of Holocaust survivors came to some 22,300, which, bearing in mind the size of the IDF at the time, is impressive indeed. At the end of 1948, the IDF consisted of 88,033 soldiers, of whom only some 60,000 were combat soldiers." Given the fact that overseas recruits "were invariably sent to join combat units, it may be concluded that, by the end of 1948, these soldiers constituted about one third of the IDF's fighting force, and that the Holocaust survivors played a significant role in Israel's War of Independence."[20] Thus, to sum up, S*he'erith Hapleitah* played an important role in helping to generate the processes that led up to the British withdrawal from Palestine and, while their contribution to the 1948–1949 War of Independence was not decisive, it was far weightier than has generally been appreciated.

Throughout this work we have chosen to translate *She'erith Hapleitah* as the Surviving Remnant. Two additional translations suggesting very different readings of the past have been used on occasion – the Saved Remnant and the Saving Remnant – and it could be said that the interplay between these contrasting representations helps to capture some of the key forces at work in the history of *She'erith Hapleitah*. The survivors themselves would have readily confirmed that they were indeed a Saved Remnant: in the first place, as the symbolism of the Day of Remembrance and Liberation made abundantly clear, were it not for the Allied victory none of them would have remained alive; the severe constraints imposed by their status as DPs, secondly, rendered them heavily dependent on outside help for the achievement of their ambitious goals. But this, of course, was not the whole story. The people of *She'erith Hapleitah* objected strenuously to the notion that they were helpless victims who could only be saved by others. Their struggle to return to a life of dignity, their political activism and bid for recognition and their willingness to do their bit in the momentous struggle for Jewish independence endowed them with a sense of being redeemers in their own right.

However, if historians can be allowed a measure of poetic license, it is our strong sense that the redeeming role of *She'erith Hapleitah* goes beyond the remarkable achievements already described. Many have warned against the deformations that could be bred by catastrophic defeat: brutalization, destructiveness and a total lack of concern for others.

---

[20] Yablonka, *Survivors of the Holocaust*: 82.

Interestingly enough, whereas the Holocaust has left its profound impress on contemporary Jewish life, it has never been allowed to become ultimately definitive of human reality. Put differently: there seems to be a cultural *a priori* at work, a fundamental affirmation of life that has largely kept the destructive and nihilistic implications of the Holocaust at bay, that has, by and large, transformed the outrage, hurt and disillusionment into a life-serving force. *She'erith Hapleitah*, in our view, filled a defining role in shaping this reality. They had every reason to surrender themselves to blind anger and wanton destruction. Such responses, however, were rare. Whereas their suffering and losses were their point of departure, the people of *She'erith Hapleitah* devoted their best energies to the reconstruction of their personal lives and the redemption of their people without forgetting broader human responsibilities. The speed and willingness with which they took up the burdens of life and civic responsibility in both Israel and, indeed, wherever they settled bear eloquent witness to their affirmation of life and their undiminished humanity.

Thus, having turned their backs on despair and rage, the survivors set the stage for the future responses of those who were not directly implicated. Once the people of *She'erith Hapleitah* refused to surrender their humanity, they created a norm which those who were not "there" cannot easily disregard.

Bibliography

ARCHIVAL COLLECTIONS

A. THE UNITED STATES OF AMERICA

YIVO Institute for Jewish Research
A rich collection of materials on *She'erith Hapleitah*. The 2,300 files assiduously collected by Leo Schwarz relate to the full panoply of the JDC operation in Occupied Germany, the files of the Central Committee for the Liberated Jews in Bavaria and its various departments, material on various DP camps, cultural activities and a wide range of movements and organizations active among the survivors.

Archive of the AJDC
Reports from the field, the shaping and implementation of JDC policy.

American Zionist Archive
The records of the American Jewish Conference, reports of emissaries from the field, visits of representatives of *She'erith Hapleitah* to the United States.

UNRRA Archive
Records of DP camps and communities administered by UNRRA, negotiations with the Central Committee, policy discussions relating to infiltrees and the care and education of children.

National Archives in Washington and Sutland
Reports of the US Army and Military Government relating to Jewish DPs, intelligence reports relating to the *Brichah* and internal developments among the survivors and the records of the Anglo-American Committee of Inquiry.

Leo Baeck Institute Archive
Material on German Jewry in the aftermath of the war and on the Deggendorf DP camp in particular.

Bund Archive
Material on the ideological differences between the Bund and Zionist groups in *She'erith Hapleitah*.

B. ISRAEL

Yad Vashem Archive and Library
The material collected by the Central Historical Commission in Munich relating to politics, culture and society in *She'erith Hapleitah*; the files of the Judicial Department of the Central Committee and a near complete collection of the newspapers, publications and posters of the Surviving Remnant; survivor testimonies.

National Library, Jerusalem
Newspapers, journals and publications of *She'erith Hapleitah.*

Central Zionist Archives
Jewish Agency policy regarding the survivors in Occupied Germany, correspondence with the Palestinian Delegation, the Central Committee and other groups in *She'erith Hapleitah*, survivor publications.

***Moreshet* Archive**
Correspondence of *Kibbutz Artzi* with *Hashomer Hatzair* in Germany, educational material prepared for *She'erith Hapleitah*, records of *Pachach* – Partisans, Soldiers and Pioneers and testimonies.

***Hashomer Hatzair* Archive – Kibbutz Merchavia**
Hashomer Hatzair in *She'erith Hapleitah*, correspondence with movement activists and emissaries, educational material and publications, internal publications of the movement and its *kibbutzim* in Germany and, in addition, analyses and policy guidelines in the private papers of Meir Yaari.

Archive of *Bet Lochamei Hagetaot* (Ghetto Fighters House)
Archive of the *Hechalutz-Dror* movement including correspondence with movement activists and emissaries in Occupied Germany, publications and the testimony of *shlichim* to *She'erith Hapleitah.*

***Ef'al* Archive**
The correspondence of *Kibbutz Meuchad* with *Hechalutz-Dror* in *She'erith Hapleitah.*

Masuah Archive
The archive of *Hanoar Hazioni* – correspondence with movement activists and emissaries in Germany, movement publications.

***Ha'avodah* – Labor Archive**
Histadrut – Labor Confederation policy regarding the Surviving Remnant, correspondence with emissaries, publications of *Nocham*, records of the central institutions of *Mapai.*

Oral History Department of the Institute for Contemporary Jewry, the Hebrew University of Jerusalem
Interviews with some of the key figures in the history of *She'erith Hapleitah.*

Private papers of Chaim Yachil (Hoffman)
Private papers of Zvi Shiloah (Langsam)

NEWSPAPERS AND JOURNALS OF *SHE'ERITH HAPLEITAH*

Dos Fraye Vort (The Free Word) the Feldafing camp paper that began to appear 4.10.1945.

Fun Letstn Khurbn: tsaytshrift far geshikhte fun yidishn lebn beysn natsirezhim (From the Recent Destruction: A Journal for the History of Jewish Life under Nazi Rule): journal of the Central Historical Commission that began to appear in August 1946.

Landsberger Lager Tsaytung (The Landsberg Camp Paper): began to appear 8.10.1945.

Nitzotz (The Spark): underground newspaper of the *Irgun Brith Zion* in the Kovno Ghetto that reappeared in Kaufering (Dachau) from November 1944.

Techiyat Hametim (Resurrection): Buchenwald, May 1945.

Undzer Veg (Our Way): organ of the Central Committee of the Liberated Jews in Bavaria that began to appear 12.10.1945.

Local camp papers and party organs that began to appear, for the most part, during the course of 1946:

A Haym (Homeward Bound): Leipheim.
Bamidbar (In the Desert): Foehrenwald.
Der Nayer Moment (The New Moment): Regensburg.
Dos Vort (The Word): *Poalei Zion* – Zionist socialist.
Dos Yidishe Vort (The Jewish Word): Agudat Yisrael.
Oyf der Fray (Set Free): Stuttgart.
Oyf der Vakh (On the Watch): *Hashomer Hatzair.*
Pachach Germaniyah Biyuletin (Pachach Germany Bulletin).
Undzer Hofnung (Our Hope): Eschwege.
Undzer Mut (Our Courage): Zeilsheim.
Undzer Velt (Our World): revisionist.
Undzer Vort (Our Word): Bamberg.
Untervegs (Underway): Frankfurt.

BIBLIOGRAPHICAL GUIDES

Feldshuh, Benzion, *She'erith hapleitah – biblyografye* (*She'erith Hapleitah – bibliography*), Directorate for Education and Education, Stuttgart: 1948.

Fuss, Felicia, *Displaced Persons: A Selected Bibliography 1939–1947*, New York: Russell Sage Foundation, 1948.

Gar, Yosef, "Bafrayte yidn" (Liberated Jews), *Fun Noentn Ovar*, vol. 3 (1957) and vol. 4 (1959).

Hebrew University-Yad Vashem, *Guide to Unpublished Materials of the Holocaust Period*, vol. III, ed. Yehuda Bauer, Jerusalem: 1975.

Krould, Harry J., *The Displaced Persons Analytical Bibliography*, Washington DC: 1950.

Moreshet – Yad Vashem, *Madrich le-archiyon moreshet be-givat haviva* (Guide to the *Moreshet* Archive in Givat Haviva), ed. Shmuel Krakowski, Jerusalem: 1979.

Robinson, Jacob, ed., *The Holocaust and After: Sources and Literature in English*, Jerusalem: Yad Vashem, 1973.

Yad Vashem, *Ha-shoah ve-sficheah be-sefarim ivriim 1933–1972* (The Holocaust and its aftermath in Hebrew books 1933–1972), 2 vols., ed. M. Piecacz, Jerusalem: 1974.

Ha-shoah be-aspeklaria shel kitvei-et ivriim (The Holocaust as reflected in Hebrew journals), ed. M. Piecacz, Jerusalem: 1978.

Ha-shoah ve-sficheah be-aspeklariat ha-itonut ha-ivrit (The Holocaust and its aftermath in the Hebrew press and journals), ed. M. Piecacz, Jerusalem: 1978.

Yad Vashem – YIVO, *Biblyografye fun yidishe bikher vegn khurbn un gvura* (Bibliography of Yiddish books relating to the Holocaust and heroism), ed. Phillip Friedman and Yosef Gar, New York: 1962.

Biblyografye fun Artikeln vegn khurbn un gvura in yidishe peryodik (Bibliography of articles on the Holocaust and heroism in Yiddish periodicals), ed. Yosef Gar, New York: 1966.

Ha-shoah ve-ha-gevurah be-aspeklaria shel ha-itonut ha-ivrit (The Holocaust and heroism as reflected in the Hebrew press), 4 vols., ed. M. Piecacz, B.Z. Ofir and V. Artzi, Jerusalem: 1966.

The Holocaust and After: Sources and Literature in English, ed. J. Robinson and Mrs. P. Friedman, Jerusalem: 1973.

A SELECTION OF SECONDARY SOURCES

Agar, Herbert, *The Saving Remnant*, London: Rupert Hart-Davis, 1960.

Amery, Jean, *At the Mind's Limits: Contemplations by a Survivor on Auschwitz and its Realities*, Bloomington: Indiana University Press, 1980.

Anissimov, Myriam, *Primo Levi: Tragedy of an Optimist*, London: Aurum Press, 1998.

Asch, Sholem, *One Destiny: An Epistle to the Christians*, New York: G.P. Putnam's Sons, 1945.

Avni, Chaim, *Im ha-yehudim be-machanot ha'akurim: rishmei shlichut 1945–1947* (With Jews in the DP camps: impressions of a mission 1945–1947), Tel Aviv: "Chaverim" Publishers, 1980.

Avriel, Ehud, *Open the Gates: A Personal Story of "Illegal" Immigration to Israel*, New York: Atheneum, 1975.

Balabkins, Nicholas, *West German Reparations to Israel*, New Brunswick: Rutgers University Press, 1971.

Barker, Pat, *Regeneration*, London: Penguin Books, 1992.

The Eye in the Door, London: Penguin Books, 1994.

The Ghost Road, London: Penguin Books, 1995.

Baron, Zvi and Levin, Dov, *Toldoteha shel machteret: ha-irgun ha-lochem shel yehudei kovno be-milchemet ha-olam ha-shniyah* (The history of an underground: the fighting organization of the Jews of Kovno in the Second World War), Jerusalem: Yad Vashem, 1962.

Bauer, Yehuda, *Flight and Rescue: Brichah*, New York: Random House, 1970.

"The Initial Organization of the Holocaust Survivors in Bavaria," *Yad Vashem Studies*, vol. 8 (1970): 127–158.

"The Holocaust and the Struggle of the Yishuv as Factors in the Creation of the State of Israel," in *Holocaust and Rebirth: A Symposium*, Jerusalem: Yad Vashem, 1974.

The Holocaust in Historical Perspective, Seattle: University of Washington Press, 1978.

The Jewish Emergence from Powerlessness, London: Macmillan, 1980.

A History of the Holocaust, New York: Franklin Watts, 1982.

"The Death Marches: January–May 1945," *Modern Judaism*, vol. 3, no. 1 (February 1983): 1–21.

Out of the Ashes: The Impact of American Jews on Post-Holocaust European Jewry, Oxford: Pergamon Press, 1989.

Rethinking the Holocaust, New Haven: Yale University Press, 2001.

Bauer, Yehuda, ed., *Machanot ha'akurim be-Germaniyah 1945–1948* (DP camps in Germany 1945–1948), Jerusalem: Institute for Contemporary Jewry, the Hebrew University, 1962–1963.

Baumel, Yehudit Tidor, *Kibbutz Buchenwald*, Tel Aviv: Ha-kibbutz Ha-meuchad – Bet Lochamei Hagetaot, 1994.

Belsen, published by the Organization of She'erith Hapleitah from the British Zone, London: 1957.

Berenbaum, Michael and Peck, Abraham J., eds., *The Holocaust and History: The Known, the Unknown, the Disputed and the Reexamined*, Bloomington: Indiana University Press, 1998.

Berlin, Isaiah, *Against the Current*, Oxford: Oxford University Press, 1981.

Bethell, Nicholas, *The Palestine Triangle: The Struggle between the British, the Jews and the Arabs, 1935–1948*, London: Andre Deutsch, 1979.

Bettelheim, Bruno, *Surviving and Other Essays*, New York: Albert A. Knopf, 1979.

Boder, David P., *I Did Not Interview the Dead*, 16 vols. (Topical autobiographies of displaced people recorded verbatim in DP camps with a psychological and anthropological analysis), Urbana: University of Illinois Press, 1949.

"The Impact of Catastrophe: Assessment and Evaluation," *Journal of Psychology*, vol. 38 (1954): 3–50.

Bogner, Nachum, *I ha-geirush: machanot ha-ma'apilim be-kafrisin, 1946–1948* (The island of deportation: Jewish illegal immigrant camps in Cyprus, 1946–1948), Tel Aviv: Am Oved, 1991.

Bowyer Bell, *Terror Out of Zion*, New York: Avon Books, 1977.

Carlebach, Azriel, ed., *Va'adat ha-chakirah ha-anglo-amerikanit le-inyanei eretz yisrael* (The Anglo-American Committee of Inquiry on Palestine), 2 vols., Tel Aviv: Leinman Publishers, 1947.

Caruth, Cathy, ed., *Trauma: Explorations in Memory*, Baltimore: Johns Hopkins University Press, 1995.

Casper, Bernard, *With the Jewish Brigade*, London: Edward Goldston, 1947.

Cholawski, Shalom, *Soldiers from the Ghetto*, New York: Herzl Press, 1980.

Clendinnen, Inga, *Reading the Holocaust*, Cambridge: Cambridge University Press, 1999.

Cochavi, Yehoyakim, *Shoresh la-akurim: tnuot ha-noar be-machanot ha-akurin be-germaniyah 1945–1949* (Roots for the uprooted: youth movements in Jewish refugee camps in Germany 1945–1949), Kibbutz Dalia: Yad Ya'ari, 1999.

Cohen, Michael J., "Why Britain Left: The End of the Mandate," *Wiener Library Bulletin – New Series*, vol. 31, no. 45/46 (1978): 74–86.

"The Genesis of the Anglo-American Committee of Inquiry on Palestine," *Historical Journal*, vol. 22, no. 1 (1979): 185–207.

Palestine and the Great Powers 1945–1948, Princeton: Princeton University Press, 1981.

"Truman, the Holocaust and the Establishment of the State of Israel," *Jerusalem Quarterly*, no. 23 (Spring 1982): 79–94.

Crossman, Richard, *Palestine Mission: A Personal Record*, London: Hamish Hamilton, 1946.

Crum, Bartley, *Behind the Silken Curtain: A Personal Account of Anglo-American Diplomacy in Palestine and the Middle East*, New York: Simon and Schuster, 1947.

Dawidowicz, Lucy S., *The Holocaust and the Historians*, Cambridge, Mass.: Harvard University Press, 1981.

Dekel, Ephraim, *Sridei cherev: hatzalat yeladim bi-shnot ha-shoah u-le-achareha* (Survivors: the rescue of children during the Holocaust and after), Tel Aviv: Ministry of Defence – Laor Press, 1963.

Des Pres, Terrence, *The Survivor: An Anatomy of Life in the Death Camps*, New York: Oxford University Press, 1976.

Dinnerstein, Leonard, *America and the Survivors of the Holocaust*, New York: Columbia University Press, 1982.

Dothan, Shmuel, *Ha-maavak al eretz yisrael* (The struggle for Palestine), Tel Aviv: Ministry of Defence – Laor Press, 1981.

Dunner, Joseph, *The Republic of Israel: Its History and its Promise*, New York: McGraw Hill, 1950.

Zu Protokoll Gegeben: Mein Leben als Deutscher und Jude, Munich: Verlag Kurt Desch, 1971.

Dvorjetski, Mark, "Adjustment of Detainees to Camp and Ghetto Life and their Subsequent Adjustment to Normal Society," *Yad Vashem Studies*, no. 5 (1963): 193–220.

Efros, Yisrael, *Heimlose yidn* (Homeless Jews), the Central Organization of Polish Jews in the Argentine and Polish Jews in Sao Paulo, 1947.

Eilat, Eliyahu, *Ha-maavak al ha-medinah: 1945–1948* (The struggle for statehood: 1945–1948), Tel Aviv: Am Oved and the Zionist Library, 1979.

Engel, David, *Bein shichrur le-brichah: nitzolei ha-shoah be-polin ve-ha-maavak al hanhagatam, 1944–1946* (Between liberation and flight: Holocaust survivors in Poland and the struggle for leadership, 1944–1946), Tel Aviv: Am Oved, 1996.

Feigenbaum, M.Y., "Peuloteha shel ha-va'adah ha-historit be-minchen" (The activities of the Historical Commission in Munich), *Dapim Le-cheker Ha-shoah Ve-ha-mered*, no. 1 (April 1951): 107–110.

Sefer biale podlaska (The Biale Podlsaka [memorial] book), edited by M.Y. Feigenbaum, Tel Aviv: the Podlaska Community Welfare Fund, 1960.

Frankel, Theodore, "My Friend Paul: One Who Survived," *Commentary*, vol. 23, no. 2 (February 1957): 147–160.

Frankl, Viktor E., *Man's Search for Meaning: An Introduction to Logotherapy*, New York: Washington Square Press, 1971.

Frei, Norbert, *Vergangenheitspolitik: Die Anfänge der Bundesrepublik und die NS-Vergangenheit*, Munich: C.H. Beck, 2nd edn., 1997.

Friedman, Philip, "Problems of Research on the European Jewish Catastrophe," *Yad Vashem Studies*, vol. 3, Jerusalem (1959): 25–40.

Friesel, Evyatar, "The Holocaust and the Birth of Israel," *Wiener Library Bulletin*, vol. 32 (1979): 51–60.

Fusell, Paul, *The Great War and Modern Memory*, New York: Oxford University Press, 1981.

Ganin, Zvi, *Truman, American Jewry and Israel*, New York: Holmes and Maier, 1979.

Garcia, Max Rodriguez, *As Long as I Remain Alive*, Tuscaloosa: A Portals Book, 1979.

Gelber, Yoav, *Toldoth ha-hitnadvut III: nosei ha-degel – shlichutam shel ha-mitnadvim la'am ha-yehudi* (A history of voluntary service III: the standard bearers – the mission of the volunteers to the Jewish people), Jerusalem: Yad Yitzchak Ben-Zvi, 1983.

Genizi, Haim, *Yoetz u-mekim: ha-yoetz la-tzava ha-amerikani u-le-she'erith hapleitah 1945–1949* (The Adviser to the American Army and *She'erith Hapleitah* 1945–1949), Tel Aviv: Sifriyat Hapoalim, 1987.

Gershon, Karen, *Postscript: A Collective Account of the Lives of Jews in Germany since the Second World War*, London: Victor Gollanz, 1969.

Giere, Jacqueline, *"Wir sind unterwegs, aber nicht in der Wüste": Erziehung und Kultur in den Jüdischen Displaced-Lagern der Amerikanischen Zone im Nachkriegsdeutschland 1945–1949*, Frankfurt a.M.: Darmstadt Copy Shop, 1993.

"We're on Our Way but We're Not in the Wilderness," in Michael Berenbaum and Abraham J. Peck, eds., *The Holocaust and History: The Known, the Unknown, the Disputed and the Reexamined*, Bloomington: Indiana University Press, 1998: 699–715.

Gilbert, Martin, *Exile and Return: The Emergence of Jewish Statehood*, London: Weidenfeld and Nicholson, 1978.

Glassgold, A.C., "The Spirit Will Rise: The Miracle of Landsberg," *Ort Economic Review*, vol. 8, no. 3 (1947/1948): 12–18.

Goldsmith, S.J., *Jews in Transition*, New York: Herzl Press, 1969.

Grinberg, Zalman, *Our Liberation from Dachau*, a private translation by Israel Eiss from *Kamah*, the Yearbook of the Jewish National Fund (Jerusalem, 1948).

Gringauz, Samuel, "Jewish Destiny as the DP's See It," *Commentary*, vol. 4, no. 6 (December 1947): 501–509.

"The Ghetto as an Experiment of Jewish Social Organization: Three Years of the Kovno Ghetto," *Jewish Social Studies*, vol. II, no. 1 (January 1949): 3–20.

"Germans Should Pay: A Reply to Leivik," *Jewish Frontier* (May 1950): 16–19.

Grobman, Alex, *Rekindling the Flame: American Jewish Chaplains and the Survivors of European Jewry*, Detroit, Mich.: Wayne State University Press, 1993.

Grodzinski, Yosef, *Chomer enoshi tov: yehudim mul tziyonim, 1945–1951* (Good human material: Jews versus Zionists, 1945–1951), Tel Aviv: Hed Artzi, 1998.

Gutman, Yisrael, "Hayehudim be-polin le-achar ha-milchamah" (The Jews in Poland after the war), *Yalkut Moreshet*, no. 33 (June 1982): 65–102.

Gutman, Yisrael and Drechsler, Adina, eds., *She'erit Hapletah 1944–1948: Rehabilitation and Political Struggle*, Jerusalem: Yad Vashem, 1990.

Hadari, Ze'ev (Venia) and Tzachor, Ze'ev, *Oniyot o medinah: korot oniyot ma'apilim ha-gedolot "pan york" ve-"pan crescent"* (Ships or state: a history of the large "illegal" immigrant ships the "Pan York" and the "Pan Crescent," Tel Aviv: the University of Ben-Gurion in the Negev and Kibbutz Hameuchad (no date).

Hakongres ha-zioni ha-kaf-bet (the 22nd Zionist Congress), Basel, 24–29 December 1946, a stenographic report, Jerusalem: Executive of the World Zionist Organization (no date).

Heller, Yosef, "Ha-mediniyut ha-tzionit ba-zirah ha-beinleumit le-achar milchemet ha-olam ha-shniyah – parashat va'adat ha-chakirah ha-anglo-amerikanit 1945–1946" (Zionist policy in the international arena in the wake of the Second World War – the case of the Anglo-American Committee of Inquiry 1945–1946), *Shalem: Studies in the History of Palestine and its Settlement*, vol. 3, Jerusalem: Yad Yitzchak Ben Zvi, 1981: 213–293.

Be-maavak la-medinah: ha-mediniyut ha-ziyonit be-shanim 1936–1948 (In the struggle for statehood: Zionist policy in the years 1936–1948), Jerusalem: the Zalman Shazar Center, 1984.

Herf, Jeffrey, *Divided Memory: The Nazi Past in the Two Germanys*, Cambridge, Mass.: Harvard University Press, 1997.

Hering, Ze'ev, *Tsvishn khurbn un geulah: in gerangl far der she'erith hapleitah* (Between destruction and redemption: midst the struggle for *She'erith Hapleitah*), Munich: Poalei Zion (Z.S.), Hitachdut and Nocham Publishing (no date).

Heymont, Irving, *Among the Survivors of the Holocaust – 1945: The Landsberg Camp Letters of Major Irving Heymont, United States Army*, Cincinnati: American Jewish Archives, Hebrew Union College, 1982.

Hilliard, Robert L., *Surviving the Americans: The Continued Struggle of the Jews after Liberation*, New York: Seven Stories Press, 1997.

Hirschmann, Ira A., *The Ember Still Burns*, New York: Simon and Schuster, 1949.

Hyman, Abraham S., "Displaced Persons," *American Jewish Yearbook*, vol. 49 (1949): 455–473.

"Victory after Liberation," *Congress Weekly*, vol. 22, no. 15 (15 April 1955): 7–10.

Ilan, Amitzur, "Messianism and Diplomacy: The Struggle for a Jewish State 1945–1948," *Wiener Library Bulletin*, vol. 30, no. 41/42 (1977): 36–46.

America, britania ve-eretz yisrael: reishitah ve-hitpatchutah shel me'uravut artzot ha-brit be-mediniyut ha-britit be'eretz yisrael, 1938–1947 (America, Britain and Palestine: the beginning and development of the involvement of the United States in British policy in Palestine, 1938–1947), Jerusalem: Yad Ben Zvi, 1979.

Jacobmeyer, Wolfgang, *Vom Zwangsarbeiter zum heimatlosen Ausländer: Displaced Persons in Westdeutschland 1945–1951*, Göttingen: Vandenhoeck und Ruprecht, 1985.

Jacoby, Gerhard, "The Story of the Jewish DPs," *Jewish Affairs*, vol. 2, no. 6 (November 1948): 3–30.

Kaplan, Yisrael, *Dos folks-moyl in nazi klem: reydenishn in geto un katzet* (Folk expression under Nazi occupation: sayings in the ghetto and concentration camp), Munich: the Central Historical Commission, 1949.

Karmi, Yisrael, *Be-derech lochamim* (On the fighters' trail), Tel Aviv: "Ma'arachot," 1964.

Katz, Jacob, *Jewish Emancipation and Self-Emancipation*, Philadelphia: Jewish Publication Society, 1986.

Ka-tzetnik 135633, *Star Eternal*, New York: Arbor House, 1971.

Kaufman, Menachem, "Atidah shel she'erith hapleitah ve-she-elat eretz yisrael be-einei ha-irgunim ha-lo-tzioniim be-artzot ha-brit bishnat 1945" (The future of *She'erith Hapleitah* and the question of Palestine in the eyes of non-Zionist organizations in the United States in 1945), *Yalkut Moreshet*, no. 21 (June 1976): 181–198.

Keynan, Irit, *Lo nirga ha-ra'av: nitzolei ha-shoah ve-shlichei eretz yisrael: germaniyah 1945–1948* (And the hunger was not staunched: Holocaust survivors and the emissaries from Eretz Yisrael: Germany 1945–1948), Tel Aviv: Am Oved, 1996.

Kimche, Jon and Kimche, David, *The Secret Roads: The Illegal Migration of a People*, London: Secker and Warburg, 1954.

Kless, Shlomo, *Bederech lo slulah: toldot habrichah 1944–1948* (On the unpaved road: a history of the *Brichah* 1944–1948), Kibbutz Dalia: *Moreshet*, 1994.

Klotz, Ben, *Memoirs 1936–1946*, Jerusalem: Yad Vashem Archives.

Kochavi, Arieh J., *Akurim ve-politika beinleumit: britanya ve-ha-akurim ha-yehudim le-achar milchemet ha-olam ha-shniyah* (Displaced Persons and international politics: Britain and the Jewish Displaced Persons after the Second World War), Tel Aviv: Am Oved, 1992.

"British Assumptions of American Jewry's Political Strength, 1945–1947," *Modern Judaism*, vol. 15, no. 2 (May 1995): 161–182.

Königseder, Angelika, *Flucht nach Berlin: Jüdische Displaced Persons 1945–1948*, Berlin: Metropol Verlag, 1998.

Königseder, Angelika and Wetzel, Juliane, *Lebensmut in Wartesaal: Die jüdischen DPs im Nachskriegsdeutschland*, Frankfurt a.M.: Fischer Taschenbuch, 1994.

Kolinsky, Eva, "Experiences of Survival," *Leo Baeck Institute Yearbook 1999*, London: Secker and Warburg (vol. 44, 1999): 245–270.

Korczak, Ruzka, "Yeladim be-machaneh rikuz buchenwald" (Children in the Buchenwald concentration camp), *Yalkut Moreshet*, no. 8 (1968): 42–74.

Korman, Gerd, "Survivors' Talmud and the US Army," *American Jewish History*, vol. 73, no. 3 (March 1984): 252–285.

Kovner, Abba, "The Mission of the Survivors," in Yisrael Gutman and Livia Rotkirchen, eds., *The Catastrophe of European Jewry: Antecedents, History, Reflections*, Jerusalem: Yad Vashem, 1976: 671–683.

Al ha-gesher ha-tzar: masot be'al peh (On the narrow bridge: spoken essays), Tel Aviv: Sifriyat Hapoalim, 1981.

"Reishitah shel "habrichah" ke-tnuat hamonim be-eiduyotav shel abba kovner" (The beginning of the "Brichah" as a mass movement in the testimonies of Abba Kovner), *Yalkut Moreshet*, no. 37 (June 1984): 7–32 and no. 38 (December 1984): 133–146.

Lagrou, Pieter, *The Legacy of Nazi Occupation: Patriotic Memory and National Recovery in Western Europe, 1945–1965*, Cambridge: Cambridge University Press, 2000.

Langer, Lawrence L., *The Age of Atrocity: Death in Modern Literature*, Boston: Beacon Press, 1978.

Lavski, Chagit, "The Day After: Bergen-Belsen from Concentration Camp to Center of Jewish Survivors in Germany," *German History*, vol. 11, no. 1 (1999): 36–59.

Leivik, H., *Mit der she'erit hapleitah* (With *She'erith Hapleitah*), Toronto: Former Publishing and Printing Company, 1947.

"No Blood-Money from the Germans," *Jewish Frontier* (May 1950): 14–15.

Levi, Primo, *Survival in Auschwitz*, New York: Collier Books, 1973.

The Drowned and the Saved, New York: Summit Books, 1986.

Levin, Dov, *Bein nitzotz ve-shalhevet: "irgun brith zion" be-milchemet ha-olam ha-shniyah* (Spark and the flame: "Irgun Brith Zion" during the Second World War), Ramat Gan: Bar Ilan University, 1987.

Liebman, Charles S. and Don-Yehiya, Eliezer, *Civil Religion in Israel: Traditional Judaism and Political Culture in the Jewish State*, Los Angeles: University of California Press, 1983.

Lifschitz, Jacob, *Sefer ha-brigada ha-yehudit: korot ha-chativah ha-yehdit ha-lochemet ve-ha-matzilah et ha-golah* (The book of the Jewish Brigade: a history of the Jewish Brigade that both fought and rescued Jews in the dispersion), Tel Aviv: Yosef Shimoni Publishers, 1950.

Lifton, Robert J., *Death in Life: Survivors of Hiroshima*, New York: Vintage Books, 1969.

Machanot ha-geirush be-kafrisin: yom iyun mukdash le-zichro shel menachem oren (The detention camps in Cyprus: a study day dedicated to the memory of Menachem Oren), no. 62, Efal: Yad Tabenkin, 1986.

Mankowitz, Ze'ev, "The Spiritual Heritage of She'erith Hapletah and Jewish Historiography," in Yisrael Gutman and Gideon Greif, eds., *The Historiography of the Holocaust Period*, Jerusalem: Yad Vashem, 1988: 749–758.

"The Affirmation of Life in She'erith Hapleita," *Holocaust and Genocide Studies*, vol. 5, no. 1 (1990): 13–21.

Marrus, Michael R., *The Unwanted: European Refugees in the Twentieth Century*, New York: Oxford University Press, 1985.

Michman, Dan, "She'erit Hapletah, 1944–1948: Rehabilitation and Political Struggle," *Holocaust and Genocide Studies*, vol. 7, no. 1 (Spring 1993): 107–116.

Monroe, Elizabeth, *Britain's Moment in the Middle East 1914–1956*, London: University Paperbacks, 1963.

Mosse, George L., *Fallen Soldiers: Reshaping the Memory of the World Wars*, Oxford: Oxford University Press, 1990.

Nadich, Judah, *Eisenhower and the Jews*, New York: Twayne Publishers, 1953.

Newman, Gemma, *Earl J. Harrison and the Displaced Persons Controversy: A Case Study in Social Action* (Temple University PhD), Ann Arbor, Michigan: University Microfilms, 1973.

Niv, David, *Ma'arachot ha-irgun ha-tzvai ha-leumi: ha-mered 1946–1947* (The battles of the national military organization: the revolt 1946–1947), Tel Aviv: Mosad Klausner-Hadar, 1976.

Ofer, Dalia, "The Leadership of the Yishuv and She'erit Hapletah," in Yisrael Gutman and Adina Drechsler, eds., *She'erit Hapletah 1944–1948: Rehabilitation and Political Struggle*, Jerusalem: Yad Vashem, 1990.

"Holocaust Survivors as Immigrants: The Case of Israel and the Cyprus Detainees," *Modern Judaism*, vol. 16 (February 1996): 1–23.

"From Illegal Immigrants to New Immigrants: The Cyprus Detainees 1946–1949," in Michael Berenbaum and Abraham J. Peck, eds., *The Holocaust and History: The Known, the Unknown, the Disputed and the Reexamined*, Bloomington: Indiana Press, 1998: 733–749.

"Nosim ve-nisaim: bein emtzaim le-tachliyot – mediniyut, olim, mehagrim ve-anashim regilim" (Subjects and objects: between means and ends – policy, *olim*, immigrants and ordinary people), *Iyunim be-tkumat yisrael*, no. 8 (1998): 630–644. (A review of Idith Zertal's *From Catastrophe to Power*.)

"Israel," in David S. Wyman, ed., *The World Reacts to the Holocaust*, Baltimore: Johns Hopkins University Press, 1996: 836–920.

Ostry, Ethel A., *After the Holocaust: My work with UNRRA*, edited by Elizabeth Fisher, Private publication, 1978. (Deposited in the Yad Vashem Library).

Peterson, Edward N., *The American Occupation of Germany: Retreat to Victory*, Detroit: Wayne University Press, 1978.

Pinson, Koppel S., "Jewish Life in Liberated Germany: A Study of the Jewish DP's," *Jewish Social Studies*, vol. 9 (April 1947): 101–126.

Modern Germany: Its History and Civilization, New York: Macmillan, 1954.

Pisar, Samuel, *Of Blood and Hope*, London: Cassell, 1980.

Porat, Dina, *Mei-eiver la-gashmi: parashat chayav shel abba kovner* (Beyond the reaches of our soul: the life and times of Abba Kovner), Tel Aviv: Am Oved, 2000.

Proudfoot, Malcolm, *European Refugees: A Study in Forced Population Movement*, Evanston: North West University Press, 1956.

Rabinowitz, Dorothy, *New Lives: Survivors of the Holocaust Living in America*, New York: Avon Books, 1976.

Reilly, Joanne, *Belsen: The Liberation of a Concentration Camp*, London: Routledge, 1999.

Ringelblum, Emmanuel, *Polish Jewish Relations during the Second World War*, Jerusalem: Yad Vashem, 1974.

Rotkirchen, Livia, "The Final Solution in its Last Stages," in Y. Gutman and L. Rotkirchen, eds., *The Jewish Catastrophe in Europe: Background, History, Implications*, Jerusalem: Yad Vashem, 1976: 671–683.

Sachar, Abraham L., *The Redemption of the Unwanted: From Liberation of the Death Camps to the Founding of the State of Israel*, New York: St. Martin's-Marek, 1983.

Sagi, Nana, *German Reparations: A History of the Negotiations*, Jerusalem: Magnes Press, 1980.

Sarid, Levi Aryeh, "Irgun 'Hanakam' – korotav, d'muto, ma'asav" (The "hanakam" [avengers] organization – its history, profile and deeds), *Yalkut Moreshet*, no. 52 (April 1992): 35–106.

Schein, Ada, *Homeless Displaced Persons as Partners in the Zionist Enterprise: Survivors in German and Austrian Displaced Persons Camps and the Jewish National Fund*, Jerusalem: Research Institute for the History of the Keren Kayemeth LeIsrael, Land and Settlement, Research Series 7, 1997.

Schwarz, Leo, "The DPs: Fiction and Fact," *American Zionist*, vol. 43, no. 15 (June 1953): 16–19.

The Redeemers: A Saga of the Years 1945–1952, New York: Farrar, Strauss and Young, 1953.

"Memorial in Munich," *Congress Weekly*, vol. 22, no. 15 (1955): 6–7.

Schwarz, Leo W., ed., *The Root and the Bough: The Epic of an Enduring People*, New York: Rinehart and Company, 1949.

Segalman, Ralph, "The Psychology of Jewish Displaced Persons," *Jewish Social Service Quarterly*, vol. 23, no. 4 (June 1947): 363–365.

Segev, Tom, *The Seventh Million: The Israelis and the Holocaust*, New York: Hill and Wang, 1993.

Semprun, Jorge, *Literature or Life*, New York: Viking, 1997.

Sha'ari, David, *Geirush kafrisin 1946–1949: ha'apalah, machanot ve-chevrat ha-ma'apilim* (Deportation to Cyprus 1946–1949: clandestine immigration, the camps and the social bonding of the illegal immigrants), Jerusalem: the University of Tel Aviv and the Zionist Library, 1981.

Shalit, Levi, *Beyond Dachau: Memories, Reflections*, Johannesburg: Kayor, 1980.

Shapira, Anita, "The Yishuv and the Survivors of the Holocaust," *Studies in Zionism* (Autumn 1986): 277–302.

"Historiah shel mithologiah: kavim le-historiografiah al odot ben-gurion ve-hashoah" (The history of a mythology – guidelines for an historiography relating to Ben-Gurion and the Holocaust), *Alpayim*, no. 18 (1999): 33–53.

Shefer, Ze'ev, ed., *Sefer ha-hitnadvut: parashat ha-hitnadvut ha-tzvait shel yehudei eretz yisrael be-milchemet ha-olam ha-shniyah* (The book of voluntary service: the voluntary military service of Palestinian Jews in the Second World War), Jerusalem: Mosad Bialik, 1949.

Shiloah, Zvi, *Eretz gedolah le-am gadol* (A great land for a great people), Tel Aviv: Orpaz, 1970.

Shils, Edward, *The Intellectuals and the Powers and Other Essays*, Chicago: University of Chicago Press, 1972.

Shimoni, Gideon, *The Zionist Ideology*, Hanover: Brandeis University Press – University Press of New England, 1995.

"Ideological Perspectives," in Moshe Davies, ed., *Zionism in Transition*, New York: Herzl Press, 1980.

Shochet, Simon, *Feldafing*, Vancouver: November House, 1983.

Skidell, Akiva, "Im ha-tzava ha-amerikani be-germaniya ha-kvushah" (With the American Army in Occupied Germany), *Yalkut Moreshet*, no. 30 (November 1980): 157–169.

Slutzki, Yehuda, *Sefer toldot ha-haganah: mi-ma'avak le-milchamah – [3]* (A history of the *Haganah*: from struggle to war – [vol. 3]), Tel Aviv: Am Oved, 1978.

Smith, Bradley F., *Reaching Judgment at Nuremberg*, New York: Basic Books, 1977.

Smith, Marcus, *The Harrowing Hell of Dachau*, Albuquerque: University of New Mexico Press, 1972.

Smolar, Moshe, *Ne'evakti al chayai* (I fought for my life), Tel Aviv: Moreshet and Sifriyat Hapoalim, 1978.

Srole, Leo, "Why the DP's Can't Wait: Proposing an International Plan of Rescue," *Commentary*, vol. 3, no. 1 (January 1947): 13–24.

Stone, I.F., *Underground to Palestine*, New York: Pantheon, 1978.

Sykes, Christopher, *Crossroads to Israel: Palestine from Balfour to Bevin*, London: Collins, 1965.

Syrkin, Marie, "The D.P. Schools," *Jewish Frontier Anthology*, New York: Jewish Frontier Association, 1967: 211–226.

Tavin, Eli, *He-chazit ha-shniyah: ha-irgun ha-tzvai ha-leumi be-eropah, 1946–1948* (The second front: the national military organization in Europe, 1946–1948), Tel Aviv: Hotza'at Ron, 1973.

Toubin, Yehuda, "Be-derech eileihem: mi-yomano shel ish brigada 1945–1946" (On the way to them: from the diary of a member of the (Jewish) Brigade 1945–1946), *Yalkut Moreshet*, no. 21 (June 1976): 57–88.

Touster, Saul, "The Treatment of Jewish Survivors of the Holocaust, 1945–1948: Dilemmas of Law, Care and Bureaucracy," the 1999 Guberman Lecture on Law and Social Policy, Brandeis University (5.10.1999).

Touster, Saul, ed., *A Survivors' Haggadah*, Philadelphia: the Jewish Publication Society, 1999.

Vida, George, *From Doom to Dawn: A Jewish Chaplain's Story of Displaced Persons*, New York: Jonathan David Publishers, 1967.

Wdowinski, David, *Anachnu lo noshanu*, (And we are not saved), Jerusalem: Yad Vashem, 1985.

Webster, Ronald, "American Relief and Jews in Germany, 1945–1960: Diverging Perspectives," *Leo Baeck Institute Yearbook 1993*, London: Secker and Warburg (vol. 38, 1993): 293–321.

Weitz, Yechiam and Lavski, Chagit, "Mi-shoah le-tkumah" (From destruction to rebirth), *Katedra le-toldot eretz yisrael ve-yishuva* (Cathedra for the history of Eretz Yisrael and its settlement), no. 55 (March 1990): 162–181.

Wetzel, Juliane, *Jüdisches Leben in München 1945–1951: Durchgangsstation oder Wiederaufbau*, Munich: Kommisions Verlag Uni-Druck, 1987.

Wiesel, Elie, *One Generation After*, New York: Avon Books, 1972.

Winter, Jay and Sivan, Emmanuel, eds., *War and Remembrance in the Twentieth Century*, Cambridge: Cambridge University Press, 1999.

Woodbridge, George, *UNRRA*, New York: Columbia University Press, 1950.

Wyman, Mark, *DPs: Europe's Displaced Persons, 1945–1951*, Ithaca: Cornell University Press, 1998.

Yablonka, Hanna, *Survivors of the Holocaust: Israel After the War*, London: Macmillan Press Ltd., 1999.

Yachil (Hoffman), Chaim, "Peulot ha-mishlachat ha-eretz yisraelit le-she'erith hapleitah, 1945–1949" (Report of the Palestinian Delegation to *She'erith Hapleitah*, 1945–1949), *Yalkut Moreshet*, no. 30 (November 1980): 7–40 and no. 31 (April 1981): 133–176.

"Displaced Persons," *Encyclopaedia Judaica*, vol. VI: 76.

Yalkut Moreshet, no. 65 (April 1998), a special issue devoted to *She'erith hapleitah ve-hakamat hamedinah* (*She'erith Hapleitah* and the establishment of the State (of Israel)).

Zemarion, Zemach, *Ha-itonut shel she'erith hapleitah ke-bitui le-ba'ayoteha* (The press of *She'erith Hapleitah* as an expression of its problems), Tel Aviv: the Organization of *She'erith Hapleitah* from the British Zone (Bergen Belsen), 1970.

Zertal, Idith, "The Poisoned Heart: The Jews of Palestine and the Holocaust," *Tikkun*, vol. 2, no.2 (1987): 47–122.

    From Catastrophe to Power: Holocaust Survivors and the Emergence of Israel, Berkeley: University of California Press, 1998.

    "Ha-meunim ve-ha-kedoshim: kinuna shel martirologiya leumit" (The tortured and the martyrs: the constitution of a national martyrology), *Zmanim*, no. 48 (1994): 26–45.

Ziemke, Earl F., *The U.S. Army in the Occupation of Germany, 1944–1946*, Washington, D.C.: Center of Military History, United States Army, 1975.

Index

Notes
1 Page numbers in *italics* indicate illustrations.
2 Most references are to **Jews** in **American** Zone of Occupied **Germany** (and Austria), except where otherwise indicated. **DPs** (displaced persons) is used to refer mainly to Jewish people. References to **Nazis** and the effects of the **Second World War** are omitted as they are implied throughout.

Studies in the Social and Cultural History of Modern Warfare

Titles in the series: